Yukon

the Bradt Travel Guide

Polly Evans

edition
I

www.bradtguides.com

Bradt Travel Guides Ltd, UK
The Globe Pequot Press Inc, USA

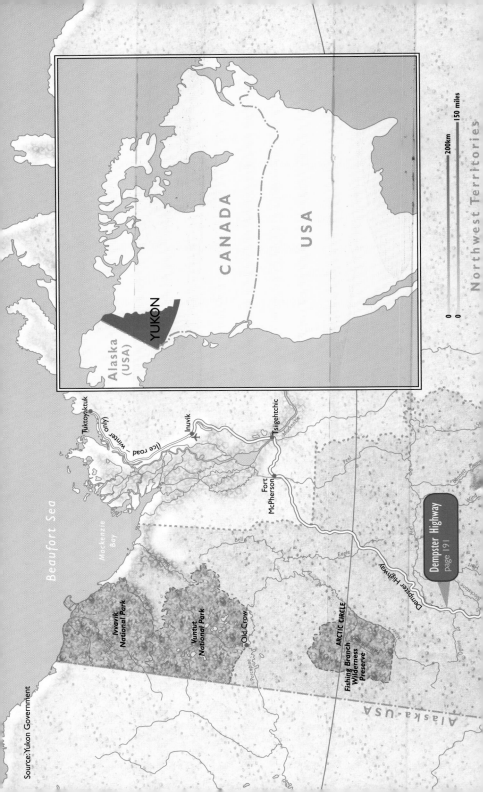

Source: Yukon Government

Beaufort Sea

Tuktoyaktuk

Inuvik

(Ice road – winter only)

Tsiigehtchic

Mackenzie Bay

Fort McPherson

Ivvavik National Park

Vuntut National Park

Old Crow

ARCTIC CIRCLE

Fishing Branch Wilderness Preserve

Dempster Highway

Alaska–USA

Dempster Highway
page 191

Northwest Territories

0 ⊢ 200km

0 ⊢ 150 miles

YUKON

Alaska (USA)

CANADA

USA

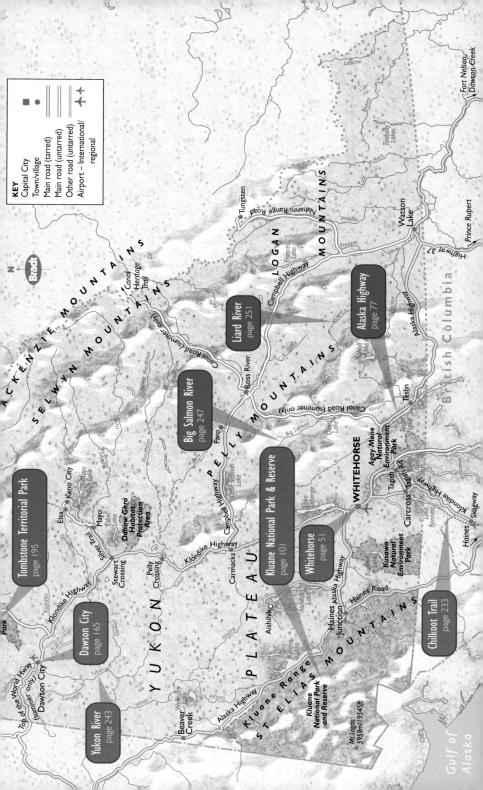

KEY
Capital City
Town/village
Main road (tarred)
Main road (untarred)
Other road (untarred)
Airport – International/regional

Bradt

N

Tombstone Territorial Park
page 195

Dawson City
page 165

Yukon River
page 243

Big Salmon River
page 247

Liard River
page 251

Alaska Highway
page 77

Kluane National Park & Reserve
page 101

Whitehorse
page 51

Chilkoot Trail
page 233

WHITEHORSE

MACKENZIE MOUNTAINS

SELWYN MOUNTAINS

LOGAN MOUNTAINS

PELLY MOUNTAINS

YUKON PLATEAU

KLUANE RANGE

ST ELIAS MOUNTAINS

British Columbia

Gulf of Alaska

Dadzw Gha Habitat Protection Area

Agay Mene Natural Environment Park

Kusawa Natural Environment Park

Kluane National Park and Reserve

Mt Logan 5959m/19545ft

Fort Nelson, Dawson Creek

Prince Rupert

Watson Lake

Tungsten

LaBiche

Ross River

Teslin

Skagway

Haines

Carcross

Haines Junction

Aishihik

Carmacks

Pelly Crossing

Stewart Crossing

Mayo

Elsa

Keno City

Dawson City

Beaver Creek

Canol Heritage Trail

Canol Road (summer only)

Canol Road (summer only)

Campbell Highway

Campbell Highway

Klondike Highway

Klondike Highway

Silver Trail

Alaska Highway

Alaska Highway

Alaska Highway

Alaska Highway

Haines Road

Haines Road

Highway 37

Nahanni Range Road

Top of the World Hwy (summer only)

Tagish Rd

Klondike Highway

Frances Lake

Wolf Lake

Teslin Lake

Atlin Lake

Bennett Lake

Tagish Lake

Marsh Lake

Laberge Lake

Little Salmon Lake

Aishihik Lake

Kluane Lake

Kusawa Lake

Wellesley Lake

Ethel Lake

Mayo Lake

Ross River

Francis Lake

Yukon

Stewart

Klondike

Sixtymile

White

Donjek

Kluane

Nisling

Big Salmon

Pelly

MacMillan

South MacMillan

North MacMillan

Hess

Paro

Frances

Yukon
Don't
miss…

Breathtaking vistas
The aurora borealis is best
seen away from city lights
(SW) page 5

**Road trips across
the Yukon**
The Dempster Highway stretches
nearly 800km from Dawson City
to Inuvik, crossing spectacular
tundra and mountain ranges
(PE) pages 191–202

Wildlife
Grizzly bears can be identified by the pronounced hump over their shoulders
(SW) page 7

A colourful history
In 1897–1898, tens of thousands of men and women made arduous journeys over the Chilkoot Trail on their way to the Klondike goldfields
(YA/AV) pages 165–8

Activities and adventure
Today, the historic trail followed by the gold rush stampeders is a popular multi-day hiking route that combines scenery and history
(SW) page 233–9

above   The Yukon Quest dogsledding race runs for 1,000 miles between Fairbanks in Alaska and Whitehorse in the Yukon each February (SW) pages 42–4

left   In the 21st century, snow machines have, for the most part, taken over dogsleds — but you'll still see signs of the old ways (PE) pages 41–4

bottom   The Donjek Route in southwest Yukon is a challenging hike — but the energetic are rewarded with views of vast valleys and tumbling glaciers (PE) pages 239–42

right Built during World War II to supply Alaska's coastal defences, the Alaska Highway now provides one of the most popular road trips in the north (SW) pages 77–100

below left Many head to the Yukon solely to fish — species include salmon, arctic char, trout and grayling (SW) page 44

below right Even novice canoeists can easily follow in the wake of the gold rush stampeders on the Yukon River (SW) page 243–47

bottom Paddlers can travel in perfect solitude on the Yukon's pristine rivers (SW) page 243–53

above   The White Pass and Yukon Route Railroad was completed in 1900; today this narrow-gauge railway, which climbs nearly 3,000ft in 20 miles, makes a breathtaking tourist trip (YG) page 70–71

below left   Robert Service arrived in Dawson after the Klondike gold rush, but his lively ballads recalling the sourdoughs' stories made him rich for life; the cabin in which he wrote many of them still stands (SW) page 183

below right   Plenty still make a living from gold mining in the Yukon and tourists, too, can try their luck with a pan (SW) page 184–6

AUTHOR

Polly Evans is an award-winning journalist and author. She's written five narrative travel books the most recent of which, *Mad Dogs and an Englishwoman*, tells the story of her learning to drive sled dogs in Canada's Yukon; a piece on the same theme led her to win the 2006 Bradt/*Independent on Sunday* Travel-Writing Competition. When not on the road, Polly teaches at Wellington College in the

AUTHOR'S STORY

I first arrived in the Yukon in the middle of January. I was heading to Muktuk Kennels, the home of veteran Yukon Quest musher Frank Turner, to research a book on learning to drive sled dogs. On my initial morning, as Frank kitted me out from the racks of winter clothing in his garage, he asked me as he asks all his guests, 'When you're in a room of ten people, are you among the five who are too hot, or the five who are too cold?' I told him I'd be among the five who were too cold. I didn't quite have the courage to add that, where nine of those people were pink-faced and perspiring, I'd be the one reaching for an extra sweater.

As I ventured out into the terrifying subzero world beyond the garage door, I felt horribly anxious – I have never been good with the cold. I was beginning to wonder what on earth I was doing there.

But as the weeks progressed, I stopped feeling the chill (and, delightfully, found I was able to eat food enough for a family without ever gaining a pound). Instead of being obsessed by the figures on the thermometer, I found myself drawn instead into the tranquil beauty of this incredible winter wonderland with its great expanses of white silence. I learned to appreciate the intricate beauty of the dazzling hoar frost and delicate snow flakes; and to take pleasure in watching the soft subarctic light shift from indigo to violet then saffron and pink as it reflected from its pale winter canvas. I developed a real fondness for the people of the Yukon who care so passionately about their largely unspoilt land – and for those mischievous, affectionate dogs who so uncomplainingly hauled me along the pristine trails of the north.

I went back – in July this time. I canoed a part of the Yukon River, and was struck by the haughty poise of the bald eagles that soared overhead as our paddles sliced though the clear jade water. I hiked the infamous Chilkoot Trail, and wondered at the gold rush artefacts, once abandoned by desperate, overladen dreamers, that still today lie littered and rusty along the way. I visited Dawson City, sauntered along its historic wooden boardwalks, and even downed a repulsive shot of 'sourtoe cocktail' – a glass of Yukon Jack whiskey garnished with a genuine, severed human toe. And when I returned home and Adrian Phillips, Bradt's Publishing Director, asked me if I thought there ought to be a Bradt guide to the Yukon, I said yes. Of course I did – to research the book I'd have to go back.

So I returned once again, and stayed a couple of months. I drove the remote Dempster Highway, and watched the Arctic tundra scream scarlet as summer turned to fall. With friends I hiked for nine days through the Kluane region, over dizzying peaks and past tumbling glaciers, and during that time we didn't spot another human soul. I poked my head round the doors of restaurants and roadhouses, bed and breakfasts and bars, and chatted with people who were quirky, colourful, and wore clothes never seen south of 60°. And by the time I'd finished my research, I found that my Yukon bug had not been cured but had, instead, intensified. And, already, I'm thumbing through my diary and planning my next trip north.

PUBLISHER'S FOREWORD *Adrian Phillips, Publishing Director*

Contrary to her claim to be 'very cowardly and not at all fond of danger', Polly Evans is one of your modern-day adventurers. She's motorcycled across New Zealand, cycled across Spain, and spent two months riding through Argentina – having never previously sat on a horse… She also happens to be a top-drawer writer. In 2006 Polly won the Bradt/*Independent on Sunday* Travel-Writing Competition with a piece based on her experiences learning to drive sled dogs in the Yukon; a few drinks and chats later, and we'd convinced her to write a Yukon guide for the Bradt list. Polly took on the task with customary relish, and there were Evans-esque scrapes along the way – including a hospital visit after her 4x4 skidded off the ice highway and rolled into a ditch. However, the result is a wonderful book that shows you exactly why Polly has fallen in love with the Yukon – a place of 'simple and almost silent pleasures that a city can never match'.

First published March 2010

Bradt Travel Guides Ltd, 23 High Street, Chalfont St Peter, Bucks SL9 9QE, England
www.bradtguides.com
Published in the USA by The Globe Pequot Press Inc, 246 Goose Lane,
PO Box 480, Guilford, Connecticut 06475-0480
Text copyright © 2010 Polly Evans
Maps copyright © 2010 Bradt Travel Guides Ltd
Illustrations copyright © 2010 Individual photographers and artists (see below)
For Bradt: Project Manager Anna Moores

British Library Cataloguing in Publication Data
A catalogue record for this book is available from the British Library
ISBN-13: 978 1 84162 310 8

Photographs Polly Evans (PE); FLPA: Theo Allofs/Minden Pictures/FLPA (TA/FLPA), Tim Fitzharris/Minden Pictures/FLPA (TF/FLPA), ImageBroker/Imagebroker/FLPA (IB/FLPA), Patricio Robles Gil/Minden Pictures/FLPA (PRG/FLPA), Mark Newman/FLPA (MN/FLPA); Norman Rich (NR); Stefan Wackerhagen (SW); YG Photo (YG); Yukon Archive: YA/Anton Vogee fonds (YA/AV) & Claude and Mary Tidd fonds (YA/CMT)
Front cover The Porcupine caribou herd migrates across northern Yukon (NR)
Back cover In cold temperatures, sled dogs on camping trips wear coats at night for warmth (PE); Alpine lakes on the Chilkoot Trail (SW)
Title page Alaskan huskies are a mixture of breeds; they run faster than heavier purebred huskies (SW); Fireweed is the one of the first plants to grow following forest fires (PRG/FLPA); Paddling Yukon's pristine rivers (SW)
Author photo © Sebastian Altenberger
Page 225 Hiking Montana Mountain, Carcross (YG Photo/D Crowe)
Illustrations Brent Liddle
Maps Dave Priestley (based on source material from Yukon Government; PR Services/yukoninfo.com; Town of Faro; The Village of Haines Junction; Haines Convention & Visitors Bureau; Parks Canada, Natural Resources Canada (Kluane National Park & Reserve)

Typeset from the author's disc by Wakewing, High Wycombe
Printed and bound in India by Nutech Print Services, New Delhi

Acknowledgements

The Yukon's people are warm and welcoming, and many of them have helped me along my way. I'd particularly like to thank Rod Raycroft of Yukon Tourism for his assistance with the research trip for this book, and Sheila Norris for her help as I travelled round. Adam Gerle of Whitehorse's Gold Rush Inn and High Country Inn, and Mary Ann Ferguson from Westmark Hotels helped me hugely with wonderfully comfortable accommodation – thank you both. Thank you, too, to Brent Liddle and Wenda Lythgoe for a fantastic few nights in their lovely cabins, and some really enlightening and enjoyable hiking with Brent.

Stefan Wackerhagen, Sebastian Altenberger and Cynthia Corriveau were good friends and outstanding research consultants who answered my most inane questions with good cheer; Stefan especially tolerated my request that he go out into the street to tell me whether the signpost said 'Seventh Avenue' or '7th Avenue', and my insistence that he scour Whitehorse Airport for a direct-dial cab phone for my readers' benefit (it turned out not to exist), with tolerance beyond the call of duty and an admirable Teutonic regard for precision. Thanks to Stefan, too, for all his input into the *Hiking and Paddling* section of this book.

In Ross River, I'd like to thank Corporal Moran and Constable Gagnon of the RCMP, and Rachel the nurse for their professionalism and kindness the day I totalled the truck – I was having a particularly awful day, and I continue to appreciate their help. Thank you, too, to the German tourists who picked me up off the road and gave me a ride – I'm sorry I never asked your names!

Last but of course not least, I'd like to thank Adrian Phillips, Anna Moores and everyone else at Bradt for their help, support and friendship.

CONTRIBUTORS

Stefan Wackerhagen is a partner of Northern Tales (*www.northerntales.ca*) tour operator; he has worked for several years as a wilderness guide in the Yukon, and is also a professional photographer. He has contributed the detailed information for the *Hiking and Paddling* section of this book.

Brent Liddle is a professional naturalist and heritage interpreter who has worked for Parks Canada in Kluane National Park for 30 years. He now operates a cabin and ecotour business at Kathleen Lake. Visit www.thecabinyukon.com and www.kluaneco.com.

Contents

LIST OF MAPS

FEEDBACK REQUEST

The Yukon may seem to move at a relaxed pace, but still its businesses open, close and change hands with sufficient regularity to give a guidebook writer nightmares. I hope that my guidebook encourages you, too, to explore the Yukon's less visited corners, and to delve into parts of this incredibly beautiful land that you might otherwise not have seen. So if you discover places that I haven't, or find that certain establishments have changed for better or worse since I visited them, please drop me a line and let me know. I'll be delighted to include your recommendations in the next edition. Please send your comments to Bradt Travel Guides, 23 High Street, Chalfont St Peter, Bucks SL9 9QE; e info@bradtguides.com.

Introduction

The Yukon is one of those places that many people have heard of, but they're not quite sure where it is. Some think it's in Alaska (it's not – Alaska is a US state while the Yukon, with which Alaska shares a border, is a territory of Canada); others ask, 'But isn't that a river?' (Answer – yes, there's a Yukon River, but the name is given to a territory as well.)

And so to clarify: perched up in the far northwest of Canada, the Yukon is almost twice the size of the UK and nearly as large as the US states of California and West Virginia stuck together. More than a century ago, an estimated 100,000 hopefuls made their way here with the Klondike gold rush; today the Yukon has just 34,000 inhabitants and 25,000 of those live in the capital, Whitehorse. But, while there may not be many humans, the Yukon is home to grizzly and black bears, moose, caribou, thinhorn sheep, bison, elk, mountain goats, wolves, wolverines, lynx and many species more.

A vast expanse of wilderness little touched by human hands, the Yukon is one of the most beautiful places I've ever visited. It's not just the scenery – though that's spectacular enough. (Those readers who examine this book closely will notice I've had difficulty finding sufficient adjectives to describe it.) I think it's the Yukon's stillness, its serenity and the vastness of its unpopulated places that make a visit here such an extraordinary experience. In the midst of such tranquillity, small moments enliven the senses: the sighting of a grizzly bear that sashays across the highway with her cubs, or a moose who nonchalantly chomps through roadside foliage; an unexpected glimpse of northern lights creeping up from the horizon and dancing green across night skies; the sound of a sled dog's paws on snow; the taste of a slightly smoky cup of tea that you drink by a campfire after a hard day's hiking. In my view, these simple and almost silent pleasures have an intensity that the noise and bright lights of a city can never match.

Since my first visit to the Yukon I've travelled extensively across the far north, from Siberia to Lapland to Greenland to Alaska. I love the light and the pristine landscapes of these remote parts, the stalwart and humorous people, and their acceptance of nature's capricious ways. But, much as I've enjoyed all these arctic and subarctic travels, it's to the Yukon that I've returned – and will continue to return – time and again. I hope that this book will inspire you to go there too, and to be touched by the magic of this quiet, little-known place that has so affected me.

Part One

GENERAL INFORMATION

Location The Yukon is a triangular-shaped territory in the far northwest of Canada. It borders Alaska to the west, the Beaufort Sea to the north, Canada's Northwest Territories (NWT) to the east, and British Columbia (BC) to the south.
Size 483,610km² (186,723 square miles)
Climate In summer Yukoners often bask in the mid-20s°C (high 70s F); while the average temperature in January is −26°C (−15°F).
Status Yukon is one of three territories, which, together with ten provinces, make up Canada.
Population Approximately 34,000, of whom about 25,000 live in Whitehorse
Main towns Whitehorse (the capital), Dawson City, Watson Lake, Haines Junction
Language English is the principal language
Currency CAN$
Exchange rate US$1=CAN$1.05, £1=CAN$1.7, €1=CAN$1.6
International telephone code +1
Time GMT-8 in winter, GMT-7 in summer
Electrical voltage 110V
Weights and measures Metric
Regional flower Fireweed
Regional bird Raven
Public holidays New Year's Day (1 January), the Friday before Easter, Victoria Day (the Monday on or before 24 May), Canada Day (1 July), Labour Day (first Monday in September), Thanksgiving (second Monday in October – note that this is not the same date as the USA's Thanksgiving), Remembrance Day (11 November) and Christmas (25–26 December). Additionally the Yukon has a holiday on Discovery Day (the third Monday in August) to mark George Carmack and co's discovery of gold in the Klondike.

Background Information

GEOGRAPHY

Located in the far northwest of Canada, the Yukon is roughly the shape of a right-angled triangle. With an area of 483,610km² or 186,723 square miles, it borders Alaska to the west, the Beaufort Sea to the north, the Northwest Territories (NWT) to the east and British Columbia (BC) to the south. Much of the territory is covered by permafrost.

The Yukon River cuts across the southwest corner of the territory. The river has its headwaters at the lakes of the southern Yukon; it runs northwest across the Yukon and Alaska for 3,185km (1,980 miles) before emptying into the Bering Sea. The territory is home to around 70 rivers in all, of which four – the Alsek, the Bonnet Plume, the Tatshenshini and the Thirtymile section of the Yukon River – are classified as Canadian Heritage Rivers (*www.chrs.ca*). The Yukon is also rich in lakes and wetlands.

The St Elias Mountains occupy the southwestern tip of the Yukon (as well as spanning into Alaska and the far northwest of BC); they contain the largest non-polar icefields in the world as well as Canada's highest peak, Mount Logan (5,959m/19,545ft). Other mountain ranges include the Coast Mountains, which, sitting in the Yukon's far south, are again shared with Alaska and BC; the Pelly Mountains in the southeast; the Mackenzie and Ogilvie Mountains, which stretch across the territory's middle; and the Richardson Mountains in the north.

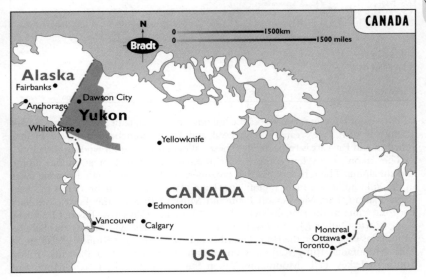

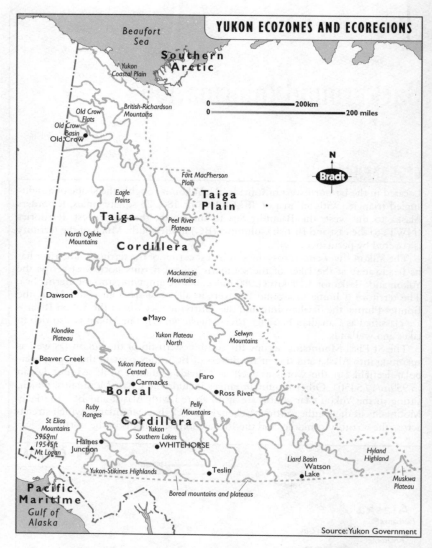

YUKON ECOZONES AND ECOREGIONS

Beaufort Sea

Southern Arctic

Yukon Coastal Plain

British-Richardson Mountains

Old Crow Flats
Old Crow Basin
Old Crow

Fort MacPherson Plain

Taiga Plain

0 ——————— 200km
0 ——————— 200 miles

N
Bradt

Eagle Plains

Taiga

Peel River Plateau

North Ogilvie Mountains

Cordillera

Mackenzie Mountains

Dawson

Mayo

Klondike Plateau

Yukon Plateau North

Selwyn Mountains

Beaver Creek

Yukon Plateau Central
Carmacks

Faro

Ross River

Boreal

Ruby Ranges

Pelly Mountains

St Elias Mountains
5959m/ 19545ft
Mt Logan

Cordillera

Haines Junction

Yukon Southern Lakes
WHITEHORSE

Hyland Highland

Yukon-Stikines Highlands

Teslin

Liard Basin
Watson Lake

Muskwa Plateau

Pacific Maritime

Gulf of Alaska

Boreal mountains and plateaus

Source: Yukon Government

Two major fault lines run across the Yukon – the Denali fault and the Tintina fault – which in turn have created the Shakwak and Tintina trenches around the Haines Junction and Faro areas respectively. These valleys create natural wildlife corridors.

The Yukon's ecosystem comprises a combination of boreal forest, tundra, alpine and subalpine. The territory has five ecozones: the Southern Arctic Ecozone takes in the Yukon Coastal Plain region; the Taiga Plain Ecozone incorporates the Peel River Plateau, Fort McPherson Plain and Muskwa Plateau; the Taiga Cordillera Ecozone contains the British-Richardson Mountains, Old Crow Basin, Old Crow Flats, North Ogilvie Mountains, Eagle Plains, Mackenzie Mountains and Selwyn Mountains ecoregions; the Boreal Cordillera Ecozone has the Klondike Plateau, St Elias Mountains, Ruby Ranges, Central and Northern Yukon Plateaus, Yukon Southern Lakes, Pelly Mountains, Yukon Stikine Highlands, Boreal Mountains and Plateaus, Liard Basin and Hyland Highland; and the Pacific Maritime Ecozone takes in the Mount Logan ecoregion.

CLIMATE

Most of the Yukon has a subarctic climate. Summers are short but generally warm and sunny (with the highest temperature ever recorded a sizzling 36°C or 97°F), and daylight hours are long: Whitehorse has nearly 20 hours of daylight on 21 June while, from the Arctic Circle up, the sun doesn't set.

Snow begins to settle from late October and melts in April. The ice on the rivers generally breaks up in May, and refreezes in October. While the sun may not rise on the Arctic coast for several weeks from December to January, in the southern Yukon daylight in winter is fairly good: on the shortest day of the year, Whitehorse has around six hours of light, including twilight.

January temperatures average –18°C (0°F) in Whitehorse and –27°C (–16°F) in Dawson; by March these have warmed to –7°C (20°F) and –12°C (11°F), and in April, average temperatures peek over zero. It may sound a little brisk but the air is dry, meaning that the cold doesn't chill the body in the same way that a damp cold does. With the right clothing, winter is a wonderful season in the Yukon – the soft yellow light and the glittering hoar frost are truly beautiful; many locals will tell you that this is their favourite time of year.

THE NORTHERN LIGHTS

The ancient Greenlanders thought the northern lights were a sign from the heavens that their ancestors were trying to contact the living. The Norwegians saw them as old maids dancing. Modern science is rather more prosaic. It tells us that the northern lights are created by solar particles ejected from the sun during explosions or flares. If these particles reach the Earth – a journey that takes two or three days – they are guided by the Earth's magnetic field towards the polar regions. As the solar particles penetrate the Earth's upper atmosphere, they collide with atoms and molecules, which absorb some of their energy. This is referred to as 'exciting' the atom or molecule, which returns to its non-excited state by emitting photons, or light particles. It's these light particles that we see as the northern lights, or aurora borealis.

The lights are best seen within the 'auroral ovals', ring-shaped areas that encircle the Earth's magnetic poles. The auroral ovals change position as the Earth rotates, and alter in shape and size according to the level of solar activity. The sky needs to be dark and free from cloud if you're going to see the northern lights; they're most visible away from the artificial building and street lights of a city, though strong displays can still be observed from built-up areas. The best times of year are around the equinox – either September or March.

For tips on how to photograph the northern lights, see page 45. Many Yukon lodges and cabins offer aurora viewing from their properties while Northern Tales (see page 25) operates packages specifically tailored to northern lights viewing.

IS THE AURORA FORECAST ACCURATE? There's a short answer to this one: yes. Northern lights are forecast on a scale ranging from one to nine. At one, you won't see a lot. At nine, you'll see a dazzling humdinger of a dance: those prone to religious experiences, beware. But remember – the sky must be dark and cloudless if you're to see the lights. And, even when activity is rated nine, they don't come out all night. Many displays only last a few minutes. They then die out; sometimes they'll come back later. You may have to be patient.

To see the current aurora forecast for the Yukon, go to www.auroraforecast.com.

CAN YOU HEAR THE NORTHERN LIGHTS? The experts say it's impossible – the air where the auroras are formed is apparently too thin to conduct sound. Across history, though, some northern people have claimed to have heard crackling and hissing sounds accompanying the northern lights. As yet, modern science has no explanation.

NATURAL HISTORY AND CONSERVATION

With its sparse population and scant roads, the Yukon is a wildlife heaven. It's home to around 160,000 caribou, 70,000 moose, 10,000 black bears and 6,000–7,000 grizzly bears, as well as arctic and red foxes, Dall, Fannin and Stone sheep, bison and wolves; more than 300 bird species have been recorded here. And you don't necessarily have to yomp off into the back of beyond to see them: large mammals, including bears and moose are regularly seen along the highways.

To improve your chances of spotting some of them, download *Yukon's Wildlife Viewing Guide Along Major Highways* from Environment Yukon's website (*www.environmentyukon.gov.yk.ca/mapspublications/documents/WVGuideEng2007.pdf*) – it tells you what to look for where. It's about 60 pages long; if you'd prefer to have a bound copy, contact **Environment Yukon's Wildlife Viewing Program** (✆ 867 667 8291, *toll-free:* ✆ 1 800 661 0408 *ext 8291;* e *wildlife.viewing@gov.yk.ca*). The Wildlife Viewing Program hosts a packed calendar of events, walks and talks. Go to www.environmentyukon.gov.yk.ca/viewing for more information, or pick up the *Wild Discoveries* leaflet from the visitor centre. The **Yukon Conservation Society** (*302 Hawkins St;* ✆ *867 668 5678;* e *ycsoffice@ycs.yk.ca; www.yukonconservation.org*) also offers interpretive walks and lectures.

For more detailed information on the Yukon's wildlife than I can offer here, go to Environment Yukon's Wildlife and Biodiversity pages: www.environmentyukon.gov.yk.ca/wildlifebiodiversity. The **Yukon Bird Club** (e *ybc@yknet.yk.ca; www.yukonweb.com/community/ybc*), **Yukon Conservation Society** (see above) and **Canadian Parks and Wilderness Society (CPAWS) Yukon Chapter** (*www.cpawsyukon.org*) are also good sources of information.

- Early morning and late evening are often the best times to see wildlife.
- Many animals come out immediately after a storm, when skies have cleared and the wind has died down. Some species are more active during wet weather so don't give up just because it's raining.
- Be quiet! You'll greatly increase your chances of seeing wildlife if you're still and silent. And once you spot wildlife, keep your distance. Never sneak up on an animal – frightened animals become stressed and could be dangerous.
- Use binoculars.
- Look for clues, such as tracks, and listen – you'll often hear wildlife before you see it.

MAMMALS Mesmerizing to watch, **grizzly bears** or **brown bears** (*Ursus arctos*) range in colour from blond to very dark brown. When walking in bear country, look out for pale-coloured hairs on the bark of trees, where grizzly bears have rubbed their backs and marked their territory. Grizzlies live all over the Yukon. In summer and fall they feast on berries, gaining up to a kilogram per day in weight; on a really gluttonous day, a grizzly can consume 200,000 berries. Most Yukon grizzlies do not have access to salmon runs though those in the Tatshenshini/Klukshu area in the southwest and near the Fishing Branch River in the northern Yukon do feed on salmon. (Bear Cave Mountain Eco-Adventures offers unique opportunities to view and photograph the Fishing Branch River bears from mid-September to mid-November – see page 224.) **Black bears** (*Ursus americanus*) are slightly more numerous in the Yukon than grizzlies. They're most common in the southern and central Yukon, and live in the forested areas of river valleys. Black bears are not always black (around a third of them are actually brown). They're smaller than grizzlies and lack the grizzly's distinctive shoulder hump; generally, a black bear will lose in a fight with a grizzly and, if a grizzly arrives at a stream where a black bear is fishing, the black bear will leave. Black bears are adept at climbing trees; look out for claw marks. (Grizzlies, too, occasionally climb but black bears are the masters due to their smaller size and better-suited claws.) Both grizzlies and black bears hibernate from October to April. Although their body temperatures do not drop more than a few degrees during hibernation (allowing them to wake up quickly if required) their heart and breathing rates slow, and they can go for up to six months without eating, drinking, urinating or defecating.

Bear attacks on people are very rare, but it's important to be familiar with – and to observe – bear safety guidelines when travelling in the Yukon. For information on bear safety, and how to tell the difference between a grizzly and black bear, see pages 228–9, download Environment Yukon's *How You Can Stay Safe in Bear Country* brochure (*www.environmentyukon.gov.yk.ca/pdf/howyoucanstaysafe.pdf*) or watch the visitor centres' bear safety video.

Polar bears (*Ursus maritimus*) are rarely spotted by visitors to the Yukon. It's reckoned around 2,000 polar bears live on and around the southern Beaufort Sea (encompassing the north shore of the Yukon, Northwest Territories and Alaska) but during the summer tourist season most bears are far offshore. In winter, polar bears are occasionally seen along the coast, on Herschel Island, and on the offshore ice. Should you be lucky enough to see a polar bear, keep in mind that it's probably out of its comfort zone, and that hungry or stressed polar bears can be extremely aggressive.

Of the Yukon's hoofed mammals, **caribou** (*Rangifer tarandus*) are the most numerous and, for thousands of years, the Yukon's First Nations people relied on caribou for food, clothing and shelter. Both barren-ground and woodland caribou inhabit the Yukon; there's a less prolific third subspecies, Peary's caribou, which lives only in the high Arctic. The largest herd is Porcupine caribou herd, which winters in the lands surrounding the Dempster Highway and migrates to its calving grounds on the coastal plain of Alaska's Arctic National Wildlife Reserve each summer. The Dempster Highway in winter provides the best vantage point for seeing caribou in the Yukon; the land around the Robert Campbell Highway is also good as this is where the Finlayson herd winters.

Caribou eat tundra vegetation and lichen, pawing the snow in winter to get at the food beneath (the word caribou comes from the Algonquin word *xalibu* meaning 'pawer'). They make a clicking noise as they walk – this is the sound of tendons slipping over the bones of their feet.

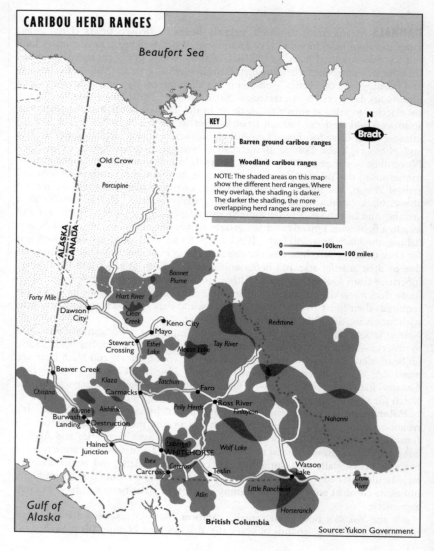

They're the same species. The word reindeer is generally used for the European animal, while caribou is used in North America.

Most European reindeer have been domesticated though there is still a small number of wild reindeer in Russia. A Lapp named Andrew Behr brought a domesticated reindeer herd to the Canadian coast near Tuktoyaktuk in the 1930s (see page 215); some descendants of that herd still survive in the area.

A **moose** (*Alces alces*) is called an elk in Europe, deriving from the old Germanic name *elch*, while the animal that North Americans call an elk (*Cervus elaphus*) is in Europe called a North American elk or a wapiti. Whatever you call it, the *Alces alces* is the largest deer in the world, and the Alaska Yukon moose (*Alces alces gigas*, sometimes called the tundra moose) is its most sizeable subspecies: a large male can weigh in at nearly 700kg (1,500lb). The Yukon also provides habitat to a second subspecies of moose, the woodland moose (*Alces alces andersoni*); the two subspecies easily interbreed.

Unlike the North American elk, which has forked antlers, the bull moose's antler consists of a flat palm from which pointed protuberances grow. Cow moose do not have antlers.

A browsing vegetarian, moose can consume up to 20kg (44lb) of twigs, leaves, and plants in a single day. Moose have self-sealing nostrils, which stop them getting water up their noses when feeding on aquatic plants. Scandinavian moose have an unfortunate habit of feasting on fermenting apples in autumn, getting drunk, and making excessively enthusiastic advances on human passers-by; fortunately, there are no apples growing in the Yukon. But be aware that moose can charge humans and kill; cows with calves and bulls in the rut (in October) are particularly dangerous.

A traditional staple for the First Nations diet, the moose continues to be popularly hunted for food in the Yukon today: residents fill their freezers with 500 to 800 animals each year.

Elk (*Cervus elaphus*) were introduced to the Yukon in the 1940s for hunting. The territory now has two elk herds: the Braeburn herd and the Takhini Valley herd, which together number less than 300 animals. They are regularly seen close to the relevant sections of the Klondike and Alaska highways, and signboards alert highway travellers when they're entering elk territory.

With their stooped, shaggy appearance and upturned horns that hug the sides of their heads, **musk oxen** (*Ovibus moschatus*) look like a throwback to a prehistoric age. Indeed, they've been around a while: musk oxen have inhabited North America for at least 150,000 years. They became extinct in Alaska and the Yukon in the mid-19th century but were reintroduced to Alaska (from where they have migrated) in 1969. The Yukon is believed to have a population of 150 to 200 musk oxen, most of which live in and around Ivvavik National Park.

While they may be called 'oxen', musk oxen are not in fact related to cows but are ruminants, as are sheep and goats. They have thick wool coats consisting of long outer hair and fine underhair (*qiviut* in Inuit), which has long been prized by northern people for its softness and warmth. Musk oxen are nervous creatures, and ready to charge. To defend against predators, herds form outward-facing circles, sheltering their young in the middle – or, where the herd is insufficiently numerous, they create straight lines of defence.

Another reintroduced species is the **wood bison** (*Bison bison athabascae*): 170 animals were released in the Nisling River valley between 1988 and 1992. The population flourished; it grew to over 1,000 and expanded its range. Wolves prey on bison to a limited degree, but the population is controlled predominantly by hunting. See page 94 for more on the reintroduction of bison to the Yukon.

The Yukon is home to around 22,000 **thinhorn sheep** (*Ovis dalli*; see page 104), divided into the more plentiful **Dall sheep** (*Ovis dalli dalli*), which number about 19,000 in the Yukon and are pure white, and **Stone sheep** (*Ovis dalli stonei*), which have white, grey or brown colouring. It's thought that the geographical obstacle of the Yukon River dissuades these two subspecies from breeding. The **Fannin sheep** (*Ovis dalli fannini*), found around the community of Faro, has different colourings again; Fannin sheep is reckoned by some to be a third thinhorn sheep subspecies, and by others to be a subspecies of the Stone sheep; this is a debate that I have no intention of wading into. Thinhorn sheep are seen across the Yukon, but particularly good places to spot them are Sheep Mountain in Kluane National Park and Reserve (see page 104) and – you guessed it – Sheep Mountain near Faro (see pages 149–50).

Mountain goats (*Oreamnos americanus*) spend their days wandering about vertiginous mountain ledges with breathtaking agility and surefootedness – the rubbery suction pads on their feet help them to perch on the most precarious-looking outcrops. There are about 1,700 animals in the Yukon, of which around half live in Kluane National Park and Kluane Wildlife Sanctuary. If you're wondering whether the distant woolly blob you're looking at is a goat or a sheep, try to determine the colour of its horns: mountain goats have black horns, while those of thinhorn sheep are brown. Additionally, goats have much shaggier coats than sheep.

The **wolf** (*Canis lupus*) is the largest wild dog and an animal that has long featured in myth and folklore. Its coat varies from black to grey to white. A wolf's howl identifies pack members and helps a pack to re-form. Like domestic dogs, wolves also bark and growl. There are about 4,500 wolves in the Yukon and they are more numerous where there are plenty of moose. Another dog species, the **coyote** (*Canis latrans incolatus*) is common in the southern Yukon. Coyotes are often confused with wolves but are, in fact, less than half the size of their relative; they're grey in colour with a white belly and throat.

The **arctic fox** (*Vulpus lagopus*) is supremely well adapted to the cold with its thick coat, small limbs and ears, and luscious insulating tail that wraps the fox like a blanket: even when temperatures drop to –60°C (–76°F), an arctic fox can maintain a body temperature of 40°C (104°F). In summer the arctic fox is brownish or grey; it grows a white coat in winter. Yukon populations are limited to the coastal plain and Herschel Island. The **red fox** (*Vulpus vulpus*) is more widespread and lives all over the Yukon, though its populations are denser south of the Arctic Circle. Red foxes are not always red, but have black and grey (called silver and cross) phases. Exact populations of foxes in the Yukon are not known.

'A ravenous monster of insatiate voracity, matchless strength, and supernatural cunning, a terror to all other beasts,' wrote 19th-century naturalist Elliott Coues of the **wolverine** (*Gulo gulo*). It's from this creature's Latin name that the word 'glutton' comes, due to its reputation for greed. Take heart, though – there's no record of a wolverine attacking a human and, despite their vicious reputation, wolverines generally prefer to scavenge than to kill – though they'll take a lamb or a caribou calf if the opportunity presents itself. Wolverines look a little bit like small, dark-coloured bears with long bushy tails. Sightings are rare – wolverines are notoriously antisocial – but the animal's pelt is much sought-after by trappers because frost will not form on it, so it makes the perfect material with which to trim a parka hood.

The Yukon has only one kind of hare and that's the abundant **snowshoe hare** (*Lepus americanus*) so named for its outsized hind feet, which allow it to move on soft snow without sinking. The snowshoe hare is white with black-tipped ears in winter, and red-brown with a grey-brown belly in summer. You can't confuse it with another species because this is the only type of rabbit or hare that lives in the Yukon.

Also numerous are **arctic ground squirrels** (*Spermophilus parryii*), also known as gophers and sik-siks due to the sound of their call. They dart in and out of their labyrinthine burrows all summer long, and are frequently sighted during the warmer months. The arctic ground squirrel hibernates for eight to ten months of the year and is the only mammal known to let its body temperature drop below freezing during hibernation – its body fluids do not solidify.

Visitors may also see **porcupines** (*Erethizon dorsatum*). Each has around 30,000 sharp quills covering its body, and these keep the Yukon's vets busy in summer as dogs have an unfortunate habit of sticking their faces into them. You may find porcupine quills made into jewellery and for sale in local craft stores.

Beavers (*Castor canadensis*) are Canada's national emblem, and they're abundant in the Yukon – indeed, it was the fur of the beaver that first brought European traders to these parts. By 1840, beavers, whose fur was highly sought after in fashionable Europe in the 18th and early 19th centuries, had been hunted almost to extinction in eastern Canada and it was the quest for richer supplies that brought Robert Campbell (see pages 142–3) and his cohorts west.

Supremely adapted to moving in water (a beaver has lips that close behind its front teeth, transparent eyelids, and can stay underwater for 15 minutes), the beaver is nature's logger; it eats the bark of willow, aspen, birch and poplar, and caches the branches for winter feeding. Indeed, even if the beavers themselves stay hidden, paddlers on the Yukon's rivers frequently see telltale gnawed logs, as well as beaver dams made from sticks and mud. During the winter, beavers do not hibernate, but feed from the food cache they've accumulated during the autumn, and stashed near their lodge. Both the entrance to their lodge and their food cache are constructed sufficiently low in the water that the beaver can move between the two beneath the ice. Beavers are most active at night, in the late evening, and at dawn.

Other mammals living in the Yukon include the **lynx** (*Lynx canadensis*), **river otter** (*Lutra canadensis yukonensis*), **least chipmunk** (*Eutamias minimus*), **marten** (*Martes americana*) – considered to be the trapper's bread and butter – **mink** (*Mustela vison*) and **ermine** (*Mustela erminea*).

Ringed seals (*Pusa hispida*) are common around the Yukon's northern coast and Herschel Island, and **Bowhead whales** (*Balaena mysticetus*) and **Beluga whales** (*Delphinapterus leucas*) can be seen in these waters as they migrate.

BIRDS The Yukon's skies play host to more than 300 species of bird, of which 195 have been recorded as breeding. **Bald eagles** (*Haliaeetus leucocephalus*) are abundant and visible. Adults are easily identified by their white heads with hooked yellow beaks, white tails and dark brown bodies; juveniles are brown with white streaks and don't gain their distinctive adult plumage until they're five years old. Bald eagles feed predominantly on fish, and during the spawning season can often be seen fishing for salmon. Thousands of bald eagles congregate around the Chilkat River near Haines, Alaska in autumn each year; see page 133.

Visitors may also see **golden eagles** (*Aquila chrysaetos*), which hunt for prey including the lambs of Dall sheep and caribou calves, **gyrfalcons** (*Falco rusticolus*), the largest of the falcon species, and the smaller **peregrine falcon** (*Falco peregrinus*), identifiable by its dark head and sideburns, barred upper wings and upper tail, blue-grey and yellow bill, yellow eye ring, pale breast and yellow legs and feet. Peregrine falcons are generally thought to be the fastest birds on earth (some claim they can swoop at up to 400km/h or about 250mph) though the prize for the fastest bird ever recorded goes to the gyrfalcon.

Ptarmigan are abundant in the Yukon. **Willow ptarmigan** (*Lagopus lagopus*) inhabit marshy tundra, forested areas and valleys; **rock ptarmigan** (*Lagopus muta*) prefer higher latitudes and altitudes. The two look virtually identical, with pure-white plumage, apart from black tail feathers, in winter, and speckled brown or grey-brown upper parts with white breast and underbody in summer; look out for the tell-tale red 'eyebrow', which is more prominent in the males than females.

During April, many birders flock to Swan Haven in M'Clintock on Marsh Lake in the southern Yukon (see page 91). Because the bay has open water at a time when the rest of the Yukon is still covered in ice and snow, many migrating waterbirds congretate here to rest and feed. The most prominent visitors are the **tundra swans** (*Cygnus columbianus*) and **trumpeter swans** (*Cygnus buccinator*). The Pacific flyway population of tundra swans is reckoned to number 63,000, and up to a thousand of the birds can be seen at one time at M'Clintock Bay. The trumpeter swan is the largest waterfowl in North America; in the 19th century the birds were widely hunted and almost became extinct. There are now about 20,000 worldwide, of which several thousand migrate through the southwest Yukon each year. It is difficult to distinguish between tundra and trumpeter swans (though tundra swans often have a yellow patch in front of the eye, which trumpeters do not). More easily distinguished are their voices: tundra swans have a melodious call, while trumpeters have a brassy and, well, trumpeting song.

As well as swans, M'Clintock Bay in spring attracts **loon** (*Gavia immer*), **horned grebe** (*Podiceps auritus*) and **red-necked grebe** (*Podiceps grisengena*), **Canada goose** (*Branta canadensis*), **teal** (*Anas crecca*), **mallard** (*Anas platyrhynchos*), **northern shoveler** (*Anas clypeata*), **wigeon** (*Anas americana*), **ring-necked duck** (*Aythya collaris*), **canvasback** (*Aythya valisineria*), **northern pintail** (*Anas acuta*), **scaup** (*Aythya affinis*), **goldeneye** (*Bucephala clangula*), **arctic tern** (*Sterna paradisaea*), **bufflehead** (*Bucephaia albeola*), **merganser** (*Mergus serrator*) and **gulls**. For more information on waterbirds at M'Clintock Bay, download Environment Yukon's booklet 'Spring Birds at Swan Haven' from http://environmentyukon.gov.yk.ca/pdf/birding.pdf.

Herschel Island (see pages 217–19) is another Mecca for birdwatchers; more than 90 species can be seen here, of which 40 breed on the island. It's home to the Western Arctic's largest breeding colony of **black guilllemots** (*Cepphus grille*), which have taken up residence in the old Anglican mission house, as well as a nesting population of **rough-legged hawks** (*Buteo lagopus*). Other species include **arctic terns** (*Sterna paradisaea*), **American golden plovers** (*Pluvialis dominica*), **red-necked phalaropes** (*Phalaropus lobatus*), **common eiders** (*Somateria mollissima*), **long-tailed jaegers** (*Stercorarius longicaudus*), **glaucous gulls** (*Larus lyperboreus*), **snow buntings** (*Plectrophenax nivalis*), **Lapland longspurs** (*Calcarius lapponicus*), **common redpolls** (*Carduelis flammea*), **long-tailed ducks** (*Clangula hyemalis*) and **surf scoters** (*Melanitta perspicillata*).

For detailed information on the Yukon's birds, download the checklist of Yukon birds from the **Yukon Bird Club** (*www.yukonweb.com/community/ybc*). The website has additional birding checklists specific to Herschel Island (*www.yukonweb.com/community/ybc/herschelbirds.pdf*) where 94 different species have been recorded; for the Tombstone Territorial Park, in which 148 species have been recorded (*www.yukonweb.com/community/ybc/tombstonebirds.pdf*); and a birdwatcher's guide to Whitehorse (*www.yukonweb.com/community/ybc/birdingwhitehorse.pdf*). The bird club also as a packed schedule of field trips. Serious birding fans may like to buy a copy of *Birds of the Yukon Territory* by Cameron D Eckert, Pamela H Sinclair, Wendy A Nixon and Nancy L Hughes (available from Mac's Fireweed Books in Whitehorse or www.yukonbooks.com) though with its $150 price tag, it won't be for everyone.

There are three major birding festivals in the Yukon each year: Celebration of Swans at Marsh Lake in April (see page 91); the Faro Crane and Sheep Festival in

Some find it surprising that, despite the abundance of majestic creatures that soar through the Yukon's skies and bob along its waterways, the territorial bird is the common old raven. Intelligent and opportunistic, this bird is seen all over the Yukon in both summer and winter – and it's a major character in First Nations stories. The Yukon First Nations call the raven 'the crow' and credit it with a major role in the creation of the world. According to Gwich'in legend, the Sky Spirit sent the crow to an unpopulated Earth with instructions to decide what to do with it. First the crow created the wolf, and then he created man.

May; and Weekend on the Wing in the Tombstone Territorial Park in June (see page 197).

FISH The Yukon's lakes and rivers are popular with anglers. Game species include **arctic char** (*Salvelinus alpinus*), whose body colour changes from bluish green to bright red when the fish is ready to spawn. Arctic char scarcely feed in the winter, but survive from fat reserves. **Arctic grayling** (*Thymallus arcticus*) in the Yukon usually only grow to around 50cm (20 inches) long. They are frequently found in the territory's rivers and have dark purple backs and sides with black spots, and a large dorsal fin spotted with green or orange. **Bull trout** (*Salvelinus confluentus*), often confused with **Dolly Varden** (*Salvelinus malma*) and arctic char, can be found in the Liard drainage area; Dolly Varden have black spots on the dorsal fin (the bull trout does not) as well as yellowish spots on their backs and orange- and pink-spotted sides. Stella Lake, off the Haines Road, has landlocked Dolly Varden. **Inconnu** (*Stenodus leucichthys*) are prolific in the Yukon, Pelly, Stewart and Porcupine river systems. They are pale in colour, and have a lower jaw that's longer than the upper. **Lake trout** (*Salvelinus namaycush*), **pike** (*Esox lucius*), **rainbow trout** (*Oncorhynchus mykiss*) and **burbot** (*Lota lota*) can also be found in the Yukon's waters.

Four species of **whitefish** are found in the Yukon: **broad** (*Coregonus nasus*), which are bottom feeders found more often in rivers than lakes; **lake** (*Coregonus clupeaformis*), found in most of the territory's lakes; **pygmy** (*Prosopium coulteri*), found in the Alsek River system and headwaters of the Yukon, as well as Squanga Lake east of Whitehorse; and **round** (*Propopium cylindraceum*), which are found across the territory.

Chinook (*Oncorhynchus tshawytacha*), **Coho** (*Oncorhynchus kisutch*), **sockeye** (*Oncorhynchus nerkaI*), **chum** (*Oncorhynchus keta*) and **Kokanee** (*Oncorhynchus nerka*) salmon all inhabit the Yukon's lakes and rivers. For more information on fishing in the Yukon, see page 44 or go to Environment Yukon's website at www.environmentyukon.com.

BUTTERFLIES About 90 species of butterfly can be seen in the Yukon; Keno Hill and the Blackstone uplands are particularly good locations. For more information, download Environment Yukon's booklet *Yukon Butterflies* from http://environmentyukon.gov.yk.ca/pdf/YukonButterflieswebfinal05.pdf or contact its Wildlife Viewing Program for a hard copy (details on page 6).

FLORA The Yukon has a rich diversity of flora due to the ice-free Beringia years (see page 15). When the ice age ended, the former land of Beringia – now divided once more by the ocean – had a huge head start on those regions that had been glaciated. Today the Yukon features more than 1,200 species of plant; the tundra areas are

TREES OF THE YUKON

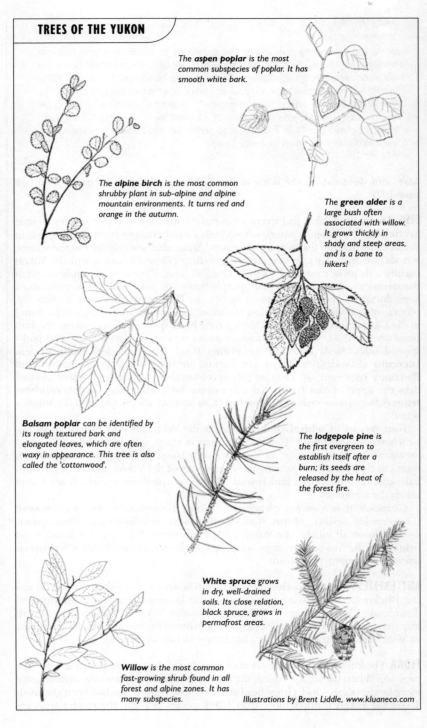

The **aspen poplar** is the most common subspecies of poplar. It has smooth white bark.

The **alpine birch** is the most common shrubby plant in sub-alpine and alpine mountain environments. It turns red and orange in the autumn.

The **green alder** is a large bush often associated with willow. It grows thickly in shady and steep areas, and is a bane to hikers!

Balsam poplar can be identified by its rough textured bark and elongated leaves, which are often waxy in appearance. This tree is also called the 'cottonwood'.

The **lodgepole pine** is the first evergreen to establish itself after a burn; its seeds are released by the heat of the forest fire.

White spruce grows in dry, well-drained soils. Its close relation, black spruce, grows in permafrost areas.

Willow is the most common fast-growing shrub found in all forest and alpine zones. It has many subspecies.

Illustrations by Brent Liddle, www.kluaneco.com

renowned for their short-lived but colourfully blooming wildflowers in summer. A few books might help enthusiasts along their way with identifying the various plants: *Flora of the Yukon Territory* by William J Cody, *Wildflowers Along the Alaska Highway* by Verna E Pratt and *Wildflowers of the Yukon, Alaska and Northwestern Canada* by John Trelawny are all available from Mac's Fireweed Books in Whitehorse, or www.yukonbooks.com.

The Yukon's official territorial flower is **fireweed** (*Epilobium angustifolium*), which blazes bright magenta across the territory through the summer. It's particularly prolific in burn areas; one of the first plants to grow following forest fires, it creates a bountiful carpet of pink beneath the blackened, beanpole-like remains of charred trees. In the UK, fireweed is sometimes called willowherb.

NATIONAL AND TERRITORIAL PARKS Ten percent of the Yukon is protected as parks. The Yukon has three national parks: Kluane (see pages 101–13), Ivvavik (see pages 222–3) and Vuntut (see page 223). It also has four territorial parks: Tombstone (see pages 195–8), Herschel Island – Qikigtaruk (see pages 217–19), Fishing Branch – Ni'iinlii'njik (see page 224) and Coal River Springs (see page 85). Additionally, the Nisutlin River Delta is protected as a National Wildlife Area; the Kluane Wildlife Sanctuary protects wildlife from hunters in certain areas bordering Kluane National Park and Reserve, and there are a number of further 'special management' and 'habitat protection' areas.

A BRIEF HISTORY

More than 20,000 years ago, the first humans are believed to have migrated into North America from Asia. They came via the Beringia land bridge: during the last ice age, ocean levels dropped as vast glaciers locked up the world's water and the floor of the Bering Sea ran dry. Beringia – the area that comprises modern-day eastern Siberia, northern Alaska and northern Yukon – never became glaciated because its climate was too dry. Instead a unique grassland flourished and became populated with mammoths, giant short-faced bears, steppe bison and scimitar cats. And where food went, human hunters followed. The first humans to arrive in the Yukon inhabited the area around Old Crow.

Around 10,000 years ago, the ice age ended and the Beringia land bridge was flooded once more. The First Nations of the Yukon continued to live off the land for thousands of years hunting and fishing as their ancestral traditions dictated and, in time, they established permanent settlements. Then the white men came.

Danish explorer Vitus Bering, sailing with the Russian navy, sighted Mount Elias (in Alaska) from the sea in 1741, and was shipwrecked off the Alaska coast a few weeks later. When his crew finally returned to Russia (Bering wasn't with them – he'd died of scurvy) they took with them the pelts of sea otters that they'd hunted for food.

Encouraged by this rich source of fur, the Russians returned and began trading with the native people of southeast Alaska and the southern Yukon. Meanwhile, the Hudson's Bay Company (HBC) had set up fur-trading stations to the east and was gradually encroaching westwards (see *The Hudson's Bay Company*, page 16). Robert Campbell (see *Robert Campbell*, pages 142–3) was the first HBC man (and, indeed, the first white man) to arrive in present-day Yukon. From 1840 he travelled across the land setting up trading posts as far west as Fort Selkirk.

On 1 July 1867 the Dominion of Canada was created. Just three months earlier, the Russians had sold Alaska to the USA for a paltry US$7.2 million. Americans reacted to the purchase with horror: the Secretary of State of the day, William Seward, may have agreed a price of just two cents an acre, but nonetheless the new

In the mid-1600s, two Frenchmen named Radisson and des Groseilliers travelled into the upper Great Lakes basin. There they traded with the First Nations for furs – but the authorities of New France (France's North American territories) accused them of trading without a licence. Their booty was confiscated, they were fined, and des Groseilliers was, for a short time, jailed.

The French were not interested in the trading networks that Radisson and des Groseilliers wished to establish and so the two entrepreneurs went to England, where they were presented to King Charles II. In 1667, the king's cousin, Prince Rupert, took enthusiastic charge of their project and the following year Radisson and des Groseilliers sailed for the New World under the English flag. The expedition returned to England in ships laden with furs. Given the journey's success, the King granted Prince Rupert a Royal Charter in 1670. This established the Hudson's Bay Company, with Prince Rupert as its governor, and granted it trading rights over the Hudson Bay drainage basin – henceforth to be known as Rupert's Land. This territory covered 3.9 million km^2 (1.5 million square miles) and comprised a third of modern-day Canada.

The North West Company was established by a group of Montreal merchants in 1779 with the aim of challenging the HBC's monopoly on North American furs. While the HBC chiefs were predominantly English, the North West Company tended to be staffed by Scots who, with their voyageurs, penetrated far into the northwest of present-day Canada. In 1821, the two rivals merged. With the merger, the HBC's trading network stretched into modern-day NWT, BC, Yukon and Alaska and covered a territory of 7.8 million km^2 (3 million square miles).

land was derided as 'Seward's folly' by his compatriots who saw no benefit in possessing a virtually uninhabited, frozen wilderness. (That, of course, was before they found the oil.) But despite the ridicule of the chattering classes, these changes in the political landscape meant that the far north now became more accessible to American and Canadian adventurers.

Gold prospectors and traders started to trickle into the present-day Yukon. Arthur Harper, Jack McQuesten and Al Mayo arrived in 1873; see *Forty miles from where?*, page 171. Over the next 20 years, several thousand prospectors would find their way into the area. In 1883, American lieutenant Frederick Schwatka made the first survey of the Yukon River; see *Frederick Schwatka*, page 72.

American whaling ships came to Herschel Island from the late 1880s (see *Herschel Island*, pages 217–19) forcing the police and missionaries to follow.

Then, in 1898, George Carmack and his brothers-in-law struck gold in the creeks of the Klondike, and the face of this land was changed forever; see pages 165–70.

The Yukon Territory was formally established at the height of the gold rush, on 13 June 1898. Dawson City became the territorial capital. In response to the gold rush, the White Pass and Yukon Route railway opened in 1900 (see pages 70–1), and the Overland Trail between Dawson and Whitehorse was completed in 1902 (see page 157).

In the early years of the 20th century, gold production declined, as did the population of Dawson. Silver instead became king, with mines in the Mayo and Keno area flourishing. The next big population rush didn't occur until 1942, when 10,000 American military and civilian personnel poured into the Yukon to construct the Alaska Highway; see pages 77–9. The creation of the highway saw Whitehorse's population boom and, in 1953, it took over from Dawson as the Yukon's capital.

GOVERNMENT AND POLITICS

Canada consists of ten provinces and three territories; Yukon is one of the territories. (The other two are Northwest Territories and Nunavut.)

Provinces have greater autonomy than territories. In practice, however, the Yukon government has much the same powers as provincial governments (except in criminal prosecution) since the Yukon Act of 2003 devolved additional powers to the territorial government, including control over land and resources.

The Yukon is governed by a Legislative Assembly consisting of 18 elected members. While, on paper, the Yukon's Commissioner reports to the federal government, and the provinces' lieutenant-governors are formal representatives of the Queen, in reality their roles are similar: the Commissioner grants assent to bills passed by the legislative assembly and represents the Yukon at protocol-related functions inside and outside of the territory. The Yukon also has a single Member of Parliament who represents the territory at federal level.

ECONOMY

In March 2009, the Yukon had a labour force of 17,800 of whom 16,600 were employed. The government is by far the Yukon's largest employer: in 2006, the Census recorded that 4,145 Yukoners were employed in public administration. This was followed by 1,735 in the retail trade, 1,650 in health care and social assistance, and 1,480 in accommodation and food services.

Mining still accounts for a strong proportion of the Yukon's economy. Tourism is also a healthy contributor: the Yukon hosts around 300,000 visitors a year (ten times its resident population). Tourism accounts for 4.4% of the Yukon's Gross Domestic Product (GDP) and 6.8% of the territory's employment.

PEOPLE

The Yukon has a population of around 34,000, roughly 25,000 of whom live in Whitehorse. Much of the population was not born in the Yukon but migrated here from elsewhere in Canada (and, indeed, from abroad). The territory attracts independent-minded individuals with little concern for the superficial trappings of fashion and other forms of consumerism, but a deep love for the expansive lands and wildlife of the north.

THE COLOURFUL FIVE PER CENT

As you travel around the Yukon you may rub up against people who are charming, excellent company and brilliant raconteurs – but their levels of eccentricity gallop off any scale known to the rest of the world. Yukoners call these offbeat personalities – drawn to the far north precisely because of its tolerance of unconventionality – the 'colourful five per cent'. Into their number fall Caveman Bill, a Dawsonite who chooses to live in a cave on the banks of the Yukon River for the very excellent reason that he likes it there; Dick Stevenson, who created the 'sourtoe cocktail' (see page 180) and Tagish Elvis (see page 129).

Illustrator Jim Robb, born in Quebec but resident in the Yukon since 1955, was the person to coin the phrase 'the colourful five per cent', and since doing so has made quite an industry of this quirky social phenomenon with his series of books, The Colourful Five Percent, for sale in bookstores across the Yukon. Robb's vibrant prints of iconic Yukon scenes are also widely available – the Midnight Sun Gallery on Whitehorse's Main Street is a good starting point.

YUKON FIRST NATIONS About 25% of the Yukon's people are of aboriginal descent. There are 14 Yukon First Nations: Carcross/Tagish First Nations (based at Carcross); Champagne and Aishihik First Nation (based at Haines Junction); Kluane First Nation (based at Burwash Landing); Kwanlin Dün First Nation (based at Whitehorse); Liard First Nation (part of the Kaska Nation, based at Watson Lake); Little Salmon/Carmacks First Nation (based at Carmacks); Na-Cho Nyak Dun First Nation (based at Mayo); Ross River Dena (part of the Kaska Nation, based at Ross River); Selkirk First Nation (based at Pelly Crossing); Ta'an Kwäch'än First Nation (based at Whitehorse); Teslin Tlingit First Nation (based at Teslin); Tr'ondëk Hwëch'in First Nation (based at Dawson City); Vuntut Gwitchin First Nations (based at Old Crow); and White River First Nation (based at Beaver Creek). The Tetlit Gwich'in (also marked on the map opposite) is based at Fort McPherson in the Northweest Territories. The Yukon once had an Inuvialuit population on Herschel Island (see pages 217–19); however, the island is now uninhabited and the islanders' descendants live for the most part in Inuvik, Aklavik and other communities of the Northwest Territories.

First Nations culture encourages respect for the land, wildlife and the forces of nature, and has rich storytelling and creative traditions. Carvings, beaded moccasins and mukluks, jewellery and weaving can be bought across the Yukon (see *Shopping*, page 40). Despite the terrible legacy of the residential schools (see below), powerful role models are emerging from these communities intent on reclaiming their history, culture, traditions and dignity, and a reviving aboriginal culture is evident throughout the Yukon.

The **Society of Yukon Artists of Native Ancestry** (SYANA; *205–302 Steele St;* ☏ *867 668 2695; www.syana.ca*) hosts workshops and exhibitions of First Nations art. It also runs the **Yukon Native Arts Festival**. First Nations storytellers also perform at the **Yukon International Storytelling Festival** each October (*www.storytelling.yk.net*).

The grim legacy of the residential schools

It is difficult, looking back on the history of Canada's residential schools, to see how anyone ever could have seen them as an acceptable way to educate the nation's aboriginal children. The stories of abuse are so horrific and the demise of the system so recent – while the government withdrew federal funding in 1969 and most schools had ceased to operate by the mid-1970s, Canada's last residential school closed only in 1996 – that the scars inflicted are still very fresh. Simply put, it was a cultural genocide: Canada's aboriginal people can never fully recover the language and cultural losses caused by the residential schools system.

Canada's prime minister, Stephen Harper, finally apologized formally to former students of the residential schools in June 2008. He said before parliament, 'The government now recognizes that the consequences of the Indian residential schools policy were profoundly negative and that this policy has had a lasting and damaging impact on aboriginal culture, heritage and language...While some former students have spoken positively about their experiences at residential schools, these stories are far overshadowed by tragic accounts of the emotional, physical and sexual abuse and neglect of helpless children, and their separation from powerless families and communities.'

The idea behind the residential schools was this: in the late 19th century, the white European-Canadian authorities decided that the best way to assimilate the Indian population into their culture was to forcibly educate its children. Taken from their homes and families at the age of five or six, they were, effectively, imprisoned in federally financed, church-run schools for ten months of each year. Forbidden from speaking their native languages (despite the fact that they at first

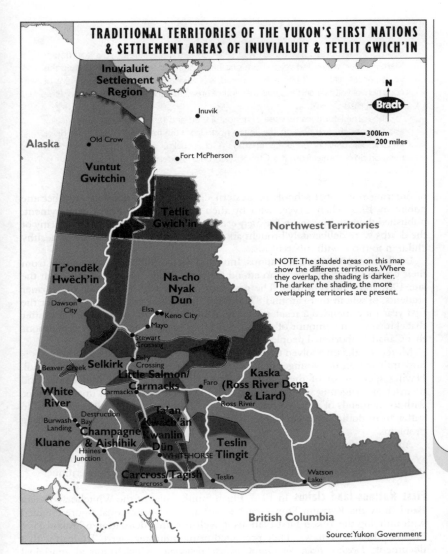

TRADITIONAL TERRITORIES OF THE YUKON'S FIRST NATIONS & SETTLEMENT AREAS OF INUVIALUIT & TETLIT GWICH'IN

Inuvialuit Settlement Region

Inuvik

Alaska

Old Crow

Fort McPherson

Vuntut Gwitchin

Tetlit Gwich'in

Northwest Territories

NOTE: The shaded areas on this map show the different territories. Where they overlap, the shading is darker. The darker the shading, the more overlapping territories are present.

Tr'ondëk Hwëch'in

Na-cho Nyak Dun

Dawson City

Elsa Keno City
Mayo
Stewart Crossing

Beaver Creek Selkirk
Pelly Crossing
Little Salmon/ Carmacks
Carmacks

Faro Kaska (Ross River Dena & Liard)
Ross River

White River

Burwash Landing
Destruction Bay
Champagne & Aishihik
Ta'an Kwäch'än
Kwanlin Dün

Kluane
Haines Junction
WHITEHORSE Teslin Tlingit

Carcross/Tagish
Carcross Teslin Watson Lake

British Columbia

Source: Yukon Government

knew no English or French, they were often beaten if they spoke in their own tongue – some were so terrified that they stopped speaking at all), and in many cases banned from speaking at all to their own siblings, the system effectively severed the children's ties with their own language and traditions. When they returned home each summer, they found themselves alienated from their former communities.

These issues were compounded by the physical and sexual abuse that ran rife in the residential schools, whose staff was not effectively monitored – and, given that residential school jobs were poorly paid and undesirably remote, they attracted applicants from the bottom of the barrel. In 1909, the general medical superintendent for Canada's Department of Indian Affairs, Dr Peter Bryce, reported that, between 1894 and 1908, 35%–60% of children died within five years

Sourdough is a bread made with wild yeast; by carrying a little of your sourdough 'starter' (flour, water and yeast) from one batch of bread to the next, you keep the yeast perpetually alive. This is how bread was always made before the advent of commercial yeasts – and this was the kind of bread that the early prospectors of the far north made.

The name later became used to denote a tried-and-tested northerner. To qualify as a sourdough, you have to stay in the north from the freezing of the Yukon River in October until its break-up in May. A cheechako, on the other hand, is a newcomer. It comes from the Chinook word for tenderfoot.

of entering residential schools in western Canada. These statistics only became public in 1922 when Bryce, who by then had left government employment, published them in his report *The Story of a National Crime*; he claimed that many of the deaths were deliberately brought about by the purposeful exposure of healthy children to those with tuberculosis.

In all, about 150,000 First Nations, Inuit and Métis children were removed from their communities and forced to attend Canada's residential schools through the late 19th and 20th centuries. The government now pays compensation; former students, of whom there around 87,000 in Canada, are entitled to $10,000 for the first year they attended a residential school and $3,000 for every school year after that. However, no amount of money can bring back the language and traditions that Canada's aboriginal people have lost.

Moreover, the unresolved trauma still suffered by residential school survivors is now inflicted on the younger generations who never attended residential school. Having spent most of their childhoods in these institutions, adults now find themselves struggling with grief, anger and low self-esteem, and unable to cope with the demands of intimacy and parenting. Aboriginal communities continue to suffer from domestic abuse, crime, increased suicide rates, and alcohol and drug problems.

Anyone wanting to learn more about the impact of the residential schools systems of the US and Canada might like to read Ward Churchill's book *Kill the Indian, Save the Man*, which provides an interesting if gut-wrenching critique.

First Nations land claims In 1973, Elijah Smith, chief of the Whitehorse Indian Band (now the Kwanlin Dün First Nation) and an inspirational figure credited with unifying the Yukon First Nations, travelled with a delegation of Yukon First Nations chiefs to Ottawa. They presented prime minister Pierre Trudeau with a document, *Together Today for Our Children Tomorrow*, which outlined aboriginal rights, defined what it meant to be Indian, and laid down principles for negotiating land claims. This was the first time a group of Canadian First Nations had created such a proposal. The Trudeau government accepted *Together Today for Our Children Tomorrow* as a basis for negotiation; the Umbrella Final Agreement was eventually signed by the governments of Canada and Yukon and the Yukon First Nations in 1993.

The Yukon's 14 First Nations have authority over 41,595km² (16,060 square miles) of land – that's to say 8.5% of the total land area of the Yukon. By 2008, 11 out of the Yukon's 14 First Nations had finalized their land claims.

The claimed land is divided into 'category A' settlement land, where a First Nation has complete ownership of both the surface and the subsurface – that's to say they own any minerals, oil and gas – and has exclusive harvesting rights over fish and wildlife, and 'category B' settlement lands, where the public is allowed to hunt and fish, and whose minerals, oil and gas are controlled by the Yukon government.

As a general rule, the public and visitors are allowed onto any undeveloped settlement land for recreational purposes (such as hiking), as long as they don't create damage.

LANGUAGE

According to the 2006 Census of Canada, 85% of Yukoners speak English as their mother tongue, while 95% said English was the language they spoke most often at home. This was followed by French (4%), German (3%) and Athapaskan languages (2%).

The Yukon's 14 First Nations share eight aboriginal languages. Seven are from the Athapaskan family (Gwich'in, Hän, Kaska, Northern Tutchone, Southern Tutchone, Tagish and Upper Tanana). Additionally, Tlingit is found in the southern Yukon, along the southeast Alaska coast and in parts of BC. Knowledge of aboriginal languages declined catastrophically as a consequence of the residential schools system (see pages 18–20); both Hän and Tagish are on the verge of extinction with just one or two very elderly speakers. According to the 2006 Census, 12% of the Yukon's aboriginal population reported having an aboriginal language as a mother tongue, and only 16% said that they were able to hold a conversation in an aboriginal language. Predictably, the majority of these were the older members of the population.

Efforts are being made to revive both the languages and other traditions of these almost-lost cultures, however. The **Yukon Native Language Centre** (*www.ynlc.ca*), based at Yukon College in Whitehorse, has developed writing systems and has trained people to read, write and teach native languages, while **Northern Native Broadcasting Yukon** (*www.nnby.net*) and the Yukon Government's Aboriginal Language Services Branch attempt to raise the profile of these languages through radio and TV.

2

Practical Information

WHEN TO VISIT

By far the majority of visitors go to the Yukon in the **summer**, between May and September, when the days are long and the weather is relatively warm. Indeed, many of the territory's museums and visitor centres, and some of its hotels and restaurants, are open only during the summer season. The **winter**, however, is truly marvellous too. Though the temperatures can dive low, the winter is glorious for outdoors enthusiasts with its dogsledding, skiing and snowshoeing opportunities – as well as the northern lights. Some say that the very best time to visit the Yukon is the end of August and beginning of September. During this short window the autumn colours are spectacular, yet the daylight hours are short enough to allow you to see the aurora borealis if you're lucky.

The 'shoulder' seasons tend to be quiet in tourist terms; however, they can be good times for birders eager to see, for example, the swan migration in April (see page 91) or the bald eagle gathering in October and November in Haines, Alaska (see page 133).

HIGHLIGHTS AND SUGGESTED ITINERARIES

HIGHLIGHTS If I were only allowed to give one piece of advice for visitors to the Yukon it would be: *get off the highway!* This is a land known for its incredible wilderness, yet many visitors see little beyond the views from the pullouts along the road. Even if your physical mobility is limited, there are easy strolls along boardwalks with interpretive boards in, for example, **Kluane National Park and Reserve** (see *Chapter 5*) and the **Tombstone Territorial Park** (see pages 195–8).

For those who can manage more than a short stroll, the Yukon's outdoor opportunities are vast. Both Kluane and the Tombstones offer outstanding walking for all levels of fitness. For the hardy, the **Chilkoot Trail** follows the path of the Klondike stampeders from the Alaska coast and makes for a truly fantastic three- to five-day journey; see pages 223–39. Paddlers relish the Yukon's pristine wilderness rivers. For more information on hiking and paddling, see *Part 3* of this book.

Now I've got all that out of my system, I'll deign to mention the roads. Many come to the Yukon to drive the **Alaska Highway**, which was built at breakneck speed during World War II in order to supply the Alaska defences. Considerably renovated since those bumpy days, it now runs for more than 2,000 breathtaking kilometres (1,250 miles) from Dawson Creek in British Columbia to Delta Junction in Alaska; see *Chapter 4* for detailed information. Even more incredible is the rough and ready **Dempster Highway** (see pages 191–202), which stretches for 736km (457 miles) from just outside Dawson City to Inuvik in the Northwest Territories.

Dawson City (see *Chapter 9*) is the town that sprung up to house the Klondike gold rush; still today it retains its wooden buildings and boardwalks, but its remote location and warmly eccentric residents mean that it keeps its slightly wild, bordertown vibe. It's an enchanting little place, and well worth making the journey north.

And now for the winter. The Yukon is definitely not a summer-only destination. On clear winter nights, the **northern lights** leap across the Yukon's skies, but for those with a good long underwear collection, there's so much more – **dogsledding**, **snowmobiling**, **skiing** and **snowshoeing** trips all take visitors into a stunning winter wonderland. With the right clothes (which tour operators will lend or rent to you), the weather really is not prohibitive.

SUGGESTED ITINERARIES Many people go to the Yukon for hiking and paddling holidays; see *Part 3* for detailed information on five multi-day routes. There are many other multi-day options besides these, which are covered in brief in the relevant destination chapters. Additionally, see *Further Information* on pages 255–7 for recommendations of books that give information on hiking and paddling.

The itineraries below assume you're travelling in summer; winter activities will often be arranged through tour operators – see pages 24–6.

One week If you only have a week in the Yukon, I'd head to Kluane National Park for a two or three days; there you can enjoy some half-day and day walks. Even if you're not the rippling muscles type, Parks Canada has created several easy strolls that allow you to get a feel for this incredible wilderness. Then drive back to Whitehorse and either fly to Dawson City or drive up the Klondike Highway (if you drive, it will be a whole day's journey from Kluane/Haines Junction). Spend two or three nights in Dawson soaking up the history and the vibe; from there, take a day trip up a part of the Dempster Highway and, if you're a keen walker, spend a day exploring the Tombstone Territorial Park.

Two weeks For a two-week journey, I'd spend a few days in Kluane and a few days in Dawson, as suggested above. With the extra time I'd drive up the Dempster Highway. Ideally, stop for a walk in the Tombstone Territorial Park on the way, and spend one or two nights in Inuvik from where you can take interesting day trips, for example to Tuktoyaktuk and Herschel Island. If there's time, treat yourself to a night or two of luxury at Inn on the Lake (see page 91) before you fly home.

Three weeks or more If you have three weeks or more in the Yukon, you'll really find time to kick back and contemplate nature. In addition to the recommendations above, think about spending a few days in the tiny but quirky village of Keno, or drinking in the wilderness in an out-of-the-way lodge – try Frances Lake Wilderness Lodge, for example (see page 144).

TOUR OPERATORS

NORTH AMERICAN WHOLESALERS
Arrangements Yukon 2101A Second Av, Whitehorse; ☏ 867 393 6070; e info@arrangementsyukon.com; www.arrangementsyukon.com

Latitude Destination Management Suite 25, 1114 First Av, Whitehorse; ☏ 867 456 7084; e bookings@latitudeyukon.com; www.latitudeyukon.com

UK WHOLESALERS
Audley Travel Group New Mill, New Mill Lane, Witney, Oxon OX29 9SX; ☏ 01993 838 000; www.audleytravel.com

Bales Worldwide Bales House, Junction Rd, Dorking, Surrey RH4 3HL; ☏ 0845 057 1819; e enquiries@balesworldwide.com; www.balesworldwide.com

Yukon Wild is a co-operative of licensed wilderness tourism operators, which aims to provide adventurous travellers with a central information source. For more information, go to www.yukonwild.com.

Canada 4U Canada House, 90 High St, Lowestoft, Suffolk NR32 1XN; ℡ 01502 565648; e sales@canada4u.co.uk; www.canada4u.co.uk

Connections 20 Port St, Evesham, Worcs WR11 1AL; ℡ 0800 988 5845; e enquiries@cnww.co.uk; cnww.co.uk

Experience Holidays 1 Town House Garden, Market St, Hailsham, East Sussex BN27 2AE; ℡ 0845 230 2131 or 01323 446550; www.experienceholidays.co.uk

Frontier Travel 6 Sydenham Av, London SE26 6UH; ℡ 020 8776 8709; e canada@frontier-travel.co.uk; www.frontier-canada.co.uk

North American Highways 10–11 Market Pl, Brewood, Staffs ST19 9BS; ℡ 01902 851138; e sales@nahighways.co.uk; www.nahighways.co.uk

Tailor Made Travel 20 Port St, Evesham, Worcs WR11 1AL; ℡ 0800 988 5887; e sales@tailor-made.co.uk; www.tailor-made.co.uk

The Independent Traveller Devonshire House, Devonshire Lane, Loughborough, Leics LE11 3DF; ℡ 01509 618800: e holidays@uni-travel.co.uk; www.itiscanada.co.uk

Titan HiTours HiTours House, Crossoak Lane, Redhill, Surrey RH1 5EX; ℡ 0800 988 5823; www.titantravel.co.uk

Travelsphere Holidays Compass House, Rockingham Rd, Market Harborough, Leics LE16 7QD; ℡ 0870 240 2426 or 01858 410818; www.travelsphere.co.uk

Windows on the Wild & **Go Fishing Canada** 2 Oxford House, 24 Oxford Rd North, London W4 4DH; ℡ 020 8742 1556; e sales@go-fishing-worldwide.com; www.gofishingworldwide.co.uk

CRUISE-SHIP COMPANIES SERVING SKAGWAY, ALASKA
Many of the Yukon's visitors arrive by cruise ship in Skagway, and then either take the White Pass and Yukon Route railway or drive over the international border.

Holland America UK: ℡ 0845 351 0557; e uksales@hollandamerica.com; www.hollandamerica.com; US: ℡ 1 877 932 4259; www.hollandamerica.com

Princess Cruises UK: ℡ 0845 355 5800; e enquiry@princesscruises.co.uk; www.princess.com; US: ℡ 1 800 7746 2377; www.princess.com

Carnival UK: ℡ 020 7940 4466; e carnivaluk@carnival.com; www.carnivalcruise.co.uk; US: ℡ 1 888 2276 4825; www.carnival.com

Royal Caribbean UK: ℡ 0845 165 8414; e infouk@rccl.com; www.royalcaribbean.co.uk; US: ℡ 1 866 562 7625; www.royalcaribbean.com

Norwegian Cruise Lines UK: ℡ 0845 658 8010; www.ncl.co.uk; US: ℡ 1 866 234 7350; www.ncl.com

Celebrity X Cruises UK: ℡ 0800 018 2525; e infoux@rccl.com; www.celebritycruises.com; US: ℡ 1 877 202 4345; www.celebritycruises.com

LOCAL TOUR OPERATORS
For tour operators offering trips exclusive to certain areas, refer to the individual destination chapters in *Part Two* of this guidebook.

Yukon tour operators are required by law to renew their licence every year. If you have any concerns about an operator's credentials, ask for their licence number. Be aware that there have been a few instances of tourists turning up in Whitehorse – as in every other destination across the globe – having booked a holiday on the internet with a tour operator that does not exist. If a company asks for money to be wired to a foreign bank account, you should be careful, and research their credentials extensively. The operators listed below are all bona fide.

Cabin Fever Adventures ℡ 867 335 0318; e info@cabinfeveradventures.com; www.cabinfeveradventures.com. Guided canoeing,

kayaking, fishing, hiking, heli-hiking, mountain- & road-biking trips, plus wilderness first-aid training.

The government tourism department has an excellent and informative website at www.travelyukon.com, and also publishes a number of helpful brochures and leaflets that can be picked up in visitor centres across the territory.

Cathers Wilderness Adventures ☏ 867 333 2186; e yukon@cathersadventures.com; www.cathersadventures.com. This is a family-run dogsledding business offering cabin-based accommodation & winter camping. Their home is on Lake Laberge & in summer they offer multi-day canoe trips & hiking with pack dogs.

Cedar & Canvas Adventures ☏ 867 633 5526; e cedar@northwestel.net; www.cedarcanvas.com. Guided canoeing, backpacking & fishing tours. As its name suggests, Cedar & Canvas Adventures uses wood & canvas canoes both for its paddling & fishing tours — its fishing boats are wood-&-canvas freighter canoes with 30 hp outboards.

Gray Line Sightseeing Tours ☏ 867 668 3225; e glainfo@HollandAmerica.com; www.graylineyukon.com. Day & part-day bus sightseeing tours, plus multi-day highway tours of Alaska & the Yukon.

Great River Journey 118 Galena Rd, Whitehorse; ☏ 867 456 2421; e info@greatriverjourney.com; www.greatriverjourney.com. 8-day river journey from Whitehorse to Dawson City, staying at Great River Journey's high-end wilderness lodges en route. Guests spend 2 nights at each of the 1st 2 lodges, and 1 night at the 3rd, which gives plenty of time for wildlife viewing, nature photography, birdwatching, hiking, paddling & participating in cultural & interpretative programs. Departures several times weekly from early Jun to mid-Sep.

Kanoe People Cnr of 1st Av & Strickland St, Whitehorse; ☏ 867 668 4899; e info@kanoepeople.com; www.kanoepeople.com. Rents both canoes & kayaks; prices start from $30 per day. Also organizes transfers, & guided package & custom trips of various local rivers. Kanoe People arranges both guided fishing day trips to lakes & rivers in the Whitehorse area, & rents boats, motors & motorized canoes. The company also has cabins & watercraft for rental at its Fox Bay Retreat on the shores of Lake Laberge, see page 156.

Nahanni River Adventures ☏ 867 668 3180; e info@nahanni.com; www.nahanni.com. Has been running guided canoe & rafting trips across the north, in Alaska, Yukon, NWT & BC, since 1972. Nahanni River Adventures operates on more than 20 rivers from easy waterways to white water.

Nature Tours of Yukon ☏ 867 667 4868; e joost@naturetoursyukon.com; www.naturetoursyukon.com. Guided canoe & hiking trips, including the historic Chilkoot Trail & Kluane National Park, as well as canoe rentals & transfers for those wishing to go it alone. In winter, Nature Tours offers mushing, ice fishing, snowshoeing and aurora viewing. Sightseeing trips by van & custom tours can also be arranged in both seasons.

Northern Tales ☏ 867 667 6054; e info@northerntales.ca; www.northerntales.ca. In winter, Northern Tales offers northern lights viewing from its comfortable heated cabin, as well as van tours, soft adventure & custom packages. Daytime activities include dogsledding, snowmobiling, ice fishing, snowshoeing, winter nature walks & trips to the Yukon Wildlife Preserve & Takhini Hot Springs. Summer activities include canoeing, kayaking, hiking, biking & van tours; packages are available, but Northern Tales specializes in custom tours to meet the client's wishes.

Ruby Range Adventure ☏ 867 667 2209; e info@rubyrange.com; www.rubyrange.com. Offers guided canoe trips on various rivers, adventure van tours & multi-day fishing tours in summer, & dogsledding, snowmobiling & van tours in winter. Ruby Range also rents canoes & arranges transfers for those who wish to paddle unguided.

CANOES AND KAYAKS

Note that when the Canadians use the word canoe, they use it to mean an open, 'Canadian' canoe propelled by a single-blade paddle. The boat with spray deck and double-bladed paddle, which the British, Australians and New Zealanders often refer to as a canoe, is always called a kayak in Canada.

Sila Sojourns ✆ 867 668 5032; e info@silasojourns.com; www.silasojourns.com. Custom hiking, skiing & boating trips from 1 day to 2 weeks. Also runs workshops & retreats incorporating activities such as creative writing, nature photography, painting, meditation, yoga, music, shaman journeying & healing practices. Some trips are for women only.

Taiga Journeys ✆ 867 393 3394; e acaltherr@northwestel.net; www.taigajourneys.ca. Taiga Journeys has 3 arms. Firstly, owners Andrea & Christoph Altherr operate 3 log cabins on the shores of Dalayee Lake (off the Alaska Highway just west of Jake's Corner, see page 90). Secondly they run guided hiking & canoeing trips for very small groups – they'll take as few as 2 people. And thirdly, Andrea offers half-day & full-day 'nature encounters' trips in the Whitehorse area.

Tatshenshini Expediting 101 Jarvis St, Whitehorse (summer only); ✆ 867 633 2742, cell: 867 333 5247; e info@tatshenshiniyukon.com; www.tatshenshiniyukon.com; ⏰ May 11am–5pm, Jun–Aug 10am–6pm. Offers courses, day trips & multi-day trips in canoeing, kayaking & rafting. Rents rafts, canoes, kayaks & inflatables. Also sells used kayaks & canoes, & provides transportation to put-in & take-out locations.

Up North Adventures 103 Strickland St, Whitehorse; ✆ 867 667 7035; e upnorth@yknet.yk.ca; www.upnorth.yk.ca. Up North is a year-round adventure travel outfitter, operating in 4 languages (English, German, French & Spanish). In summer it offers half-day, full-day & multi-day canoeing & kayaking trips, both guided & self-guided; half-day & full-day guided fishing tours; half-day & full-day guided mountain-bike tours; & full-day ATV tours. The company also offers canoe & kayak courses, wilderness first-aid courses in spring & fall, & avalanche instruction. In winter there's half- & full-day snowshoeing & ice fishing, & half-, full- & multi-day snowmobiling, plus aurora viewing. Up North also has a retail shop selling related clothing & equipment.

Walden's Guiding & Outfitting ✆ 867 667 7040; e info@waldensguiding.com; www.waldensguiding.com. 5- to 12-day canoe trips, all fully guided. Walden's specializes in the Peel River watershed's 5 tributaries – the Wind, the Snake, the Hart, the Blackstone & the Bonnet Plume – plus trips on the Yukon, Teslin, Hart & Big Salmon rivers. Custom trips can also be arranged.

Yamnuska CJ Link ✆ 867 668 3660; e inq@yamnuskaguides.com; www.cjlink.yk.net. Caters mainly to the Japanese market with aurora tours & hiking.

Yukon Horsepacking Adventures Nov to mid-May, ✆ 250 263 7903, mid-May to 1 Nov, ✆ 867 633 3659; e yukonhorsepacking@gmail.com; www.yukonhorsepacking.com. Day & multi-day rides in the Fox Lake & Lake Laberge areas.

Yukon Pride Adventure Tours ✆ 867 668 2932; e info@yukonpride.com; www.yukonpride.com. Introduces gay & lesbian travellers to the Yukon with activities including hiking, rafting, river trips, van tours, aurora viewing, dog mushing & more.

Yukon Wide Adventures ✆ 867 393 2111; e info@yukonwide.com; www.yukonwide.com. Guided river & hiking tours across the Yukon; also rents log cabins in wilderness locations on Big Salmon Lake & Pilot Mountain in both summer & winter.

RED TAPE

Citizens of many countries, including the United States, United Kingdom, France, Germany, Spain, Australia, New Zealand, Mexico, the Republic of Korea and Japan, may enter Canada for a limited period without a visa. For full information on Canada's visa requirements, go to www.cic.gc.ca/english/visit/visas.asp.

International visitors, other than US citizens and US permanent residents, must present a passport to enter Canada. Visitors from the US do not need to carry a passport to enter Canada if they can present proof of citizenship, such as a birth certificate, plus photo ID, such as a driver's licence – but this is now academic if they ever wish to return home again as from 1 June 2009 US citizens re-entering the United States by air, land or sea must present either a passport or NEXUS card.

ⓔ EMBASSIES

International embassies and the UK High Commission are all located in Ottawa; some have offices in other major cities but there are no offices in the Yukon.

Australia ✆ 613 236 0841; e dima-ottawa@
dfat.gov.au; www.canada.embassy.gov.au
France ✆ 613 789 1795; e politique@
ambafrance-ca.org; www.ambafrance-ca.org
Germany ✆ 613 232 1101; e info@
ottawa.diplo.de; www.ottawa.diplo.de
Japan ✆ 613 241 8541; e infocul@embjapan.ca;
www.ca.emb-japan.go.jp

New Zealand ✆ 613 238 5991; e info@
nzhcottawa.org; www.nzembassy.com
UK ✆ 613 237 1530 or ✆ 613 239 4288 for
emergency consular assistance outside office hours;
e consular.assistanceottawa@fco.gov.uk;
www.ukincanada.fco.gov.uk
USA ✆ 613 688 5335; e web1@
ottawa.usembassy.gov; http://ottawa.usembassy.gov

CANADIAN EMBASSIES AND HIGH COMMISSIONS ABROAD

Australia Canberra: Commonwealth Av, Canberra ACT
2600; ✆ +61 2 6270 4000; e cnbra@
international.gc.ca; Sydney: Level 5, 111 Harrington
St, Sydney, NSW 2000; ✆ +61 2 9364 3000; email
for enquiries not related to visas or immigration
e sydny@international.gc.ca (note spelling of
Sydney without an e); www.australia.gc.ca
France 37, av Montaigne, 75008 Paris; ✆ +33 1 44
43 29 00; e paris_webmaster@international.gc.ca;
www.amb-canada.fr
Germany Leipziger Platz 17, 10117 Berlin; ✆ +49 30
20312 0; www.germany.gc.ca/www.deutschland.gc.ca
Japan 7-3-38 Akasaka, Minato-ku, Tokyo; ✆ +81 3
5412 6200; e tokyo-cs@international.gc.ca;
www.japan.gc.ca

New Zealand Level 11, 125 The Terrace, Wellington,
6011; ✆ +64 4 473 9577, freephone from
Auckland ✆ (09) 309 8516; e wlgtn@
international.gc.ca; www.newzealand.gc.ca
UK Macdonald House, 1 Grosvenor Sq, London, W1K 4AB;
✆ +44 207 258 6600; passport services during
working hours ✆ 020 7258 6356 (voicemail) or ✆ 020
7258 6346 (emergencies only); e ldn.passport@
international.gc.ca; consular services: e ldn.consular@
international.gc.ca; visas & immigration: 38 Grosvenor
St (use Grosvenor Street entrance, not Grosvenor Sq),
London W1K 4AA; go to the website for visa &
immigration forms; www.unitedkingdom.gc.ca
USA 501 Pennsylvania Av, NW, Washington, DC
20001; ✆ +1 202 682 1740; www.washington.gc.ca

GETTING THERE AND AWAY

✈ **BY AIR** Most people flying to the Yukon land at **Whitehorse International Airport**
(✆ 867 667 8440, toll-free: ✆ 1 800 661 0408: e yxy@gov.yk.ca). **Air Canada** (from
Canada & US ✆ 514 393 3333, toll-free: ✆ 1 888 247 2262; www.aircanada.com or from the
UK ✆ 0871 220 1111; www.aircanada.co.uk) connects Vancouver to Whitehorse daily;
one-way tickets start from $165. The Yukon's airline is **Air North** (✆ 867 668 2228,
toll-free: ✆ 1 800 661 0407; e customerservice@flyairnorth.com; www.flyairnorth.com). It flies
daily to Vancouver and regularly to Edmonton, Calgary, Dawson City, Old Crow,
Inuvik and Fairbanks, Alaska (summer only). Tickets start from $165 for a single fare
from Vancouver to Whitehorse. It's around $130 for a one-way ticket between
Whitehorse and Dawson, and $195 from Dawson to Inuvik; you get a bit of a discount
if you go the whole hog from Whitehorse to Inuvik with a one-way ticket costing
$260. **First Air** (Northwest Territories and Nunavut's airline, ✆ 1 800 267 1247;
e reservat@firstair.ca; www.firstair.ca) flies three times a week between Whitehorse and
Yellowknife in Canada's Northwest Territories. **Condor** (from Canada & US: ✆ 1 800
364 1667, from all other countries: ✆ +49 (0) 180 5 707202; e reservation.en@condor.com;
www.condor.com) runs direct charter flights twice a week from May to September and
once a week during spring and autumn from Frankfurt, Germany.

BY SEA Cruise-ship and ferry passengers dock at Skagway, Alaska. From Skagway
you can travel by the White Pass and Yukon Route railway to Carcross and then by
bus to Whitehorse, or by road all the way; see pages 70–1.

🚗 **BY ROAD** The Alaska Highway crosses from BC into the Yukon just outside Watson
Lake (see page 80) and from the Yukon into Alaska at Beaver Creek (see pages
99–100). Alternatively the Top of the World Highway leads from Alaska to Dawson

27

City (see *Chapter 9*). The South Klondike Highway runs north from Skagway to join the Alaska Highway just outside Whitehorse.

For distances by road and approximate driving times from Whitehorse, see page 53.

BY BUS See page 53 for details of bus companies serving Whitehorse from Alaska and western Canada, and page 170 for details of bus routes to Dawson from Alaska via the Top of the World Highway.

HEALTH with Dr Felicity Nicholson

Whitehorse's **hospital** has a 24-hour emergency department and outpatient unit; see page 67. The smaller communities all have **health centres** with nursing care and regular doctor visits. **Yukon Healthline** is a free, 24-hour service offering everyday health advice to anyone travelling in the Yukon; call ＼ 811.

Be aware of the risk of **hypothermia** if you're doing outdoors activity – even in summer you should carry a good-quality waterproof jacket and trousers, and a warm hat and gloves.

In cold winter weather, exposed skin can freeze in minutes. Cover as much skin as possible to prevent **frostbite**, and keep a close eye on any exposed areas. Frostbitten skin turns numb, hard and waxy white, and may throb with pain. It flushes red when it warms and blisters. If you suffer from frostbite, seek medical help.

SAFETY

The Yukon people do not present any particular threat to tourists, despite their sometimes unkempt appearance and outspoken ways. The territory's natural resources are far more likely to damage you if you don't treat them with respect.

Bear attacks are very rare; however, you should always adhere to bear safety guidelines. If you see a bear when you're driving along the highway, always stay in your vehicle, and keep your distance. Be aware of traffic behind you: don't execute an emergency stop in the middle of the road so that you can take a photo, but find a safe place to pull over. If the bear approaches your vehicle, this is your cue to leave. Never feed a bear, and never stand between a female and her cubs. See pages 228–9 for more detailed bear safety advice, download Environment Yukon's *How You Can Stay Safe in Bear Country* brochure (*www.environmentyukon.gov.yk.ca/pdf/howyoucanstaysafe.pdf*) or watch the visitor centre bear safety video.

Moose kill more people than bears do (they batter with their hooves) but the problem is greater in Alaska than in the Yukon as moose are more numerous there. Keep a distance of at least 15m (50ft) from a moose. Don't stand between a female and her calf. If the moose lays back its ears, or its hackles (the hairs on its hump) rise, this is a sign that the moose is annoyed or afraid, and it may charge: this is a good moment for you to leave.

The **weather** presents the Yukon's greatest dangers. If you're travelling in summer and not venturing far from the highways and towns, or if you're on an organized tour, the risks are negligible. Winter driving, however, can present hazards (see page 33). If you're hiking or paddling in summer, be aware that the Yukon's weather is highly capricious (I have been snowed on at low altitude in Kluane National Park in August) and pack accordingly. In winter, take precautions for every eventuality: when the temperatures dive low, small mistakes kill.

Water from the taps is safe to drink. Water from creeks, rivers and lakes, however, should be boiled, filtered or purified before drinking.

In the case of **emergencies**, dial ☎ 911 if you're within the Whitehorse area. Beyond a 50km (30-mile) radius of Whitehorse, the 911 emergency service doesn't operate. **RCMP (Royal Canadian Mounted Police)** and **health centre** telephone numbers are listed for each town and village in the relevant chapters; otherwise you can call connect to the RCMP in Whitehorse on ☎ 867 667 5555. Note that there is no cell-phone coverage in the Yukon outside the towns (and that European cell phones don't work at all anywhere in territory, see page 46): if you break down or crash on a remote highway, you'll have to wait for the next vehicle to give you a ride to civilization.

WHAT TO TAKE

Do not confuse the Yukon with Milan: this is no glamour capital and the people dress functionally rather than for style. Even at dinners and banquets, there's often little in the way of a dress code.

In summer, temperatures can rise to 30°C (86°F); they can also drop to very cool. Bring sweaters and jackets alongside your T-shirts. Make sure you have good rainwear, both jacket and trousers if you're planning on doing any outdoors

Lieke Scheewe (with advice from Gordon Rattray; www.able-travel.com)

Canada has relatively high accessibility standards. There has been an increasing awareness that many people need special services, from various diet requirements to accessibility arrangements and protection from animal allergies. As such, its beach resorts as well as its wilderness are becoming a joy for everyone. Nevertheless, since Yukon is one of the most remote areas, getting around will be a challenging adventure.

GETTING THERE AND AROUND Access to Travel (*www.accesstotravel.gc.ca*) is a comprehensive resource that emerged from a co-operative effort between federal and local governments as well as the private and non-profit sectors. It provides up-to-date information on accessible transportation services across Canada, including information on transportation by air, bus, as well as local public and private transportation.

By air Erik Nielson Whitehorse International Airport (867 667 8440) should be contacted for information about accessibility. Assistance needs to be arranged directly with the airlines: First Air (800 267 1247; *www.firstair.ca*) and Air Canada (888 247 2262; *www.aircanada.com*) both offer services for disabled travellers.

By bus Greyhound Canada (800 661 8747; *www.greyhound.ca*) is a bus line that reaches the city of Whitehorse. It offers various services to those with limited hearing, sight and mobility. Mobility-impaired must book their seat 72 hours prior to departure. A travel escort or service animal can travel free of charge for those who need assistance during the trip.

In and around Whitehorse accessible Low-Floor Buses are available, although not all bus routes and stations are fully accessible. To ensure that a Low-Floor Bus is on your route contact the Transit Control Centre at 800 668 8394.

ACCOMMODATION Accessible accommodation is not very difficult to find, although the amount of accessible rooms is usually very limited. Travellers with special needs are urged to make their reservations in advance of arrival and to mention any specific requirements at the time of booking. A few useful resources include **Access Guide Canada** (*www.abilities.ca/agc*) which provides an overview of the level of accessibility for many lodgings in towns throughout the Yukon. The website of **Cottage Portal**™ (*www.cottageportal.com*) is very useful in finding wheelchair-accessible accommodation.

TRAVEL INSURANCE Most insurance companies will cater for disabled travellers, but it is essential that they are made aware of your disability. Examples of specialized companies that cover pre-existing medical conditions are Free Spirit (0845 230 5000; *www.free-spirit.com*) and Age Concern (0845 601 2234; *www.ageconcern.org.uk*), who have no upper age limit.

FURTHER INFORMATION The most comprehensive accessibility information website is offered by Access Guide Canada, a voluntary program compiling information on a wide variety of services, from transportation to lodgings and entertainment venues. Start your search by entering your destination province and community within Canada at www.abilities.ca/agc.

activities, as well as a warm hat and gloves. If you're intending to camp, I recommend tucking some long underwear into your rucksack, even in the height of summer. Bring comfortable walking shoes if you're planning a soft, highway- and town-based trip. Obviously if you're doing hardier stuff, you'll need good boots. See pages 230–2 for a comprehensive list of recommended gear for hiking and paddling trips.

Mosquitoes are the bane of the north in summer. Whitehorse has a highly effective 'mosquito control program' that eradicates larvae populations using a bacterium called *Bacilus thuringiensis var israelensis* (or Bti) – it does not harm humans, fish or wildlife. As a result, you don't tend to suffer from mosquito bites in Whitehorse. If you're planning on spending much time in rural areas, however, a bug shirt might be the answer: a bit like bee-keeping outfits, they're loose, fabric and mesh garments with hoods and zip-up mesh that covers the face. You can usually buy them in Coast Mountain Sports (see page 65) in Whitehorse. Even if you have a bug shirt, be sure to pack some DEET (50% concentration is sufficient); it's poisonous stuff, though, and you may prefer to use it sparingly.

In midsummer the Yukon has very long hours of daylight. Most hotels have effective blackout curtains, but it's a good idea to pack an eye mask (of the kind that airlines give out on long-haul flights) just in case – and particularly if you're intending to camp.

The Yukon is very photogenic so remember your camera, while binoculars add considerably to the pleasure of wildlife and birdwatching outings. Most of the Yukon's hotels, bed and breakfasts, and commercial campgrounds and RV parks have wireless internet connectivity so, if weight isn't an issue, carrying a laptop works well for those who wish to be in contact with home. Cell-phone connectivity is less widespread (see page 46) – a laptop may perform more reliably than a BlackBerry, especially if your BlackBerry doesn't understand CDMA technology.

WINTER CLOTHING In winter, you must have a good down jacket and insulated trousers if you're planning on spending any time outdoors, as well as excellent winter boots – preferably the white rubber 'bunny boots' first dreamed up by the American military, or otherwise a felt-lined boot such as those made by Sorel if you're going to embark on activities such as dogsledding or snowmobiling. The advantage of bunny boots over Sorels is that, if you get water in your boot, you can tip it out and carry on whereas a wet felt liner may freeze to your skin. Tour operators will usually lend or rent these expensive items.

Packaged carbon warmers can be bought in outdoors shops in the far north, and are a good solution for cold hands and feet. You shake them up to activate them, then slip them in your gloves or boots; they stay warm for around eight hours. Bring good, warm wool socks (cotton is no good), and always carry an extra couple of pairs in case your feet become damp: wet feet soon become frostbitten feet. Remember that keeping your clothing dry is of the greatest importance when travelling outdoors in winter as water soon turns to ice. Before leaving home, don't stand in wet patches on the floor when wearing just socks as then your feet will be wet and may freeze when you go outdoors. Once outside, never leave mitts or clothing with their insides facing out in case snow falls on them.

Hat and gloves, of course, are a must. It's a good idea to bring both a thin pair of gloves that allows you the use of your fingers, and a thicker pair of gloves or, better, mitts to wear over the top. A spare pair is also a good idea – if you lose a glove in the Great Outdoors you could be in trouble very fast. You'll also need a balaclava or Buff that you can pull over your face. In seriously low temperatures, skin can freeze in minutes – keep it covered whenever possible.

The best material to wear next to your skin is merino wool (Icebreaker and Ulfrotte are both reliable brands); wool, polypropylene and fleece all stay warmer than cotton, which soon turns cold and clammy. It's better to be a little on the cool side than to wear too much and sweat: damp clothing will make you cold. The Inuit don't mince words. They say, 'If you sweat, you die.'

HIKING AND PADDLING GEAR See pages 230–2 for sample packing lists for hiking and paddling expeditions.

BOOKS AND MAPS Mac's Fireweed Books (*203 Main St, Whitehorse;* ↘ *867 668 2434;* e *orders@macsbooks.ca; www.yukonbooks.com or www.macsbooks.ca;* ⊕ *summer: 8am–midnight daily, winter: 8am–9pm daily*) has a wide selection of Yukon-related books, and the full range of topographical maps and river guides. You can order them online if you want to refer to them before you arrive in the Yukon.

ELECTRICITY The Yukon has a 120V/60Hz electricity supply, and uses flat two-pin plugs.

$ MONEY AND BUDGETING

Bank opening hours vary: in Whitehorse, Dawson and Watson Lake you'll find banks open roughly from 9am or 9.30am to 4pm or 4.30pm Monday to Friday, but hours are often reduced – where banks exist at all – in the smaller communities. There are several banks with 24-hour ATMs in Whitehorse (see page 67 for location and opening hours), and at least an ATM in most of the smaller communities. Credit cards are widely accepted. Banks can arrange money transfers. See page 2 for the exchange rate at the time of going to print.

The far north is never a cheap destination due to the fact that so many goods need to be flown in from the south. However, the Yukon isn't truly exorbitant either, and budget-conscious travellers carrying tents can survive well as campsites are good and plentiful (government campsites cost just $12 per night per tent), and supermarket food, bought ahead in Whitehorse, is reasonably priced. Public transport is limited, however, so unless you're driving your own vehicle from the US or elsewhere in Canada, you'll need to hire a car if you're going to travel independently off the beaten track; see page 53. For outdoors expeditions, cost depends on accessibility: trips with road access cost less than those that require a float-plane fly-in.

For those with deep pockets, the top-end lodges and wilderness experiences come in at up to $1,000 a night, all-inclusive, once you've paid GST, alcohol, tips and the rest. For example, Tincup Wilderness Lodge (see page 35) offers all-inclusive fishing packages at $4,495 for seven nights or $3,750 for four nights; Great River Journey's Yukon River trip (see page 25) costs $7,800 for eight days.

Note that Yukon shops add on a goods and services tax (GST) of 5% at the point of payment rather than including it in the marked-up price, so you end up paying a little bit more than is marked on the price tag. GST isn't charged on groceries or prescription drugs.

In restaurants, most people **tip** between 10% and 20%.

GETTING AROUND

BY CAR The roads in the Yukon vary from the Alaska Highway, which is paved almost throughout and is in generally good condition, to tiny, rutted minor roads that would only just pass as a farm track elsewhere. Even on paved roads, however, the Yukon's weather can create hazards. Permafrost causes heaves where the water freezes, thaws and shifts the tarmac, and freezing conditions break up the road's surface to leave potholes. Little red flags by the side of the road alert drivers to these potholes and heaves. Note also that if there's a change of colour on the surface of the road ahead, this is probably an indication of a pothole or other damage even if no red flag is present.

Drive slowly on unpaved roads, and allow plenty of time – many visitors find that road journeys on the Yukon's more remote highways take considerably longer than they had expected. Soft gravel can have disastrous effects on one's steering (I speak from bitter experience – see page 141). After wet weather, potholes in gravel roads can become particularly severe. Allow extra time for road construction, which on the Yukon's gravel roads involves driving through great soft heaps of dirt – a far more hazardous affair than the asphalt replacement that urbanites and southerners are used to and especially difficult in wet weather when the roads can become slick with fresh mud.

The Yukon's law requires you to drive with headlights on at all times, and to wear a seatbelt. For up-to-date road conditions go to www.yukon511.ca or dial ℩ 511.

Car hire The only city in the Yukon to offer car hire is Whitehorse; see page 53. There are also car-hire companies in Inuvik, over the border in the NWT; see page 205 and in Skagway, Alaska; see page 121..

Road maps The government's free Yukon Highway Map is available from visitor centres across the territory.

Winter driving A week or so into my three-month stay at Muktuk Kennels, a journalist came to interview a musher about the forthcoming Yukon Quest. On leaving, she had difficulty negotiating the steep driveway in her car. 'I think she just thought she could put her foot on the gas and go,' the musher's girlfriend laughed as everyone else guffawed derisively. I sat rather quietly and concluded that, during my stay in the Yukon, it might be better if I sat in the passenger seat.

Independent winter travel is possible, and it's beautiful, but one must take precautions. In other parts of the world, if the car breaks down or if you accidentally slide into the ditch, you can use your cell phone to call the tow company. In the Yukon, outside the towns, cell phones don't work and the next vehicle may not come along for some time. If the temperature's 40 below, if you can't keep your vehicle's engine running, and if you're not carrying sufficient winter clothing, you'll be in big trouble – fast.

Take local advice before setting out. If you're driving your own vehicle, make sure it is winterized. Always carry winter clothing and an emergency survival kit that includes a torch or headlamp, a shovel, sand or kitty litter, and a survival candle. Drive slowly, and check out road conditions before you leave at www.yukon511.ca, or by calling ℩ 511.

If you do have an accident or breakdown, and if you must leave your vehicle's engine running to keep warm, try to avoid asphyxiating yourself – it would be annoying to survive an accident but then to expire from carbon-monoxide poisoning. Make sure the vehicle's exhaust pipe is not blocked with snow and keep a window slightly open to let in fresh air. You may prefer to burn a survival candle than to keep the vehicle's engine running. Lastly, if you pass a broken-down vehicle, you *must* stop. Your failure to help could be critical.

For winter driving, most vehicles in the Yukon have block heaters, which connect via a cable running from the front of the vehicle to an electrical socket. Plug the vehicle in overnight, or an hour or two before you wish to drive, in order to warm the engine's vital parts.

OTHER TRANSPORT There are **bus** services along the Alaska Highway, and connecting Whitehorse to Skagway and Dawson in the summer; see pages 53, 121 and 170. Otherwise, regular flights connect Whitehorse, Dawson, Inuvik and Old Crow; see page 27.

Float and **ski plane** and/or **helicopter charters** operate out of all major communities. For float plane charters call **Alpine Aviation** (↘ *867 668 7725, cell: 867 393 1482;* e *alpine@polarcom.com; www.alpineaviationyukon.com*) or **Black Sheep Aviation** (↘ *867 668 7761;* e *blacksheep@northwestel.net; www.flyblacksheep.ca*). Both companies are licensed to carry external loads such as canoes and kayaks. Helicopter charter companies are listed in the relevant chapters.

 ACCOMMODATION

Almost all of the Yukon's **hotels** are clean and comfortable. Most will not win any design awards for ultra-sleek décor but they're perfectly pleasant and they work just fine. The only thing to watch out for is the fact that the Yukon's licensing laws require any bar to be attached to a 'hotel' – a couple of these have rooms that are very rudimentary (for example, the 98 in Whitehorse and, to a lesser extent, the Westminster in Dawson) and their accommodation is not geared to the tourist trade. The better in-town hotels cost $150+ while mid-range rooms come it at between $75 and £150.

There are also plenty of very good **bed and breakfasts**, which offer a more personal touch. The **Bed & Breakfast Association of the Yukon** (e *stay@yukonbandb.org; www.yukonbandb.org*) is an excellent resource, and its website has comprehensive listings of its members. B&Bs will generally set you back between $95 and $150.

For a comfortable wilderness experience, book into one of the many out-of-town **lodges**. Some of these are just a short drive from Whitehorse; others are in remote bush locations. Levels of luxury vary but generally they have electricity (though not always in their outlying cabins) and some kind of access to running water. They tend to offer full board as well as outdoor activities. Wilderness lodges can cost in the region of $200–$300 in high season per person per night including all meals and activities, but prices vary considerably depending on location and facilities. There are also a lot of **cabins** for rent in the Yukon. Some of these have electricity and running water; others do not. Check before you book if such mod cons are important to you – while remembering that, often, the fewer the facilities, the more serene the wilderness experience. Cabins range from around $200 per double per night for high-end accommodation with full facilities, while you can usually rent a simpler cabin for around $75–$100. If you're planning an extended stay in the Yukon, many of the cabin owners will give you a good deal.

The only **backpackers' hostel** in Whitehorse (the Beez Kneez, see page 60) charges $25 for a dorm room or $50 for a private double; in Dawson the cheapest hostel accommodation you'll find is the Bunkhouse (see page 177) at $72 for a double, while Dawson City River Hostel (page 178) has good-value cabins.

Some of the Yukon's accommodation is open in the summer only; where this is the case, I have noted it in each listing. Where there is no mention of seasonal opening, the establishment operates year round.

The price codes used in this guide are listed on the inside front cover.

CAMPGROUNDS AND RV SITES There are plenty of commercially run campgrounds and RV parks across the territory, which generally offer a high level of facilities. RV sites range from around $20–$35 per night depending on the level of service; commercially run campgrounds usually charge $15–$20.

The Yukon government additionally manages more than 40 campgrounds. **Government campgrounds** don't have electricity or running water (there are outhouses) but do provide free firewood, picnic tables and fire pits, and they are all in fantastically scenic spots on the shores of lakes and rivers.

Government campground sites cost $12 per night. The fee applies to each tent or RV; children's tents go free when children are camping with their parents. Everyone staying at a campground must self-register either by depositing payment at the campground itself or by buying campground permits in advance from visitor centres, highway lodges, gas stations, local stores or Environment Yukon offices. Once at the campground, you should choose your site and note down both the site number and your vehicle registration number. Take this information to the fee station where you'll fill in a self-registration envelope and deposit either your $12 or your pre-paid permit inside. Remove the receipt stub, seal the envelope, and put it in the deposit vault. Then fill out the receipt stub and attach it to the site number post.

Campground stays are limited to 14 days in a 30-day period, and sites may not be reserved for campers who have not yet arrived. All garbage should be put in bear-resistant containers. Quiet hours are between 11pm and 7am and generators should be shut down between those times. Note that popular campgrounds near to Whitehorse can become very busy during summer weekends.

FISHING LODGES AND CAMPS The following lodges are specifically geared towards fishing packages and must be pre-booked. They all offer genuine wilderness experiences (only Dalton Trail Lodge has road access); as such, you will not find chi-chi décor or silk drapes, but solid, functional style.

⌂ **Dalton Trail Lodge** (10 rooms in main lodge plus 4 cabins) On Dezadeash Lake, Haines Rd; ☎ 867 634 2099; e grayling@lincsat.com; www.daltontrail.com; ⊕ end May–early Oct. Accesses 24 different lakes & rivers. Also has outpost cabins in remote locations & fly-outs. The lodge is comfortable with a bar & restaurant; there's wireless internet via a satellite connection. Hiking, mountain biking & canoeing are also offered.

⌂ **Inconnu Lodge** (accommodates 12 guests) ☎ 250 860 4187; e info@inconnulodge.com; www.inconnulodge.com; ⊕ mid-Jun to mid-Sep. Fly-in lodge in southeast Yukon offers 5-day & 7-day packages. Activities include heli-hiking, canoeing, kayaking & gold panning in addition to fishing.

⌂ **Tincup Wilderness Lodge** (accommodates 8–10 guests) ☎ 604 762 0382; e tincup@axion.net; www.tincup-lodge.com; ⊕ mid-Jun to mid-Sep. High-

end fly-in lodge on the edge of Kluane National Park. In addition to fishing, there are boating, glacier-viewing & photography outings.

⌂ **Wilderness Fishing Yukon** ☎ 867 667 2846; e info@fishingyukon.com; www.fishingyukon.com. Fishing at fly-in camps on 9 different Yukon lakes. The camps can accommodate parties from 2 to 12. There is only 1 camp per lake, and only 1 party in each camp at a time: you'll never have to share your space. The camps are rustic with propane fuel & outhouses. You're provided with boats with 9.9 hp motors, but must bring your own sleeping bags, groceries, fishing licence & tackle. Wilderness Fishing Yukon also takes guests on an annual 10-day moose-hunting trip on horseback but note – this is not trophy hunting. Clients hike, canoe, watch wildlife, pick berries & fish, & help search for the moose but do not shoot.

2

RV DUMP STATIONS

It is illegal, not to mention morally heinous, to dump your RV holding tank into the Yukon's lakes, rivers and forests. (Bears may dump in the woods, but your RV may not.) Most RV parks will allow you to use their dump stations for a small fee, even if you're not a registered guest; some service stations also have RV dump facilities. Note that Yukon government campgrounds do not have RV dump stations.

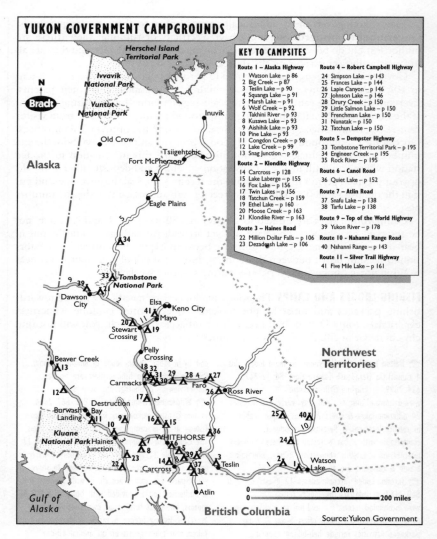

YUKON GOVERNMENT CAMPGROUNDS

N

Bradt

Herschel Island
Territorial Park

Ivvavik
National Park

Vuntut
National Park

Inuvik

Old Crow

Tsiigehtchic

Fort McPherson

Alaska

35

Eagle Plains

34

33 Tombstone
National Park

9 39

Dawson
City

Elsa

41 Keno City

Mayo

20 19

Stewart
Crossing

Pelly
Crossing

Beaver Creek
13

12

18 32

31 29 28 4 27

Carmacks 30

Faro

26 Ross River

17

Destruction
Bay

Burwash 11 10 9 16 15

Landing

Kluane
National Park Haines
Junction

WHITEHORSE 36

6

4 4

8

22 23

14 39

Carcross 3 37 Teslin

38

Atlin

Northwest
Territories

25 40

24

2 1 Watson
Lake

Gulf of
Alaska

British Columbia

0 ———————— 200km
0 ———————— 200 miles

Source: Yukon Government

KEY TO CAMPSITES

Route 1 – Alaska Highway
1 Watson Lake – p 86
2 Big Creek – p 87
3 Teslin Lake – p 90
4 Squanga Lake – p 91
5 Marsh Lake – p 91
6 Wolf Creek – p 92
7 Takhini River – p 93
8 Kusawa Lake – p 93
9 Aishihik Lake – p 93
10 Pine Lake – p 93
11 Congdon Creek – p 98
12 Lake Creek – p 99
13 Snag Junction – p 99

Route 2 – Klondike Highway
14 Carcross – p 128
15 Lake Laberge – p 155
16 Fox Lake – p 156
17 Twin Lakes – p 156
18 Tatchun Creek – p 159
19 Ethel Lake – p 160
20 Moose Creek – p 163
21 Klondike River – p 163

Route 3 – Haines Road
22 Million Dollar Falls – p 106
23 Dezadeash Lake – p 106

Route 4 – Robert Campbell Highway
24 Simpson Lake – p 143
25 Frances Lake – p 144
26 Lapie Canyon – p 146
27 Johnson Lake – p 146
28 Drury Creek – p 150
29 Little Salmon Lake – p 150
30 Frenchman Lake – p 150
31 Nunatak – p 150
32 Tatchun Lake – p 150

Route 5 – Dempster Highway
33 Tombstone Territorial Park – p 195
34 Engineer Creek – p 195
35 Rock River – p 195

Route 6 – Canol Road
36 Quiet Lake – p 152

Route 7 – Atlin Road
37 Snafu Lake – p 138
38 Tarfu Lake – p 138

Route 9 – Top of the World Highway
39 Yukon River – p 178

Route 10 - Nahanni Range Road
40 Nahanni Range – p 143

Route 11 – Silver Trail Highway
41 Five Mile Lake – p 161

Wolf Lake Lodge (4 cabins each sleep up to 3 people) ☎ 306 873 7733 year round or call the satellite phone at the lodge, ☎ 250 483 6919 from Jun to mid-Sep; e wes.walker@sasktel.net; www.wolflake.ca; ⏰ early Jun to mid-Sep. Fly-in lodge on the shores of Wolf Lake, 160km (100 miles) east of Whitehorse.

✕ EATING AND DRINKING

FOOD This is Canada, and there won't be much on the menu that travellers don't recognize. In Whitehorse, Dawson City and Haines Junction there's a handful of excellent restaurants, including those serving international fare from Mexican to Japanese to Greek. A main course will usually cost in the range of $10 to $25. Outside the larger towns, the range becomes reduced but you'll usually find burgers, fish and chips, soups, salads and sandwiches. Much of the food served in the Yukon's restaurants and cafés is homemade and of high quality.

You may notice when eating out in the Yukon that the menus generally feature meats like beef and chicken. It seems odd, when there's a not a cow or a hen to be seen, and the forests and roadsides are instead are filled with wild moose, caribou and bison. So why are the restaurateurs using imported meats rather than local fare? Answer: restaurants aren't allowed to serve wild game. They may serve farmed game, so when you see bison, elk or caribou on the menu, that will be its provenance. But if you want to eat a moose fresh from the forest, you'll have to make friends with a hunter.

Self-catering You'll find food shops in all the Yukon's communities, but the best choice and best prices are in the Whitehorse supermarkets; see page 67.

DRINK The local beers are Yukon Gold, Yukon Red and Chilkoot, all brewed by the **Yukon Brewing Company** (*102A Copper Rd;* ☎ *867 668 4183; www.yukonbeer.com*), which offers free tours; call for more information. In common with many northern communities, alcohol tends to be more expensive than it is in, for example, the UK.

The Yukoners (or maybe it's North America in general) are strangely puritanical about the purchase of alcohol. You can't buy it in a normal grocery store, so either you must go to a dedicated liquor store or to a hotel. Even when you have tracked down a bottle, you must leave with it wrapped in a paper bag. If you drive to the liquor store, don't leave with your bottle of wine sitting on the passenger seat – it's illegal. Alcohol must be stowed in the trunk. And under no circumstances whatsoever must you carry an open bottle of alcohol in the main compartment of the car, even if you had not the remotest intention of drinking from it. It's very illegal – and while these rules seem absurdly uptight to us lax and wayward Europeans, to North Americans they apparently appear entirely right and proper. (Think of it like the right to bear arms, which we Europeans can never understand, but in reverse.)

PUBLIC HOLIDAYS, FESTIVALS AND EVENTS

PUBLIC HOLIDAYS The Yukon observes Canadian public holidays on New Year's Day (1 January), the Friday before Easter, Victoria Day (the Monday on or before 24 May), Canada Day (1 July), Labour Day (first Monday in September), Thanksgiving (second Monday in October – note that this is not the same date as the USA's Thanksgiving), Remembrance Day (11 November), and Christmas (25–26 December). Additionally the Yukon has a holiday on Discovery Day (the third Monday in August) to mark George Carmack and co's discovery of gold in the Klondike.

FESTIVALS AND EVENTS For a place with few inhabitants, the Yukon has a surprisingly jam-packed cultural schedule (not to mention a heart-pumping calendar of sporting races including running, biking, skiing, paddling and dogsledding; see page 39.

February

Available Light Film Festival Whitehorse; www.yukonfilmsociety.com. Features more than 20 screenings as well as guest filmmakers, workshops, industry events & panel discussions.
Frostbite Music Festival Whitehorse; www.frostbitefest.ca. 3 days of concerts & workshops with Yukon, Canadian & international musicians.

Kiki Karnival Watson Lake; ☎ Town of Watson Lake 867 536 8000. 3-day winter carnival featuring hockey, bonspiel, food & the like.
Outdoor Bonspiel Watson Lake; ☎ Town of Watson Lake 867 536 8000. 3 days of jam-packed curling.
Trek over the Top Dawson; www.trekoverthetop.com. 3 1-day snowmobile rides in Feb & Mar over the

Top of the World Highway between Dawson & Tok, Alaska; see page 187.

Yukon Sourdough Rendezvous Festival Whitehorse; www.yukonrendezvous.com. Whitehorse's winter festival features 4 days of dog racing, skijoring, ice carving & all those other events that northerners consider so much fun: log tossing, chainsaw chucking & the rest.

March

Ice Worm Squirm Extravaganza Faro; www.faroyukon.ca. Carnival featuring winter sports, games & dancing.

Muskrat Jamboree Inuvik; e muskratjamboree@ hotmail.com. 4-day celebration includes muskrat-skinning, snowshoe racing, log sawing, tea boiling, ice chiselling, nail driving, egg tossing, & snowmobile & dog races.

Thaw-Di-Gras Spring Carnival Dawson; www.dawsoncity.ca. Dawson's winter carnival with frolics including showshoe baseball.

Trek over the Top See *February*, above.

Easter weekend

Aklavik Mad Trapper Rendezvous Aklavik; ⟍ Aklavik Hamlet office at: 867 978 2351. Dog races, snowmobile races, traditional dances, cultural events & a community feast. Visitors are welcome.

Dawson City International Short Film Festival Dawson; www.dawsonfilmfest.com. 4 days filled with more than 100 films as well as workshops & masterclasses.

April

Celebration of Swans M'Clintock Bay, Marsh Lake; www.environmentyukon.gov.yk.ca/viewing. See page 91.

May

Annual Crane and Sheep Viewing Festival Faro; www.faroyukon.ca.

June

Aboriginal Day Celebrations Dawson & Whitehorse; www.trondek.com (Dawson) & www.yfnta.org (Whitehorse). Cultural celebrations with the region's First Nations.

Alsek Music Festival Haines Junction; www.alsekfest.com. The focus is on Yukon musicians, & performers from other northern communities, playing folk to jazz to country to classical, plus there are arts & crafts activities for the kids.

Commissioner's Ball Dawson City; www.dawsoncity.ca. Pack your ball gown if you're going to join Dawson for its annual knees-up in the Palace Grand Theatre.

Klondike Motorcycle Run Dawson City; www.dawsoncity.ca. Canada's northernmost motorbike rally lasts 3 days.

Kluane Mountain Bluegrass Festival & Music Camp Haines Junction; www.kluanemountainbluegrassfest.com.

The festival features musicians from around the world, while the Music Camp is held at The Cabin Bed & Breakfast & Kathleen Lake Retreat; it offers instruction in guitar, mandolin, fiddle, banjo & bass. Note that this festival is now held on a different w/end to the Alsek Music Festival, above.

Mayo Arts Festival Mayo; http://mayoarts.wordpress.com. Takes place on 21 June, coinciding with the Midnight Marathon, see page 162.

Ride Yukon – Motorcycles, Music and Midnight Sun www.rideyukon.com. Golden Circle route from Whitehorse to Haines Junction, Haines, Skagway & back to Whitehorse.

Weekend on the Wing Tombstone Territorial Park; www.environmentyukon.gov.yk.ca/wildlifebiodiversity/birds.php. See page 197.

July

Annual Faro Open Golf Tournament Faro; www.faroyukon.ca. Try your skills on this quirky 'urban' golf course.

Atlin Arts & Music Festival Atlin, BC; www.atlinfestival.ca. Musicians, artists, storytellers & film makers flock to the tiny but scenic town of Atlin for 3 days of live performances, workshops & exhibitions.

Coca-Cola Golf Championship Whitehorse; www.mountainviewgolf.ca. A 1-day stroke play

If you like a competitive edge to your outdoor activities, these are the major events on the Yukon calendar.

FEBRUARY
Yukon Arctic Ultra www.articultra.de. Mountain-bike, running, cross-country ski and skijoring race over 100 and 300 miles (160 and 480km).
Yukon Quest International Sled Dog Race www.yukonquest.com. Teams run for 1,600km (1,000 miles) between Whitehorse and Fairbanks, Alaska via Dawson; see pages 42–4.

MARCH
Percy DeWolfe Memorial Mail Race www.thepercy.com. Dogsled race between Dawson and Eagle, Alaska, which commemorates the life of 'the iron man of the north' – he carried the mail along this route from 1910 to 1949; see page 188.
NorthwesTel Yukon Loppet www.xcskiwhitehorse.ca. 30, 20, 7.5 or 3km cross-country ski races.

JUNE
24 Hours of Light Mountain Bike Festival Whitehorse; www.24hoursoflight.ca. Team or solo event; the course runs through the night along mountain biking trails outside Whitehorse. No lights allowed!
Annual City of Whitehorse Triathlon www.whitehorse.ca. Olympic and sprint distance events; it's a pool swim.
Kluane Chilkat International Bike Relay www.kcibr.org. Bike relay race runs from Haines Junction to Haines, Alaska.
Mayo Midnight Marathon www.kenocity.info/marathon_detail.html. See page 162.
Yukon River Quest Canoe and Kayak Race www.yukonriverquest.com. Participants paddle 740km (460 miles) from Whitehorse to Dawson.

JULY
Yukon 1000 Canoe & Kayak Race www.yukon1000.com. The course runs for 1,600km (1,000 miles) from Whitehorse to the Alaska Pipeline Bridge on the Dalton Highway, Alaska. The event was scheduled for the first time in 2009; check the website for dates of future races.

AUGUST
Yukon River Trail Marathon Whitehorse; www.yukonmarathon.com. Off-road course on the trails around Whitehorse.
Yukon 360 Canoe & Kayak Race www.yukon1000.com/360. The smaller sibling of the Yukon 1000 (see July), this race runs over Discovery Day weekend, from Johnson's Crossing to Carmacks.

SEPTEMBER
Klondike Trail of 98 International Road Relay www.sportyukon.com. Teams of up to ten runners race overnight from Skagway to Whitehorse.

championship, over 18 holes, with dinner & prizes. Non-members welcome.
Dawson City Music Festival Dawson; www.dcmf.com. 3 days of music & dancing under the midnight sun, with genres ranging from folk to blues to hip-hop.
Great Northern Arts Festival Inuvik; www.gnaf.org. See page 213.

Midway Music Festival Midway Lake, 30km (48 miles) southwest of Fort McPherson on the Dempster Highway. See page 199.
Mini Arts Festival Faro; www.faroyukon.ca. Local artisans display their work, & there's a wild-game BBQ.

Moosehide Gathering Moosehide, near Dawson. The Tr'ondëk Hwëch'in First Nation & its guests celebrate northern heritage every 2nd year; see page 189.
Yukon Gold Panning Championships Dawson; www.dawsoncity.ca. Visitors are welcome to try their chances against the pros in these gold-panning time trials.

August
Discovery Days Festival Dawson; www.dawsoncity.ca. A week of events celebrating Discovery Day (17 Aug).
End of the Road Music Festival Inuvik; ✆ 867 777 3054; e eotr_musicfestival@yahoo.ca. Showcases local & Canadian artists.
Fireweed Festival Faro; www.faroyukon.ca. Horticultural festival, plus arts & crafts workshops & sales.

Great Klondike International Outhouse Race Dawson; www.dawsoncity.ca. Teams race decorated outhouses on wheels through the streets of Dawson.
Northern Games Inuvik; www.northerngames.org. See page 214.

October
Yukon International Storytelling Festival Whitehorse; www.storytelling.yk.net. International, national & Yukon

performers take to the stage for 3 evenings that celebrate the rich storytelling tradition of the north.

December
Dawson City Old-Fashioned Christmas Party Dawson; www.dawsoncity.ca. Festivities to brighten Dawson's dark winter days.

🛍 SHOPPING

The Yukon has a surprisingly rich and diverse arts scene considering its small population; this is particularly true of Whitehorse and Dawson, but even tiny communities such as Keno attract creative types looking for a simpler pace of life. Given the Yukon's high number of artists, both indigenous and non-indigenous, it's a good place to buy paintings, prints, photographs, jewellery and carvings. In many cases it is possible to buy direct from the artist. Yukon Tourism and Culture publishes an informative booklet entitled *Art Adventures on Yukon Time*, which lists nearly 200 local artists, with their contact details and website URLs where available, and tells visitors where they can buy their work. You can pick the booklet up at the visitor centre or at the Yukon Arts Society's home, **Arts Underground** (see page 65).

In Whitehorse, both **Arts Underground** and **Yukon Artists@Work** (see page 65) make for excellent browsing. Locally crafted gold jewellery and nuggets of Klondike gold are sold in various shops in Dawson and Whitehorse.

First Nations artwork, clothing, leatherwork and beadwork are for sale in communities across the Yukon. For carving, the **Sundog Carving Studio & Gallery** in Whitehorse (see page 65) is particularly worth a visit.

Note that if you buy (or indeed find) **antlers, horns, pelts or other wildlife parts** in the Yukon, you must get an export permit from **Environment Yukon** (*10 Burns Rd, Whitehorse – across from the airport;* ✆ *867 667 5652, toll-free:* ✆ *1 800 661 0408 ext 5652;* e *environmentyukon@gov.yk.ca; www.environmentyukon.gov.yk.ca)* before you take them out of the territory.

For equipment and clothing for **outdoor activities**, go to Coast Mountain Sports in Whitehorse; see page 65. Books and maps can be bought at Mac's Fireweed Books in Whitehorse (see page 65) or ordered ahead from www.yukonbooks.com. Maximilians's Gold Rush Emporium in Dawson (see page 180) also has a reasonable range of books.

All the communities have well-stocked **food stores**; inevitably, the best choice is in Whitehorse.

ARTS AND ENTERTAINMENT

Due to the large number of artists, musicians and filmmakers living in the territory, the Yukon benefits from frequent events and festivals. See *Public Holidays, Festivals and Events* on pages 37–40 as well as the individual chapters in *Part Two* of this book – particularly the chapters on Whitehorse and Dawson – for information on events and venues.

Events listings are uploaded onto the Yukon Arts & Events Calendar (*www.yukonarts.com*); also check out *What's Up Yukon* (*www.whatsupyukon.com*).

MUSIC Those interested in the Yukon music scene should check out Whitehorse's cafés for their regular live performances (see *Chapter 3, Whitehorse*, pages 63–4). You can download local musicians' sample tracks from MusicYukon's website, www.musicyukon.com. There are also links to local artists at Triple Js Music Café's (see page 66) website, www.jjjmusiccafe.ca.

One of the most popular – and enduring – musicians in the Yukon is Hank Karr, who has lived in the territory since 1963. He sings and plays country music, sometimes with a Yukon theme. His song 'After Yukon' seems to blast out from local radio stations with great regularity – you can download a sampler from www.musicyukon.com (click on 'List Music by Artist', then scroll down to Hank Karr). Hank Karr's CDs are available in Mac's Fireweed Books on Whitehorse's Main Street (see page 65), and other shops across the Yukon.

OUTDOOR ACTIVITIES

Given its tremendous expanses of untrammelled wilderness, the Yukon makes a paradisiacal playground for outdoors enthusiasts. In summer there are boundless hiking options, pristine wilderness rivers to be paddled, as well as biking and horse-riding adventures. In winter there's dogsledding, cross-country skiing and snowshoeing through a breathtakingly beautiful winter landscape.

Possibilities for half-day and day trips are numerous, but to really get a feel for the vast magnificence of this incredible land, longer trips are all the better. Information on short hikes and skiing routes, and summaries of navigable waterways are provided in the individual chapters of *Part Two*, while *Part Three* of this book is dedicated to detailed route descriptions of three of the Yukon's most popular paddling rivers (the Yukon between Whitehorse and Carmacks, the Liard and the Big Salmon), its most infamous hike (the Chilkoot), and one long, arduous, but utterly wonderful eight- to ten-day hike in and around Kluane National Park (the Donjek Route).

DOGSLEDDING I spent three months in early 2006 living at Muktuk Kennels (see page 56) near Whitehorse, learning the art of mushing, and researching my book *Mad Dogs and an Englishwoman*. Before leaving home, I was nervous about my trip. I was terrified of the prospect of the cold and I didn't know much about dogs. (My last close canine encounter had been the year before in Argentina – the dog in question had sunk its teeth into my bare leg.) I feared that the Yukon's mushing fraternity would be too formidable for me, a soft urbanite, to befriend. But over my weeks in the Yukon, I slowly fell in love with the far north, with the silent expanses of snow, with the sharp blue skies, the bright-turquoise overflow ice, the dusky pink sunsets, the warm yellow light of noon. I also developed a deep fondness for the hundred-odd joyful, mischievous huskies with whom I shared my days.

There are few experiences that compare to driving your own team of dogs along a wilderness trail – but the pleasure comes not from any alpha-male satisfaction with one's own bravado, but from the relationship that a musher builds with the dogs. I always cringe at the TV shows we see in the UK (and I dare say the US is the same) which celebrate some well-known 'adventurer' courageously heading out with a team of dogs into the subzero beyond, while a voiceover regales the viewers with enthusiastic assertions about this 21st-century Tarzan's tremendous grit, courage and resolve. The narrative overlooks the fact that the musher on the back of the sled would go nowhere without the dogs, and that the dogs will go nowhere unless they love and respect the musher. Given that these celebrity adventurers often appear not even to know the names of the individual members their teams, much less how to engage their love and respect, we can only assume that there is a dog handler somewhere behind the scenes doing the work – or otherwise a shambles ensues, and our 'hero' is warmly congratulated for surviving the canine chaos of his own creation. I always sit there and think, 'Poor, poor dogs being stuck out there with a fool like that.' And then I generally change channel.

Enough of my ranting. Dogsledding is a truly wonderful way to spend a week or two's vacation. While a couple of hours' riding in the sled while someone else drives has its pleasures, it's infinitely better to take a longer trip, and to drive your own team under the supervision of an experienced guide. This gives you an opportunity to bond with the dogs, to learn their names and personality quirks, to feed and care for them, and even to love them a little. As the days go by, you'll notice that your dogs – who can scent a novice at a hundred metres and then behave like a class of six-year-olds with a supply teacher – respond more keenly to your commands. Dogs work better for people they know.

Many dogsledding tour operators offer winter camping trips. Some operators use designated trails on which they set up wall tents for the entire season, which reduces the workload of guides and guests. Others take a freer approach, allowing a greater diversity of trails, but then you have to set up camp from scratch each evening. Even with the tent ready pitched, though, winter travel with dogs is hard work. Just to melt enough snow for water for a group of dogs and humans takes hours each day.

Do you need to be physically fit to drive a team of dogs? Well, if you're chugging happily along a flat trail, the dogs are behaving like four-legged angels and snow conditions are good, you won't need to exert yourself a great deal. Dogs can be unpredictable, however, and it's easy to lose control of the sled on sloping ice. You may fall from the sled or be dragged (you should never let go of the sled as you may then lose the team), and this requires some resilience.

For longer trips, you'll want to be in better shape, particularly where hills are involved. A musher should help the dogs in uphill sections either by running alongside the sled, or by pedalling with one foot. The dogs have a remarkably expressive way of turning their heads and delivering withering looks if you try to ride the runners during an ascent. As for the issue of speed, dog mushing is not really an adrenalin junky's sport: you're aiming for a steady pace so that you don't strain the dogs' legs and shoulders. If it's speed you're after, you might be better off hiring a snowmobile instead.

The Yukon Quest The Yukon Quest is one tough race. It runs each February for 1,600km (1,000 miles) over historic gold-rush and mail-run routes between Whitehorse in the Yukon and Fairbanks in Alaska. The direction of the race alternates year on year: one year it starts at Whitehorse and finishes in Fairbanks, the following year it's the other way round.

If the Quest is less famous than the Iditarod, that's partly because it was intended to be. The race's founders set it up in 1984 precisely because they felt that the Iditarod was becoming too commercialized. The Quest's entrants are fewer, its prize money is less – but it's in many respects a more arduous race. The Iditarod has 25 checkpoints over its thousand-mile course. The Yukon Quest has just ten, and some of those are more than 300km (188 miles) apart. To complete the Quest, mushers must have real knowledge of how to survive, and to care for a team of dogs, in temperatures that can drop into the minus 40s.

Anyone who feels sorry for the dogs should just take a visit to the start line of the Yukon Quest. These dogs know what's in store for them – all have been on long training runs, and many have run thousand-mile races before – yet they bark and whine and leap up down in the harness, tongues lolling and tails wagging. They are beside themselves with excitement. They can't wait to start. And just in case any musher isn't caring sufficiently for his or her dogs, there are mandatory vet checks along the way. If the vets are concerned about the state of any dog or team they can – and do – require the musher to take a longer rest, or even to scratch from the race.

The winners generally complete the course in around ten days. During this time, the musher gets little sleep: the dogs rest frequently but, as they do so, the musher must prepare food and water, and check the state of every dog's feet. There's a mandatory 36-hour layover in the middle of the race, at Dawson City. This is the only time in the race when anyone other than the musher, or the race's vets and officials, may help a musher with his or her dogs. Now the mushers head off for food and rest, and the handlers care for the dogs in camps set up in the government campground on the west bank of Dawson City.

It's possible for tourists to follow the Yukon Quest – though even following this race is a gruelling business. Most of the checkpoints are in tiny, out-of-the-way settlements where there's no such thing as a comfortable hotel, and the mushers often come through the checkpoints in the middle of the night. If you're interested in following the race, **Muktuk Adventures** (see page 56) runs 'Follow the Quest' packages; these are rough-and-ready expeditions that follow the race from checkpoint to checkpoint – be aware that your bed may be the back seat of the truck. For more comfort (but fewer of the out-of-the-way checkpoints) **Northern**

WHAT IS AN ALASKAN HUSKY?

Purebred dogs such as Siberian huskies and Malamutes are considered too heavy and slow for contemporary sled-dog racing. The type of dog favoured by today's mushers is the Alaskan husky – which isn't a purebreed at all, but a mixture of many such as Siberian husky, Alaskan village dog and hound. The musher's aim in breeding is to create an athletic animal suited to northern temperatures, not a thoroughbred beauty.

In recent years, the top mushers have increasingly introduced hound breeds into their Alaskan husky hybrid. As a result, dogs today tend to be smaller and shorter-haired than they used to be. But visit a sled dog kennels and you'll find dogs of all colours and markings – white, black, tan, speckled and patched. Some have ears that stick up, others have ears that flop down, and dogs may sport either blue eyes or brown – some even have one of each.

As for why huskies howl, it's not a sign of discontent (though dogs do howl pitifully when their companions have been harnessed and taken out for a run and they are left behind). Huskies often howl after they've eaten and sometimes, it seems, they just like a good, lusty singalong.

Tales (see page 25) runs Yukon Quest packages taking in the 36-hour stopover in Dawson as well as the start or finish line, and other Yukon attractions such as the Tombstone and Kluane parks and northern lights viewing. Otherwise, you can always watch the start or finish in Whitehorse or Fairbanks, and follow the action online at the Quest's website, www.yukonquest.com.

Volunteering Many of the dogsledding kennels take on volunteers to help feed and care for the dogs, clean the yard, and so on in return for food, board and mushing; stays can range from a couple of weeks to a couple of months – some volunteers can't tear themselves away and stay a couple of years. It's not just the tourist operations that take on volunteers: the professional mushers who don't run tourism programs also require dog handlers. If you're interested in learning about the world of mushing from the inside, contact the individual tour operators, or look for non-tourist operations in need of handlers in the classified ads pages of www.sleddogcentral.com (go to the 'Wanted' section and click on 'Help/Handlers').

The **Yukon Quest** also needs volunteers to help with the race in February each year; go to www.yukonquest.com/site/for-volunteers or contact the Quest office (✆ 867 668 4711; e questadmin@polarcom.com) for more information. The Quest office may also know of local mushers looking for handlers.

FISHING If you're going to fish in the Yukon, you must have a licence. It costs $10 per day, $15 per week or $25, plus GST, per season if you're a Canadian (non-Yukon) resident, or $10, $20, $35 if you're not Canadian or Alaskan. Licences can be bought at the **Environment Yukon** office in Whitehorse (*10 Burns Rd, across from the airport,* ✆ *867 667 5652, toll-free:* ✆ *1 800 661 0408 ext 5652;* e *environmentyukon@ gov.yk.ca; www.environmentyukon.gov.yk.ca*), the **Fisheries and Oceans Canada** office (*100–419 Range Rd, Whitehorse;* ✆ *867 393 6722*) and most gas stations, sporting goods stores and convenience stores.

The Yukon Angling Licence is not valid in Kluane, Ivvavik or Vuntut national parks, where you must buy a national park fishing licence from a park office. For more information call ✆ 867 634 7250.

If you wish to **fish for salmon** in the Yukon (other than in stocked lakes) you must buy a Salmon Conservation Catch Card in addition to your angling licence, $20 (non-Yukon Canadian residents), $50 (non-Canadian residents).

Many tour operators offer guided fishing trips; see pages 24–5 and the tour operator listings in individual chapters. For details of dedicated fishing lodges, see page 35. For more information on regulations and on where and what to fish in the Yukon go to www.yukonfishing.com. For details on stocked lakes, download Environment Yukon's booklet *Angler's Guide to Stocked Lakes in the Yukon*, www.environmentyukon.gov.yk.ca/yukonfishing/angler_guide_2006.pdf.

HUNTING Species that may be hunted, within designated seasons, include caribou, moose, mountain sheep and goats, grizzly and black bears, wolves and bison. Non-residents (including Canadians not resident in the Yukon) may only hunt for big game when guided by a registered outfitter, and must pay trophy fees. Non-residents may hunt rabbits, ground squirrels and porcupines on their own without a licensed guide and, in the fall (after 1 September) they may also hunt grouse, ptarmigan and waterfowl without a guide. To hunt small game, however, you must still have a licence.

The **Yukon Outfitters' Association** (*B4 – 302 Steele St, Whitehorse;* ✆ *867 668 4118;* e *info@yukonoutfitters.net; www.yukonoutfitters.net*) represents the 20 outfitting concessions in the Yukon. The association adheres to strict environmental guidelines, and states that its members must recover meat from those animals harvested and ensure that it is not wasted. For more information on hunting in the Yukon, contact **Environment Yukon** (*10 Burns Rd, Whitehorse, across from the airport;* ✆ *867 667 5652, toll-free:* ✆ *1 800 661 0408 ext 5652;* e *environmentyukon@ gov.yk.ca; www.environmentyukon.gov.yk.ca/huntingtrapping*).

A number of hunting outfitters operate out of Inuvik and Tuktoyaktuk in the Northwest Territories; for information on licensed outfitters contact the **Western Arctic Regional Visitor Centre** in Inuvik (*eastern end of Mackenzie Rd;* ✆ *867 777 4727;* e *travel_westernarctic@gov.nt.ca;* ⊕ *mid-May to mid-Sep 9am–8pm daily, in winter call Judith Venaas on* ✆ *867 777 7237*).

Firearms regulations Firearms brought into Canada for sport purposes, or for protection against wildlife, must be declared at the border. More information is available from the **Canadian Firearms Centre** (✆ *1 800 731 4000 from the US & Canada only;* e *cfp-pcaf@rcmp-grc.gc.ca; www.rcmp-grc.gc.ca/cfp-pcaf*).

PHOTOGRAPHY

With its stunning scenery, wonderful arctic and subarctic light, and wildlife viewing opportunities, you will definitely want to pack your camera when travelling to the Yukon. If you need to refresh your photographic supplies, **Photovision** in Whitehorse (*205A Main St;* ✆ *876 667 4599*) is well stocked. There's also a small photography store in Dawson (**Peabody's Photo Parlour**, *Second Av & Princess St;* ✆ *867 993 5209;* e *peabody@northwestel.net*).

One word of warning: don't let your enthusiasm for photographing cute furry things lead you into the jaws of danger. Those grizzly cubs may look adorable but mother bears can get awfully tetchy if you march up to their young with your camera, and angry moose can charge and kill.

HOW TO PHOTOGRAPH THE NORTHERN LIGHTS Firstly, remember that the northern lights can only be seen when the sky is clear and dark – so you'll never see them during midsummer in the Arctic. The aurora forecast is very accurate so, rather than sit up all night with your camera hoping to see them, go first to www.auroraforecast.com to find out if the current activity is low or high.

Assuming it's medium to high, dress up warmly. Even when activity is high, the northern lights are whimsical and don't dance on demand. You will almost certainly have to wait for some time before you see them. Wear a thin pair of gloves underneath a thick pair of mitts – when the lights come out, you can take off the mitts but still operate your camera without succumbing to frostbitten fingers.

A tripod is essential for photographing the aurora – you'll need long exposures given the low light. Make sure you don't touch a metal tripod with bare fingers as your skin will stick fast to the metal. Many experienced northern photographers tape foam around their tripod legs to avoid this.

Battery power dies very quickly in the cold. If you have an SLR camera, consider buying a battery pack and filling it with lithium AA batteries, which last much better. Otherwise, stash a spare battery in an inside pocket, where your body heat will keep it warm. Don't take the camera indoors as the contrast in temperature will fog the lens, and when you go outdoors again the fog will turn to ice.

So, you're all set up and the lights are leaping. Now what? Set your camera's focus to infinity and open the aperture as wide as your lens will allow. If you're using a digital camera, it's best to switch the ISO to 200 or 400 – more than that and your pictures will suffer from too much noise. If you can, turn off the LSD display as its illumination interferes with your vision through the viewfinder on a dark night. Ideally, you should select a view with foreground such as trees, a tent or a building as these will give your image some perspective. Then all you have to do is press the button. And pray.

A LAYMAN'S GUIDE TO PHOTOGRAPHING WILDLIFE The tips below aren't for the serious photographer hauling a 400mm telephoto lens and a hulking great tripod. This is for those carrying simpler gear who would just love, one day, to take a photograph of a grizzly that's actually in focus.

The first thing to remember is that you shouldn't let your enthusiasm for photography endanger your wellbeing. Bear cubs and moose calves may look sweet, but their mothers may not approve of you rushing up to snap their portrait.

Professional wildlife photographers will tell you that good wildlife photography requires a telephoto lense. If you're not carrying one, however, all is not lost. In the Yukon, you'll often see bears and moose at close range from your car and may have the opportunity to get great shots through an open window (don't, of course, get out of your vehicle if a bear is close!) Turn your engine off, so the vehicle is no longer vibrating, and you can use the frame of your window as a tripod. Try not to become fixated on the big game though. Consider also taking shots of smaller, tamer creatures: engaging little arctic ground squirrels, for example, are frequently seen in the Yukon in summer, you can often walk up close to them, and they're sometimes even kind enough to stand still while you snap.

With all wildlife, you should focus on the eyes. (Experts will tell you to look for the 'catchlight' – the twinkle where the light reflects in the animal's eye.) Always use a fast shutter speed (eg: 1/000 second). To achieve this, you'll need a wide aperture; you may also have to up your ISO to 400. Stay still and silent when you can.

Lastly, don't just hammer away on the shutter button hoping against hope that one of your hundred shots will come out OK. You'll do better if you take your time and compose your shot.

COMMUNICATIONS

TELEPHONE

Mobile phones So you thought that in the 21st century, an era of all-bleeping, ever-ringing mobile connectivity, a time when your phone hums to life in the smallest village in China, your cell phone would work in the Yukon? Think again. It seems incredible, but mobile phones from many countries, including the UK, do not work at all in the Yukon. This is because the Yukon has signed up to a CDMA-based service while the rest of us are on something called GSM. North American phones do, generally, seem to pick up a signal but if your cell phone is vital to you, you should call your service provider and ask before you travel.

There is no cell phone coverage in the Yukon outside the towns, even if your phone understands CDMA technology. Landline telephones work in all communities; some remote lodges rely on radio and satellite phones.

Calling cards Calling cards are widely available, and are by far the best way of making long-distance calls. You simply buy a card for a certain amount of money, eg: $10 or $25 (which you can then top up by phone), dial the number on the card, enter the card's pin code, and dial your destination number. It works out considerably cheaper than calling directly from hotel-room phones. You can buy calling cards from convenience stores, gas stations and many other places besides.

Toll-free numbers Note that the toll-free telephone numbers listed in this guidebook will usually work in North America only.

INTERNET Internet accessibility in the Yukon is rather more reliable than cell-phone coverage. Most hotels, bed and breakfasts, and commercial RV parks and campgrounds offer a wireless connection (Yukon government campgrounds do not); some have guest computers. Most hotels etc offer internet usage to their guests for free. Otherwise, there are good-value internet cafés in Whitehorse and Dawson, while several of the smaller communities offer free internet use in their libraries.

POST Goodness knows why, in this age of aeroplanes, but international post to and from the Yukon often takes aeons to arrive. I have no explanation to offer. There are post offices in all the major communities, however. Their opening hours vary.

MEDIA

The Yukon's **newspapers** are the *Yukon News* (*www.yukon-news.com*) and *Whitehorse Star* (*www.whitehorsestar.com*) in Whitehorse, and the *Klondike Sun* (*www.klondikesun.com*) in Dawson. All are fairly parochial.

More interesting are the **magazines**. *Up Here* (*www.uphere.ca*), published in Yellowknife in the NWT, is an excellent magazine covering stories on the whole of the Canadian north. Also well worth reading is *Yukon: North of Ordinary* (*www.northofordinary.ca*) published in Dawson. It covers local personalities, news and issues and is carried by Air North, the Yukon's airline, as well as being for sale on the newsstand. *What's Up Yukon* (*www.whatsupyukon.com*) focuses on arts, entertainment and recreation.

A number of excellent **websites** carry information and articles on the Yukon. **Yukon Tourism**'s website, www.travelyukon.com, has a wealth of information for visitors as does **PR Services**' website www.yukoninfo.com – this is the online version of the free mini-guides to Yukon communities and Skagway that you'll find distributed around the territory. **Environment Yukon** publishes huge amounts of information and advice on everything outdoors at www.environmentyukon.gov.yk.ca. Owned and operated by the **Arctic Borderlands Ecological Knowledge Society**, www.taiga.net publishes articles and reports relating to wildlife and ecological issues. The **aurora forecast** is at www.auroraforecast.com. Current **road conditions** are at www.yukon511.ca, or to hear them by phone, dial ╲ 511.

There's a whole range of local **radio** stations in the Yukon covering community issues, news and talk. There's no coverage outside the towns but as you approach each community on the highway you'll see a signboard telling you that you're now in range, and giving you the frequency.

CULTURAL ETIQUETTE

Yukoners are passionate about their (largely) unspoilt land. They take conservation issues seriously. When hiking, stick to trails where they exist so as not to damage delicate flora; if the path is narrow, you should walk in single file rather than widening it. Observe the principles of Leave No Trace (www.lnt.org or there's a summary in *Into the Yukon Wilderness*, see page 227).

Burial sites are sacred to the First Nations people, and should be left undisturbed. If you come across camps that are being used by First Nations for traditional pursuits, bear in mind that these are not a tourist attraction. Some First Nations people feel uncomfortable having their photograph taken: ask first.

Lastly, the caprices of the northern weather mean that things don't always happen when they're meant to. Charter flights may be delayed and journeys postponed. Grin and bear it – it's not just his own life the pilot is protecting by refusing to fly in inclement conditions.

TRAVELLING POSITIVELY

The **Yukon Conservation Society** (✆ *867 668 5678;* e *ycs@ycs.yk.ca; www.yukonconservation.org*) is a registered charity that aims to encourage the conservation of Yukon wilderness, wildlife and natural resources.

Part Two

THE GUIDE

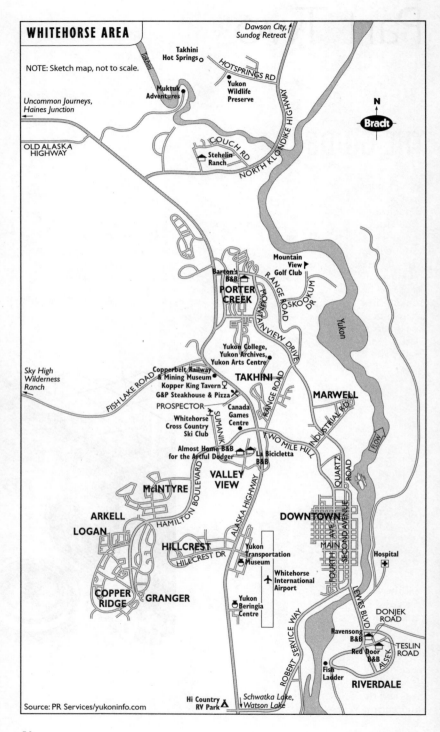

WHITEHORSE AREA

NOTE: Sketch map, not to scale.

Dawson City,
Sundog Retreat

Takhini
Hot Springs

HOTSPRINGS RD

Muktuk
Adventures

Yukon
Wildlife
Preserve

Uncommon Journeys,
Haines Junction

N

Bradt

OLD ALASKA
HIGHWAY

COUCH RD

NORTH KLONDIKE HIGHWAY

Stehelin
Ranch

Mountain
View
Golf Club

Yukon

Barton's
B&B

PORTER
CREEK

RANGE ROAD

MOUNTAINVIEW DRIVE

SKOOKUM DR

Sky High
Wilderness
Ranch

FISH LAKE ROAD

Yukon College,
Yukon Archives,
Yukon Arts Centre

Copperbelt Railway
& Mining Museum
Kopper King Tavern
G&P Steakhouse & Pizza

PROSPECTOR

Whitehorse
Cross Country
Ski Club

TAKHINI

RANGE ROAD

MARWELL

INDUSTRIAL RD

Canada
Games
Centre

SUMANIK

TWO MILE HILL

QUARTZ ROAD

FLOW

Almost Home B&B
for the Artful Dodger

La Bicicletta
B&B

**VALLEY
VIEW**

McINTYRE

HAMILTON BOULEVARD

ALASKA HIGHWAY

DOWNTOWN

ARKELL

LOGAN

MAIN

FOURTH AVE

SECOND AVENUE

LEWES BLVD

Hospital

HILLCREST

HILLCREST DR

Yukon
Transportation
Museum

Whitehorse
International
Airport

DONJEK
ROAD

**COPPER
RIDGE**

GRANGER

Yukon
Beringia
Centre

Ravensong
B&B

Red Door
B&B

**TESLIN
ROAD**

ALSEK

ROBERT SERVICE WAY

Fish
Ladder

RIVERDALE

Hi Country
RV Park

Schwatka Lake,
Watson Lake

Yukon

Source: PR Services/yukoninfo.com

3

Whitehorse

With its population of 25,000, Whitehorse is the big city, the scary metropolis, the place whose mere mention makes rural Yukoners shudder and look slightly afraid (though they reserve their real horror for the moment you tell them where *you* come from). On weekdays, for a few minutes around 5pm, Whitehorse even stretches to fairly busy traffic. Locals call it their rush minute.

Whitehorse's architecture isn't going to win any prizes: the buildings are mostly boxy and functional. The streets are in a grid. This is a place designed to work, not to look pretty. And work it does. Whitehorse makes an excellent base of operations for those heading out on wilderness journeys, and for cruise-ship passengers drinking in the Yukon's rich history and panoramic landscapes. Its shops stock pretty much everything you'll need; it has some fantastic cafés, and several good restaurants. And, while first impressions can be a little blah, within a short time most visitors are seduced by Whitehorse's blend of funky artistic vibe, derring-do history and rufty-tufty outdoors adventure.

HISTORY

Whitehorse, essentially, is a war baby. It existed as a settlement well before World War II, but it was the Japanese bombing of Pearl Harbor and the subsequent construction of the Alaska Highway to supply coastal defences (see pages 78–9) that saw the town boom.

Archaeologists have shown that the First Nations occupied seasonal fish camps on the banks of the Yukon in the Whitehorse area for thousands of years. The name of White Horse, however, only came into being during the Klondike gold rush (see pages 165–9). The majority of stampeders came from the Alaska coast to the south and crossed either the Chilkoot Pass or White Pass to Lake Bennett on the border of present-day British Columbia and Yukon. There, in the spring of 1898, they built boats and when on 29 May the ice broke, more than 7,000 hand-hewn vessels set off across the lake to the Yukon River and Dawson. Just south of present-day Whitehorse, they came to notorious rapids whose foaming crests recalled the white manes of galloping horses. These deathly waters – 150 boats were wrecked and several people drowned in the first few days alone – became known as the White Horse Rapids. (Since the construction of the hydroelectric dam in 1958, the rapids have been replaced by the serene Schwatka Lake.)

Enter Superintendent Sam Steele of the Northwest Mounted Police.

'There are many of your countrymen who have said that the Mounted Police make the laws as they go along, and I am going to do so now, for your own good,' he told the assembled Americans who sat desolate at the water's edge, wrecked boats and ruined goods strewn between them. Steele pronounced that women and children must circumnavigate the rapids by land; that boats would be inspected before entering the rapids; and that inexperienced steersmen would have to hire skilled pilots to take their boats through. And so the first major settlement in this area appeared to house the bottleneck: a tent city, known as Canyon City, sprung up 8km (five miles) upriver of present-day Whitehorse.

But Canyon City's days were short-lived. Already, supplies were arriving in Skagway for the construction of the White Pass and Yukon Route railway (see page 71). Completed in 1900, the railway needed a transportation hub at its inland terminus, and so the town of White Horse was born. Supplies and people were transported by rail from the Alaska coast; from White Horse they proceeded by river to Dawson. But White Horse was little more than a depot. It housed few people and scant diversions. Then came World War II.

On 7 December 1941, the Japanese attacked Pearl Harbor. In 1942, they moved in on Alaska's Aleutian Islands, invading and occupying the islands of Kiska and Attu. The Americans were gripped by the urgent need to strengthen their defences on the Alaska coast – and those defences required a supply route. The US Navy considered that it could do the job but the politicians decided otherwise. They would build a road from Dawson Creek in Canada's British Columbia, through the Yukon, to Delta Junction in Alaska.

In 1941 White Horse had a population of 400. Work on the Alaska Highway started in March 1942; due to its railroad links and location roughly in the middle of the new highway's proposed route, White Horse was chosen as the base for US servicemen and contractors. By the time the road was opened in November that year, the town had a population of 8,000.

In 1950, White Horse became a city. In 1953, it took over from Dawson as the capital of the Yukon. And in 1957, it changed its name to a single word: Whitehorse.

GETTING THERE

BY AIR Whitehorse International Airport (☎ 867 667 8440, toll-free: ☎ 1 800 661 0408: e yxy@gov.yk.ca) is located at km 1423, mile 887 of the Alaska Highway, a five-minute drive from downtown. Daily flights connect to regional and international airports. See *Chapter 2* for details. Most hotels, bed and breakfasts and tour operators offer airport transfer. Otherwise, there are usually a couple of cabs outside the airport; if not see page 55 for phone numbers of Whitehorse cab companies. The car-hire firms (see page 53) have desks at the airport.

BY CAR Downtown Whitehorse is just a few minutes' drive from the Alaska Highway. There are two turn-offs: Robert Service Way at km 1419, mile 884 and Two Mile Hill at km 1425, mile 887. Distances by road from Whitehorse are as follows:

9/11 DIVERSION

During the 9/11 attacks of 2001, a Korean Air 747 approaching Anchorage, Alaska, from Asia started sending out a signal that it had been hijacked. It was impossible to evacuate such a large city as Anchorage so Whitehorse – very nobly – allowed the plane to divert to its airport. Nearby city buildings were evacuated, military jets escorted the flight into Whitehorse, and the RCMP ordered the crew off the plane at gunpoint. But there were no terrorists. The plane's transponder, it turned out, was malfunctioning and had emitted the wrong signal: the plane had not been hijacked, it was simply low on fuel.

Beaver Creek	451km, 280 miles	Haines Junction	158km, 98 miles
Carcross	71km, 44 miles	Haines, Alaska	393km, 244 miles
Carmacks	177km, 110 miles	Ross River	407km, 253 miles
Dawson City	533km, 331 miles	Skagway, Alaska	179km, 111 miles
Dawson Creek	1,427km, 887 miles	Teslin	179km, 111 miles
Delta Junction, Alaska	805km, 500 miles	Tok, Alaska	634km, 394 miles
Destruction Bay	264km, 164 miles	Watson Lake	441km, 274 miles
Fairbanks, Alaska	962km, 598 miles		

Approximate driving times

Whitehorse–Watson Lake:	5hrs	Whitehorse–Haines Junction:	2hrs
Whitehorse–Skagway:	2hrs	Whitehorse–Dawson City:	6hrs

Car hire Car hire starts at around $50 per day or $250 per week; Rent-a-Wreck is slightly cheaper. See pages 32–3 for general information about driving conditions and regulations in the Yukon.

🚗 **Budget** 4178 Fourth Av, cnr of Black St; ✆ 867 667 6200, toll-free: ✆ 1 800 661 0411; e budget@ whitehorsemotors.com; www.budgetyukon.com

🚗 **Canadream** Unit 2, 17 Burns Rd; ✆ 867 668 3610; e whitehorse@canadream.com; www.canadream.com

🚗 **Fraserway** RV 9039 Quartz Rd; ✆ 867 668 3438; e john.whitehorse@fraserway.com; www.fraserway.com

🚗 **National Car Rental** ✆ 867 456 2277; www.nationalcar.ca

🚗 **Norcan** 213 Range Rd; ✆ 867 668 2137, toll-free: ✆ 1 800 764 1234 (from USA), 1 800 661 0445 (from western Canada); www.norcan.yk.ca; also has airport & Alaska Highway locations

🚗 **Rent-a-Wreck** 17 Chilkoot Way; ✆ 867 456 7368; e whitehorse@rent-a-wreck.ca; www.rentawreck.ca

BY BUS

Greyhound Canada (*2191 Second Av;* ✆ *867 667 2223; www.greyhound.ca;* ⊕ *9am–5pm Mon–Fri*) The Greyhound comes to Whitehorse three times a week and connects to various western Canada destinations including Vancouver, Calgary and Edmonton. It operates year round. Within the Yukon, it comes via Watson Lake making various stops, but does not connect to the Yukon north of Whitehorse. It's not a quick journey, though. The fastest trip from Vancouver takes one day, 19 hours and 15 minutes (including three transfers) and costs from around $95 for a 21-day advance ticket to around $320 for a fully refundable fare.

Alaska Direct Bus Line (*Toll-free:* ✆ *1 800 770 6652 from Canada & US only;* e *info@alaskadirectbusline.com; www.alaskadirectbusline.com*) Alaska Direct runs buses between Whitehorse and Tok, Alaska (US$135), with stops in Haines Junction, Burwash Landing, Beaver Creek, and Northway Junction on Sundays and Wednesdays from 1 October to 15 May, and on Wednesdays, Fridays and Sundays from 16 May to 30 September. From Tok you can make connections with the same company to Fairbanks, Anchorage and other Alaska destinations.

Alaska/Yukon Trails (*Toll-free:* ✆ *1 800 770 7275 from Canada & US only;* e *alaskashuttle@yahoo.com; www.alaskashuttle.com*) Alaska/Yukon Trails operates a shuttle between Whitehorse and Dawson stopping at Braeburn Lodge and Carmacks from mid-May to mid-September. Leaves Whitehorse Sunday, Tuesday, Friday and leaves Dawson Monday, Wednesday, Saturday; US$149. There's also a Fairbanks–Whitehorse (Alaska Highway) route operating once a week on a Thursday from mid-May to mid-September, stopping at Tok, Scotty Creek, and Haines Junction; US$195.

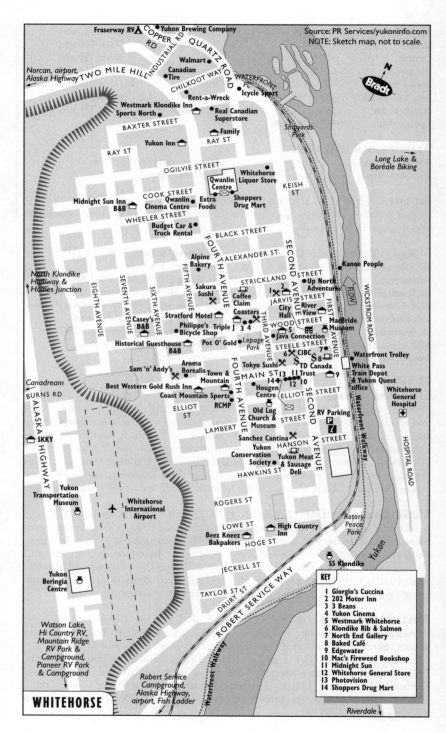

Source: PR Services/yukoninfo.com
NOTE: Sketch map, not to scale.

Fraserway RV Yukon Brewing Company

COPPER RD
INDUSTRIAL RD
QUARTZ ROAD

Norcan, airport,
Alaska Highway TWO MILE HILL CHILKOOT WAY

Walmart
Canadian
Tire

WATERFRONT
PL

Rent-a-Wreck Icycle Sport

Westmark Klondike Inn
Sports North

Real Canadian
Superstore

Shipyards
Park

BAXTER STREET

Family

Yukon Inn RAY ST

RAY ST

Long Lake &
Boréale Biking

OGILVIE STREET

Whitehorse
Liquor Store

Qwanlin
Centre

KEISH
ST

Midnight Sun Inn
B&B

COOK STREET

Qwanlin
Cinema Centre

Extra
Foods

Shoppers
Drug Mart

WHEELER STREET

Budget Car &
Truck Rental

BLACK STREET

Alpine
Bakery

ALEXANDER ST

FOURTH AVENUE

SECOND

Kanoe People

STREET

STRICKLAND

Up North
Adventures

FLOW

WICKSTROM ROAD

Sakura
Sushi

Coffee
Claim

STREET

City
Hall

River
View

JARVIS

Coasters

WOOD

Stratford Motel

Philippe's Triple
Bicycle Shop

STREET

Java Connection

MacBride
Museum

FIRST

Casey's
B&B

SIXTH AVENUE

FIFTH AVENUE

SEVENTH AVENUE

EIGHTH AVENUE

North Klondike
Highway &
Haines Junction

Historical Guesthouse
B&B

Pot O' Gold

Lepage
Park

STEELE STREET

CIBC

Waterfront Trolley

Sam 'n' Andy's

Aroma
Borealis

Tokyo Sushi

MAIN ST

TD Canada
Trust

White Pass
Train Depot
& Yukon Quest
office

Canadream

BURNS RD

ALASKA HIGHWAY

Best Western Gold Rush Inn

Town &
Mountain

Coast Mountain Sports

FOURTH AVENUE

Hougen
Centre

ELLIOT

SECOND

Whitehorse
General
Hospital

HOSPITAL ROAD

SKKY

RCMP

ELLIOT
ST

Old Log
Church &
Museum

STREET

RV Parking

LAMBERT

HANSON

STREET

Yukon
Transportation
Museum

Whitehorse
International
Airport

Sanchez Cantina

Yukon
Conservation
Society

Yukon Meat
& Sausage
Deli

Waterfront Walkway

HAWKINS ST

ROGERS ST

Rotary
Peace
Park

Yukon
Beringia
Centre

LOWE ST

Beez Kneez
Bakpakers

HOGE ST

High Country
Inn

SS Klondike

Yukon

JECKELL ST

DRURY ST

TAYLOR ST

Watson Lake,
Hi Country RV,
Mountain Ridge
RV Park &
Campground,
Pioneer RV Park
& Campground

ROBERT SERVICE WAY

Robert Service
Campground,
Alaska Highway,
airport, Fish Ladder

Waterfront Walkway

WHITEHORSE

Riverdale

KEY
1 Giorgio's Cuccina
2 202 Motor Inn
3 3 Beans
4 Yukon Cinema
5 Westmark Whitehorse
6 Klondike Rib & Salmon
7 North End Gallery
8 Baked Café
9 Edgewater
10 Mac's Fireweed Bookshop
11 Midnight Sun
12 Whitehorse General Store
13 Photovision
14 Shoppers Drug Mart

BY SEA The nearest port is Skagway, Alaska. Passengers leaving ferries and cruise ships there can travel in summer only by the historic White Pass and Yukon Route railway to Carcross, and then connect by bus to Whitehorse (see pages 70–7 for details). Many cruise companies provide bus connections; see page 24 for a list of cruise-ship companies that include Skagway on their itineraries.

If cruising's not your thing, the **Alaska Marine Highway** (↘ *907 465 3941; www.ferryalaska.com*) runs ferries connecting Skagway to Haines and Juneau, and from there across its entire system from Bellingham in Washington State along Alaska's Inside Passage and across to the Aleutian Islands. A passenger fare from Juneau to Skagway is $50 with vehicles starting from $63; to go the whole way from Bellingham to Skagway costs US$363 per person with vehicles from US$478.

Yukon Alaska Tourist Tours (↘ *867 668 5944, ticket office* ↘ *867 668 4414 May–Sep only; www.yukonalaskatouristtours.com*) offers a bus connection from Skagway to Whitehorse in the summer only for US$40–55.

Note the time difference when travelling between Alaska and the Yukon: the Yukon is one hour ahead. Also remember that you'll need to show your passport or other approved ID at the international border.

GETTING AROUND

Whitehorse is small, and the downtown area can be navigated easily on foot.

The **Whitehorse Transit** is the city's bus service. It connects downtown Whitehorse with residential neighbourhoods and the Canada Games Centre. Cash fares cost $2.50. For information on routes and timetables go to www.city.whitehorse.yk.ca, or pick up a schedule at the visitor centre (see page 56).

Whitehorse and its surroundings are good for cycling – in the summer, at any rate. You can rent a bike from **Philippe's Bicycle Shop** (*508 Wood St,* ↘ *867 633 5600;* e *synclastic@hotmail.com;* ⊕ *10am–6pm Mon-Fri, 10am–5pm Sat, closed Sun*) for $20–25 per day (sliding scale for longer periods). Philippe also sells his 'purple bikes' – these are bikes he cobbles together from bits and sprays purple, then sells for $100. If you bring your purple bike back to him when you're done, he'll refund you $50, so if you want a basic bike to get around on for more than a couple of days, this is a good option. Bike rental is also available from **Up North** (*103 Strickland St;* ↘ *867 667 7035;* e *upnorth@yknet.yk.ca; www.upnorth.yk.ca*) and **Kanoe People** (*cnr of First Av & Strickland St;* ↘ *867 668 4899;* e *info@kanoepeople.com; www.kanoepeople.com*).

Cab companies include **5th Avenue Taxi** (↘ *867 667 4111*), **Whitehorse Taxi** (↘ *867 393 6543*) and **Yellow Cab** (↘ *867 668 4811*).

PARKING Whitehorse is fairly straightforward for parking, with all but the very centre of town unrestricted. In the town centre, there are some meters and time limits. Visitors can pick up a free three-day parking permit from **City Hall** (*2121 Second Av;* ↘ *867 667 6401; www.city.whitehorse.yk.ca;* ⊕ *8.30am–4.30pm Mon–Fri*),

HIKES AND BIKES

The Yukon Conservation Society has published a great book called *Hikes & Bikes*, which gives detailed trail information on more than 30 routes suitable for hiking and/or mountain biking in the Whitehorse area. It's available from Mac's Fireweed Books on Main Street (see page 65), or from www.yukonbooks.com.

which entitles them to park at most metered spots. Hotel car parks can sometimes be limited, and generally work on a first-come first-served basis, but even if you can't squeeze in you should be able to park in the street just a couple of minutes' walk from your hotel.

TOURIST INFORMATION

The **Whitehorse Yukon Visitor Information Centre** (*100 Hanson St – cnr of Second Av;* ✆ *867 667 3084;* e *vic.whitehorse@gov.yk.ca; www.travelyukon.com;* ☺ *10am–6pm mid-May to mid-Sep, 8.30am–noon & 1pm–5pm late Sep to early May, opening hrs may vary in the shoulder season*) has helpful staff plus a wide selection of brochures, trip ideas and videos. The short bear safety video is recommended for anyone planning hiking, paddling or other wilderness outings. There is enough parking for the most gas-guzzling of RVs.

The **City of Whitehorse** (*Smith House, LePage Park, 3128 Third Av;* ✆ *867 668 8687;* e *tourism@whitehorse.ca; www.visitwhitehorse.com*) has information on Whitehorse's tourism attractions.

Parks Canada's Whitehorse office (*Suite 205, 300 Main St;* ✆ *867 667 3910, toll-free:* ✆ *1 800 661 0486;* e *whitehorse.info @pc.gc.ca; www.pc.gc.ca*) can provide information on Kluane National Park and Reserve, the Chilkoot Trail and other Parks-managed areas and historic sites.

The **Yukon First Nations Tourism Association** (*1109 First Av;* ✆ *867 667 7698;* e *admin@yfnta.org; www.yfnta.org*) is an umbrella organization for tourism products involving the Yukon's aboriginal cultures.

TOUR OPERATORS

Also see pages 24–6 for tour operators offering trips Yukon-wide; many of these are based in Whitehorse.

Alpine Aviation Schwatka Lake; ✆ 867 668 7725, cell: 867 393 1482; e alpine@polarcom.com; www.alpineaviationyukon.com. Offers flightseeing tours as well as charter flights.

Boréale Biking Km 6, mile 4 Long Lake Rd (to get there, follow Second Av over the bridge by the *SS Klondike*. Turn left onto Hospital Rd then left onto Wickstrom Rd. This turns into Long Lake Rd. Boreale Biking is 5km down the road on the left); ✆ 867 332 1722; e info@borealebiking.ca; www.borealebiking.ca; ☺ May–Sep. Offers half-day, full-day & multi-day mountain bike tours from its base 5km (3 miles) from downtown Whitehorse. Half-day trips $75–90, full-day trips $130–175 based on groups of 1–3 people. Enquire for prices for larger groups. Bike rental included in the price. Boréale Biking also runs drop-in rides on weekday evenings, which you don't have to book. Drop-in rides last about 1½hrs & cost $20; bike rental $10. Also has yurt accommodation, see *Where to stay*, page 60.

Equinox Adventure Learning ✆ 867 456 7846; e equinox@northwestel.net; www.equinoxyukon.com. Runs the climbing wall & zipline at Takhini Hot Springs in summer, & the ice-climbing towers in Whitehorse in winter. Also organizes kids' adventure & leadership camps.

Muktuk Adventures ✆ 867 668 3647; e muktuk@ northwestel.net; www.muktuk.com. Owned by Frank Turner, a musher who has run the thousand-mile Yukon Quest more than 20 times, & his wife Anne, Muktuk's main business is winter dogsledding experiences from half-day & day trips to multi-day packages & camping trips. In summer they rent their cabins on a B&B basis & offer kennel tours, talks & BBQ dinners. Muktuk is located off the Alaska Highway about 24km (15 miles) from downtown Whitehorse. The word '*muktuk*', incidentally, means 'whale blubber' in the Inuit language. Frank is not Inuit (he's from Toronto) & has no profound connection to whale blubber, but his friend Victor Allen (see *My Father, My Teacher*, page 211) used to give him *muktuk* for his dogs & Frank liked the sound of the word sufficiently to name his kennels for it.

Shadow Lake Expeditions ✆ 867 393 2232; e aquadog@shadowlake.ca; www.shadowlake.ca. Rents canoes, rafts, power boats, expedition gear &

camping equipment. Also runs day & part-day trips out of Whitehorse, such as evening boat trips to Miles Canyon & Canyon City, evening waterfowl-viewing trips & excursions to wilderness lakes.

SIR North Country Ranch Km 4.9, mile 3 Takhini Hotsprings Rd; ☏ 867 393 3492; www.travel-yukon.com. Multi-day & day horse-riding packages, plus cabin rentals.

Sky High Wilderness Ranch End of Fish Lake Rd, off the Alaska Highway in the northerly Haines Junction direction; ☏ 867 667 4321; e_info@skyhighwilderness.com; www.skyhighwilderness.com. About a 30min drive from town, Sky High has horseriding in the summer (1hr & 3hr rides as well as multi-day), dogsledding in the winter, & lodge & cabin accommodation year round. The owners also run a campground on the shores of Fish Lake.

Tom's Touring Service ☏ 867 393 3848; e info@tomstouring.com; www.tomstouring.com. Day & part-day trips & sightseeing in Whitehorse & the surrounding area. Destinations include Takhini Hot Springs, Yukon Wildlife Preserve & a Whitehorse city tour.

Uncommon Journeys ☏ 867 668 2255; e info@uncommonyukon.com; www.uncommonyukon.com.

Uncommon Journeys is based up on the Old Alaska Highway (off the present-day Alaska Highway) just outside Whitehorse. In winter, the owners Rod & Martha Stewart specialize in high-end dogsledding packages. All are at least a week long. Most guests are based at the lodge; others stay a few nights at Uncommon Journeys' base camp in the nearby Ibex Valley where they sleep in yurts furnished with beds & heaters. Adventurous mushers can take more arduous camping trips, for example, along the Yukon Quest trail or in the Tombstones Range north of Dawson during the month of April. In the summer, Uncommon Journeys runs multi-day guided hiking & canoeing trips, some of which are based at the Ibex Valley camp.

Yukon River Cruises 68 Miles Canyon Rd; ☏ 867 668 4716; e info@yukonrivercruises.com; www.yukonrivercruises.com; ⊕ daily at 2pm 1 Jun–1 Sep, additional cruise at 4pm 15 Jun–15 Aug; adults $30, children aged 6–12 $15. Part-day cruises on the Yukon River aboard the MV Schwatka with narration about the river & Whitehorse's history.

⌂ # WHERE TO STAY

Whitehorse has a good selection of hotels, bed and breakfasts, and RV and camping options. The city doesn't tend towards chi-chi boutique establishments where you'll 'ooh' over the raw-silk drapes, but rather towards solid, reliable hotels that work. A note on seasonal opening: all the hotels, etc below are open year round unless I've stated otherwise.

DOWNTOWN
Hotels
⌂ **SKKY Hotel** (32 rooms) 91622 Alaska Highway; ☏ 867 456 2400, toll-free: ☏ 1 866 799 4933; e info@skkyhotel.com; www.skkyhotel.com. The SKKY is up on the Alaska Highway, by the airport, so a drive from downtown. Having opened only in 2009, it's a sleek new addition to Whitehorse's hotel collection, & features those high-end accoutrements that mean something to the hotel marketing folk but not much to the rest of us (luxury rain showers, anyone?). More comprehensibly, there are plasma TVs and fireplaces in some rooms, & free Wi-Fi & hardwire internet throughout. $$$$–$$$$$

⌂ **Edgewater Hotel** (31 rooms) 101 Main St; ☏ 867 667 2572; e edgewater@northwestel.net; www.edgewaterhotelwhitehorse.com. The Edgewater has a great location at the end of Main St, almost on the waterfront. It's a particularly good spot for foodies who don't like to walk: the Baked Café opposite is Whitehorse's most popular spot for coffee & cake, & the steakhouse in the hotel's cellar serves up superlative meat. The rooms are perfectly comfortable, though won't win any prizes in the interior design department; all have high-speed DSL & wireless internet connection. $$$$–$$$$$

⌂ **Westmark Whitehorse Hotel** (180 rooms) 201 Wood St; ☏ 867 393 9700; www.westmarkhotels.com. Part of the Holland America empire, this place is slick. The coaches full of cruise passengers roll in & out, all with their different itineraries, yet the staff at the Westmark never seem to miss a beat — they are remarkably cheerful & courteous. While you may not think you want to share a hotel with several hundred cruise-ship passengers, if you want a hotel that works, the Westmark Whitehorse delivers. A word of advice for those with laundry requirements: the Holland America coaches arrive in the evening, & leave early in the morning. In the evening, therefore, there are queues for most facilities. If you have the liberty to do so, do your laundry during the day when you'll have the machines to yourself. In addition to washing machines there's wireless internet, full conference facilities, & even a Frantic Follies vaudeville show. The hotel's Steele Street restaurant is good. $$$–$$$$$

🏠 **Yukon Inn** (99 rooms) 4220 Fourth Av; 🔧 867 667 2527, toll-free: 🔧 1 800 661 0454; e info@ yukoninn.com; www.yukoninn.com. This is a good mid-range option. It's owned by 6 First Nations groups, & the artwork on the walls reflects their heritage: each room features 2 signed prints by local artists. Free wireless internet connection, plus computer room. All rooms have microwave & fridge; kitchenettes also available. $$$–$$$$$

🏠 **High Country Inn** (81 rooms) 4051 Fourth Av; 🔧 867 667 4471; e info@highcountryinn.yk.ca; www.highcountryinn.yk.ca. This is the sister hotel to the Gold Rush Inn (below); it's operated by the Best Western chain. Renovations (new beds, curtains, bedding & some furniture) are planned for spring 2010. On a sunny evening, the High Country Inn's deck is one of the most pleasant places to enjoy a beer in Whitehorse. Free wireless internet. $$$–$$$$

🏠 **Best Western Gold Rush Inn** (103 rooms) 411 Main St; 🔧 867 668 4500; e fdsupervisor@ goldrushinn.ca; www.goldrushinn.com. This hotel underwent extensive renovations in 2008; it has stylish up-to-date décor & wonderfully comfortable beds. Free wireless internet. $$$–$$$$

🏠 **Westmark Klondike Inn** (99 rooms) 2288 Second Av; 🔧 867 668 4747; www.westmarkhotels.com; 🕐 May–Sep. This is the Westmark Whitehorse's smaller, plainer sister. The Klondike Inn has a less central location (not that it matters much in Whitehorse), but it's hospitable & reliable. $$$

🏠 **River View Hotel** (52 rooms) 102 Wood St; 🔧 867 667 7801; e info@riverviewhotel.ca;

www.riverviewhotel.ca. There's nothing the matter with the hotel. Though it looks like a big green box from the outside, inside the rooms are large, bright & comfortable, the bathrooms (all en suite) are good, & the staff are efficient & friendly. There's wireless internet & a computer in reception — in theory there's a one-off $5.25 charge for wireless, but in practice this isn't always charged. Combine all this with its central, riverside location & good-value prices, & the River View ought to be a winner. There's one but, however — and that's the neighbours. The River View is located right next door to the 98 Hotel, which is a notorious drinking den. I'd scarcely closed the car door before I was accosted by a lost soul asking for money. Noise at night can also be a problem (& forget the hotel part of the 98 — rumour has it that there are a few curtained-off mattresses to comply with licensing regulations, but I've never met anyone who's dared go inside to verify this). $$$

🏠 **Town & Mountain Hotel** (30 rooms) 401 Main St; 🔧 867 668 7644, toll-free: 🔧 1 800 661 0522; e lizard@yknet.yk.ca; www.townmountain.com. This hotel was fully renovated in 2008 yet it's still rather plain. Its downstairs bar, Lizards, is popular locally: whether this is a plus or a minus depends on your own point of view. $$$

🏠 **Family Hotel** (44 rooms) 314 Ray St; 🔧 867 668 5558. This one won't be top of your list — it's a little bit dingy & brusque, & at these prices you can do better — but it's perfectly adequate if needs must. All rooms have wireless internet & en-suite bathroom. There's a public Laundromat attached so no worries about where to do the washing. $$–$$$

🏠 **Stratford Motel** (49 rooms) cnr of Fourth Av & Jarvis St; 🔧 867 667 4243; e reservations@ thestratfordmotel.com; www.thestratfordmotel.com. It's nothing glam but it's not badly priced, & its 11 kitchenette units are a good size. There's one internet computer in the reception area. Personally I'd spend an extra $20 and move up a rung to a B&B or the Yukon Inn, though. $$

BED AND BREAKFASTS There are three bed and breakfasts in central Whitehorse. All are excellent (higher quality than the hotels in the same price bracket) and very different in character.

🏠 **Casey's Bed and Breakfast** (1 queen, 1 king, 1 twin) 608 Wood St; 🔧 867 668 7481; e carol@ caseybandb.com; www.caseybandb.com. This is the homey one: the owner, Carol, has a gratifying penchant for baking. The room with the king-size bed has its

own kitchenette & private bathroom. The other 2 rooms share facilities & can be rented as a suite or separately. Guests are also welcome to enjoy the flower-filled garden in summer, & the hot tub. There's also a laundry & internet access. Guests are given ingredients to cook themselves a substantial breakfast, plus Carol provides an evening snack — usually something she has baked that day. $$–$$$

🏠 **Historical Guest House Bed and Breakfast** (3 rooms) Cnrr of Fifth Av & Wood St; ☎ 867 668 2526; e info@yukongold.com; www.yukongold.com. This is the heritage one — the house is more than 100 years old, which, for Whitehorse, is positively ancient. They say it was originally built for Sam McGee & his family (see *The real Sam McGee*, page 68). It's a really lovely place, full of atmosphere, excellent value, & guests have the run of the house — the owners live in the green log building next door. The downstairs basement suite has 2 queen beds, en-suite shower room, full kitchen, & living area. Upstairs are 1 room with a queen bed, 1 with a queen & a single. These 2 rooms share a ground-level kitchen & living area with wood stove. Their bathrooms are also on the ground level — they are private but not en suite. Wireless internet connection. $$–$$$

🏠 **Midnight Sun Inn Bed and Breakfast** (4 rooms) 6188 Sixth Av, cnr of Cook St; ☎ 867 667 2255, toll-free: ☎ 1 866 284 4448; e midnightsunbb@northwestel.net; www.midnightsunbb.com. The Midnight Sun is a bright, pleasant place with good-sized, comfortable rooms & efficient, enthusiastic owners. It has won a raft of accolades & awards. Each of the rooms has an en-suite bathroom; other facilities include wireless or cable internet ($5 a day), large guest kitchen & living area (the freezer is kept stocked with ice cream), laundry & BBQ. B/fast & evening snack included. $$–$$$

BEYOND DOWNTOWN There are a number of bed and breakfasts in the residential suburbs of Whitehorse. These are all pleasant places, though personally I wonder why a visitor would want to stay in a Whitehorse suburb. In my view, you'd either want to be in downtown Whitehorse, within walking distance of all the amenities, or experiencing the 'real' Yukon in a wilderness setting. On the other hand, many of these places are not that far from the town centre – just a few minutes in the car – and if you're watching your pennies, you can get comfortable accommodation here at a better price than the central locations.

Riverdale Riverdale's lawns are spotlessly tended and flowers duly bloom – in summer at least. It's all fantastically clean and tidy, perhaps a little too much so. It reminds me slightly of *Asterix in Britain*. Having said that, it's not far from downtown – about 25 minutes' walk or a couple of minutes in the car, and there are some good bed-and-breakfast options.

🏠 **Red Door B&B** (4 rooms) 61 Teslin Rd; ☎ 867 633 4615; e boily@northwestel.net; http://reddooryukon.tripod.com/bnb.htm. The owner is a charming, hospitable woman, whose doll collection is much in evidence. The rooms are homey & comfortable, with brass bedsteads & floral counterpanes. There's a good-sized deck, wireless internet, laundry, & full b/fast. 1 room has en-suite bathroom; the other 3 share. $$–$$$$

🏠 **Ravensong B&B** 11 Donjek Rd; ☎ 867 667 4059, cell: 867 333 5619; e ravensong@northwestel.net; www.ravensongbb.com. Owned by a local musician & singer, Ravensong consists of 3 suites each with their own entrance. There's a deck with BBQ, continental b/fast including organic produce, internet access & laundry facilities. $$–$$$

Valleyview This is at the top of Two Mile Hill, just across from the Canada Games Centre. Again, it's a few kilometres out of town (and the hill is a killer to boot) but easy enough in the car. And the pool is so close there's no excuse for missing your morning swim. It's also near to the skiing, hiking and biking trails of Mount McIntyre.

🏠 **La Bicicletta B&B** (2 rooms) 342 Valleyview Crescent; ☎ 867 668 2659/335 0327; e info@bicicletta.ca; www.bicicletta.ca. The pine interiors are all brand new, & guests have the run of this lovely house, which comes complete with sitting room, kitchen, deck with BBQ & garden — so if you rent both rooms, you'll have the place to yourselves. There's wireless internet. Both rooms are queens with en-suite bathrooms. $$–$$$

3

⌂ Almost Home Guest House and Bed and Breakfast for the Artful Lodger (3 rooms) 124 Valleyview Dr; ☏ 867 633 4844; e stay@almosthomeyukon.com; www.almosthomeyukon.com. Its name is a mouthful, but this is a delightful place. The artist owner comes & goes (she also has a country home), & she encourages independence in her guests — you make your own b/fast from the stocked fridge & cupboards, & you're welcome to use the kitchen or BBQ to cook other meals, too. There are 2 small dbls upstairs with shared bath, plus a beautiful downstairs suite. There's wireless internet & a computer for those without laptops. $$

Porter Creek This really is a drive out of town, but the more rural feel, combined with all mod cons, may be a good half-way house for those who don't want to venture into the real wilderness. And the non-central location brings the prices down.

⌂ Barton's B&B 19 Boxwood Crescent; ☏ 867 668 7075; e dbarton@klondiker.com; www.bartonsbb.com. There's a separate entrance for guests who can choose between a self-contained 1-bedroom apt with separate entrance & full kitchen, & a bedroom & family suite within the house, both of which have a private bathroom & kitchenette (no hob but there's a microwave, fridge, sink etc). There's also wireless internet, off-street parking with plug-in for the winter, & a patio with BBQ for the summer. The views over mountains & spruce forest are spectacular. $$–$$$

HOSTELS Or should that heading read 'hostel'? There's currently only one:

⌂ The Beez Kneez Bakpakers (1 4-bed dorm, 1 6-bed dorm, 1 dbl room indoors, 2 private cabins — outdoor cabins are summer only) 408 Hoge St; ☏ 867 456 2333; e hostel@klondiker.com; www.bzkneez.com. This is a friendly place with cosy communal areas & basic but comfortable bedrooms. Guests are welcome to use the BBQ on the deck; there are laundry & kitchen facilities, free internet computers & wireless connection, free bicycle loan, & book swap. $–$$

LUXURY YURTS Boréale Biking's yurts (Km 6, mile 4, Long Lake Rd – see page 56 for directions; ☏ 867 332 1722; e info@borealebiking.ca; www.borealebiking.ca; ☼ May–Sep; $$) deserve a category all of their own, and so I shall give them one. This isn't camping as you know it – it's comfortable living beneath canvas. All the yurts have hardwood floors and attractive furniture. The main yurt, which acts as a communal living area, has a full kitchen, electricity, water and an internet connection. The bedroom yurts (there are currently three) don't have electricity or running water, but they're beautiful constructions, each with three beds (a queen, a futon, and a single). And the location is phenomenal – just 5km (3 miles) from the centre of Whitehorse, yet it's a full-on wilderness setting, on the edge of a hill with incredible views over the city to the coastal mountains beyond. And it's all temporary – in winter, owners Marsha Cameron and Sylvain Turcotte dismantle and remove their operation so there's no long-term disturbance to the landscape. Boréale Biking also arranges mountain biking tours on trails that start right out of its driveway, hence the name. See page 56.

LODGES AND WILDERNESS CABINS IN THE WHITEHORSE AREA
⌂ Inn on the Lake (sleeps 30) Km 1370, mile 855 Alaska Highway; ☏ 867 660 5253; e carson@exceptionalplaces.com; www.exceptionalplaces.com. Located a 40min drive from downtown Whitehorse on the Alaska Highway, Inn on the Lake is, in my opinion, the top accommodation choice in the area. See page 9 for more information. $$$–$$$$$
⌂ Sundog Retreat (5 cabins) Lot 1160, Policeman's Point Rd (follow the signs off the North Klondike Highway); ☏ 867 633 4183; e info@sundogretreat.com; www.sundogretreat.com. These cabins (2 1-bedroom & 3 2-bedroom) have a rural location, yet are convenient for Whitehorse. All have full bathroom with running hot & cold water & electricity, living room, kitchen, satellite TV, wireless internet, deck & BBQ. There's also a hot tub & a sauna. This is one of the better options for those wanting wilderness plus mod cons. $$$

☂ **Stehelin Ranch** (4 rooms) 40 Couch Rd; ✆ 867 633 6482; e stehelinbandb@yknet.ca; www.stehelinranch.com. Located off the North Klondike Highway (Couch Rd is on the left as you head away from the Alaska Highway, before the Takhini River Bridge), the Stehelin Ranch is only 20mins' drive from downtown Whitehorse (& they'll arrange airport transfer if you don't have a car). It has an attractive deck & garden, & guests are welcome to use both outdoor & indoor living spaces. The b/fast menu is such that you won't need to eat again for a while. $$$

☂ **Hotsprings Valley Retreat** (10 cabins & 2 bunkhouses with 4 bunks each) Km 10, mile 6 Takhini Hotsprings Rd, off North Klondike Highway; ✆ 867 456 8000; e hotsprings@yknet.yk.ca; www.yukonretreat.ca. Part of the Takhini Hot Springs complex, the cabins have electric heat, phone & internet; washrooms & shower are shared & in a separate building. Guests receive a complimentary pass to the hot springs. $$$ ·

☂ **Sky High Wilderness Ranch** (5 rooms in the lodge, plus 4 cabins that sleep 2–4 people; additional wall tent & cabin accommodation available for dogsledding & horse tours; lakeside campground has space for about 8 tents) End of Fish Lake Rd, off the Alaska Highway in the northerly Haines Junction direction; ✆ 867 667 4321; e info@skyhighwilderness.com; www.skyhighwilderness.com. Sky High has a fantastic location on the shores of Fish Lake. They keep around 20 horses & 150 sled dogs, but not everyone who comes here rides or mushes. Some just enjoy the wilderness location from the comfort of the newly renovated lodge, which is built from the original cedar telegraph poles that used to line the Alaska Highway. There are also a number of cabins & wall tents for rental, some more rustic than others. The history here is interesting. In 1960, a woman named Sylvia Heikilla left her home near Bella Colla with a covered wagon, a few horses & her 3 children. Her destination was the Yukon, where she hoped to set up a trail-riding & pack-horse business. She picked up 2 more children along the way (as one does) so when she finally arrived, they were 6. She homesteaded on this plot of land, way out in the wilderness (in those days there was no road), home-schooling her children until, in 1975, she

found company in the form of a trapper named Ian, whom she met while grocery shopping in town. Sylvia passed away in 2003 & Ian has since taken on additional business partners, but her original cabin still stands in fascinatingly dilapidated condition. $–$$$

☂ **Muktuk Adventures** (1 room in the main lodge & 4 cabins) Located about 4km (2½ miles) off the Alaska Highway as you head in the Haines Junction direction from town — in total it's about 24km (15 miles) from downtown Whitehorse; ✆ 867 668 3647, toll-free: ✆ 1 866 968 3647; e muktuk@ northwestel.net; www.muktuk.com. Owner Frank Turner says that Muktuk's cabins don't offer B&B but BB&E — that's to say bed, breakfast & experience. The experience comes in the form of 130-plus Alaskan huskies — Frank is a professional musher who has competed in the thousand-mile Yukon Quest dogsledding race 24 times. Visitors are welcome to talk to the dogs — they're all friendly (if you're lucky there may be puppies to play with) — & Frank is full of stories from his 3 decades of Yukon mushing. He also runs tours of the kennels & gives talks. Sometimes there's the option of a BBQ dinner. The cabins are clean & comfortable but rustic — there's no electricity or running water. Guests can use the shower, power points & Wi-Fi access in the main lodge, however. $$

☂ **The Country Cabins B&B** (4 cabins) Km 8.8, mile 5.5 Hotsprings Rd; ✆ 867 633 2117; e bona@ polarcom.com; www.countrycabinsyukon.com. These cabins sit in the woods between the Yukon Wildlife Preserve & Takhini Hot Springs — that's about 28km or 17.5 miles from downtown Whitehorse. They're not high tech (think kerosene lamps & wood stoves & note that there's no running water) but this is a nice spot to kick back & contemplate nature. $$

☂ **Northview B&B Cabin** Km 7.7, mile 4.8, Hotsprings Rd; ✆ 867 633 2362; e northviewyukon@gmail.com; www.northviewcabins.com; ⊕ May–Sep. This may be an option for those who want a wilderness experience plus electricity (though the loo is an outhouse, not a flushing job: there's no running water). Kitchenette includes fridge & microwave, but not hob. If you want to take a shower, you'll need to go to Takhini Hot Springs. $$

CAMPGROUNDS AND RV PARKS

⛏ **Mountain Ridge RV Park** (15 sites plus 7 cabins) Km 1418, mile 883, historical mile 912 Alaska Highway; ✆ 867 667 4202; e info@mtnridge.ca;

ww.mtnridge.ca. A small & rather plain site with 11 RV sites with full hook-up, plus sites for 3 or 4 more with electricity only. There's also a line of terraced 1-bedroom cabins with separate living area, kitchenette & full bathroom, plus a studio cabin (no bathroom — you have to use the communal shower). The cabins are pleasant & customer testimonials praise the owner's hospitality, the views from the kitchen windows, the cleanliness & the convenient highway location. Personally I'd stay downtown or in a more rurally located cabin rather than right on the highway — & the price here isn't cheap — but people seem to like it. Wireless internet free of charge. RV sites $, studio cabin $$, 1-bedroom cabins $$$

Å Robert Service Campground (68 sites) 120 Robert Service Way; ☎ 867 668 3721; e robertservicecampground@yahoo.ca; www.robertservicecampground.com; ⏰ mid-May to the end of Sep. This is most centrally located dry camping site in Whitehorse — it's about 15–20mins' walk from downtown along the riverside Millennium Trail. Filled with flowers & trees, it's a campground for the sociable — the 'living room' area is a covered outdoor nook that's furnished with sofas & has a wireless internet connection. The office (⏰ 7.30am–11pm daily) sells coffee, cakes & sandwiches. Hot showers cost $1 a go; you can also rent gas stoves. Firewood is provided for $4 per evening. Each site has a fire pit & picnic table. Dogs are welcome. This is dry camping only: RVs are welcome to park, but there are no hook-ups. $

Å Hi Country RV Park (130 sites) Km 1419, mile 884, historical mile 913 Alaska Highway; ☎ 867 667 7445, toll-free: ☎ 1 877 458 3806; e hicountryrv@polarcom.com; www.hicountryrvyukon.com; ⏰ early May to late Sep. Located on the Alaska Highway just above downtown Whitehorse (this is the nearest of the highway RV parks to town), the Hi Country has 130 RV sites with full & partial hook-ups, & 15, 20 & 30 amp power. There are good facilities — hot showers are free, there's a Laundromat, store, free wireless internet, free cable TV & fire pits & picnic tables at all sites. There are plenty of trees around & between sites, & a pleasant atmosphere. Tent sites also available. All buildings are accessible by wheelchair ramp. $

Å Pioneer RV Park & Campground (150 sites) Km 1414, mile 880, historical mile 911 Alaska Highway; ☎ 867 668 5944, toll-free: ☎ 1 866 626 7383 (reservations only); e info@pioneer-rv-park.com or info@prvp.ca; www.pioneer-rv-park.com; ⏰ mid-May to end Sep & longer if the weather is good though some facilities may not be available after mid-Sep. Full & partial hook-up, 15 & 30 amp power. Dry sites also available. Facilities include free cable TV, wireless internet, BBQ pits, showers, store, fuel, mechanic & Laundromat. It's a pleasant site with plenty of trees. $

Å Takhini Hot Springs Campground (about 100 sites) Km 10, mile 6 Takhini Hotsprings Rd, off North Klondike Highway; ☎ 867 456 8000; e hotsprings@yknet.yk.ca; www.takhinihotsprings.com; ⏰ 15 May–30 Sep. This is an attractive campground, especially if you have kids, as the Hot Springs amenities — the pools, the café, the climbing wall & zipline, & the horseriding, see page 74 — are right there. There are 57 RV sites (30 of which are pull-through) with power plus about 50 tent sites. There's also a separate shelter that can accommodate groups of up to 50. $

✕ WHERE TO EAT

RESTAURANTS

✕ Cellar Steakhouse and Wine Bar Edgewater Hotel, 101 Main St; ☎ 867 667 2572; www.edgewaterhotelwhitehorse.com; ⏰ from 6pm Tue–Sat. The décor may be dated but the steaks are outstanding & the service super-friendly. The restaurant is located in the basement of the Edgewater Hotel; salmon, Alaska king crab & lobster tails are also on the menu. $$$

✕ G&P Steakhouse & Pizza Km 1477, mile 918 Alaska Highway; ☎ 867 668 4708; e gpsteakhouse@hotmail.com; www.gandpsteakhouse.com; ⏰ 4pm–10pm daily. Located at the Kopper King on the Alaska Highway, a 5min drive from downtown, this steakhouse is rated by locals as one of Whitehorse's best eateries. It doesn't just serve steak & pizza but also BBQ ribs, chicken, fish & souvlaki. $$$

✕ Giorgio's Cuccina 206 Jarvis St; ☎ 867 668 4050; www.giorgioscuccina.com; ⏰ 11.30am–2pm & 4.30pm–11pm daily. The food at this Italian-Greek restaurant receives consistently good reviews from travellers & locals alike, though some complain it's a little over-priced. It serves up pasta, pizza & souvlaki alongside Alaska salmon, arctic char & king crab. $$$

✕ Volare Restaurant SKKY Hotel, 91622 Alaska Highway; ☎ 867 456 2400, toll-free: ☎ 1 866 799 4933; e info@skkyhotel.com; www.skkyhotel.com;

🕐 11am–2pm & 5pm–10pm Mon–Sat. SKKY is Whitehorse's nod to contemporary style, & this carries through to its upscale restaurant, where international cuisine meets Caribbean fusion. Lunch $, dinner $$$

✗ **Klondike Rib & Salmon Barbecue** Cnr of Second Av & Steele St; ☎ 867 667 7554; e krs@ klondiker.com; 🕐 mid-May to early Sep from 11am (they stop serving at roughly 9pm but there's no fixed closing time) Mon–Sat. This is probably Whitehorse's most popular restaurant (in summer, at any rate). They don't take bookings: they don't have to because the place is always packed. If you want a table, you'll either have to arrive at an unfashionable hour, or stand in the queue that usually snakes onto the street. It's popular with good reason. Klondike Rib & Salmon is an atmospheric little joint which, strangely enough, serves its drinks in jam jars. It gets away with it. The food – halibut & chips, fresh local salmon, bison & caribou – is outstanding. The only thing that might stop you from scraping the pattern off your plate is the sight of the drool-worthy desserts that sit in a cabinet & taunt you not to fill up too soon. $$–$$$

✗ **Coasters** 302 Wood St; ☎ 867 456 2788; 🕐 summer: 11am–8pm Mon–Sat, 11am–4pm Sun, winter: 11am–4pm daily. There's a good front deck here & a back garden too making for pleasant alfresco dining in summer. The vibe is young & lively, & the food is for the most part good ole North American – burgers, steak sandwiches, California salad & such. $$

✗ **Sakura Sushi** 404 Wood St; ☎ 867 668 3298; 🕐 11am–10.30pm Mon–Wed, 11am–11pm Thu–Fri, noon–11pm Sat, 4pm–10.30pm Sun. Whitehorse is good on its sushi (due, presumably, to the large numbers of Japanese who flock here in winter to see the northern lights) & this is generally reckoned to be the best of the sushi bunch. It has an attractive, Japanese-themed interior & the food is excellent. Takeaway is also available. $$

✗ **Sanchez Cantina** 211 Hanson St; ☎ 867 668 5858; 🕐 11.30am–2pm, 5pm–9pm Mon–Sat. This is reckoned to be the more authentic of Whitehorse's 2 Mexican restaurants. (The other is Sam 'n' Andy's at 506 Main St; ☎ 867 668 6994, which is more Tex Mex). Personally I think I've had better Mexican, but let's face it, this isn't Mexico. It's tasty enough & the restaurant is cosy & atmospheric. $$

There are two other sushi restaurants in Whitehorse. **Oishi Sushi** (*208, 211 Main St;* ☎ *867 668 7570;* 🕐 *10am–6pm Mon–Fri, 11am–6pm Sat, closed Sun;* $$) is really just a takeaway joint with a few stools at a bar, but the food is great. I've taken dinner from there back to my hotel room plenty of times. It's not obvious to find – go in the entrance of the post office building on the corner of Third and Main and take the stairs up to the shopping centre. Then just follow the mall around till you find the sushi counter. Beware of its early closing time. The other is another proper restaurant: **Tokyo Sushi** (*204 Main St;* ☎ *867 633 4567;* $$). I have to confess that I've never eaten there as I was told that Sakura was the place to go and, loving it there, I didn't move on. But others now tell me that Tokyo Sushi, too, is good.

CAFÉS Whitehorse has a vibrant café culture, and several of these independent establishments host exhibitions of local artists' work and live performances from local musicians as well as serving up coffee and cake.

🍴 **Alpine Bakery** 411 Alexander St; ☎ 867 668 6871; e info@alpinebakery.ca; www.alpinebakery.ca; 🕐 8am–6pm Tue–Fri, 8am–4pm Sat, closed Sun. Head here if you're low on vitamins – they'll stick some carrots, apple & beets in the juicer to pep you up. There are also organic chocolates, muffins etc, & a wide selection of organic breads including European varieties. There are just a few tables – more people take out than eat in – but it's a good place to stop & watch the bread-buying world go by.

🍴 **Baked Café** 100 Main St, cnr of First Av & Main St; ☎ 867 633 6291; 🕐 summer: 7am–7pm daily,

winter: 7.30am–6pm Mon–Fri, 8.30am–5pm Sat–Sun. This is Whitehorse's most popular café; it buzzes at all hours. The baked goods – scones, muffins, filled croissants – are always outstanding. At lunchtime there are sandwiches & a daily lunch special. Note that some people still call this café by its former name, the Bäckerei.

🍴 **Bean North** Km 9.3, mile 5.7 Takhini Hotsprings Rd; ☎ 867 667 4145; e info@beannorth.com; www.beannorth.com; 🕐 early Jun to 1 Sep: 11am–4pm Tue–Wed, 11am–5pm Thu–Sun, closed Mon; Sep to early Jun: 11am–5pm Thu–Sun, closed

Mon–Wed. This is outside Whitehorse, but definitely worth stopping by if you're in the Takhini Hot Springs area: it's just before the hot springs on the Hotsprings Rd. It's a colourful little shack with delightful outdoor space. The coffee is organic (Bean North roasts its own fair-trade beans), as are most of Bean North's wares: cakes & cookies, chocolates, fruit & nuts. The owners make a point of supporting local businesses such as the farmers' community market; they also sell local artists' work.

Chocolate Claim 305 Strickland St; ✆ 867 667 2202; e chocolateclaim@northwestel.net; www.chocolateclaim.com; ⊕ 7.30am–6pm Mon–Thu, 7.30am–7pm Fri, 8.30am–6pm Sat, closed Sun. Another good choice for a caffeine injection, the Chocolate Claim also sells handmade Belgian chocolates. It serves up very good soup at lunchtime as well as sandwiches & so on. It also exhibits local artists' & photographers' work (a different artist each

month) & on Fri there's a guest musician. Note though that sandwiches etc here are a few dollars more expensive than in most of the other cafés in town.

Java Connection 3125 Third Av (between Steele & Wood Sts); ✆ 867 668 2196; ⊕ 7am–5pm Mon–Fri, closed Sat–Sun. Sells beans & coffee-related paraphernalia as well serving coffee & snacks. There's often a quieter atmosphere here than in some of the other coffee joints in town.

Yukon Meat and Sausage Deli 203 Hanson St; ✆ 867 668 4848; ⊕ 8.30am–5.30pm Tue–Sat, closed Sun–Mon, lunch special served from 11.30am until it runs out. A good spot for a simple lunch or to buy up your picnic supplies, the Deli has an excellent selection of meats & cheeses, ice cream, fresh brownies & cakes. There's a sandwich bar, plus soup & a lunch special. The atmosphere is functional rather than stylish but the food is good.

ENTERTAINMENT AND NIGHTLIFE

It's a funny thing for a place with so many lively cafés, but Whitehorse does not do bars well. The principal reason is that, many years back, the powers-that-were instigated a law that forbade any establishment without lodging to serve alcohol. So all the bars and clubs in Whitehorse (and the rest of the Yukon) are attached to hotels. Added to this, a small segment of the population – predominantly among the First Nations, some of whose people still carry the terrible legacy of the residential schools and other misguided social policies (see page 18), but the white community is not immune – suffers from deep-seated social issues that sometimes express themselves through alcohol and drug consumption; Whitehorse is a small place, and it's impossible to avoid the sight of substance abuse spilling onto the streets. There's rarely a physical threat, but neither is it pretty to look at. The one place that's squeaky clean is the **High Country Inn** (*4051 Fourth Av;* ✆ *867 667 4471;* e *info@highcountryinn.yk.ca; www.highcountryinn.yk.ca*). The hotel's deck is a fantastic place to drink a beer in summer. During the winter I spent at Muktuk Kennels we used to go for a few beers to the **Kopper King Tavern** (*km 1477, mile 918 Alaska Highway;* ✆ *867 668 6236*) out on the Alaska Highway. I always liked it, and its tables, imprinted with historic Yukon photos, are a nice touch. Don't come here if you're after a classy cocktail, however. It's a little rough around the edges. But at least nobody cares if your clothes are covered in dog hair.

Coasters (*202 Motor Inn, 206 Jarvis St;* ✆ *867 633 2788*) and Lizards (*T&M Hotel, 401 Main St;* ✆ *867 668 7644*) are both popular locally. All the other major hotels have bars too; they're fine, but nothing to include on your postcards home.

Since I did the research trip for this book, the **SKKY Hotel** up by the airport (*91622 Alaska Highway;* ✆ *867 456 2400, toll-free:* ✆ *1 866 799 4933;* e *info@ skkyhotel.com; www.skkyhotel.com*) has opened. Its bar, called **VOLARE euroBARcaffé**, is said to be sleek, stylish and a good place to visit for an upmarket drink. It claims to have the most extensive martini list of any bar in the Yukon – to be frank, it wouldn't take a lot to achieve this, but cocktail lovers: this is probably your drinking hole.

For information on performing arts and film, see page 70.

BOOKS For books, maps, and magazines go to **Mac's Fireweed Books** (*203 Main St;* ✆ *867 668 2434;* e *orders@macsbooks.ca; www.yukonbooks.com or www.macsbooks.ca;* ☉ *summer: 8am–midnight daily, winter: 8am–9pm daily*). Topographical maps and travel guides are in the basement. For second-hand books, **Well-Read Books** (*4137 Fourth Av, between Jarvis & Wood Sts;* ✆ *867 393 2987;* e *wellreadbooks@northwestel.net; www.wellreadbooks.yk.net*) has a huge selection of mass-market fiction, as well as non-fiction, literary fiction and children's books. They also have a trade-in policy.

ARTY STUFF **North End Gallery** (*118–1116 First Av, between Main & Steele sts;* ✆ *867 393 3590;* e *info@northendgallery.ca; www.northendgallery.ca;* ☉ *10am–6pm Mon–Sat, open Sun & extended hrs during the summer*) is a high-quality arts and gift shop with a northern theme. It stocks prints and paintings, sculpture (eg: sculpted moose and polar bears) ceramics and jewellery. This is a long way from a tacky gift shop: there are many things here you might tastefully hang on your wall. Also worth a visit is **Midnight Sun Gallery & Gifts** (*205C Main St;* ✆ *867 668 4350;* e *sales@midnightsunyukon.com; www.midnightsunyukon.com;* ☉ *9.30am–6pm Mon–Sat with late opening till 8pm Fri*), which sells prints and cards by local artists, as well as mouthwatering fudge.

Arts Underground (*basement of the Hougen Centre, Suite 15, 305 Main St;* ✆ *867 667 6058;* e *yukonart@polarcom.com; www.artsunderground.com;* ☉ *9am–5.30pm Mon–Fri, 11am–5pm Sat*) is run by the Yukon Arts Society. It showcases and sells work of local artists in various disciplines, and hosts regular workshops and talks.

It's a trip out of downtown, but if you're driving south (towards Watson Lake) on the Alaska Highway, it's definitely worth dropping in on **Yukon Artists@Work** (*3B Glacier Rd;* ✆ *867 393 2391; www.yaaw.com;* ☉ *noon–5pm daily in summer, Mon–Fri in winter*). It's a co-operative of 35 Yukon artists who exhibit and sell their work – paintings, sculpture, photographs and art cards – in this space that they operate themselves. It's about a ten-minute drive from downtown at McCrae. Take the Alaska Highway in the Watson Lake direction and follow the signs, left down Fraser Road, left again into Denver Road and follow it round.

The **Sundog Carving Studio & Gallery** (*4194 Fourth Av, across from the Qwanlin Centre;* ✆ *867 633 4186;* e *info@sundogretreat.com; www.sundogretreat.com;* ☉ *9am–4.30pm Mon–Fri*) is home to a youth program that teaches artists aged 16 to 30 the skills in the artistic, business and social arenas needed to make a career from carving. Many of the participants have not succeeded in conventional education and while Sundog's programs are not, in theory, restricted to First Nations students, these groups are the main focus and the carving reflects First Nations traditions. Visitors are welcome to drop in during working hours. The artists are happy to explain their work, and visitors can buy direct from the studio, which means that the artist receives 100% of the price paid: the studio takes no commission.

PHOTOGRAPHY Whitehorse's photographic supplies store is **Photovision** (*205A Main St;* ✆ *876 667 4599*). It has a pretty good stock of most things you'll need.

OUTDOORS CLOTHING AND EQUIPMENT **Coast Mountain Sports** (*cnr of Fourth Av & Main St;* ✆ *867 667 4074;* e *cmsmanager@klondiker.com*) is Whitehorse's most comprehensive outdoor goods and clothing store, selling everything from tents to merino-wool knickers.

For cycling matters, go to **Icycle Sport** (*9002 Quartz Rd;* ✆ *867 668 7559; www.icyclesport.com;* ☉ *summer: 10am–6pm Mon–Fri, 10am–5pm Sat, closed Sun, winter: hrs are variable & posted outside the shop*). Icycle also sells skiing equipment.

Up North Adventures (*103 Strickland St;* ☎ *867 667 7035;* e *upnorth@ upnorthadventures.com; www.upnorthadventures.com*) has a shop that sells canoeing, kayaking, and other outdoors gear in summer, and skis, snow shoes and winter clothing in winter. There's also a ski tech shop here that will help with mounting, tuning and repairs. **Kanoe People** (*cnr of First Av & Strickland St;* ☎ *867 668 4899;* e *info@kanoepeople.com; www.kanoepeople.com*) also has a small shop selling outdoors equipment.

Canadian Tire (*18 Chilkoot Way – you can see it on the left as you drive down Two Mile Hill;* ☎ *867 668 3652;* ⊕ *8.30am–9pm Mon–Fri, 8.30am–6pm Sat, auto centre* ⊕ *8am–5pm Mon–Sat, closed Sun*) has the best prices on fishing gear. **Sports North** (*406 Baxter St;* ☎ *867 667 7492*) is a dedicated fishing store with a good selection. **Hougen's Sportslodge** (*105–305 Main St;* ☎ *867 668 2103;* e *hunting@hougens.com; www.sportslodge.ca;* ⊕ *9am–6pm Mon–Sat*) sells fishing and hunting gear.

SOUVENIRS AND GIFTS The **Whitehorse General Store** (*205C Main St;* ☎ *867 393 8203; www.yukonqueststore.com*) sells souvenirs and clothing as well as Yukon Quest (see pages 42–4) memorabilia.

Another great place to buy gifts to take home is **Aroma Borealis Herb Shop** (*504B Main St;* ☎ *867 667 4372; www.aromaborealis.com*), which sells fabulous lotions and potions with suitably northern names, such as its Arctic Woman range. The Yukon sled dog pad and paw cream is particularly good for humans who suffer from chapped lips.

For artfully crafted Yukon gold, try **Pot o' Gold** (*4129 Fourth Av;* ☎ *867 668 2058;* e *pog@northwestel.net*). Around a third of the jewellery sold here is locally made from Yukon gold; there's also First Nations-produced jewellery. Particularly quirky is the shipglass jewellery made by Yukoner Colleen Slonski (*www.cslonski.etsy.com*). It's made from old bottles that were thrown from paddlewheelers into Yukon lakes during the gold rush and the years that followed.

The **White Pass and Yukon Route railway** ticket office (*1109 First Av, at the junction with Main St;* ☎ *867 633 5710, toll-free:* ☎ *1 800 343 7373;* e *info@ whitepass.net; www.wpyr.com*) has a small memorabilia stand selling books, model trains, caps and so on.

MUSIC **Triple Js Music Café** (*4121A Fourth Av, between Wood & Steele Sts;* ☎ *867 456 7555;* e *jjjmusic@klondiker.com; www.jjjmusiccafe.ca*) is the only independent music store in Whitehorse. It sells CDs, vinyl, art and clothing. They also do body piercing and host visiting tattoo artists. Triple Js organizes regular music events in the Whitehorse area.

FOOD AND DRINK **3 Beans Natural Foods** (*308 Wood St;* ☎ *867 668 4908; www.3beansnaturalfoods.com;* ⊕ *10am–5.30pm Tue–Sat*) sells a lot more than three types of beans. It also stocks organic vegetables, vitamins, and all sorts of other frighteningly healthy fare. Good meats, cheeses and bakery items can be found at **Yukon Meat and Sausage Deli** (*203 Hanson St;* ☏ *867 667 7583*). The **Alpine Bakery** (*411 Alexander St;* ☏ *867 668 6871;* e *info@alpinebakery.ca; www.alpinebakery.ca*) sells fresh breads and bakery items, including 'expedition bread' which apparently lasts four to five weeks without refrigeration.

The two major supermarkets in Whitehorse are more or less next door to each other. The **Real Canadian Superstore** (*2270 Second Av – just follow the northern end of Second Av round to the bit before it joins with Fourth;* ⊕ *7am–10pm Mon–Sat, 8am–10pm Sun*) is generally reckoned to pip **Extra Foods** (*Qwanlin Centre, 303 Ogilvie St, between Third & Fourth Avs;* ☏ *867 667 6251;* ⊕ *8am–7pm Mon–Wed, 8am–9pm Thu–Fri; 8am–7pm Sat, 8am–6pm Sun*) to the post, but both are comprehensive.

For wine and beer, the **202 Motor Inn** and **Town and Mountain** hotels have off sales (or off licences to the British) but it's better to walk a few minutes or drive to the **Whitehorse Liquor Store** (*cnr of Second Av & Ogilvie St;* ⊕ *summer: 9.30am–7pm Mon–Thu, 9.30am–8pm Fri, 9.30am–6pm Sat, closed Sun, winter: 10am–6pm Mon–Thu & Sat, 10am–8pm Fri, closed Sun*) where the choice is greater and prices marginally less astronomical.

PRACTICAL SHOPPING Most of the boring but useful shops are located in the sprawling amalgamation of corrugated metal and parking lots that lies on the north side of town to the east of Fourth Avenue before it turns into Two Mile Hill. **Walmart** is at 9021 Quartz Rd (☏ *867 667 2652;* ⊕ *7am–10pm Mon–Sat, 8am–9pm Sun*). **Canadian Tire** (*18 Chilkoot Way;* ☏ *867 668 3652;* ⊕ *8.30am–9pm Mon–Fri, 8.30am–6pm Sat, auto centre* ⊕ *8am–5pm Mon–Sat, closed Sun*) is good for camping, fishing and hunting equipment, and hardware and motoring conundrums.

OTHER PRACTICALITIES

POST The downtown branch of **Canada Post** is in the basement of the Shoppers Drug Mart building on the corner of Main Street and Third Avenue (*100–211 Main St;* ☏ *867 667 2485;* ⊕ *9am–6pm Mon–Fri; 11am–2pm Sat, closed Sun*). There's another branch at the Qwanlin Centre (*303 Ogilvie St;* ⊕ *8am–10pm daily*) and at Range Road (*300 Range Rd;* ⊕ *8.30am–5pm Mon–Fri, closed Sat–Sun*).

BANKS There are several banks and ATMs in Whitehorse including **CIBC** (*110 Main St;* ☏ *867 667 2534, toll-free:* ☏ *1 800 465 2422; www.cibc.com;* ⊕ *9.30am–4pm Mon–Thu, 9.30am–4pm Fri, closed Sat–Sun*), **RBC** (*4110 Fourth Av;* ☏ *867 667 6416; www.rbc.com;* ⊕ *9.30am–4pm Mon–Thu, 9.30am–4pm Fri, closed Sat–Sun*) and **TD Canada Trust** (*200 Main St;* ☏ *867 668 8100; www.tdcanadatrust.com;* ⊕ *9am–5pm Mon–Fri, 9am–4pm Sat, closed Sun & 9016 Quartz Rd Unit 103;* ☏ *867 456 3622;* ⊕ *9.30am–4.30pm Mon–Thu, 9.30am–5.30pm Fri, closed Sat–Sun*).

HOSPITAL Whitehorse General Hospital (*5 Hospital Rd;* ☏ *867 393 8700;* e *info@ wgh.yk.ca; www.whitehorsehospital.ca*) has a 24-hour emergency and outpatient unit. The hospital is located on the other side of the river to the downtown area. Cross the bridge at the end of Second Avenue (by the *SS Klondike*) then turn left into Hospital Road.

PHARMACY There's a **Shoppers Drug Mart** downtown (*211 Main St;* ☏ *867 667 2485;* ⊕ *8am–9pm Mon, 9am–9pm Tue–Fri, 9am–6pm Sat, 10am–6pm Sun*). The Shoppers Drug Mart at the Qwanlin Centre (*303 Ogilvie St – right by Extra Foods;* ☏ *867 667 6633;* ⊕ *8am–10pm daily*) keeps longer hours for those seeking pharmaceutical relief after the Main Street branch has closed.

POLICE The emergency number is ❭ 911. The RCMP detachment is located at 4100 Fourth Avenue (between Main and Elliott streets); ❭ 867 667 5551.

WHAT TO SEE AND DO

MUSEUMS Whitehorse may not be bulging with high-budget displays, but it's a city with a vibrant history that its handful of museums succeeds in bringing to life.

MacBride Museum of Yukon History *(1124 First Av;* ❭ *867 667 2709;* e *info@ macbridemuseum.com; www.macbridemuseum.com; $8 adults, $7 seniors & students, $4.50 children under 18, $20 family;* ☉ *May–Aug 9.30am–5.30pm daily, Sep–Apr noon–4pm Tue–Sat)* This is Whitehorse's premier museum, which is not to say that it's enormous. It was, however, expanded in summer 2008 and can now display 50% of its collection at any one time (previously just 10% was on show). In any case, size isn't everything. This is a good, lively display that tells of First Nations history, and the wildlife and environment of the Yukon, but most of the museum's space is dedicated to gold-rush and post gold-rush days. Stories of the Yukon's more colourful inhabitants are exhibited, alongside all sorts of nooks and crannies that house, for example, a children's classroom from the *SS Portland* (the ship that took the first miners to the Outside in 1897 and started the Klondike stampede) and the confectionary shop of former Whitehorse residents Grandma and Granddad Puckett – Grandma moved to Whitehorse in 1900 with three children and three dollars. There's also a Cluttertorium whose information board explains: 'What do a magic lantern, a 50-year-old vacuum cleaner and a deck of cards from the White Pass and Yukon Route railway have in common? Nothing? Well that's the point. This exhibit is a literal cluttertorium of interesting objects from the MacBride Museum of Yukon History's collection.' Daily activities through the summer include gold panning, performances by local musicians, talks from local historians, and readings of Robert Service poetry outside the *real* Sam McGee's cabin.

THE REAL SAM MCGEE

'Now Sam McGee was from Tennessee, where the cotton blooms and blows,' Robert Service wrote in one of his most famous poems, 'The Cremation of Sam McGee.' But the real Sam McGee didn't come from Tennessee at all. He was from Peterborough, Ontario. He came to the Yukon in 1898 via the Chilkoot Trail but was involved predominantly in road construction rather than prospecting. He lived in the cabin that's now exhibited at the MacBride Museum for ten years, from 1899 to 1909.

McGee was one of Robert Service's customers at the Bank of Commerce (for more on Robert Service, see page 182). Service liked the sound of his name and asked McGee's permission to use it in a poem. McGee said yes, little realizing the levels to which Service's fame – and in particular his poem 'The Cremation of Sam McGee' – would soar.

McGee was plagued for the rest of his life by the poem, and by passing wits asking him if he was warm enough. When McGee made a return visit to the Yukon in the 1930s, he found urns supposedly containing his own ashes for sale in the souvenir shops.

The real Sam McGee died in 1940. Robert Service attempted to attend his funeral, but the story goes that he went to the wrong church and missed the service. He arrived, apparently, just in time to see McGee's coffin lowered into the ground. McGee had decided against cremation.

SS Klondike (*Located in Rotary Park on the banks of the river by Second Av; for information call Parks Canada on* ↘ *867 667 3910;* e *whitehorse.info@pc.gc.ca; www.pc.gc.ca/ssklondike; $6.05;* ⊕ *tours run every half hour, on the hour & half hour, mid-May to mid-Sep 9am–4.30pm Mon–Fri, & every hour Sat–Sun*) Whitehorse's other really worthwhile historical display is the *SS Klondike*, which was one of the sternwheelers that once plied the Yukon River between Whitehorse and Dawson City. First launched in 1937, she was the largest of the sternwheelers owned by the British Yukon Navigation (BYN) Company; she used to take 36 hours to travel to Dawson from Whitehorse, and four or five days to return upriver. In 1952 she was transformed into a cruise ship, and was retired in 1955: that was the year the Dawson spur of the Whitehorse–Mayo Road opened and the demand for river travel plummeted. The ship was moved to her present location from the shipyards on the other side of town in 1966. She couldn't be moved by water because her hull had been damaged and, in any case, by now a bridge had been built that was too low for her to pass under. And so they brought her by road. The move took four bulldozers, four wooden skids – and eight tonnes of Palmolive soap flakes that were used to lubricate the road.

The best bit of the visit, perhaps, is the 20-minute video that's played before each tour of the boat. It shows historical footage from the 1930s of the wood camps, the deck hands wheeling the cords of wood on board, and so on. Anyone planning to paddle the Yukon River should definitely see this, as they'll pass these very camps, now abandoned, and this footage really brings to life this aspect of the river's history. The boat itself is also interesting. It was surprisingly comfortable – in first class, it even verged on luxurious. Second-class women weren't expected to sleep on the cots downstairs with the men. They were given cabins upstairs – but were locked in from 9pm so they couldn't mix with their social superiors and, first thing the following morning, they were packed back down below.

Note that the visit to the *SS Keno* in Dawson, also run by Parks Canada, is very similar to the *SS Klondike* in Whitehorse, and the video is the same.

Old Log Church Museum (*Cnr of Third Av & Elliot St;* ↘ *867 668 2555;* e *logchurch@ klondiker.com; $3;* ⊕ *mid-May to early Sep 10am–6pm daily*) This museum tells the stories of the missionaries from Archdeacon Robert McDonald (see page 200), who travelled extensively in northern Yukon and Alaska in the late 1800s and was the first person to create a written form of the Gwich'in language, to Bishop Isaac Stringer, known as the Bishop Who Ate His Boots (see page 218). There are also small exhibits on the First Nations, whalers and explorers. It's a slight museum, with limited information on the truly courageous characters who made such arduous journeys to spread the word of God through this remote and frigid land, but it's intriguing enough if you're only after the basics. The Old Log Church Museum also organizes tours of Whitehorse's Pioneer Cemetery.

Yukon Beringia Centre (*Km 1473, mile 914 Alaska Highway;* ↘ *867 667 8855;* e *beringia@gov.yk.ca; www.beringia.com; $6, or $9 for combined entrance to the Transportation Museum & Beringia Centre;* ⊕ *May–Sep 9am–6pm daily, 1–5pm Sun only or by appointment Oct–Apr*) This is up on the Alaska Highway, right by the airport and, predictably enough, it focuses on Beringia – the unglaciated continent that formed during the last ice age, comprising modern-day eastern Siberia and northern Alaska and Yukon. Beringia was home to the mammoth, the giant short-faced bear, the steppe bison, the scimitar cat – and the early North American people. Whitehorse's Beringia Centre is dedicated to this prehistory. It features recreations of the now-extinct animals and exhibits of their remains. Films are shown in its theatre, which is also used as a lecture and film venue by the Yukon Science Institute and others.

Yukon Transportation Museum *(30 Electra Crescent;* ✆ *867 668 4792;* e *info@ goytm.ca; www.yukontransportationmuseum.ca; $6, or $9 for combined entrance to the Transportation Museum & Beringia Centre, seniors $5, students aged 12–17 $4.50, children aged 6–12 $3, children under 6 free;* ⊕ *mid-May to end Aug 10am–6pm daily)* Located next door to the Beringia Centre, this is dedicated to the Yukon's historical trains, planes and rugged ole bush pilots – oh yes, and dog sleds too.

For more information on the Yukon's museums, go to the Yukon Museum Guide at www.yukonmuseums.ca.

YUKON ARCHIVES *(400 College Dr, next to Yukon College;* ✆ *867 667 5321, toll-free:* ✆ *1 800 661 0408 ext 5321;* e *yukon.archives@gov.yk.ca; www.yukonarchives.ca; free entry;* ⊕ *year round 9am–5pm Tue–Wed, 1pm–5pm Thu, 1pm–9pm Fri, 10am–1pm & 2pm–6pm Sat, closed Sun–Mon)* This is a fascinating place to spend a few hours (or days, or weeks) for those with clean hands and an interest in history. Most accessible perhaps is its collection of almost 120,000 historical photographs that show everything from First Nations fish camps, to the Klondike gold rush, to the Mounties' dog sled patrols, to the construction of the Alaska Highway, to sternwheeler travel along the Yukon River. The Archives also houses a vast collection of documents (including Jack London's 1897 placer claim application to mine for gold), diaries, manuscripts and scrapbooks, and there are films, sound recordings, maps, old newspapers and a library. It's an incredible treasure trove, and most amazingly of all, you can just walk in off the street and explore it for free.

PERFORMING ARTS AND GALLERIES The **Yukon Arts Centre** *(300 College Dr, Yukon Pl;* ✆ *867 667 8485; http://yukonartscentre.com; box office* ⊕ *10am–3pm Mon–Fri & 1hr before showtime, tickets also available from Arts Underground on Main St, see page 65 for details; public art gallery:* ⊕ *noon–6pm Tue–Fri, noon–5pm Sat–Sun, closed Mon, also open during performance intermissions)* has an excellent music, dance, and theatre program. Check out the schedule at the centre's website. There's an art gallery here too but, unless there's an event on, it's pretty dead. If you're interested in the Yukon's art scene, **Arts Underground** and **Yukon Artists@Work** (see *Shopping*, page 40) offer a more dynamic environment.

During the summer, the Yukon Arts Society runs **Arts in the Park**. Every weekday at noon, musicians, dance groups, storytellers and visual artists give concerts and demonstrations in LePage Park, at the corner of Third Avenue and Wood Street.

For up-to-date listings for theatre, music, poetry readings, talks and more, pick up a copy of *What's Up Yukon* magazine or go to www.whatsupyukon.com.

FILM The **Yukon Film Society** *(cnr of Fourth Av & Jarvis St – enter off Jarvis St beside China Garden;* ✆ *867 393 3456;* e *yukonfilmsociety@yknet.ca; www.yukonfilmsociety.com)* has an active program screening documentaries, foreign films, film classics, and independent Canadian film and media art at the Old Firehall *(First Av & Main St)* in Whitehorse.

The **Yukon Cinema** *(304 Wood St;* ✆ *867 668 6644)* and the **Qwanlin Cinema** *(4188 Fourth Av;* ✆ *867 668 6644)* both show mainstream movies. Go to www.tribute.ca for the current schedule.

WHITE PASS AND YUKON ROUTE RAILROAD Construction of the railway started in 1898 during the Klondike gold rush (see *The rise and fall of the White Pass and Yukon Route railroad*, page 71). It now runs as a tourist attraction – and truly spectacular it is, too. It's tortuously steep, terrifically tight on the bends, and takes in bridges, tunnels and trestles that still in the 21st century make the heart beat a little faster.

THE RISE AND FALL OF THE WHITE PASS AND YUKON ROUTE RAILROAD

It took 35,000 men, 450 tons of explosives, $10 million and 26 months to blast through the coastal mountains of Alaska and the southern Yukon and create the White Pass and Yukon Route railway. It was a task that many considered impossible – but Michael J Heney, the railroad's labour contractor, wasn't one to give in. 'Give me enough dynamite and snoose, and I'll build the railroad to hell,' he once proclaimed.

Construction began on 28 May 1898 and, as winter set in, conditions were arduous. Men with pick axes and shovels worked in temperatures that dipped to around –50°C (about –60°F). Their task was extreme: they were to build a 180km (110-mile) narrow-gauge railway that climbed almost 879m (2,885ft) in just 32km (20 miles), and took in inclines of almost 4%. The track was completed on 29 July 1900 when the teams heading north and south met in Carcross. They tried to drive in a golden spike to mark this historic meeting, but the metal was too soft and it buckled.

Perhaps it was a sign: by now the Klondike gold rush had died. In its place, however, companies had been created to mine copper, silver and lead as well as gold, and the railway was used principally to transport their freight. It was also vital to the US military in the early 1940s to supply construction materials and men for the building of the Alaska Highway.

The White Pass and Yukon Route suspended operations in 1982: profits had dropped off due to the decline in the Yukon's mining industry. It reopened, however, in 1988 as a seasonal tourist attraction and now carries thousands of passengers each year.

From the train, you can still see traces of the trail of '98 over which so many men, women and horses tramped (and died) during the stampede to the Klondike. See page 119 for Jack London's description of the White Pass route in 1898.

The railway does not run all the way to Whitehorse any more; however, you can buy a bus–train–bus combination running Whitehorse–Carcross–Fraser–Whitehorse or Whitehorse–Carcross–Skagway–Whitehorse (the latter requires an overnight in Skagway). The railway runs from the end of May to the beginning of September. The Whitehorse ticket and information office is at the old White Pass train depot on the river's edge; it shares the building with the Yukon Quest office (*1109 First Av – at the junction with Main St;* ❧ *867 633 5710, toll-free:* ❧ *1 800 343 7373;* e *info@whitepass.net; www.wpyr.com;* ⊕ *mid-May to mid-Sep 8am–4.30pm daily*). Note that Skagway is in Alaska, USA. There's an hour's time difference (the Alaskans are behind) and you'll need to take your passport or other accepted ID for the border crossing.

WHITEHORSE WATERFRONT TROLLEY (*Run by the Miles Canyon Historic Railway Society, 1093 First Av;* ❧ *867 667 6355;* e *mchrs@northwestel.net; www.yukonrails.com; $2;* ⊕ *mid-May to early Sep 1st trolley leaves Rotary Park at 9am, then it runs continuously until the last trolley leaves Spook Creek at 8.30pm, daily*) This is a refurbished 1925 trolley that trundles along the Whitehorse waterfront. It leaves Rotary Peace Park, across from the *SS Klondike*, on the hour to travel north, and leaves Spook Creek Station, across from Walmart, on the half hour. Passengers can get on and off at stops *en route*; a commentary tells of the history of the sternwheelers and White Pass and Yukon Route railroad.

BEYOND DOWNTOWN
Miles Canyon Miles Canyon is about 10km (6 miles) from town, but it definitely merits the detour. In summer, the energetic can rent a bike (see page 55) and cycle there – the round trip takes around two hours. Otherwise, hop in the car or take a

tour (see Yukon Conservation Society, below, or Shadow Lake Expeditions, pages 56–7). To get there, head out of town in a southerly direction, along Robert Service Way, then take the first left after Yukon Energy. You're now on the Miles Canyon Road, a tiny back road that takes you past Schwatka Lake (Whitehorse's float plane base). This used to be the site of the Whitehorse rapids, before the hydroelectric dam was built in 1958. After a couple of steep hills, you come to a wide pull-out with interpretive boards and wonderful views over the canyon. Follow the road downhill to the canyon itself, cross the footbridge, and then either turn right for the ride/hike to Canyon City or, if you're on a bike or on foot, you can turn left to return to Whitehorse along wooded paths; if you're in a vehicle, you'll obviously need to stick to the road. The Schwatka Lake section of Miles Canyon Road is open to vehicles in summer only; in winter it's popular with walkers and skiers.

The **Yukon Conservation Society** (*302 Hawkins St;* ☎ *867 668 5678;* e *ycsoffice@ycs.yk.ca; www.yukonconservation.org*) runs free interpretive walks from Miles Canyon to Canyon City from the beginning of July to mid-August. Walks leave at 10am and 2pm from the Robert Lowe suspension bridge, beneath the parking lot at Miles Canyon. It's 1.75km (about one mile) from Miles Canyon to Canyon City.

Birders should look out for belted kingfishers and violet-green, cliff and bank swallows, which nest here. Townsend's solitaires, least chipmunks and arctic ground squirrels live on the south-facing slopes.

McIntyre Marsh This is straightforward to get to: it's located 3.4km (2 miles) up the Fish Lake Road, whose surface is good and easy at this early stage (following bad weather, it goes to the dogs a little further on). McIntyre Marsh is one of the few wetlands in the Yukon that doesn't freeze over in winter. It's therefore an important

FREDERICK SCHWATKA

Frederick Schwatka, for whom Schwatka Lake is named, was, according to Allen A Wright in his book *Prelude to Bonanza*, 'a dapper, arrogant little man with a goatee and pince-nez'. He was a lieutenant in the US Cavalry, but spent rather more time exploring than soldiering: in 1879 he led one of many expeditions through the Canadian Arctic to look for written records thought to have been left on King William Island by members of the Franklin expedition (see *John Franklin*, page 210). He also found time to complete a medical degree, and to be admitted to the Nebraska bar. In 1883, at the age of 34, he embarked on his exploration of the Yukon River travelling over the Chilkoot Pass and down the river to its mouth at the Bering Sea. As he went, he indulged in a bit of a naming spree, and many of the names that Schwatka gave to the lakes and rivers he passed are still used to this day.

Schwatka was the first white man to write a detailed description of the Chilkoot crossing. He renamed the Chilkoot Pass – he called it Perrier Pass after Colonel J Perrier of the French Geographical Society, but the name didn't stick. His naming of Lake Lindeman did, however – Schwatka named the body of water where he and his men constructed their raft, as would so many thousands of gold stampeders 15 years later, after the secretary of the Bremen Geographical Society. Lake Bennett was for James Gordon Bennett, founder and editor of the *New York Herald*, and a patron of Schwatka's (Bennett also put money into Stanley's search for Livingstone). He named Marsh Lake after Professor Othaniel Charles Marsh, a professor of palaeontology at Yale University, and Miles Canyon after General Nelson Miles, who later became Commanding General of the US Army.

Schwatka died young. He met his end in 1892, at the age of just 43, from an accidental overdose of laudanum, which he used to treat a stomach disorder.

stopping point for migratory birds in spring. Dead trees standing in the marsh provide nesting sites for tree swallows, boreal chickadees, and Barrow's goldeneye. Otters, beavers, muskrats, coyotes and foxes are also seen regularly. There's an interpretive gazebo, and an easy walking loop. For those wanting a longer walk, the Trans Canada trail passes through here. See *Trans Canada Trail*, above.

Whitehorse Fish Ladder (✆ *867 633 5965; www.yukonenergy.ca; suggested donation of $3 pp; ⊕ Jun 9am–5pm daily, 1 Jul–1 Sep 9am–9pm daily*) This is a slightly quirky one, but it sits on the route of a pleasant riverside walk, making an interesting focus to one's stroll. The story is this: in the late 1950s, the dam at the Whitehorse rapids was built to harness hydroelectric power for the growing community. This created a problem for the fish. For thousands of years, Chinook salmon had travelled upstream along this section of the Yukon River to the streams where they hatched in order to spawn. A new generation of salmon duly hatched, travelled down the river to the Bering Sea, and returned a few years later to spawn themselves. Now the dam was in the way.

In 1959, therefore, the Whitehorse Fishway was constructed so that the salmon could, quite literally, climb up and down the dam and, in the mid-1980s, this was expanded to include a hatchery and salmon transplant program that would help to maintain the salmon populations.

While I can't confess in any way to be an expert on the mechanics of fish ladders, it apparently works something like this: a concrete wall is built at an angle across the dam to funnel the fish into the fishway. The ladder itself is built in a series of steps – it's about 366m (1,200ft) long, making it the longest wooden fish ladder in the world, and rises over 15m (50ft) in height – and in each section the water flows in a series of eddies that allow the fish to rest, but provide enough current to encourage them to swim. Each eddy flows in the opposite direction to those above and below, and each step has a vertical baffle and a submerged opening which allow the fish either to jump over, or swim through. There will be those reading this who can get their heads round this kind of thing. I am not among their number but what I do know is that, somehow or other, the fish swim up stairs.

About halfway along the ladder, the fish enter a holding area: this is where visitors can view the fish, and where staff can record the size, sex and condition of the fish for their records.

The Fishway also hosts regular talks from Environment Yukon and storytelling from First Nations elders.

Yukon Wildlife Preserve (*Km 8, mile 5 Takhini Hot Springs Rd; ✆ 867 633 2922; e info@yukonwildlife.ca; www.yukonwildlife.ca; adults bus tour $22, walking tour $15, seniors $20/$12, children aged 6–17 $10/$8, children under 6 free; ⊕ mid-Jun to end Sep 8am–6pm daily, bus tours last 75mins & depart 10am, noon, 2pm & 4pm, walking tours are 2.5 or 5km long & take 1–2½hrs, last walking tour entry 4pm; reduced hrs early May to mid-Jun – see website or call for info; in winter walking, snowshoeing or cross country skiing tours are available by appointment Thu–Sun, call ✆ 867 456 7300*) You may see moose as you

It doesn't start out too badly. After all, the Chinook salmon that hatch around the Whitehorse area get to do their first 3,000km (1,865-mile) swim downstream, along the creeks in which they were born and then down the Yukon River to the Bering Sea. There they spend a few relatively peaceful years. And then, it all goes pear-shaped.

In order to spawn, a salmon must return to the very same stream in which it was born. And for the salmon you'll see at the Whitehorse fish ladder, that means swimming 3,000km (1,865 miles) against the current – the Yukon River is the site of the longest upstream migration of Pacific salmon in the world.

It takes the fish three months to complete the journey. During that time, they don't eat but rely on body fat for sustenance. As they progress towards their hatching and spawning waters, the streams along which they swim narrow. Sometimes the current surges and froths against them. Sometimes rocks block the way, and the salmon must attempt, seemingly impossibly, to flip themselves over. And everywhere there are bears, picking them off in a big summer feeding frenzy.

Those that arrive lay around 5,000 eggs of which 90% die – as does the poor Chinook salmon itself, shortly after spawning.

drive down the Yukon's highways; if you head out into wilderness areas you might see mountain goats and Dall sheep. Visit the Wildlife Preserve, however, and you will definitely be able to take home photographs of ten northern mammal species: moose, musk oxen, mountain goats, wood bison, mule deer, woodland caribou, elk, lynx and two species of thinhorn sheep; Dall and Stone sheep. Tours of this 285ha (700-acre) facility are greatly informative.

Takhini Hot Springs (*Km 10, mile 6 Takhini Hotsprings Rd;* ☎ *867 456 8000;* e *hotsprings@yknet.yk.ca; www.takhinihotsprings.com; adults $9.50, youth/seniors $7, children $6, under 3 free;* ⊕ *summer: 8am–10pm daily, winter: 4pm–10pm Mon, Thu, Fri, noon–10pm Sat, 11am–10pm Sun. Opening hrs may change during the shoulder & winter seasons, call or check the website for the latest information*) The good news is that there's no sulphur in the Takhini Hot Springs, so they're not stinky. There are two pools, one hottish and one warm – the water flows in at about 40°C and flows out at about 35°C. There are also changing rooms and a café (⊕ *8am–11pm daily May–Sep, 4pm–10pm Mon, Thu, Fri, 11am–10pm Sat–Sun in other months*) that focuses on home-cooked food.

If you're in the Yukon in winter, this is definitely the best time to visit the hot springs – you stay warm in the water and rising steam, yet your hair turns to white icicles. If you're lucky you may even see the northern lights as you soak.

Note: you should bring your own flip-flops or Crocs as you're not allowed to walk around barefoot or in outdoor footwear. The hot springs are 30km (18 miles) from Whitehorse; the journey takes about 25 minutes by car.

At the same site there's a 10m (32ft) climbing wall and zipline run by **Equinox Adventure Learning** (*seasonal – at the wall:* ☎ *867 456 7846, year round:* ☎ *867 456 7846;* e *equinox@northwestel.net; www.equinoxyukon.com;* ⊕ *May to early Sep; drop-in climbing hrs are: 6pm–9pm Fri, 1pm–6pm Sat–Sun*). There's also a Kidz Club, and lessons and courses can be arranged. Call, email, or visit Equinox's website for information and current rates.

From June to September, there's a **horseriding centre** at the hot springs offering trail rides into the surrounding hills for both adults and children. Hours and rates are variable; call: ☎ 867 456 8000 for up-to-date information.

Takhini Hot Springs also has a campground. See page 62.

Copperbelt Railway and Mining Museum (*Km 1428, mile 889, historical mile 919 Alaska Highway, ie: you leave Whitehorse in the northerly Haines Junction direction;* \ *867 667 6355 or 867 667 6198;* e *mchrs@northwestel.net; www.yukonrails.com;* ⊕ *May–Sep 10am–5pm daily*) Located on the site of historic copper claims, this is now home to a 1.8km (1.1-mile) railway that runs through an 8ha (10-acre) park. The engines are one-cylinder ten- and 20-HP diesel mining engines called Lokies. There's also a small museum and a picnic area.

SPORTS AND ACTIVITIES

Whitehorse has a positively exhausting schedule of running, biking, skiing and dogsledding races – competitive types should turn to page 39 for a calendar of the major races. For details of guided activities, see *Tour operators*, pages 56–7.

SUMMER HIKES AND STROLLS For details of multi-day hikes across the Yukon, see *Chapter 12*. For details of operators offering guided hikes see pages 24–6. The following are shorter walks of an hour to a day in the Whitehorse area; all are straightforward with no difficult terrain.

For a gentle summer walk, take the paved 5km (3-mile) **Milliennium Loop** along the river. Start at the *SS Klondike* and turn right onto the river path (heading upstream). There's a brief stretch along the highway but then the path dips down behind the Robert Service campground and continues to the dam and fish ladder (see page 73). Cross the bridge to visit the fish ladder, then continue on the path down that side of the river until the bridge by the *SS Klondike* allows you to cross back into the town centre. Interpretive boards explain wildlife, history and so on as you walk.

For the more energetic, there's also a 15km **Yukon Loop**, which starts up where the Millennium Loop ends.

In the summer only, the **Yukon Conservation Society** (*302 Hawkins St;* \ *867 668 5678;* e *ycsoffice@ycs.yk.ca; www.yukonconservation.org*) organizes guided hikes every day. Most last two or three hours though some are full-day. There's a twice-daily Canyon City Historical Hike (see *Miles Canyon*, pages 71–2), plus other themed hikes on different days of the week. Guides explain about wildlife, history and environmental issues as you walk. Pick up a leaflet at the visitor centre or around town, or go to the Conservation Society's website for more information.

Additionally, the Yukon Conservation Society's book *Hikes & Bikes* gives detailed trail information on more than 30 day routes in the Whitehorse area; it's available from Mac's Fireweed Books on Main Street or www.yukonbooks.com.

For those who wish to twitch as they stroll, the **Yukon Bird Society** offers birdwatching field trips from April to October. Go to www.yukonweb.com/community/ybc/yukonbirdclub-fieldtrips.pdf or email yukonbirdclub@gmail.com for more information. Membership costs $10.

MOUNTAIN AND ROAD BIKING The **Contagious Mountain Bike Club** (e *info@cmbcyukon.ca; www.cmbcyukon.com*) has information on maintained trails, and organizes group rides every Thursday evening in summer. To go on the ride you must be a member ($15 per year). The club also hosts the **24 Hours of Light Mountain Bike Festival** each June (*www.24hoursoflight.ca*) for which you must have Cycling Association of Yukon Insurance ($25). **Yukon Dirt Girls** (e *yukondirtgirls@gmail.com; http://groups.google.com/group/yukondirtgirls*) offers recreational mountain bike rides and skills clinics for girls and women. They have regular Tuesday-evening rides in the Whitehorse area. **Boréale Biking** (see page 56) offers guided mountain biking as well as yurt accommodation just outside Whitehorse, while rentals are available from **Philippe's Bicycle Shop, Up North** and **Kanoe People** (see page 55).

Velo North (*www.velonorth.ca*) is a general hub for Yukon cycling, though the website is less than user-friendly at the time of writing.

GOLF Whitehorse has two golf courses that are open to visitors:

Meadow Lakes Golf & Country Club Km 1411, mile 878 Alaska Highway, ie: in the southerly Watson Lake direction as you leave Whitehorse, ☎ 867 668 4653; e info@meadowlakesgolfandcountry.com; www.meadowlakesgolfandcountry.com; $25 for 9 holes outside peak hrs, $30 evenings, w/ends & holidays. ⏰ 1 May to mid-Oct 8am–8pm (last tee time) Mon–Sat, 8am–6pm Sun. A 9-hole course situated on the banks of the Yukon River, a 10min drive from the centre of Whitehorse.

Mountain View Golf Club 250 Skookum Dr (off Range Rd & Mountain View Dr); ☎ 867 633 6020/6030; e mvgc@yknet.ca; www.mountainviewgolf.ca; ⏰ mid-May to late Sep 7am–10pm (last tee time) daily; green fees $30 (9 holes), $49 (18 holes) for adults, concessions for seniors & juniors. This is an 18-hole, par-72 course with driving range & putting green. Clubs & power carts can be rented.

CROSS-COUNTRY SKIING If you're looking for groomed trails, the best place for cross-country skiing in Whitehorse is Mount McIntyre, base of operations for the **Whitehorse Cross Country Ski Club** (*#200, 1 Sumanik Dr;* ☎ *867 668 4477 or 867 668 7742 – trail conditions & event information only;* e *info@xcskiwhitehorse.ca; www.xcskiwhitehorse.ca*). It's five minutes out of central Whitehorse, near the Canada Games Centre. The ski club maintains 75km (46 miles) of groomed trails and offers day, three-day and five-day passes ($10, $25, $40) for out-of-town visitors. There are some trails for use with dogs. It also rents skis, skates, poles and boots, and has an indoor waxing area with benches, vices, irons and power outlets as well as changing rooms, lockers, showers and sauna. Ski lessons are available for both adults and children. The Ski Base Service Centre, from where you buy your pass and rent equipment, has hours of operation that vary according to the weather and season. Check the ski club's website for up-to-date information. You can also find information and book ski lessons at Coast Mountain Sports on Main Street.

DOWNHILL SKIING AND SNOWBOARDING Mount Sima (*Mount Sima Rd;* ☎ *867 668 4557;* e *info@mountsima.com; www.mountsima.com; $29 for a day, $20 for half day for adults; concessions for children & seniors;* ⏰ *mid–Dec to Apr 10am–3pm Thu–Fri, 10am–3.30pm Sat–Sun;*) is Whitehorse's only alpine ski hill. It has 12 runs and two lifts (a chair and a tow). Ski, board, boot and pole rental, and lessons are available. Mount Sima is a 15-minute drive from downtown Whitehorse. Take the Alaska Highway in a southerly direction, towards Watson Lake, then follow the signs – the ski centre is 5km (3 miles) up Mount Sima Road.

ICE CLIMBING Equinox Adventure Learning (☎ *867 456 7846;* e *equinox@ northwestel.net; www.equinoxyukon.com*) builds ice towers for climbing in Whitehorse each winter. Instruction is available from 1½ hours ($45) to a full day ($150). Experienced climbers may buy a day pass for $15; gear is available for rent.

SNOW KITING Kite Yukon (☎ *867 667 6683;* e *info@kiteyukon.com; www.kiteyukon.com*) runs snow kiting courses and expeditions for beginners and advanced snow kiters alike.

4

The Alaska Highway

'Where are you heading?' I asked a white-haired American couple who were staying at my hotel at Watson Lake. I was just making light chat; I assumed they were going to the next town.

'Aw, Florida,' they replied in a tone of voice that implied they were popping out to buy milk. 'We're dropping our granddaughter off in California on the way.' They made the woman I met later in Beaver Creek – travelling with her dog from Idaho to start a new life in Alaska – seem rather unadventurous.

That, for me, was one of the great joys of driving this famous highway that stretches more than 2,000km (1,200 miles) from Dawson Creek in British Columbia to Delta Junction in Alaska. I'd driven parts of the road plenty of times before – I knew it was both stunningly scenic and historically extraordinary – but until I began the research for this guidebook, I'd never stopped to talk to my fellow travellers along the way. Once I did so, I found that the stories of these people, who were fulfilling the road-trip dream of a lifetime, gave the Alaska Highway a dimension that I'd never imagined.

HISTORY

In the heart of the primeval forest men of the United States Army Engineering Corps …lived up magnificently to their frontier traditions. Bridging unpredictable glacial streams, scaling white-capped peaks, wrestling with quaking bog and muskeg; fighting mosquitoes and bulldog flies in summer, and stinging, searing winter cold that froze the very marrow in their bones – through tropical heat and Arctic cold they ploughed ahead. And, in seven short months, the pioneer Hudson's Bay fur trail…was converted into a 1,600-mile military highway.

So wrote Philip H Godsell in his book *Alaska Highway*, which was published in 1944 – a time when the terrors of World War II ran fresh, and patriotism pumped through robust American veins.

It took more than 10,000 troops eight months and 12 days to hack their way through those interminable miles of frozen, forested muskeg and build the Alaska Highway (sometimes called the Alcan) in the fear-filled year of 1942. There had been talk of a road through Alaska and the Yukon to the south for years. Then, on 7 December 1941, the Japanese attacked Pearl Harbor. The Americans were panic-stricken by the vulnerability of their western flank. They urgently needed to strengthen their defences on the Alaska coast – and they needed a supply route. The US Navy considered that it could do the job but the politicians decided otherwise. They would build a road from Dawson Creek in Canada's British Columbia (the point where the Northern Alberta Railway, which connected with towns to the south, ended) through the Yukon Territory, and into Alaska. The Americans would pay; after the war the Canadians would take over maintenance of their section.

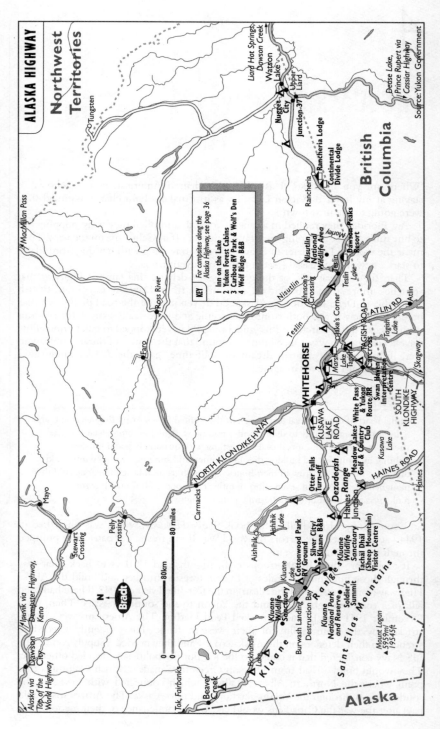

British
Columbia

Alaska

KEY *For campsites along the Alaska Highway, see page 36*

1 Inn on the Lake
2 Yukon Forest Cabins
3 Caribou RV Park & Wolf's Den
4 Wolf Ridge B&B

Source: Yukon Government

Liard Hot Springs,
Dawson Creek
Watson
Lake
Upper
Liard
Nugget
City
Junction-37
Dedsa Lake,
Prince Rupert via
Cassiar Highway
Rancheria Lodge
Continental
Divide Lodge
Rancheria
Morley
Dawson Peaks
Resort
Nisutlin
National
Wildlife Area
Teslin
Teslin
Lake
Johnson's
Crossing
Jake's Corner
Atlin
Nisutlin
ATLIN RD
Tungsten
MacMillan Pass
Ross River
Faro
Teslin
WHITEHORSE
Marsh
Lake
Tagish
Tagish
Lake
TAGISH ROAD
CARCROSS
Skagway
SOUTH
KLONDIKE
HIGHWAY
Swan Haven
Interpretation
Centre
White Pass
& Yukon
Route/RR
KUSAWA
LAKE ROAD
Kusawa
Lake
HAINES ROAD
Haines
Meadow Lakes
Golf & Country
Club
Otter Falls
Turn-off
Dezadeash
Haines Range
Junction
Ross River
NORTH KLONDIKE HWY
Carmacks
Pelly
Crossing
Stewart
Crossing
Mayo
Aishihik
Aishihik
Lake
Kluane
Lake
Cottonwood Park
RV Ground
Silver City
Kluane B&B
Kluane
Wildlife
Sanctuary
Tachäl Dhäl
(Sheep Mountain)
Visitor Centre
Kluane
National Park
and Reserve
Soldier's
Summit
Destruction Bay
Burwash Landing
Kluane
Wildlife
Sanctuary
Pickhandle
Lake
Beaver
Creek
Tok, Fairbanks
Alaska via
Top of the
World Highway
Dawson
City
Inuvik via
Dempster Highway,
Keno
Mount Logan
▲5959m/
19545ft
Saint Elias Mountains
Kluane Range Mountains

N
Bradt
0   80km
0   80 miles

78

Various routes were discussed, but military planners in the end settled for one that linked the existing airports of the Northwest Staging Route, which supplied goods across the north and into Russia: the air bases and the highway would complement each other (see *Watson Lake and the Alaska–Siberia Airway*, page 83).

Work started in March 1942. It was finished an astonishing eight months later (the sense of urgency increased when the Japanese moved in on Alaska's Aleutian Islands, invading and occupying the islands of Kiska and Attu in June 1942). But this wasn't the kind of road that we know. It was a tortuous pioneer route, with interminable corduroy sections – logs laid side by side over muskeg and permafrost – and devastatingly steep gradients. Where possible, it connected existing First Nations trapping and trading trails. So heinous were the twists and turns that many believed the military must have designed it that way on purpose so that the Japanese could not easily bomb the road.

They've been straightening it out ever since. Almost as soon as it was 'completed' in October 1942, civilian contractors were working on the highway, trying to turn it into a less terrifying driving experience. The road was opened to the public in 1948, but they're still working on it today, improving bridges, ironing out permafrost heaves and trying to keep up with the havoc wreaked on the tarmac by the extreme weather of the north.

DRIVING THE HIGHWAY

ROAD CONDITIONS Most of the Alaska Highway is in good condition, and almost all of the Yukon section is paved. The unpaved stretches are between Burwash Landing and Beaver Creek. Here the road surface deteriorates in general; even in the paved sections there can be severe potholes and permafrost heaves, which turn the road into something of a rollercoaster ride. Look out for the little red flags on the side of the road: these indicate a hazard. And if the road surface in front of you changes colour, slow down – the change in colour is almost certainly a sign of a broken-up road or of road repairs – and even the repairs can be surprisingly bumpy. When the road is empty, locals drive on the smoothest part of the road, even if that's on the left, but obviously you'll need to keep to the right on corners and hills.

For up-to-date road reports, call ☏ 511 from within the Yukon or Alaska, or go to www.511yukon.ca. You can also call ☏ 250 774 7447 for road reports specific to the Alaska Highway.

HISTORICAL MILES, OUT-OF-DATE MILES AND ACTUAL MILES Think of it like Yukon time, but for mileposts. If you look at three different sources for the mile or kilometre number of any site on the Alaska Highway, you seem to get three different figures: they reckon there's only one accurate milepost on the whole of the highway, and that's at mile zero in Dawson Creek. Ever since the original route was completed in 1942, engineers have been upgrading and straightening the Alaska Highway – and so the road has shortened. It was 2,700km (1,680 miles) on the road's 'completion' in 1942; by the time the Canadian section was handed over in 1946 the highway as a whole had already shrunk to 2,288km (1,422 miles).

Today…well, today nobody really knows how long the Alaska Highway is. It's managed and maintained by three different governments – BC, Yukon and Alaska – and they all do things their own way. To add to the confusion, Canada went metric in the 1970s, and so the Canadians have now replaced the mileposts with kilometre markings. The Yukon section was recalibrated in 2005, but just as far as Kluane Lake; after that, the kilometre posts are based on the historical miles, not the actual distance. The BC part was recalibrated in 1990. And the Alaska section hasn't been recalibrated at all, with the result that the Canadians reckon that their section of the highway ends at 1,910km or 1,187 miles, but the first milepost of the Alaska part says 1,222.

In this guidebook, I've taken the miles to tally with those of *The Milepost*: they refer to the actual miles driven from Dawson Creek, with the historical miles added in where relevant. The kilometres ought to – for the most part! – tally with the kilometre posts on the road. But you'll almost certainly find that somebody somewhere has measured things differently. Lodges, restaurants and so on along the way often use the historic miles to refer to their location.

Also note that locals refer to driving north and south along the highway rather than east and west, even in those sections, for example between Watson Lake and Whitehorse, where there's little change in latitude.

GAS STATIONS There are plenty of gas stations along the Alaska Highway, but be careful in winter, when some may close or operate for reduced hours; even in summer, gas stations in the smaller communities close up in the early evening. Take local advice before setting out.

REST STOPS AND PULL-OUTS There are many pull-outs along the highway with interpretive boards and outhouses. Usually these are located in places of beauty and historical or geographical interest.

WATSON LAKE (km 980, mile 613)

Read this sentence quietly: the town of Watson Lake is not the centre of the universe. Its signpost forest and northern lights centre are mildly interesting for a quick stop, and you'll find practical conveniences here – bank, bed and food that's likely to be mediocre. More interesting are the lesser-sung attractions that lie a little way out of town, such as the waterslide at Lucky Lake on a sunny afternoon, or the surrounding hiking and cross-country ski trails. There are also a couple of really delightful bed and breakfasts just outside town where one could happily lay one's hat for several days of swimming, skiing or snoozing – or even all three.

HISTORY There seems to be consensus that Watson Lake is named after Frank Watson, though the stories surrounding him vary somewhat. Most agree that at the age of 14 he travelled with his father from their home in Tahoe City, California to the Klondike goldfields. About five years later, after his father had gone back south, Frank came here, to the shores of what was then called Fish Lake, where he met and married local Kaska First Nation girl Adela Stone. He lived, worked as a hunter and trapper, and raised a family on the shores of the lake. Frank Watson died of pneumonia in 1938, but his descendants live in the area to this day.

Watson Lake's airstrip was used from 1941 with the advent of the Alaska–Siberia Airway that supplied war-ravaged Russia (see *Watson Lake and the Alaska–Siberia Airway*, page 83) and Watson Lake, the town, was born the following year when it served as a barracks and supply centre during the construction of the Alaska Highway. It now has a population of around 1,700.

GETTING THERE Watson Lake sits at the junction of the Alaska Highway and the Robert Campbell Highway, which leads north towards Frances Lake, Ross River and Faro. For more on the Campbell Highway and those communities, see *Chapter 7: Campbell Country*. The turn-off for Highway 37, which goes south through BC, is about 20km (12 miles) west of Watson Lake.

Greyhound Canada (*office in Recreation Centre, 912 Lakeview Dr;* \ *867 536 8020; www.greyhound.ca;* ⊕ *9am–noon Mon–Sat, 6pm–8.30pm Mon, Wed, Fri,*

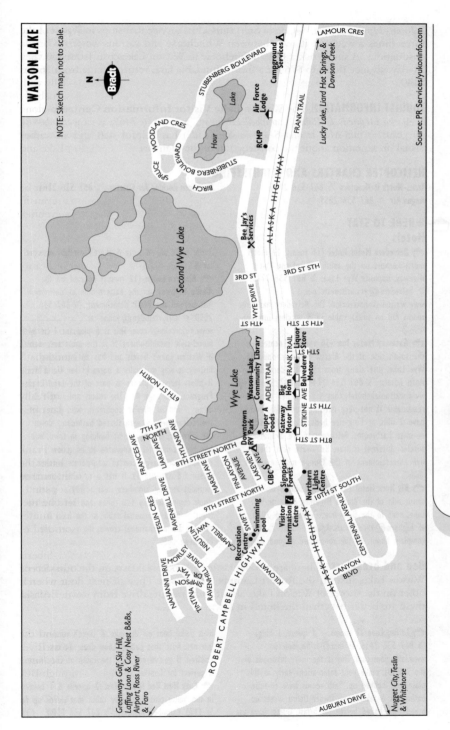

WATSON LAKE

NOTE: Sketch map, not to scale.

N

Bradt

Source: PR Services/yukoninfo.com

STUBENBERG BOULEVARD

Hour Lake

Lake

WOODLAND CRES

SPRUCE

BIRCH

STUBENBERG BOULEVARD

Air Force Lodge

Campground Services

RCMP

FRANK TRAIL

LAMOUR CRES

ALASKA HIGHWAY

Lucky Lake, Liard Hot Springs, & Dawson Creek

Second Wye Lake

Bee Jay's Services

3RD ST

3RD ST STH

WYE DRIVE

4TH ST

4TH ST STH

Wye Lake

Watson Lake Community Library

ADELA TRAIL

FRANK TRAIL

LS STH

Liquor Store

Big Horn

Belvedere Motor

LS STH

6TH ST NORTH

7TH ST NORTH

7TH ST

8TH STREET NORTH

Downtown RV Park

Super A Foods

Gateway Motor Inn

STIKINE AVE

7TH ST STH

8TH ST STH

FRANCES AVE

LIARD AVE

MARSH AVE

8TH HYLAND AVE

LAKEVIEW AVE

FINLAYSON AVENUE

CIBC $

Signpost Forest

Northern Lights Centre

9TH STREET NORTH

10TH ST SOUTH

TESLIN CRES

RAVENHILL DRIVE

WRATSIN

CAMPBELL WY

SWIFT PL

Visitor Information Centre

Recreation Centre

Swimming pool

ALASKA HIGHWAY

CANYON BLVD

CENTENNIAL AVENUE

NAHANNI DRIVE

MORLEY

SIMPSON

TININA

RAVENHILL DRIVE WAY

NISUTLIN

KILOWATT

ROBERT CAMPBELL HIGHWAY

Greenways Golf, Ski Hill, Loffing Loon & Cosy Nest B&Bs, Airport, Ross River & Faro

Nugget City, Teslin & Whitehorse

AUBURN DRIVE

8.30pm–11pm Tue, Thu, Sat, closed Sun) runs a bus service that stops in Watson Lake three times a week on its way between Whitehorse and various western Canada destinations. A single ticket from Whitehorse to Watson Lake costs from $30 for a 21-day advance ticket to $76 for a fully refundable fare; returns range from $60 to $140.

TOURIST INFORMATION The **Watson Lake Visitor Information Centre** (*junction of Alaska Highway & Robert Campbell Highway;* ☎ *867 536 7469;* e *vic.watsonlake@ gov.yk.ca;* ⊕ *mid-May to mid-Sep 8am–8pm daily*) has helpful staff and an audio-visual presentation about the construction of the highway.

HELICOPTER CHARTERS AND FLIGHTSEEING

Trans-North Helicopters ☎ 867 536 2100   **Northern Rockies Air Charter** ☎ 867 536 2364
Angus Air ☎ 867 536 2059

WHERE TO STAY
Hotels

🏠 **Belvedere Motor Hotel** (31 rooms, 17 motel units) Located on the south side of the Alaska Highway, opposite Wye Lake; ☎ 867 536 7712; e belvedere@yt.northwestel.net; www.watsonlakehotels.com. The Belvedere has large rooms (all en suite), cable TV & wireless internet. $$$

🏠 **Gateway Motor Inn** (50 rooms) Located on the south side of the Alaska Highway, opposite Wye Lake, just along from the Belvedere & Big Horn hotels; ☎ 867 536 7744; f 867 536 7740; www.watsonlakehotels.com; ⊕ summer only. A reasonable if not very exciting hotel. All rooms have 2 dbls or king-size beds, plus sofa beds & en-suite bathrooms. Kitchenettes are available; wireless internet is free. Be aware that there's live entertainment in the lounge most evenings. $$$

🏠 **Big Horn Hotel** (29 rooms) Located on the south side of the Alaska Highway, opposite Wye Lake, next to the Belvedere; ☎ 867 536 2020; e bighorn@yknet.yk.ca. Again, nothing to complain about. All the rooms are a good size with 2 dbl beds, all en suite & there's wireless internet for $2. $$–$$$

🏠 **Airforce Lodge** (12 rooms) Located on the Alaska Highway, on the eastern side of 'downtown', just beyond the RCMP detachment; ☎ 867 536 2890; e airforcelodge@yahoo.ca; www.airforcelodge.com. This is a pleasant 1-storey motel-style establishment. It is the most personable of Watson Lake's hotels and has an interesting history: it was originally a barracks for World War II pilots ferrying planes as part of the Lend Lease Program (see page 83). The rooms are simple & clean – indeed, they've apparently won prizes for their cleanliness – with shared bathrooms down the corridor. It's the oldest building in town, but has been completely renovated to be a low consumer of energy, and to incorporate wireless internet & satellite TV. It has a sociable atmosphere (without verging anywhere near rowdy – guests drink complimentary tea, coffee and hot chocolate together at a communal table in the hall) & attracts an international crowd; the owners are European. $$

Bed and breakfasts There are two fantastic bed and breakfasts on the outskirts of Watson Lake, just off the Robert Campbell Highway. They sit next door to each other on the shores of Watson Lake, about a ten-minute drive from town. Both of these are better bets than the hotels in town.

🏠 **Laffing Loon** (2 rooms – 1 queen, 1 king) ☎ 867 536 7636; e info@laffingloon.com; www.laffingloon.com. This is the more luxurious of the 2 B&Bs: make your reservations early as this place gets booked up. Both rooms have en-suite bathrooms & lake views. Owner Debra serves up bread she's baked herself for b/fast. Guests have use of a pedal boat on the lake, & there's wireless internet. Note that Laffing Loon does not take children. If you've got kids, the cabin at Cozy Nest is perfect for families. $$$

🏠 **Cozy Nest Bed & Breakfast** (2 queens & 1 twin in the house plus a lakeside cabin that sleeps up to 5) 1175 Campbell Highway; ☎ 867 536 2204;

'Give us the tools,' Winston Churchill told the American people in February 1941, 'and we will finish the job.' A month later, the Americans signed the Lend-Lease Act: America would supply with food, ammunition and equipment those nations whose survival was considered essential to the defence of the United States.

The Lend-Lease Agreement began to affect the Yukon and Alaska in June that year, when the Nazis invaded Russia. Russia's defence was, with Great Britain's, considered vital for the wellbeing of the US, and so the Alaska–Siberia Airway was born: between 1942 and 1945, its pilots delivered almost 8,000 aircraft and billions of dollars worth of goods from the United States to Russia. Starting in Great Falls, Montana, where the planes were manufactured, they flew across western Canada to Ladd Field (now known as Fort Wainwright) near Fairbanks in Alaska, where the planes were handed over to Soviet pilots. From there, the Russians flew them across Siberia and to the fronts.

These men's journeys were dangerous: 133 planes crashed in North America and 44 in Siberia over the three years of the Alaska–Siberia Airway. Most of the land over which these men flew was remote wilderness, and they made their journeys in hops from one rudimentary airfield to the next. Watson Lake was one of these airfields, and the Air Force Lodge was the barracks at which the pilots slept.

e cozynest@northwestel.net; www.cozynestbandb.com. This place has a great deck overlooking Watson Lake, & owners & guests swim here year round — the water was a toasty 20°C when I visited. In winter you'll need to be tougher as they cut a hole in the ice, but give a few hrs' notice & the owners will stoke up the sauna before you jump in. It's all tremendous fun, I'm sure. The B&B rooms in the house share a bathroom & a living & kitchen area with microwave & fridge. The cabin has a BBQ & electricity but no running water (there's an outhouse) but who needs running water when there's a lake right there? Free wireless internet. $$

Campgrounds and RV parks

⚑ **Campground Services** (62 full hook-ups, 38 water & electricity only, 30 tent sites) Km 976, mile 611, historical mile 633 Alaska Highway (on the east side of town, beyond the RCMP & Air Force Lodge); ☎ 867 536 7448; ⏰ May–Sep. Facilities include grocery store, Laundromat, gas, a mechanic & free wireless internet. $

⚑ **Downtown RV Park** (84 full hook-ups) Junction of Lakeview Av & 8th St North; ☎ 867 536 2646; e selliott@yknet.yk.ca or atannock@hotmail.com; ⏰ summer only. Rather spartan, with rows of hook-ups in a gravel yard, but some might appreciate the central location. Offers full hook-ups, laundry & free wireless internet. $

✗ **WHERE TO EAT** There's no nice way of saying this: Watson Lake is not a gourmet's paradise. Your best bet is to eat before you get here – if you're coming from the Whitehorse direction, I recommend Wolf It Down at Nugget City (see pages 86–7). Failing that, try one of the following.

✗ **Belvedere Motor Hotel** Located on the south side of the Alaska Highway, opposite Wye Lake; ☎ 867 536 7712; e belvedere@yt.northwestel.net; www.watsonlakehotels.com. There's a basic coffee shop serving sandwiches & burgers, where I ate a perfectly acceptable burger & fries. The hotel also advertises a 'fine dining' restaurant; I've heard that standards can be sketchy. $$–$$$

✗ **Bee Jay's Services** ☎ 867 536 2335; ⏰ 6.30am–7.30pm. Located just along from the RCMP detachment, this is basically a truckers' café, but it has a good reputation. $$

SHOPPING Try not to confuse Watson Lake with New York's Fifth Avenue. Still, there's a good grocery store in town if you need to stock up: **Super A Foods** (*on* *the cnr of 8th St North & Adela Trail;* ✎ *867 536 2250).* The **liquor store** is at 603 Frank Trail (✎ *867 536 7311;* ⊕ *10am–6pm Tue–Sat).*

OTHER PRACTICALITIES

Bank CIBC, Adela Trail, between 8th & 9th Sts; ✎ 867 536 7495; ⊕ 9.30am–4pm Mon–Thu, 9.30am–5pm Fri. ATM available 24hrs.
RCMP Adela Trail, by Stubenberg Boulevard junction; ✎ 867 536 5555
Watson Lake Health Centre ✎ 867 536 7483

Post office 20b Adela Trail; ✎ 867 536 7325
Internet There are internet computers in the Watson Lake Community Library (*Adela Trail*), in the Northern Lights Centre (*opposite 9th St on Frank Trail*), & in the Recreation Centre (*912 Lakeview Dr*).

WHAT TO SEE AND DO
Downtown

Signpost Forest (*Junction of the Alaska Highway & Robert Campbell Highway*) Back in 1942 during the construction of the Alaska Highway, a US soldier named Carl Lindley from Danville, Illinois, was stationed at Watson Lake. He was homesick, and so he planted a sign pointing in the direction of his hometown, stating that it lay 2,835 miles away. The planting of signposts caught on and now everyone's at it: Watson Lake's signpost forest has more than 65,000 signs. It's an intriguing site in that it tells the story of those who have driven the highway, from every corner of the United States and beyond, in a powerfully visual way. Bring a sign from your own hometown, and you can add it to the collection.

Northern Lights Centre (*Opposite 9th St on Frank Trail, running parallel to the Alaska Highway on the south side;* ✎ *867 536 7827;* e *nlc@northwestel.net; www.northernlightscentre.ca;* ⊕ *summer: 12.30pm–4pm, 6pm–9.30pm daily, winter: Tue–Sat with varying hrs*) The main attraction is the 55-minute show, which runs six times daily (*$10 adults; 1pm, 2pm, 3pm, 6:30pm, 7:30pm & 8:30pm from mid-May to mid-Sep*). It's divided into two parts, one on Canada's role in space exploration, and the other on the Yukon northern lights, including science, mythology and folklore. You can pick up a $1-off voucher at the visitor centre. In winter, when you can watch the northern lights outside, the auditorium is used to screen regular movies. Also of note: the Northern Lights Centre has free internet access year round.

Wye Lake This is the lake just behind the main 'downtown' area. There's a pleasant boardwalk surrounding it, which makes for a good stroll. It's about 1.5km (1 mile) long, and interpretive boards give information on flowers and birds. Look out for red-necked grebes, tree and violet-green swallows, pileated woodpeckers, and clay-coloured, white-throated and swamp sparrows. There are further hiking trails in the 26ha (64-acre) Wye Lake Park. Ask at the visitor centre for directions.

Recreation Centre (*912 Lakeview Dr – it's the big green & red building behind the Signpost Forest;* ✎ *867 536 8020;* e *alyssa.magun@watsonlake.ca; $3 adults, $2 seniors, children under 12 go free;* ⊕ *8am–8.30pm Mon, Wed, Fri, 8am–5pm Tue, Thu, 8am–noon Sat, closed Sun*) When you consider that these prices are for unlimited use of the gym, squash courts, bowling alley, rollerblading and more, this is a definite bargain. There's internet access, too.

Swimming pool (*The small brown & white building behind the Recreation Centre – it's rather tucked away but if you come out of the Rec Centre, turn right & keep walking round, you'll find it; adults $3.50, discounts for children & seniors;* ⊕ *Jun–Aug*) The pool is separately run from the Rec Centre; ask at the visitor centre or Rec Centre for the daily schedule. Note that there's only one lifeguard in Watson Lake, so when the Lucky Lake pool (see below) is open, the swimming pool is closed.

Beyond Downtown

Lucky Lake If it's a warm weekend, and you've put in the driving or cycling hours, Lucky Lake Recreation Site makes the perfect stop. It's more or less bang on the Yukon/BC border, about 8km (5 miles) out of Watson Lake on the Alaska Highway. The pretty lake is lined by a sandy shore and spruce trees, and there's a fabulous waterslide (the only outdoor waterslide in the Yukon). It's open on summer weekends only, when the weather is fine, and because the lake is fairly shallow, it warms up fast once the sun comes out. Note that when the lake is open, the swimming pool in town is closed: the same lifeguard works at both and modern medicine hasn't yet found a way to clone him. There's also a scenic 2.2km (1.4-mile) trail that goes down the west side of Lucky Lake to Liard Canyon. Look out for gray jays, northern flickers and black-capped or boreal chickadees. As for the lake's name: like the highway itself, it dates back to the war. It's due, apparently, to the work of an entrepreneurial woman who set up a tent here to provide 'services' for soldiers during the construction of the highway.

Albert Creek Banding Station Set up and run by bird biologist Ted Murphy-Kelly, the Albert Creek bird banding station lies near Upper Liard, 12km (8 miles) northwest of Watson Lake. It operates during the migratory season: May to mid-June and end of July to end of September. Visitors are welcome to drop by and learn about the banding station's work. The volunteers that do the banding are only there in the morning though: they start at around 5am and work until lunchtime. For more information, call the Yukon Government Environment Office in Watson Lake at ☏ 867 536 7365, or ask for a map at the Watson Lake visitor centre.

Watson Lake Airport The airport is a drive out of town, off the Robert Campbell Highway – it's about ten minutes up the highway, and signed off to the left. It's housed in an historic log building, and photographs on the walls document the use of the airstrip during World War II. It's mildly interesting, if largely an excursion for aviation buffs. Note that scheduled flights don't serve this airport.

COAL RIVER SPRINGS TERRITORIAL PARK

Adventurous souls might like to consider an excursion to Coal River Springs. This tiny territorial park – it measures in at 16km^2 or about 6 square miles – is known for its limestone terraces containing pools of blue water. The pools' walls are made of tufa, a precipitate of dissolved limestone; they build at a rate of two or three centimetres a year. You're not allowed to bathe in the pools (whose water is cold) as you may damage the tufa.

To get there, you'll have to charter a helicopter from Watson Lake (see *Helicopter charters and flightseeing*, page 82) unless you're an experienced outdoors person. Flights take about an hour. Advanced hikers and routefinders can bushwhack in from an old logging road, or advanced paddlers can take a float plane from Watson Lake, then line upstream on the Coal River – but they're then committed to a week-long trip through grade III and IV rapids before reaching the take-out where the Coal River meets the Alaska Highway in British Columbia. There's a camping and recreation area 200m (220yds) east of the main formations. For more information go to www.environmentyukon.gov.yk.ca/parksconservation/CoalRiverSprings.php, call Yukon Parks at ☏ 867 667 5648 or e yukonparks@gov.yk.ca.

The **Liard Hot Springs** (*km 765, mile 478 Alaska Highway;* ✆ *250 427 5452;* e *ekparks@telus.net; www.env.gov.bc.ca/bcparks/explore/parkpgs/liard_rv_hs; $5 adults, $3 children, $10 families;* ⊕ *year round but the larger, deeper pool is usually closed 1 Aug–1 Oct due to bear activity, followed by danger from icy conditions on the boardwalk*) are not in the Yukon but in British Columbia – but given they're a major attraction of this part of the highway, and only a couple of hours beyond the border, they warrant a mention.

The second-largest hot springs in Canada, there are two pools ranging from 42°C to 52°C (107°F–126°F). A boardwalk leads over swamps that link the two pools; moose often feed here.

There's a campground at the hot springs, operated by BC Parks and open year round. In the summer, it gets very full so it's wise to make a reservation via **Discover Camping** (✆ *604 689 9025, toll-free:* ✆ *1 800 689 9025; www.discovercamping.ca*). Reservations may be made for stays from mid-May to the beginning of September only.

Greenway's Greens Golf and Country Club (*Turn off the Alaska Highway at km 993, mile 620.3;* ✆ *867 536 2477*) A nine-hole, par-35 course, open daily in summer.

Watson Lake Ski Club (*Access road to Mount Maichen is on the right 7km, 4.3 miles up the Campbell Highway;* ✆ *867 536 8031 (seasonal); www.watsonlakeskiclub.ca; adult pass $16 for a half day, $22 for a full day, or $50 for the w/end inc Fri night, concessions for juniors; ski rental available;* ⊕ *call or go to website for current operating hrs*) The ski club (which is entirely volunteer run) is based at Mount Maichen. The longest run is 1.5km (just under a mile); elevation is 275m (900ft). There are two T-bar lifts and nine groomed runs. Cross-country ski trails (and hiking trails in the summer) connect to the ski hill. The ski hill closes if temperatures dip lower than –25°C (–13°F).

FROM WATSON LAKE TO TESLIN

It takes around two hours to drive the 179km (111 miles) between Watson Lake and Teslin – if you don't stop. But that would be missing the point. To start with, the food at Nugget City is fantastic, and that's only 23km (14 miles) out of town. In fact, you may be well advised to skip breakfast in Watson Lake and eat it there instead. Then, just a little further along, there's Rancheria, a quirky little spot at which to grab an ice cream, or a home-baked cookie or six, or even a full meal. Admittedly, by this time your stomach might be starting to hurt, but there's a wholesome stroll to a waterfall nearby which may help work off the calories.

KM 984, MILE 615: WATSON LAKE CAMPGROUND (55 sites) A pleasant government campground, though the sites are not directly on the lake. See page 35 for information on how government campgrounds work.

KM 992, MILE 620, HISTORICAL MILE 642: UPPER LIARD This is a small settlement of fewer than 200, populated almost entirely by the Liard First Nation. It sits 7km (4.3 miles) west of Watson Lake. There are services, a bar, a motel and a campground, but the vibe is very local, and this isn't a great stop for those driving the road.

KM 1003, MILE 627, HISTORICAL MILE 650 NUGGET CITY (✆ *867 536 2307, toll-free:* ✆ *1 888 536 2307, 1 866 494 0131 Nov–May;* e *nuggetcity@telus.net;*

www.nuggetcity.com; ⊕ *restaurant open year round, RV park & gift shop summer only*) This is not a city. It's handful of buildings at the side of the road, owned by Scott and Linda Goodwin, and Linda's one woman you may choose not to mess with: she shot the stuffed moose in the Northern Beaver Post Gift Shop herself, and it probably wasn't giving her any trouble. Linda was raised in the Yukon. Her parents Gwen and Don Lee came here to mine, and they told their story in their book, *Rivers of Gold*, which is for sale in the shop. Beyond lively characters and stuffed dead things, the shop's also known for its wood carvings by local craftsman Roger Latondress.

There are also cabins, ranging from luxury jacuzzi suites ($$$$$), to en suites ($$$), to basic rooms with bathrooms down the hall ($). They're perfectly nice on the inside, but rather plonked in a gravel yard with no surrounding landscaping. Nugget City also has an RV park (*89 sites with power & water but no sewerage, plus 6 tent sites,* $). Other amenities include a service centre with licensed mechanic, wireless internet, Laundromat and best of all, Wolf It Down restaurant and bakery ($$–$$$). Mains include buffalo steak, roast beef, schnitzel and fish and chips, there's delicious homemade pie for dessert, and a good deck on which to, erm, wolf it down.

KM 1042, MILE 651: BIG CREEK CAMPGROUND (15 sites) Another government campground, see page 35.

KM 1100, MILE 683, HISTORICAL MILE 710: RANCHERIA LODGE (☏ 867 851 6456)
This place is somehow cool and kooky in an I've-never-clapped-eyes-on-a-razor kind of a way. It's very Yukon and the people, with their big facial hair and paint-spattered clothing, are a total delight. Accommodation consists of a basic hotel (13 rooms, $$), which has something of a truck-stop feel to it, six lakefront cottages ($$), 22 RV hook-ups with power and water, and 28 tent sites ($). There's wireless internet in the restaurant and hotel but not the RV site. All the food in the restaurant is homemade. The folk at Rancheria Lodge are in the process of cutting further trails and renovating old horse trails for walking and snowmobiling, which will make this a good spot to stop off along the highway for a breath of fresh air. There's also a short (ten-minute) boardwalk trail leading to a waterfall at Rancheria Falls from the Rancheria Falls Recreation Site (*km 1113, mile 695*). Look out for least chipmunks and American dippers.

On a historical note, Rancheria was one of the first lodges to open along the highway in the 1940s – it was one of four establishments financed by the British Yukon Navigation Company when it started its bus service between Dawson Creek and Whitehorse in 1946, and was run from that date for 28 years by Bud and Doris Simpson. Rancheria is one of the only early highway lodges still operating today.

KM 1118, MILE 698, HISTORICAL MILE 721: CONTINENTAL DIVIDE LODGE (☏ 867 851 6451) There's a grocery store with gas, a motel, RV park and café, open summer only.

KM 1232, MILE 770, HISTORICAL MILE 797: DAWSON PEAKS RESORT (☏ 867 390 2244, toll-free: ☏ 1 866 402 2244; e *info@dawsonpeaks.ca; www.dawsonpeaks.ca;* ⊕ *mid-May to mid-Sep*) I'm going to stick my neck out and say that, with the exception of Inn on the Lake, which falls into a higher-end bracket, Dawson Peaks is the best place to stay between Whitehorse and Watson Lake during the summer months. The resort sits on the shores of Teslin Lake. There are three lakefront cabins, all with private deck ($$). They are plain but clean, all with en-suite bathrooms,

fridge and TV. There are additionally eight motel rooms ($$) and two 'camping cabins' ($), which are very basic and have no running water but you can shower in the main lodge. Dawson Peaks also has 18 RV sites with power and water, and eight tent sites ($). There's wireless internet throughout. There are also boat and canoe rentals, and chartered fishing. Plus, there's a gift shop and the restaurant has an excellent reputation ($–$$$). It serves up fresh fish, steak and an apparently prize-winning rhubarb pie; all the food is homemade. *And*, as a little added extra, owner David Hett is a marriage commissioner so, should driving the Alaska Highway bring on that loving feeling, you can get hitched here.

TESLIN (km 1244, mile 777, historical mile 804)

Once a summer camp of the Tlingit First Nation, Teslin sits at the confluence of Teslin Lake and the Nisutlin River. The Hudson's Bay Company opened a trading post here to serve the stampeders to the Klondike, but closed it again in 1903 when Tom Smith and George Geddes opened the Nisutlin Trading Post. Nowadays, Teslin has a population of just over 400 people. One point of interest is the Nisutlin Bay Bridge, which is the longest on the Alaska Highway at 584m or 639yds. More fascinating by far, though, is the George Johnston Museum, a quirky little establishment which, in my view, is one of the most interesting stops along the Yukon section of the Alaska Highway.

TOUR OPERATORS

Nisutlin Outfitting 867 390 2123, cell: 867 334 7364; e dmartens@northwestel.net; www.nisutlinoutfitting.com. This family-run business offers fishing & boat rental on Teslin Lake, guided & self-guided canoe trips on the Nisutlin, Teslin & Big Salmon rivers, & transfers. They also have 2 cabins for rent.

WHERE TO STAY AND EAT

🏠 **Yukon Motel** (10 rooms, 63 RV full & partial hook-ups) ☎ 867 390 2443 (office), 867 390 2575 (restaurant); e yukonmotel@northwestel.net; www.yukonmotel.com. Rooms are simple in décor, but large & clean, & all have private bathrooms. The restaurant serves up homemade soup, salads, burgers & wraps ($$). Free wireless internet. Motel rooms $$$, RV sites $

🏠 **Nisutlin Trading Post & Motel** (8 rooms) ☎ 867 390 2521; closed at Christmas. There's also a good-size general store here ⊕ summer: 6am–11pm, winter: 7am–10pm. $$
🏠 **Nisutlin Outfitting** ☎ 867 390 2123; cell: 867 334 7364; e dmartens@northwestel.net; www.nisutlinoutfitting.com. Has 2 cabins for rent. $–$$. See *Tour operators*, page 88.

OTHER PRACTICALITIES
RCMP ☎ 867 390 5555

Teslin Health Centre ☎ 867 390 4444; e hc.teslin@gov.yk.ca

WHAT TO SEE AND DO

George Johnston Museum (*Km 1244, mile 777 Alaska Highway;* ☎ *867 390 2550; e gjmuseum@hotmail.com; www.gjmuseum.yk.net; adults $5, children $2.50; ⊕ Jun–end Aug 9am–5pm daily*) This is one of my favourite stops along the road, though admittedly I'm attracted to things that are a little offbeat. But what a character George Johnston was. Born in coastal Alaska around 1884, he was a Tlingit trapper and fur trader with a fantastically creative mind. He bought himself a brownie box camera by mail order and taught himself to use it; his rich archive of photographs gives wonderful insights into the Inland Tlingit people of the early 20th century. Most amazing, though, was Johnston's decision to buy himself a car at a time when Teslin had neither vehicles nor roads. He took the boat to Whitehorse where he purchased a 1928 Chevrolet, which he ferried back to Teslin. He persuaded some of his friends to help him lay logs to build a rough corduroy road along a three-mile stretch near the village, and then charged his fellow villagers $2 for his 'taxi' service (he then paid them, in return, for helping him to maintain the road). Even more extraordinary, in winter he camouflaged the car by painting it white and driving it out onto the lake to hunt. The footage is all there (and the lake driving looks terrifying) in the DVD *Picturing a People: George Johnston, Tlingit Photographer*, made by the National Film Board of Canada and shown at the museum, which also displays Johnston's car among other Tlingit artefacts. If you don't have time to sit and watch the film for 50 minutes, you can buy the DVD ($25) and watch it later.

Tlingit Heritage Centre (*3km, 1.8 miles, west of Teslin;* ☎ *867 390 2070, toll-free:* ☎ *1 866 854 6448; www.tlingit.ca; ⊕ late May–early Sep 9am–5pm Mon–Fri, 10am–5pm Sat–Sun, by appointment only in winter*) This tiny museum tells the story of the Tlingit people, and exhibits a few attractive masks and some clothing. The gift shop sells authentic Tlingit artefacts.

FROM TESLIN TO WHITEHORSE

This section of the highway takes in the jaw-droppingly pretty southern lakes, which positively shimmer on a sunny summer's afternoon. The lakes, needless to say, attract waterfowl so this is a good area for birders. And the waterfowl attract predators, so there's plenty of meat-munching wildlife, too. About 40 minutes short of Whitehorse, on the shores of Marsh Lake, there are a couple of really lovely bed and breakfasts, plus the wonderful Inn on the Lake if you feel like a night of real comfort. And, a little way off the highway, there are some great wilderness cabins – perfect for a few days of total tranquillity.

You'll need at least a couple of days and a canoe to explore this wildlife area that lies just north of the highway at Teslin. The Nisutlin River valley and delta is a network of mudflats, marshes, channels and islands. It supports one of the largest concentrations of breeding trumpeter swans in Canada, as well as Canada and white-fronted geese, American widgeon and Barrow's goldeneye, bears, wolves, caribou, deer and elk; it is a vital early-spring feeding ground for cow moose and their calves. Traditionally an important hunting ground for the Teslin Tlingit people, the Nisutlin River Delta National Wildlife Area was created in 1995 as a result of land claim negotiations.

To paddle through the Nisutlin River Delta, put in at the boat launch on Teslin Lake and paddle northeast, towards Nisutlin Bay. An alternative route is to put in at Nisutlin River Recreation Site on the South Canol Road (km 68, mile 42), and paddle for 180km (108 miles) back to Teslin Lake. This trip takes four to six days. For canoe rentals, see *Tour operators*, page 88. Note that the Nisutlin River Delta is an undeveloped wilderness area with no staff, facilities or services.

KM 1257, MILE 785: TESLIN LAKE CAMPGROUND (27 sites) Government campground, see page 35.

KM 1273, MILE 795: DEADMAN CREEK Look out for Stone sheep on the east side of the highway. Stone sheep are a kind of thinhorn sheep, but unlike the more abundant Dall sheep they're not pure white in colour, but brown with white rumps; see *Dall sheep*, page 104.

KM 1296, MILE 808, HISTORICAL MILE 836: JOHNSON'S CROSSING CAMPGROUND SERVICES (✆ 867 390 2607) There's an RV park ($) and a little grocery store here; it sells home-baked food (cinnamon buns, pastries, meat pies and fries, fried chicken, soups) and souvenirs. To be honest, though, you're probably better off at Dawson Peaks a little further on.

Johnson's Crossing was named for Colonel Frank Johnson, of the US Army's 93rd Engineers: he was the commanding officer of the engineers that built the Teslin River Bridge. The Bechtel-Price-Callahan supply camp was based at Johnson's Crossing from 1942 to 1944 while the Canol pipeline and road were built; see pages 150–1.

KM 1314, MILE 820: TRAILHEAD TO DALAYEE WILDERNESS CABINS (✆ 867 393 3394; e *acaltherr@northwestel.net*; *www.taigajourneys.ca*; $$$) Owned by Andrea and Christoph Altherr of Taiga Journeys (see page 26), these three log cabins sit on the shore of Dalayee Lake, just west of Jake's Corner. You can fly in by float plane from Whitehorse (it costs around $400), or hike, ski or snowshoe the 9km (5.5 miles) from the highway. Many people choose to fly in with their food and supplies, then hike, ski or snowshoe out when their load is lighter. Although there are three cabins, each of which sleep four to six people, Andrea and Christoph have a policy that they only rent to one party at a time: even if you only take one cabin, you'll still have total privacy. The cabins have wood stoves for heating and propane burners for cooking; there's also a sauna. Canoes are supplied free of charge, and there's a motorboat available for a small fee for those wishing to fish for lake trout, arctic grayling and pike. In winter, guests may see the Carcross caribou herd, plus moose, lynx, wolverines, and black and grizzly bears year round. If you wish, you can hire a guide and cook for the duration of your stay. Minimum stay three nights.

KM 1316, MILE 821: SQUANGA LAKE CAMPGROUND (16 sites) A quiet, cosy government campground (see page 35) with a stunning location overlooking the lake – which, incidentally, is named for the rare Squanga pygmy whitefish that live here.

KM 1321, MILE 821: SQUANGA AIRSTRIP Keep an eye out for the pair of osprey that nest on top of the tower.

KM 1370, MILE 855: INN ON THE LAKE (*867 660 5253;* e *carson@ exceptionalplaces.com; www.exceptionalplaces.com;* $$$–$$$$$) Located a 40-minute drive from downtown Whitehorse on the Alaska Highway, Inn on the Lake is one of the – oh heck, let's stop mincing words and say *the* – top accommodation choice in the area. Between the main lodge and the independent cabins, it can sleep up to 30 people. The newest cabin, designed for two, has a private deck, with hot tub, which looks north for the best views of the aurora. The main lodge also has a hot tub and an extensive deck overlooking the lake; make full use of the honesty bar system to enjoy your evening sundowners – in full summer, with almost round-the-clock daylight, you could be at it for hours. Inn on the Lake has kayaks, canoes, pedal boats and passes for Meadow Lakes golf course in the summer, and toboggans and snowshoes in the winter, all included in the price. Use of snowmobiles costs extra; the Inn can also arrange ice fishing and dogsledding outings. Dinner – for those that wish – is four courses, and the guests eat together at a long and sociable table. In all, it's entirely delightful.

KM 1379, MILE 860: MARSH LAKE CAMPGROUND (41 sites) Another superb government campground (see page 35) – it's the turning after the recreation ground as you head in the Watson Lake direction. Some of the sites are on the shore of Marsh Lake.

KM 1381, MILE 861: SWAN HAVEN INTERPRETATION CENTRE (*For information call Environment Yukon:* * 867 667 8291, toll-free:* * 1 800 661 0408 ext 8291;* e *wildlife.viewing@gov.yk.ca; www.environmentyukon.gov.yk.ca/viewing;* ⊕ *Apr only 5pm–9pm Mon–Fri, noon–7pm Sat–Sun*) Swan Haven is at M'Clintock Bay, at the north end of Marsh Lake where the lake is joined by the M'Clintock River. Each April, thousands of tundra and trumpeter swans stop here for R&R during their spring migration. The water of M'Clintock Bay melts earlier than the other Yukon lakes and rivers giving the birds access to food, yet the surrounding ice offers protection from predators; Canada geese, green-winged teal and northern pintail take advantage too, while bald eagles come fishing and coyotes and wolves are attracted by the prolific bird life. Yukoners mark this welcome sign of spring with a Celebration of Swans, which lasts for eight days in the third week of April. There are birding tours, photography workshops, talks and children's activities. In other months, when the centre is closed, visitors can still enjoy the deck with its interpretive boards overlooking the bay.

KM 1393, MILE 867, HISTORICAL MILE 897: YUKON RIVER BRIDGE There's a good-sized deck with interpretive boards here, and binoculars. Look out for northern pintail, canvasback, American wigeon and common merganser on the water, American kestrels and bald eagles nesting on the banks, and mule deer on the south-facing slopes.

JUDAS CREEK SUBDIVISION There are a couple of lovely bed and breakfasts off the highway on Judas Creek Drive. They're signed ages back, but nonetheless you have to drive slowly and keep your eyes peeled as the turnings are tiny. You can turn down either Doehle Drive past Marsh Lake Community Centre, or Judas Creek Drive (*km 1360, mile 849*) – the road is U-shaped so if you accidentally drive past one turning, you can always take the next.

Where to stay

Andreas's Inn (2 rooms in main house, plus 1 cabin that sleeps 3) Lot 117 Judas Creek Subdivision; ↘ 867 660 4813; e andreasm@ northwestel.net; www.yukonweb.com/tourism/andreas. Andreas's is a large log cabin on a hill with wonderful views over the lake. Winter visitors enjoy the cross-country ski trails that run for 25km (15.5 miles) from his door; these can be used for mountain-biking & hiking in summer. He also rents out kayaks, canoes & skidoos. Guests have use of the kitchen, but there's a restaurant here as well, & Sat is Thai night – Andreas's wife is from Thailand so the food should be authentic. Cyber-addicts, relax: the house has wireless internet. $$

Old Screen Door B&B (3 rooms) 121 Judas Creek Drive; ↘ 867 660 4410; e Mo17@ marshlake.polarcom.com; www.oldscreendoor.homestead.com; ☼ summer only. Situated about 2.5km (1.5 miles) off the highway, this B&B has an incredible location on a quiet country road overlooking Marsh Lake. It's surrounded by hiking & skiing trails. The twin room has a private bathroom; the 2 dbls, 1 of which has its own deck, share. There's also a sitting room & kitchen for guests' use. No internet. Mo's only officially open in summer, but in reality she's often home for parts of the winter too (the rest of the time she heads to Jamaica to escape the snow). Call ahead &, if she's there, she'll probably open up for you. No children or pets. $$

YUKON FOREST CABINS (*Located 6.6 km, 4 miles east of the Carcross cut-off,* ↘ *867 668 7082; www.yukonforestcabins.com;* ☼ *year round but in winter cabins are available for long-term rental only;* $$$$) Two log cabins with electricity and running water. Mod cons include fridge, microwave and electric stove, a jacuzzi in one cabin and a claw-foot bathtub in the other (both have showers as well). Activities include canoeing, hiking and biking in summer, and skiing, snowshoeing or just lying back and watching the aurora in winter. And as if all that weren't enough, you can even get married here – owner Liesel Briggs is a licensed marriage commissioner.

KM 1403, MILE 874, HISTORICAL MILE 904: CARIBOU RV PARK & WOLF'S DEN RESTAURANT (↘ *867 393 3968; e wolfsden@northwestel.net or caribourvpark@ northwestel.net; www.wolfsden.yk.ca or www.caribou-rv-park.com*) Run by a Swiss couple, the restaurant (☼ *summer: 8am–10pm daily, winter: hrs vary so check the website or call ahead;* $$–$$$) This place has an excellent reputation among expatriate Germans, Swiss and Austrians living in the Whitehorse area; they flock here when they yearn for a taste of home. The menu features fondues, bratwurst and Bavarian sausage alongside local barbecue and international dishes. The RV site/campground (☼ *May–Sep;* $) has pull-through sites with power, plus dry sites in the woods for tenting. There are showers, satellite TV, wireless internet and laundry. It's all located 1.5km (just under a mile) east of the Carcross cut-off.

KM 1408, MILE 877: WOLF CREEK CAMPGROUND (40 sites) Yet another pleasant, wooded government campsite (see page 35). This one is just a few kilometres outside Whitehorse, though if you're tenting and you want to enjoy the bright lights of the city, you'd do better to opt for the more centrally located, privately owned Robert Service Campground (page 62). On the other hand, if you're after peace, quiet and serenity, this will probably be perfect. If you don't have a tent about your person but fancy a short walk, there's a 2km (1.2-mile) trail that leads from the campground to a viewing point over the Yukon River and back along Wolf Creek. An interpretive map at the campground tells you where to go and what to look out for.

KM 1411, MILE 878: MEADOW LAKES GOLF AND COUNTRY CLUB See page 76.

WHITEHORSE See *Chapter 3*, page 51.

FROM WHITEHORSE TO HAINES JUNCTION

This section takes around 1½–2 hours to drive. It's a pleasant enough stretch, though scenically not a patch on either the Southern Lakes to the east, or Kluane Lake and the mountains that come after Haines Junction.

KM 1460, MILE 909, HISTORICAL MILE 941: WOLF RIDGE BED AND BREAKFAST (✆ 867 456 4101; e info@wolfridge-cabins.com; www.wolfridge-cabins.com; $$) Two delightful cabins with kitchenettes, electricity, wood stoves, picnic tables and barbecues; one sleeps four people, the other sleeps two to three. The cabins don't have running water but Heide Hofmann, the gregarious German owner, invites guests to shower in the main house, where she also serves breakfast.

KM 1489, MILE 927: KUSAWA LAKE ROAD There are two government campgrounds down this gravel road that leads south from the Alaska Highway. The first, the **Takhini River Campground** (13 sites), is 15km (9 miles) along the road; the second, the **Kusawa Lake Campground** (56 sites), lies 22.5km (14 miles) from the highway intersection. For more on government campgrounds see page 35. From the Kusawa Lake Campground, you may be able to see Dall sheep on the mountain across the road.

KM 1546, MILE 964.6: OTTER FALLS TURN-OFF The Aishihik Road heads north off the highway towards Otter Falls, which are located 30km (18 miles) along this gravel road and were once pictured on Canada's five-dollar bill. There's a picnic area and walking trail. **Aishihik Lake Campground** (16 sites) is a government campground (see page 35) situated a further 12km (8 miles) along the Aishihik Road. You may see wood bison in this area; they were re-introduced to the Yukon in the 1980s. See page 94.

KM 1572, MILE 980: PINE LAKE CAMPGROUND (42 sites) Government campground; see page 35.

TAKHINI ELK HERD

Between the Takhini River bridge and the Mendenhall River, you may see elk on the south-facing slopes and in open aspen woodland. In recent years, these elk have been found to suffer from winter tick infestations, however, and have been kept in captivity during the spring and early summer until the ticks have fallen off. While the ticks pose no real danger to the elk, they can be fatal to moose if they spread, and there is fear that they could decimate the Yukon's moose population.

Unlike moose, elk are a non-indigenous species in the Yukon. They were introduced from Alberta in the 1950s.

WOOD BISON RECOVERY PROJECT

Back in the days of Beringia, bison were common in the Yukon. It's reckoned that Pleistocene bison inhabited this land as far back as 700,000 years ago, and that wood bison evolved from them. Estimates suggest that in 1800 there were 160,000 wood bison in North America. Then came men with guns, and the fur trade. By the beginning of the 20th century, only a few hundred wood bison remained.

In response to the decimation of these herds, Wood Buffalo National Park was established on the Northwest Territories–Alberta border in 1922, and numbers rallied. By 1925, it was reckoned that the protected herd comprised between 1,500 and 2,000 animals. But then plains bison were brought in to join them. They interbred, and disease spread. By the 1960s, just a few pure wood bison remained.

In 1978, wood bison were designated as endangered in Canada and, in the early 1980s, the Yukon government began to participate in Canada's Wood Bison Recovery Project: the aim was to create at least four separate, free-ranging herds of 400 or more animals. The first bison arrived in the Yukon from Elk Island National Park near Edmonton in 1986; they were brought to an enclosure 80km west of Carmacks. The first of them were released into the wild two years later. By 1992, 170 wood bison had been released. The wild herd is now thought to number more than a thousand.

HAINES JUNCTION (km 1579, mile 985)

Haines Junction came into being in 1942: it was originally a construction camp at the intersection of Haines Road and the Alaska Highway. There was already an old mining and mail road in this area (gold was discovered near Kluane Lake in 1904) and the Alaska Highway's planners incorporated that route, together with the Champagne and Aishihik First Nations trails, into the original path of the highway.

Today, it's for Kluane National Park and Reserve (see *Chapter 5*) that most people come to Haines Junction. The village per se is neither very big (its population is less than a thousand) nor tremendously exciting: the surrounding mountains, lakes and wilderness walks are the attraction. For athletic types, this is the base point for many incredible adventures. But even if you don't wish to yomp for miles, it's worth stopping here for a couple of days as there are plenty of short, easy trails in Kluane that will give you a taste of the area's natural grandeur. One further note: Haines Junction and Haines are not the same place. Haines is 235km (146 miles) away, in Alaska, and is covered on pages 130–7.

GETTING THERE For information on bus routes to Haines Junction, see *Chapter 5: Kluane National Park and Reserve*.

TOUR OPERATORS For Haines Junction tour operators, see pages 104–5.

 WHERE TO STAY

⌂ **Raven Hotel** (12 rooms) 181 Alaska Highway; ☏ 867 634 2500; e kluaneraven@yknet.ca; www.yukonweb.com/tourism/raven; ⊕ end Apr–beginning Oct. Pleasant dbls with all mod cons & wireless internet. Rates include b/fast. $$$

⌂ **Alcan Motor Inn** (23 rooms) Junction of Alaska Highway & Haines Rd; ☏ 867 634 2371, reservations toll-free: ☏ 1 888 265 1018; e alcanmotorinn@northwestel.net; www.alcanmotorinn.com. Decent, good-value, clean & comfortable motel-style accommodation. Wireless internet. $$–$$$$

⌂ **Paddlewheel Adventures** (2 cabins) ☏ 867 634 2683; e pwadventures@hotmail.com;

www.paddlewheeladventures.com. Pleasant, comfortable cabins each with kitchenette (cold running water, propane stove & fridge), electricity & wood heater. They share a bathroom. These cabins would be a good place to base oneself for a few days of outdoors day trips in Kluane. $$

🏠 **Kluane RV Kampground** (60 fully serviced hook-ups plus 40 campsites) Km 1636, mile 1016 Alaska Highway; ✆ 867 634 2709, toll-free: ✆ 1 866 634 6789; e kluanerv@yknet.yk.ca; www.kluanerv.ca; ⊕ Apr–Oct. This place is better by far than the only other RV option in town, which is the roadside yard by the Fas Gas station. There are trees here, at least. There's also free wireless internet, cable TV, Laundromat & so on. $

Outside Haines Junction Those wanting to spend a few days in the Kluane area should see further accommodation options on pages 105–6. I particularly recommend The Cabin B&B.

✖ WHERE TO EAT

✖ **Raven Hotel** 181 Alaska Highway; ✆ 867 634 2500; e kluaneraven@yknet.ca; www.yukonweb.com/tourism/raven; ⊕ end Apr–beginning Oct. Haines Junction seems an unlikely place for a gourmet restaurant to flourish, but the dining room at the Raven has a seriously good reputation. The menu has a European flavour & features plenty of fish & game. $$$$

✖ **Kluane Park Inn** Km 1578, mile 1016 Alaska Highway; ✆ 867 634 2225; e kpi@northwestel.net. The restaurant serves up a mixture of burgers & Chinese food. It's fine, though nothing spectacular. $$

✖ **Northern Lights Restaurant** Junction of Alaska Highway & Haines Rd; ✆ 867 634 2033; e alcanmotorinn@northwestel.net; www.alcanmotorinn.com. Next door to the Alcan Motor Inn (& owned by the same people) this place offers steak, seafood & pasta dishes. $$

✖ **Frosty Freeze** Cnr of Alaska Highway & Jacquot St; ✆ 867 634 2674. A simple roadside affair selling burgers, fries, fish & chips, ice cream & so on. You order through the window, then can either take out or eat on their deck or in the basic dining room. Unless you're desperate for a fried-food fix, the bakery (see below) is better. $–$$

🍴 **Village Bakery & Deli** Logan St – located across the car park from the visitor centre; ✆ 867 634 2867; ⊕ 7am–9pm daily. The Bakery & Deli is

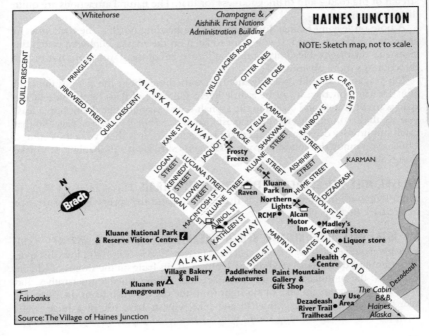

Source: The Village of Haines Junction

a great option for a light meal or snack — it has delicious homemade pizza, quiche, fruit pies, cakes, breads & other baked goods. There's also local smoked salmon for sale. There are a few tables for eating in, both indoors & on a deck, & wireless internet. $

SHOPPING **Madley's General Store** (✆ 867 634 2200; e madleys@northwestel.net) is pretty much the only shop in town; it sells everything from groceries to fishing tackle to souvenirs. The **liquor store** is at 112 Haines Rd (✆ 867 634 2201; ⊕ 10am–6pm Tue–Sat). For gifts there's **Paint Mountain Gallery & Gift Shop**, located next to the bakery, which sells myriad souvenirs.

OTHER PRACTICALITIES

RCMP Junction of Alaska Highway & Haines Rd; ✆ 867 634 5555

Haines Junction Health Centre Bates St; ✆ 867 634 4444; e hc.haines-junction@gov.yk.ca

Bank TD Canada Trust, 176 Lucania St; ✆ 867 634 2820; ⊕ 1pm–4pm Mon–Fri.

Post office Within the same building as the bank. ⊕ 9am–5pm Mon–Fri, but closes for lunch.

WHAT TO SEE AND DO

See *Kluane National Park and Reserve Visitor Centre*, page 103.

FROM HAINES JUNCTION TO BEAVER CREEK

Oh you lucky, lucky thing. Now you're driving through Kluane country. In good summer weather, Kluane Lake is bluer than blue and stretches for mile upon happy mile, while the mountains of the Kluane Ranges are outrageous in their exhibitionism. (If they were a small child, you'd tell them to stop showing off.) In winter, the whole wonderful lot of it is beautiful, glistening white with tinges of dusky pink, indigo blue, sunflower yellow and turquoise depending on the whims of the low subarctic sun. There isn't a whole lot of manmade interest along this stretch of the road – and thank goodness for that. The natural attractions are quite distracting enough.

A note on leaving Haines Junction if you're heading north – the road straight ahead is the Haines Road. If you want to keep on the Alaska Highway, watch the signs and turn right. Heading south, you'll turn left at the T-junction, but in this direction it's more obvious.

Oh yes, and I should probably mention something about the state of the road after Destruction Bay: it can be a little lively. Cheery red flags by the side of the road warn of craters and cracks in the asphalt – you may not like them, but at least you see these coming. It's the permafrost heaves (see *Permafrost heaves*, page 99) that catch out unwary drivers and send them bouncing towards their vehicles' ceilings. Unless you enjoy the sound of your passenger's shrieks, it's probably best to take things slow.

KM 1597, MILE 992: SPRUCE BEETLE INTERPRETIVE TRAIL This is an easy 1.6km (1-mile) loop with interpretive boards that explain about the spruce bark beetle. See *Spruce Bark Beetle*, page 97.

KM 1636, MILE 1021: KLUANE BED & BREAKFAST (*4 cabins;* ✆ 867 841 4250; e kluanecabins@northwestel.net; www.kluanecabins.com; ⊕ Feb–Nov; $$) I love this spot, 5km (3 miles) down a dirt road off the highway. It sits bang on the shores of Kluane Lake with the mountains beyond. There are four cabins, suitable for families, and you can hike, mountain bike or ski right from the door, or fish from the shore for lake trout, arctic grayling, whitefish and pike. Guests have use of a huge, well-equipped kitchen and dining room, which has a good supply of books and board

SPRUCE BARK BEETLE

'So what's with the ghostly grey spruce trees?' you ask as you drive north of Haines Junction. Don't worry – it's not your eyes. The trees really have turned grey. They're the victims of the longest and most intensive spruce bark beetle (*Dendroctonus rufipennis*) infestation that Canada has known.

Spruce bark beetles are only about the size of a grain of rice, yet they've affected 350,000 hectares of forest in southwest Yukon. This most recent outbreak started in 1990; while infestations usually last two to five years, it ran for more than 15.

Environmentalists blame warmer-than-usual summers, whose drought conditions lowered the spruce trees' resistance to infestation. Warm summers also meant that the beetles could complete their life cycles in a single year, as opposed to the normal two years, which led to a creepy crawly baby boom, and a succession of mild winters meant that a greater number of larvae and beetles survived the snowy months.

So how do the beetles kill the trees? Each spring, the females emerge from the trees where they've spent the winter and look for a host on which to lay their eggs. Usually they'll attack sick or old trees, but while beetle populations have been high they've gone for healthy trees as well. Once she's found a suitable host, the female releases pheromones to attract males, who die after mating. She then bores a tunnel under the bark where she lays her eggs. A healthy tree will produce resin to flush out the beetles and seal the hole: you can sometimes see this resin. If the tree fails to eliminate the beetles, the eggs hatch and the larvae feed on the tree's phloem – that's essentially the tree's plumbing system, which transports sugar made into the needles down into the roots. When the system is cut off, the roots starve. The new shoots receive no sustenance from the roots the following spring; the spruce needles turn a reddish colour, and then the tree dies.

games should the weather turn iffy, and there's a deck, barbecue and fire pit for when it's fine. Bathrooms and showers are in the kitchen building (the cabins have electricity but no running water). There's no internet connection – owner Cecile Sias, a sixth-generation Yukoner, very wisely says that's not the point of this place.

KM 1636, MILE 1021: SILVER CITY The tumbledown cabins along the end of the road that leads to Kluane Bed & Breakfast are the remains of Silver City, which was created to serve the mining community that came here after the discovery of gold in the Kluane Mountains in 1904. The buildings used to house a North West Mounted Police barracks, a trading post and a roadhouse.

KM 1707, MILE 1029: TACHÄL DHÄL (SHEEP MOUNTAIN) VISITOR CENTRE See *Chapter 5: Kluane National Park and Reserve*, page 104.

KM 1710, MILE 1031: SOLDIER'S SUMMIT This is where the ribbon was cut on 20 November 1942 signalling the opening of the Alaska Highway. Temperatures were –35°C (–31°F) that day – though this piece information was censored from contemporary broadcasts. Soldier's Summit is no longer on the Alaska Highway; if you want to stand on the spot you have to hike up a path from the parking area.

KM 1717, MILE 1035: COTTONWOOD PARK RV GROUND (*50 RV & tenting sites both serviced & unserviced plus 2 cabins:* \ *summer: cell: 2M3972, Destruction Bay Channel – dial 0 & ask for a mobile operator who will connect you, winter:* \ *613 968 9884;* e *glen.brough@sympatico.ca; www.yukonweb.com/tourism/cottonwood;* ⊕ *1 Jun–1 Sep;*

RV & tenting $, *cabins* $$) Cottonwood Park is right on the shores of Kluane Lake; there's electricity, hot showers, a small store and a hot tub. Activities include hiking, fishing and mini-golf.

KM 1725, MILE 1040: CONGDON CREEK CAMPGROUND (81 sites) Government campground (see page 35) with a pretty location on the shores of Kluane Lake. Tent camping is not recommended from mid-July to September as the soapberries are ripe and plentiful at this time, and they attract bears. When bears are sighted, the campground is closed to tenters.

KM 1743, MILE 1052: DESTRUCTION BAY This is a tiny settlement of 50-odd people. There's gas and food and beds and booze, but not a great deal else. The name comes from a particularly ferocious windstorm that struck the place in the 1940s and blew many of the buildings down.

Where to stay

Talbot Arm Motel (32 rooms) ☎ 867 841 4461. Those who have spent too much time in British pubs might, like me, initially find themselves confused by the name of this motel. Shouldn't it be the Talbot Arms? Answer: no, it's named not for human limbs but for the Talbot Arm of Kluane Lake of which there is just the 1. Moving swiftly on: I've only visited this motel while passing through, but have a feeling it might be an intriguing spot to stop for the night if you're looking to make some new friends in the middle of nowhere. It has the air of a place that attracts interesting types — truckers, travellers & the like. The rooms themselves are functional & clean, though unlikely to blow your socks off. There's also a rather Spartan gravel yard with RV hook-ups. The food gets good reports. The owner is friendly & no doubt has some stories to tell to those who settle down in the lounge for the evening. His parents built this place in 1967 & he's been here in Destruction Bay running it since 1981. Wireless internet is free; there's also a general store & gas. $$

KM 1759, MILE 1062, HISTORICAL MILE 1093: BURWASH LANDING Burwash Landing is one of the Yukon's earliest settlements: a trading post was established here in 1904

SHAKWAK RECONSTRUCTION PROJECT

The Alaska Highway was, from its conception, an American rather than a Canadian project. Still, today, 85% of the traffic north of Haines Junction is of American origin, according to Yukon Highways and Public Works. And this is one expensive road, which has been under reconstruction since the day it was 'completed'.

When the Americans handed maintenance and management of the highway to the Canadians in 1946, the Canadians found themselves the not-so-proud owners of a very rough bush trail. The road was not of the standard that had originally been agreed between the two countries. (In fact, the project had turned out so complicated that the Americans tried to give it back to the Canadians before the war ended, but the Canadians refused to take it.) By the 1970s, the Canadians had managed to straighten and smooth most of the southern section, but the stretch north of Haines Junction was still very rough.

And so, in the end, the Americans agreed to get out their cheque book. In 1977, the Canadians and Americans signed the Shakwak Agreement (named for the geological fault that creates the valley in this area), by which the Americans promised funds for the upgrading of the Alaska Highway north of Haines Junction, and for the Haines Road. Funds dried up in the 1980s, but have since continued; it's hoped that the bulk of the work will be completed by 2010, with the replacement of the Duke and Slims River bridges the last major projects.

North of Destruction Bay, the ground beneath the highway is permafrost – that's to say, it's 'permanently' frozen. Except that it's not.

Permafrost is covered by an active layer of ground, which thaws in summer and refreezes in winter. With warmer temperatures in recent years, and disturbance from construction, the active layer has become deeper. Any infrastructure built on top of this melting permafrost becomes unstable, and if the liquid refreezes in low temperatures, it expands or 'heaves'. This is what causes the rollercoaster effect in northern roads.

Engineers are continually trying to find ways to stabilize roads built over permafrost. They use gravel pads and embankments in an attempt to create insulation. But this is nature they're arguing with, and nature has a habit of winning – as motorists along this section of the highway will very soon attest.

by two brothers, Eugene and Louis Jacquot, who came from their home in Alsace-Lorraine (now part of France) to the Klondike gold rush in 1898. They followed the lure of the yellow metal to the Kluane region when gold was discovered here in 1904. During the construction of the highway, the Jacquot brothers flourished, selling meals and goods to the soldiers. The dugout and ice house used by the Jacquot brothers to keep food cool and fresh before the days of refrigerators still stand on the shore of the lake – see the map in the Burwash Landing Walking Tour leaflet, which you can pick up from the visitor centre in Haines Junction.

Where to stay

Burwash Landing Resort & RV Park (25 rooms/cabins) ☎ 867 841 4441; e blr@ yt.sympatico.ca. This building was constructed in 1944–45, & the lodge was run by Eugene Jacquot until he died in 1950. It's pretty basic & the RV sites (💲) are close together. However, if you're hungry, there's still food to be had here. The restaurant (💲–💲💲💲) specializes in lake trout. 💲💲

What to see and do

Kluane Museum (☎ 867 841 5561; e kluanemus@yknet.ca; adults $3.95; ⊕ mid-May to mid-Sep 10am–6pm daily) If you've not yet seen enough of stuffed moose, Dall sheep and wolves on your Yukon journey, this is the stop-off for you. It's small but nicely done. There's also a video on the construction of the Alaska Highway.

KM 1853, MILE 1119: LAKE CREEK CAMPGROUND (27 sites) This government campground (see page 35) has stunning mountain views. Sites are surrounded by trees, and sit on the shores of a flowing creek.

KM 1865, MILE 1128: PICKHANDLE LAKE This is a particularly scenic spot in an area that's jam-packed with them. There's a spacious area for parking your vehicle if you want to get out and take photos.

KM 1912, MILE 1155: SNAG JUNCTION CAMPGROUND (15 sites) Yet another pretty lakeside government campground (see page 35) with a panoramic mountain backdrop, just 15 minutes' drive from Beaver Creek. Some might find this preferable to Beaver Creek's accommodation options.

BEAVER CREEK (km 1935, mile 1169, historical mile 1202)

Beaver Creek is the border town: the crossing into Alaska is just 3km (2 miles) away. Like so many of the other settlements along the highway, it's really just a bunch of buildings strung out along the road. Of historical interest: Beaver Creek is one of two places where the bulldozers from opposite ends met when they were building the highway.

🏠 WHERE TO STAY AND EAT None of Beaver Creek's hotels falls anywhere near the luxury end of the market; however, they are generally comfortable enough.

🏠 **Westmark Inn** (174 rooms, 67 RV hook-ups) 🌂 867 862 7501; www.westmarkhotels.com; ⊕ mid-May to early Sep. This Westmark is not on the same level as the Westmark hotels in Whitehorse, Dawson or Skagway. It's a basic motel-style establishment, with worn décor & thin walls. It also has an RV park; there's no wireless internet but you can plug into a guest computer. However, its big plus is its nightly 'Rendezvous' show, an hour-long musical about the Yukon's historical characters, which is reputed to be a barrel of laughs. Having heard great things from fellow travellers, I put my foot down on the highway and hurtled horribly over the permafrost heaves to be sure of arriving in time — only to be told when I skidded into reception with moments to spare that there was no show that evening. 'So when it says here, "every evening", that's not actually every evening, then?' I jabbed my finger at the flyer on the desk & hissed to the girl on reception, who was entirely pleasant & totally undeserving of my barbed tone. She said that it really meant every evening when Holland America had a coach party staying — which is pretty much every evening. I was there, after all, on the hotel's last night of the season. *Almost* every evening, then, the reception starts 6.30pm, dinner starts 7.30pm, show starts 8.45pm. You can buy tickets for the show only if you don't want to do the whole dinner-theatre shebang, or if you're just plain late. $$$
🏠 **1202 Motor Inn** (11 rooms) 🌂 867 862 7600; e 1202motorinn@northwestel.net. I stayed at the

1202 Motor Inn back in early 2006 when I was writing my book on dogsledding, *Mad Dogs and an Englishwoman*. We were driving with truck full of dogs to Fairbanks for the start of the Yukon Quest (see pages 42–4). We arrived at about 1am, then left again before dawn, but even in that short time I formed an impression of this as a friendly, homey place that served up a superlative b/fast. There's a large family room in addition to standard dbls, plus a souvenir shop & gas. The place is easily recognizable — it's on the northern side of the village, & is decorated on the outside with a giant polar bear & Dall sheep. Well, isn't your home? $$
🏠 **Ida's Motel & Restaurant** (25 rooms) 🌂 867 862 7223; e famhotel@polarcom.com. Standard motel-style accommodation with mixed reviews from travellers — but, to be honest, this is true of every hotel in Beaver Creek. $$
🏠 **Buckshot Betty's** (4 cabins) 🌂 867 862 7111; e buckshotbetty@hotmail.com; ⊕ closed Tue. I'm not sure if the woman who served me was Betty. I was far too frightened of her to dare to ask her name. The service may be a little slam-'em-down — at least it gives those who've been on the road for 1,000-odd miles something new to talk about — but the food ($–$$) is definitely good & the portions are hearty. There are 3 large tables which diners share. B/fast runs pretty much all day; there's also soup, sandwiches, burgers, pasta, pizza & homemade baked goods. Plus there's a gift shop, & cabins for those who want to sleep here. $$

WHAT TO SEE AND DO There's a tiny **government visitor centre** right on the highway (🌂 867 862 7321; e vic.beavercreek@gov.yk.ca; ⊕ May–Sep daily), which supplies brochures and information to those passing through.

OTHER PRACTICALITIES
RCMP 🌂 867 862 5555

Health Centre 🌂 867 862 4444

5

Kluane National Park and Reserve

At 21,980km² or 8,487 square miles, Kluane (pronounced Kloo-AH-nee) National Park and Reserve is more than half the size of Switzerland. Together with the adjoining wildernesses of British Columbia's Tatshenshini–Alsek Park, and the Wrangell–St Elias and Glacier Bay national parks in Alaska (together these parks comprise 97,520km² or 37,650 square miles of unbroken wilderness – that's almost the size of the state of Kentucky), it is UNESCO World Heritage listed. The park is traversed by the St Elias Mountains, which comprise two ranges, the lower Kluane Ranges (visible from the Alaska Highway and Haines Road) and the higher Icefield Ranges behind. The latter contain 21 peaks over 4,000m (about 13,000ft) and one of the largest non-polar icefields on the planet with hundreds of glaciers; they're also home to Canada's highest peak, Mount Logan, which measures in at 5,959m (19,545ft).

This massive natural wonderland provides habitat for numerous mammals, including grizzly and black bears, Dall sheep, wolves, lynx, mountain goats and moose, as well as more than 150 bird species, from trumpeter swans, peregrine falcons and gyrfalcons, to bald and golden eagles. Kokanee salmon live in Kluane's Kathleen, Louise and Sockeye lakes; lake trout, arctic grayling and northern pike also thrive in the park's waters.

For outdoors enthusiasts, Kluane National Park and Reserve is an adventure paradise. One can hike for days or even weeks without seeing another human soul. For mountaineers there are challenging peaks to be scaled, while the Alsek and Tatshenshini Rivers, which cross into the Tatshenshini–Alsek Park of BC before draining into the Gulf of Alaska, provide outstanding day or multi-day kayaking and rafting trips. In winter, there's cross-country skiing, backcountry ski touring and snowshoeing. But even those who aren't natural born athletes can enjoy Kluane. Parks Canada has created a few short trails that demand nothing more than a gentle stroll, and a couple of companies offer flightseeing trips over the mesmerizing icefields.

HISTORY

Kluane National Park and Reserve overlaps the ancestral lands of the Champagne and Aishihik First Nations and the Kluane First Nation; these peoples are a part of the larger Southern Tutchone group that has inhabited these parts for thousands of years.

White men didn't arrive here till the late 19th century though the area was sighted from the sea much earlier by Danish explorer Vitus Bering, aboard a Russian navy ship: he named Mount St Elias on 16 July – St Elias Day – 1741. A small number of explorers and prospectors travelled in the area from the 1880s. The first non-native trading posts in the area were established by Jack Dalton in the mid-1890s; Dalton also upgraded the old Chilkat trading trail to create a 400km

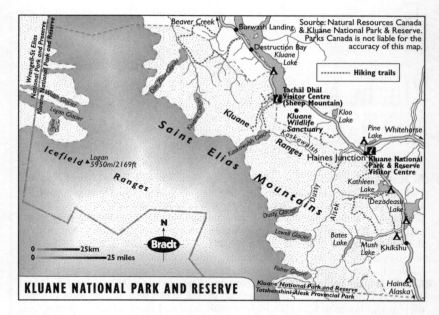

Beaver Creek

Burwash Landing

Destruction Bay

Kluane Lake

-------- **Hiking trails**

Wrangell-St Elias National Park and Preserve

Kluane National Park and Reserve

Kluane Wash Glacier

Logan Glacier

Dan Zhúr Glacier

Kaskawúlsh Glacier

Ogilvie Glacier

Kluane Glacier

Tachäl Dhäl Visitor Centre (Sheep Mountain)

Kloo Lake

Kluane Wildlife Sanctuary

Kaskawúlsh

Pine Lake

Whitehorse

Saint Elias

Kluane Ranges

Icefield Ranges

Logan ▲5950m/2169ft

Ranges

Haines Junction

Kluane National Park & Reserve Visitor Centre

Mountains

Kathleen Lake

Dusty

Dezadeash Lake

Alsek

Dusty Glacier

Lowell Glacier

Bates Lake

Mush Lake

Klukshu

0 ────25km

0 ──────25 miles

N

Bradt

Fisher Glacier

KLUANE NATIONAL PARK AND RESERVE

Kluane National Park and Reserve Tatshenshini-Alsek Provincial Park

Haines, Alaska

(250-mile) route that ran from Pyramid Harbor, to the west of Haines, to Fort Selkirk in the Yukon interior. He ran a packhorse business to supply local prospectors and charged a toll for the use of his road, which became a popular route for stampeders streaming to the Klondike in the late 1890s. The trail's popularity waned following the completion of the White Pass and Yukon Route railway in 1900. Today, the Haines Road follows part of its route.

The yellow stuff was found at Ruby Creek, near Kluane Lake, on 4 July 1903 by one of the men that discovered the Klondike riches, Tagish Charlie. He named his creek, a tributary of the Jarvis River, Fourth of July Creek. A bit of a rush ensued the following year – with the settlement of Silver City (see page 97) springing up to service it – though this was on nothing like the scale of the Klondike stampede five years previously. It soon transpired that there was less gold here than had been hoped, and most prospectors quickly moved on. Subsequently, there was some copper mining in the Kluane area.

The first attempt to summit Mount St Elias was made by American military man and explorer Frederick Schwatka (see *Frederick Schwatka*, page 72) in 1886, but the peak wasn't conquered until Italian nobleman the Duke of Abruzzi led his expedition there in 1897. Mount Logan was first summitted in 1925, when a team from the Alpine Club of Canada under the leadership of A H MacCarthy made the ascent.

As with so much in the southern Yukon, it was the construction of the Alaska Highway in 1942 that really changed things. Now the natural wonders of Kluane were discovered by the outside world; the Yukon Council created the Kluane Game Sanctuary in 1943 in response to the military personnel's and highway construction workers' overhunting of local game. However, the sanctuary's regulations also blocked native hunting and trapping (while allowing outsiders to stake claims and mine), and deprived the First Nations people of their traditional connection with the land.

Kluane National Park and Reserve was established in 1972, and the park's boundaries were formally gazetted four years later in 1976. From the time of the park's initial establishment in 1972, the regulations of the former game sanctuary were annulled and hunting by First Nations was once more allowed in the lands then designated as a national park reserve. This change in the rules was not well communicated, however, and some years passed before First Nations people relearned their old territory and began, once more, to hunt and trap in their traditional lands.

Today, the local First Nations are jointly responsible with Parks Canada for the management of the park's natural and cultural resources.

GETTING THERE

The park is bordered by the Alaska Highway and Haines Road. Haines Junction (see pages 94–6) is the gateway village to the park.

BY BUS Alaska Direct Bus Line (*toll-free:* ✆ *1 800 770 6652 from Canada & US only;* e *info@alaskadirectbusline.com; www.alaskadirectbusline.com*) runs buses between Whitehorse and Tok, Alaska with stops in Haines Junction on Sundays and Wednesdays from 1 October to 15 May, and on Wednesdays, Fridays and Sundays from 16 May to 30 September. A one-way ticket from Whitehorse to Haines Junction costs $75.

Alaska/Yukon Trails (*toll-free:* ✆ *1 800 770 7275 from Canada & US only;* e *alaskashuttle@yahoo.com; www.alaskashuttle.com*) runs a bus between Whitehorse and Fairbanks each Thursday in summer. Currently, the company takes passengers from Fairbanks to Haines Junction ($160) but Canadian restrictions prevent it from carrying passengers from Haines Junction to Whitehorse. (You may however travel from Fairbanks to Whitehorse, or vice versa.)

At the time of writing, the company is in talks with the Canadian authorities to ease these confusing restrictions, so it would be worth giving them a call to find out the current situation.

TOURIST INFORMATION

Kluane National Park and Reserve is administered by Parks Canada. There's detailed information at www.pc.gc.ca/pn-np/yt/kluane.

The park has two visitor centres. If you're going to camp overnight in the park outside of Kathleeen Lake Campground (see page 106), you're required to register at one of these visitor centres first. Park permits cost $9.80 per person per night or $68.70 for an annual pass. When you return from your trip, you must tell Parks that you have safely completed your journey. If you fail to do this, you may be liable for the cost of any search and rescue teams sent out to find you.

ⓔ Kluane National Park and Reserve Visitor Centre

Turn off the Alaska Highway in Haines Junction at Kluane St (by The Raven): it's across the car park at the end of the street — just follow the signs; ✆ 867 634 7207 (Parks Canada phone number for information on trails & park specifics) or 867 634 2345 (Yukon Tourism number for general tourism information); e kluane.info@pc.gc.ca (Parks) or vic.hainesjunction@gov.yk.ca (Yukon Tourism); www.pc.gc.ca/kluane (Parks); ⊕ Parks Canada: mid-May to mid-Sep 9am–5pm daily & by appointment the rest of the year, arrive by 4.30pm to register for overnight trips in the park; Yukon Tourism: mid-May to mid-Sep 8am–8pm daily. Run jointly by Parks Canada & Yukon Tourism & Culture, the visitor centre offers information & advice on everything from short strolls to major backcountry adventures. It also has a small number of interpretive displays on, for example, gold mining in the Kluane area, the Southern Tutchone First Nations, a history of mountaineering including the first conquests of Mt Logan & Mt Elias, & information on Tatshenshini–Alsek Park. There's also an audio-visual show about the park & a video on how to stay safe in bear country.

Sheep Mountain is not the English translation of the Southern Tutchone words 'Tachäl Dhäl'. The native name translates as 'Skin Scraper Mountain' in English: a *tachäl* was the flat stone scraper that women traditionally used to prepare hides.

☑ Tachäl Dhäl (Sheep Mountain) Visitor Centre Km 1707, mile 1029 Alaska Highway (an hour's drive north of Haines Junction); ☏ 867 841 4500; e kluane.info@pc.gc.ca; www.pc.gc.ca/kluane; ⊕ mid-May to early Sep, 9am–4pm daily, arrive by 3.30pm to register for overnight trips in the park. This small visitor centre has information on Dall sheep, displays on the Southern Tutchone people & telescopes looking out onto the mountain – this is the sheep's winter range, so you stand the best chance of seeing them between late Aug & May. The face of the mountain is a 'special preservation zone'; ask visitor centre staff about designated hiking areas.

TOUR OPERATORS AND GUIDES

The following specialize in Kluane and are based in the local area. However, some of the Whitehorse-based and Yukon-wide tour operators also cover Kluane; see pages 56–7 and 24–6.

Icefields Discovery ☏ summer: 867 841 4561, winter: 867 633 2018; e icefields@yukon.net; www.icefields.org. Operates flightseeing trips over the St Elias Mountains & organizes expedition charters for mountaineers. Icefields Discovery also has a Discovery Camp in the heart of the mountains,

The periglacial areas of Kluane are home to high densities of Dall sheep. It's thought that, during the last ice age, two distinct groups of North American mountain sheep found separate ice-free zones: in central Alaska and in the mountains of the northwestern United States. The latter group is now known as bighorn sheep (*Ovis canadensis*) and is still found in the Rocky Mountains, while the former evolved to become thinhorn sheep (*Ovis dalli*), found in Alaska, the Yukon, the western Northwest Territories, and northern BC.

There are three subspecies of thinhorn sheep: the white Dall sheep (*Ovis dalli dalli*), the darker-coloured Stone sheep (*Ovis dalli stonei*), which breeds in the southern Yukon and northern BC (see page 10), and Fannin sheep (*Ovis dalli fannini*), which has varying colour and is found in the Faro area of central Yukon. Confusingly, the term Dall sheep can also be used to refer to the overall thinhorn sheep species (that's to say *Ovis dalli*). Some naturalists also recognize the thinhorn sheep of Alaska's Kenai Peninsula, *Ovis dalli kenaiensis*, as another subspecies.

Both rams and ewes have horns, though the rams' are longer and curlier – they grow to around a metre (3ft) in length, while the ewes have straighter horns of around 25cm (10 inches). The sheep's horns grow throughout their lives – they are never shed – and the rams' take seven or eight years to grow a full curl. You can count the growth rings on the horns to determine a sheep's age. As it reaches its teens a Dall sheep is considered to be long in the tooth, not to mention the horn: in Kluane rams generally live to be about 12 years old while ewes reach roughly 16, though both can be older.

As for William Healy Dall, he was an American naturalist who spent considerable time in Alaska, and a little time in the Yukon. He first saw the white sheep that would later be named for him when he was exploring the Mount McKinley area in 1879.

between the Kaskawulsh, Logan & Hubbard glaciers, which provides a comfortable base for those wanting to explore the icefields. Tents provide sleeping quarters for up to 12 people, & staff cook meals for guests.

Kluane Ecotours ☎ summer: 867 634 2600, winter: 867 634 2626; e kluaneco@yknet.ca; www.kluaneco.com. Brent Liddle, who runs Kluane Ecotours, worked in Kluane for Parks Canada for 30 years: he knows pretty much every leaf of every tree, & is responsible for the very existence of many of the trails. Now retired from Parks, Brent takes guests on what he calls 'ed-ventures' — that's to say, you learn something as you go along. The trips are generally custom day trips for individuals or small groups, though Brent can also take you on overnight hiking, canoeing or kayaking journeys. He's a charming, entertaining & highly knowledgeable man.

Kruda Ché Boat Tours ☎ 867 634 2378; www.krudache.com. Ron Chambers, born in the Yukon of Tutchone & Tlingit ancestry, has been a park warden for 22 years. His boat trips on Kathleen Lake feature cultural & historical interpretation, & wildlife viewing.

Paddlewheel Adventures ☎ 867 634 2683; e pwadventures@hotmail.com; www.paddlewheeladventures.com. ⏰ Jun—Aug (Lee Drummond, the co-owner, is a teacher in Whitehorse so only operates his tour business during the summer vacation). Guided fishing, raft-floating, interpretive hikes, mountain bike adventures & canoeing, plus canoe, fishing gear & mountain bike rentals. All trips are half-day or a day long;

Paddlewheel doesn't offer multi-day trips. Lee's mother Val also sells her handmade jewellery from the Paddlewheel office, which sits across the car park from the visitor centre (Logan St, between Kathleen St & Auriol St). Paddlewheel also has 2 cabins for rent, see pages 94–5.

Parks Canada Contact the visitor centres, pages 103–4. Parks runs a series of guided walks from mid-Jun to late Aug, for example a 2hr Dezadeash (pronounced DEZ-dee-ash) River Stroll, a 3hr walk to Shepherd's Knoll at Sheep Mountain, & a full-day guided hike on Sheep Creek Trail. Prices range from $4.90 to $19.60 pp. Parks staff also give campfire talks on Sun evenings at Kathleen Lake campground (free of charge). The program & fees change from year to year, so ask at the visitor centre for the latest events schedule.

Sifton Air ☎ 867 634 2916. Offers flightseeing tours over the mountains & icefields. There are trips of different lengths, but the cost comes in at roughly $150 per hr pp. Trips depart from Haines Junction's airport, off the Alaska Highway 1km (0.6 miles) south of the village.

Tatshenshini Expediting ☎ Whitehorse office: 867 633 2742, Haines Junction office: 867 634 2683, cell: 867 333 5247; e info@tatshenshiniyukon.com; www.tatshenshiniyukon.com. Offers day & multi-day rafting on the Tatshenshini & Alsek rivers, plus river trips elsewhere in the Yukon. See page 26.

Trans North Helicopters ☎ Haines Junction office: 867 634 2242, Whitehorse office: 867 668 2177, cell: 867 335 2242; e email@tntaheli.com; www.tntaheli.com. Helicopter flightseeing & charters.

WHERE TO STAY AND EAT

For accommodation in Haines Junction village, see page 94. Most of the following are south of Haines Junction, on the Haines Road.

🏠 **The Cabin B&B** (5 cabins) Km 219, mile 130 Haines Rd (26km, 16 miles, south of Haines Junction); ☎ summer: 867 634 2600, winter: 867 634 2626; e thecabin@northwestel.net; www.thecabinyukon.com; ⏰ May–Sep. If you're planning to spend a few days doing day trips in the Kluane area, I would recommend this as the best place to spend the night, as long as you don't mind having to walk a little to find a hot shower & a flushing loo. It's a way out of Haines Junction on the Haines Rd. The cabins don't have electricity or running water but there are gas lamps & propane heaters, & hot showers & flush loos in a separate washhouse. The location, very close to Kathleen Lake,

is outstanding & the views over the mountains from the cabins' private decks are sensational. Moreover, the cabins are sufficiently spaced out that you feel as if you're in your very own patch of wilderness. Owner Brent Liddle worked for Parks Canada for 30 years & now runs Kluane Ecotours; see above. Another point of interest: Brent and his wife Wenda are the co-founders of the bakery in Haines Junction. $$$

🏠 **Kathleen Lake Lodge** (3 cabins) Km 220, mile 131 Haines Rd (26km, 16 miles, south of Haines Junction); ☎ 867 634 2888; ⏰ May–Sep. Very different in feel to The Cabin's accommodations (above), these are on the highway, catering more to passing traffic than to those wanting a quiet wilderness experience. The cabins have electricity & water, & there's a small café (🕐 7.30am–7.30pm; $–$$). It serves a limited but tasty menu of burgers, salads, soups & sandwiches, plus great homemade pie, all at excellent-value prices. $$

🏠 **Dalton Trail Lodge** Fishing lodge offering pre-booked packages; see page 35.

🏠 **Icefields Discovery Stellar Hut** Km 142, mile 83 Haines Rd (110km, 68 miles, south of Haines Junction – the hut is on the right, 3km or 1.8 miles after the Blanchard River bridge, just after the BC border); ☎ 867 634 2729; e icefields@ yukon.net; www.icefields.org; 🕐 Jan–Apr. The Stellar Hut is a good base for accessing the backcountry of the Tatshenshini area for kite skiing, back-country & cross-country skiing. The hut has wood heat, propane stove & lights, & all kitchen hardware. You will need to bring your sleeping bag, mattress, food & personal equipment. Sian & Lance from Icefields Discovery will light the fire so it's warm when you get there; they supply drinking water, & there is a well for washing water. The toilet is an outhouse. Phone ahead to register. $

CAMPGROUNDS

🏕 **Kathleen Lake** (39 sites) Km 219, mile 130 Haines Rd (27km, 17 miles, south of Haines Junction). This delightful campground is managed by Parks Canada. It's the only designated campground within the park boundaries and has basic facilities – picnic tables, outhouses, firewood for purchase – but no electricity or running water. Prices are different from those of the government campgrounds (at the time of writing the fee was $15.70 plus $8.80 if you want to purchase firewood), & payment operates from mid-May to mid-Sep by a self-registration system very similar to that of the Yukon government campgrounds: you choose your site, then put money in an envelope, which you post into a box at the campground. Reservations are not taken, nor are they usually needed as the campground doesn't tend to be busy unless there's a major happening in Haines Junction. $

🏕 **Dezadeash Lake** (20 sites) Km 196, mile 116 Haines Rd (50km, 31 miles, south of Haines Junction). This is another well-placed government campground; the regulations on page 35 apply. $

🏕 **Million Dollar Falls** (33 sites) Km 159, mile 94 Haines Rd (87km, 53 miles, south of Haines Junction). Again, a government campsite, so see page 35 for the rules and prices. There's a short boardwalk trail to the falls themselves. $

🏕 **Pine Lake Campground** (42 sites) Km 1572, mile 980 Alaska Highway. A government campground just outside the boundary of the park and close to Haines Junction. See page 35. $

KLUKSHU *(Km 183, mile 108 Haines Rd or 63km, 38 miles, south of Haines Junction)*

Kluskshu is a seasonal First Nations fish camp that sits just outside the National Park boundary. It used to buzz with activity as the Champagne and Aishihik First Nations gathered here to bring in the salmon during the summer sockeye and chinook runs. In recent years, however, salmon numbers have declined and, in summer 2008, these First Nations closed their fisheries here altogether due to the low numbers. The reason for the declining salmon numbers is unknown. Still, Klukshu is right on the highway and an interesting stop for the interpretive boards that explain about the salmon runs and First Nations traditions. And in future years the salmon numbers may again pick up.

HIKING IN KLUANE NATIONAL PARK

EASY WALKS AND STROLLS

Kokanee *(Distance: 1km, 0.6 miles, round trip; Time: 10–30mins; Difficulty rating: very easy; Trailhead: Kathleen Lake day use area)* This is a wheelchair-accessible boardwalk that goes along the shore of Kathleen Lake.

Rock Glacier *(Distance: 1.6km, 1 mile, round trip; Time: ½–2hrs; Difficulty rating: easy; Trailhead: 50km, 30 miles, south of Haines Junction on the Haines Rd; www.pc.gc.ca/*

KATHLEEN LAKE AND ITS KOKANEE SALMON DECLINE

A kokanee salmon is a landlocked sockeye salmon (kokanee and sockeye are similar in appearance except that the kokanee is much smaller); Kluane is the only national park in Canada where kokanee naturally occur. It's thought that Kluane's kokanee evolved from sockeye salmon that once migrated from the Gulf of Alaska, up the Alsek River and into the Kathleen Lake system. When the Lowell Glacier created an ice dam across the river, they became landlocked.

Park staff have monitored the numbers of kokanee salmon in the Kathleen Lake system for the last 30 years. Traditionally, spawning runs have averaged around 2,800 fish – but in recent years the decline in numbers has been dramatic. Just 730 fish were counted on the spawning beds in 2002; this had plunged to 44 by 2008. Sport fishing was closed in the park in 2004, and research is underway to identify the reason for the decline. Possible causes include climate change: warmer temperatures could kill off temperature-sensitive kokanee eggs, or they could encourage kokanee fry to emerge before sufficient food is available to feed them. Equally, increasing water temperatures might force the fish to deeper levels, where predators are more prolific. Diseases and parasites are also being investigated, as is the possibility that the change in numbers could be part of the kokanee's natural cycle.

pn-np/yt/kluane/activ/activ1/activ1bv_e.asp) This self-guided interpretive walk follows a raised boardwalk through a forest of spruce and poplar, then continues along large, flat slabs of rock to the toe of a rock glacier. There are interpretive boards that explain about the formation of rock glaciers.

Dezadeash River Trail (*Distance: 6.5km, 4 miles, round trip; Time: 1–2hrs; Difficulty rating: easy; Trailhead: day use area at the south end of Haines Junction, just north of the Dezadeash River bridge; www.pc.gc.ca/pn-np/yt/kluane/activ/activ1/activ1bviii_e.asp*) The trail starts by following the shore of the Dezadeash River, then crosses wetland, meadows and forest; the first 300m (330yds) of boardwalk are suitable for wheelchairs. There are benches and viewing points, from where you may see beaver, moose and waterfowl.

Soldier's Summit (*Distance: 1km, 0.6 miles round trip; Time: 1hr; Difficulty rating: easy; Trailhead: 1km, 0.6 miles north of visitors' centre at Tachäl Dhäl*) Soldier's Summit is the point where the Alaska Highway was officially opened in 1942; see pages

ROUTE DESCRIPTIONS

I've given web links to Parks Canada's website for further information on all these walks; if you don't have access to a computer (or indeed a printer) you can find all this information ready printed onto good, old-fashioned paper at the Parks visitor centres in Haines Junction and Tachäl Dhäl.

There are also detailed route descriptions of all these walks and hikes in *The Kluane National Park Hiking Guide* by Vivien Lougheed. Now in its third edition, this guide gives reliable information on more than 50 hikes in Kluane National Park and Reserve and Tatshenshini–Alsek Park.

Note that Parks staff draw a distinction between 'trails' and 'routes'. Trails are marked and maintained, while routes are just suggestions of they way people sometimes hike following the flow of the natural landscape.

77–9. There are interpretive boards about the history of the highway, and good views over Kluane Lake and the highway.

HIKES FOR THE MORE ENERGETIC The following are day and half-day hikes. See the box on page 110 or *Part 3* for information on multi-day trips.

St Elias Lake Trail (*Distance: 7.6km, 4.8 miles, round trip: Time: 2–4hrs; Difficulty rating: easy; Trailhead: 60km, 37 miles, south of Haines Junction on the Haines Rd; www.pc.gc.ca/pn-np/yt/kluane/activ/activ1/activ1bi_e.asp; topo map: Mush Lake 115 A/6, though the trail is clear enough that you don't really need it*) This is a wheelchair-accessible boardwalk that goes along the shore of Kathleen Lake. It is a pleasant, easy trail which comes alive with wild flowers in summer and it offers good wildlife-viewing opportunities. There's a primitive campsite at the east end of the lake. Vivien Lougheed recommends this as a good first backpacking experience for children. But if you've got a comfortable bed to come back to, why bother? It's simple enough to walk there and back in a day.

Auriol Trail (*Distance: 15km, 9.3 miles, round trip; Time: 4–6hrs; Difficulty rating: moderate; Trailhead: 7km, 4.3 miles, south of Haines Junction on Haines Rd; www.pc.gc.ca/pn-np/yt/kluane/activ/activ1/activ1bvii_e.asp; Topo map: Auriol 115 A/12*) This is a great option for a day walk through boreal forest and into the subalpine. It offers fabulous views of the Auriol Range above the alpine meadows; the trail is cut and maintained, and there are bridges over the creeks, so you won't even need to get your boots wet.

King's Throne Trail and Route (*Distance: 10km, 6 miles, round trip; Time: 6–8hrs; Difficulty rating: strenuous; Trailhead: Kathleen Lake day use area 27km, 17 miles, south of Haines Junction on Haines Rd; www.pc.gc.ca/pn-np/yt/kluane/activ/activ1/activ1bvi_e.asp; topo map: Kathleen Lakes 115 A/11*) This is one of Kluane's most popular day routes; some would say it has become too popular. The fabulous views from the summit draw the numbers but be warned: it can be very windy at the top, even when the weather seems quite pleasant down below.

Sheep Creek Trail (*Distance: 10km, 6 miles, round trip; Time: 3–6hrs; Difficulty rating: moderate; Trailhead: Tachäl Dhäl visitor centre; www.pc.gc.ca/pn-np/yt/kluane/activ/activ1/activ1bx_e.asp; Topo map: Congdon Creek 115 G/2, but the trail is clearly marked*) During the spring, this trail offers good opportunities to see Dall sheep as they move to their summer grounds. It also gives fantastic views over the Slims River Valley and Sheep Mountain. The trail itself starts 2.6km (1.6 miles) from the visitor centre, but Parks staff advise that you check in at the visitor centre before you start so that they can advise you on bear sightings, creek conditions and other potential hazards.

Tachäl Dhäl (Sheep Mountain) Ridge Route (*Distance: 11km, 6.8 miles, loop; Time: 6–10hrs; Difficulty rating: challenging; Trailhead: 2km, 1.2 miles north of Tachäl Dhäl (Sheep Mountain) visitor centre; www.pc.gc.ca/pn-np/yt/kluane/activ/activ1/activ1bxvi_e.asp; Topo map: Congdon Creek 115 G/2*) Steep off-trail sections make this is an energetic day's

FOOD CANISTERS

It's a good idea to pack your food in bear-resistant food canisters; in some parts of the park this is mandatory. You can borrow canisters (you'll need to leave a deposit) from either of the two visitor centres.

CROSSING CREEKS

When water is high and fast, crossing creeks can be highly dangerous. Visitor centre staff will advise on creek-crossing techniques if requested; in the meantime, here are a few points to bear in mind.

- Find the slowest, shallowest place to cross, even if this means walking a bit further.
- Don't cross barefoot. You should carry shoes, such as running shoes, for crossing creeks. Some people like to use Crocs (as they don't stay soggy) or sandals, but a running shoe will stay on your foot better and protect your feet from rocks tumbling down the creek.
- Undo the waist strap of your backpack so that you can take it off easily. If you fall face first, you can drown in just a few centimetres of water if the weight of your pack forces your face under the water.
- Hiking sticks, or a sturdy stick you've found on the trail, give you extra stability.
- Always face upstream when you cross as leaning downstream increases the chance of having your feet swept from under you, and walk sideways like a crab.
- Crossing in pairs or in a group, holding onto each other's waists or shoulders and facing upstream with the weaker members of the group in the middle, can also help.
- Unless it's rained overnight, creeks are at their lowest early in the day as the ice that fills them does not melt at night.
- If in doubt, don't cross. Wait for water levels to subside – or go back the way you came.

hiking, but the route rewards those prepared to climb with panoramic views. You may see Dall sheep during the summer.

Bullion Plateau Trail (*Distance: 24km, 15 miles, round trip; Time: 6–9hrs; Difficulty rating: moderate; Trailhead: Tachäl Dhäl (Sheep Mountain) visitor centre; www.pc.gc.ca/ pn-np/yt/kluane/activ/activ1/activ1bxi_e.asp; Topo map: Congdon Creek 115 G/2, Slims River 115 B/15*) This is a long day hike, with tricky terrain and creek crossings – you'll need to carry shoes for the latter. It's a great route for wildflowers in spring, and gives good views of Slims River, Sheep Creek and Red Castle Ridge. You can also see the toe of the Kaskawulsh glacier. Parks Canada recommends that hikers don't walk this route in groups of fewer than six as this is good habitat for grizzly sows with cubs, and family groups of bears are often seen in the area. Larger groups of hikers are less likely to have problems with bears. As with the Sheep Creek Trail, Parks staff recommend you stop by the visitor centre before starting out so that they can give you up-to-date information on bear activity and creeks.

Mount Decoeli (*Distance: 18km, 11 miles, round trip; Time: 7–11hrs; Difficulty rating: advanced; Trailhead: 19km, 11.8 miles, north of Haines Junction on the Alaska Highway; www.pc.gc.ca/pn-np/yt/kluane/activ/activ1/activ1bxiii_e.asp; Topo map: Kloo Lake 115 A/13*) Mount Decoeli is designated by Parks Canada as a 'route' rather than a trail – that's to say, it's not maintained or marked, and should only be attempted by hikers experienced in route-finding. It's not a technical climb, but is steep with loose rock in places. The views are fabulous – Mt Logan, Mt Vancouver, Mt Kennedy, Mt Hubbard and many other peaks in the icefields can be seen on a clear day – and wildlife viewing opportunities are excellent.

For detailed route descriptions of a couple of the Yukon's most interesting hikes, see *Chapter 12: Hiking*. There are, however, many more multi-day hikes possible in Kluane National Park and Reserve – and in the Yukon in general – than are included in this chapter. Popular routes in Kluane include the **Cottonwood Trail**, a route of 85km (53 miles) that usually takes four to six days; you can start either at the Kathleen Lake day use area 27km (17 miles) south of Haines Junction on the Haines Road, or at Mush Lake Road, 54km (33 miles) south of Haines Junction. The trail is marked though difficult to see in places; you'll need to cross creeks. Bear-resistant food canisters are mandatory – you can pick them up when you register at the Kluane National Park and Reserve Visitor Centre in Haines Junction. For more information, see *The Kluane National Park Hiking Guide* by Vivien Lougheed, or www.pc.gc.ca/pn-np/yt/kluane/activ/activ1/activ1biv_e.asp.

Alternatively, the **Slims River West to Canada Creek** trail starts at the Tachäl Dhäl (Sheep Mountain) visitor centre. When the 'trail' ends a 'route' takes over, climbing Observation Mountain, which overlooks Kaskawulsh glacier. This is the most accessible glacier in the park but it's popular with the bears, and the route is often closed. Again, the use of bear-resistant food canisters is mandatory. This trail/route is 60km (37 miles) return and, apart from the climb up Observation Mountain, it's a straightforward hike on a maintained trail; the round trip takes most people three to five days. See www.pc.gc.ca/pn-np/yt/kluane/activ/activ1/activ1bxii_e.asp for more information. If the Slims River West trail is closed, an alternative is the **Slims River East** route, which is slightly shorter (40km, 25 miles) and usually takes two to four days. It's an easier route than Slims River West, and ends up at the toe of the glacier. See www.pc.gc.ca/pn-np/yt/kluane/activ/activ1/activ1bxiv_e.asp for more information – or, again, Vivien Lougheed's *The Kluane National Park Hiking Guide*.

More challenging is the fantastic (but exhausting!) **Donjek Route**, an eight- to ten-day trip without a trail, for which you'll need good route-finding and bushwhacking skills. You'll be rewarded, however, with stunning views, including those over the Donjek glacier. There's a detailed trail description on pages 239–42, as well as in Lougheed's guide and at www.pc.gc.ca/pn-np/yt/kluane/activ/activ1/activ1bxv_e.asp.

FISHING

Anglers come to Kluane for lake trout, arctic grayling, rainbow trout and northern pike, among other species. Popular lakes include Kathleen Lake, Mush Lake, Bates Lake, St Elias Lake and Louise Lake; only Kathleen Lake is easily accessible by vehicle. Note that you'll need a National Parks fishing licence if you're going to fish within the park's boundaries; this is separate from the territorial fishing licence required to fish elsewhere in the Yukon. Licences cost $9.80 per day (or $34.30 per year) and can be bought at the visitor centres in Haines Junction and Tachäl Dhäl, and Madley's General Store in Haines Junction.

CANOEING, KAYAKING AND RAFTING

You can canoe and kayak on the major lakes in Kluane – but be careful. Strong winds can whip up suddenly, and the water is treacherously cold if you get into trouble. On Kathleen Lake, for example, the average water temperature is just 5°C (41°F), and swells can blow up within an hour. Stick to the shore: don't paddle out any further than you can comfortably swim to land bearing in mind that, should you tip, you'll be considerably weakened by the cold. Cold water and waves make even kayak recovery almost impossible. The most sheltered area of Kathleen Lake is around the day use area and the dock.

Motorized boats are allowed on Kathleen Lake and Mush Lake. Be aware that Mush Lake is accessed by a 26km (16-mile) narrow, rough road that crosses numerous creeks. If you're going to attempt it, you'll need a high-clearance 4x4 and experience with this kind of driving.

THE ALSEK AND TATSHENSHINI RIVERS The Alsek and Tatshenshini rivers, which after their separate beginnings converge to drain into Dry Bay on Alaska's Pacific Coast, are reckoned to provide two of the most scenic wilderness river journeys in the world, with sensational views of glaciers and icebergs, and good opportunities for grizzly spotting. They're both white-water rivers and can be navigated by raft or by kayak. Inexperienced paddlers can join guided rafting trips: for example Tatshenshini Expediting (see page 26) offers either one-day rafting trips on the Tatshenshini, or 11-day journeys all the way to Dry Bay.

The Alsek route starts on the Dezdeash River in Haines Junction; you paddle along the Dezadeash for 27km (17 miles) until it meets the Alsek. For the first 151km (94 miles) of the trip, you'll encounter nothing greater than class III rapids; then you come to the aptly named Turnback Canyon, whose rapids are class V+. Turnback Canyon falls within the Tatshenshini–Alsek Park and is administered by BC Parks (*www.env.gov.bc.ca/bcparks*); they recommend against even expert kayakers attempting to run this canyon. Given that land portage is either extremely arduous or downright impossible (at best, it's two days dragging a kayak through bushes and difficult terrain in the middle of bear country), they recommend portage by helicopter.

A more accessible route is via the Tatshenshini River (this is the route taken by Tatshenshini Expediting). The route is 219km (136 miles) and usually takes between six and ten days; the fastest rapids are class III. The put-in is at Dalton Post on the Haines Road. After 124km (77 miles) the Tatshenshini joins the Alsek. At Alsek Lake, glaciers flow into the water, creating incredible iceberg surrounds, while the mountains tower overhead.

These trips should be booked months in advance. The take-out in Dry Bay requires a charter flight. If you're going to do this trip privately, you'll need a put-in date from Kluane if you're going to be travelling on the Alsek, and a take-out date from Glacier Bay National Park whether you're taking the Alsek or Tatshenshini routes. You'll also need a permit both for overnighting in Kluane National Park, and for the Glacier Bay National Park section in Alaska – and for the latter there is a waiting list. Alternatively you can book through a tour operator, but operators can only obtain permits for group trips, which they guide, and not for private parties.

For more information, and to get your name on the waiting list, you need to send your name, address, telephone numbers, email address, and payment of US$25 to cover administrative charges to: National Park Service, Yakutat Ranger Station, River Permits, PO Box 137, Yakutat AK 99869, USA, or call the Yakutat Ranger Station at ☎ +1 907 784 3295.

SKIING AND SNOWSHOEING

The following trails are maintained by Kluane National Park for cross-country skiing, snowshoeing and hiking in winter. This information is taken from the Parks Canada website; for more details go to www.pc.gc.ca/pn-np/yt/kluane/activ/activ11_e.asp#a13 or call Parks Canada on ☎ 867 634 7250.

DEZADEASH RIVER (*Distance: 5km, 3 miles, loop; Difficulty rating: easy; Trailhead: Dezadeash River day use area*) This is a forested, riverside trail, suitable for novices.

AURIOL TRAIL (*Distance: there are 2 options, a longer 15km, 9.3-mile, loop or a shorter 9km, 5.5-mile, loop; Difficulty rating: intermediate to advanced; Trailhead: 7km, 4.3 miles, south of Haines Junction on the Haines Rd*) The trail runs through open meadows and forest, and has some lovely views, but some sections are steep so you'll need skiing experience.

KATHLEEN LAKE (*Distance: 7km, 4.3 miles, with various looping options; Difficulty rating: easy to moderate; Trailhead: Kathleen Lake day use area*) This trail runs through poplar and spruce forest; it's suitable for beginners.

COTTONWOOD TRAIL (*Distance: 85km, 52.5 miles, loop; Difficulty rating: advanced; Trailhead: Kathleen Lake day use area or you can pick it up 55km, 34 miles, south of Haines Junction on the Haines Rd*) Most people take four or five days to complete this trail, which is not usually packed or track set.

MUSH LAKE ROAD (*Distance: 43.2km, 26.6 miles, round trip; Difficulty rating: intermediate; Trailhead: 55km, 34 miles, south of Haines Junction on the Haines Rd*) Again, this isn't usually packed or track set. It follows the route of an old mining road from the Haines Road to Mush Lake.

ST ELIAS LAKE (*Distance: 8km, 5 miles, round trip; Difficulty rating: intermediate; Trailhead: 60km, 37 miles, south of Haines Junction on the Haines Rd*) This trail follows an old road to an alpine lake; there are some steep sections.

Icefield Discovery is also developing a network of ski trails from its Stellar Hut on the Haines Road. See page 106 for details.

MOUNTAINEERING

This information is taken from the Parks Canada website. You'll find more detailed coverage at http://www.pc.gc.ca/pn-np/yt/kluane/activ/activ3/activ3_e.asp.

The Icefield Ranges of the St Elias Mountains are one of the largest non-polar icefields in the world. Within Kluane National Park and Reserve, major mountains include Mount Logan (5,959m, 19,545ft), Mount St Elias (5,489m, 18,004ft), Mount Lucania (5,226m, 17,141ft), King Peak (5,173m, 16,967ft), Mount Steele (5,073m, 16,639ft), Mount Wood (4,842m, 15,882ft) and Mount Vancouver (4,812m, 15,783ft).

It takes a week or two to hike into the Icefield Ranges from the nearest road; many climbers prefer to fly in. Note that high winds and heavy snowfall are common in the Icefield Ranges year round, and that temperatures can range from -40°C (-40°F) to above freezing.

ICEFIELDS MOUNTAINEERING PERMIT Anyone planning to climb the mountains within the icefields of Kluane National Park must have an Icefields Mountaineering Permit. To obtain a permit, send a completed application form together with itinerary detailing your air carrier, radio communications, arrival and departure date, and a list of your equipment to the Mountaineering Warden at the Parks Office in Haines Junction. You'll need to prove that you have the knowledge and equipment for self-rescue before the permit will be issued. Additionally, you're required to watch the *Mountaineering in Kluane National Park & Reserve* video before

- Mount Logan has the largest circumference of any mountain on earth.
- A total of 11 peaks run along Mount Logan's summit ridge, which stretches for more than 16km (10 miles).
- Mount Logan is getting taller. In 2007, a University of Alaska survey calculated that it was 5,966m (19,568ft) high – 7m (23ft) higher than its official level, which was measured in 1992. Some believe that climate change is leading to greater snowfall, leading to accumulated snow and ice on the mountain.
- On 26 May 1991, a temperature of –77.5 °C (–106.6 °F) was recorded on Mount Logan; this is the coldest temperature recorded anywhere outside of Antarctica.
- The icefield that surrounds Mount Logan is about 300m thick.

departure, and must register back with the warden, either in person or by phone, when you return from your expedition. There's more information at www.pc.gc.ca/pn-np/yt/kluane (click on 'activities', then on 'mountaineering') or ☎ 867 634 7279.

TOPO MAPS Mount St Elias 115 B and C, and Kluane National Park & Reserve Lake 115 F and G at a scale of 1:250,000 cover the entire Icefield Ranges of Kluane National Park & Reserve. You can buy them in Mac's Fireweed Books in Whitehorse (see page 65) or from www.yukonbooks.com.

MOUNTAIN BIKING

The park has plenty of disused mining roads that make for good mountain biking. It's easy to surprise bears when you're mountain biking, as you're moving quickly and quietly. Try to make noise!

ALSEK RIVER VALLEY TRAIL (*Distance: 58km, 36 miles, round trip; Trailhead: 10km, 6.2 miles, north of Haines Junction on the west side of the Alaska Highway, just across the road from Bear Creek Lodge; www.pc.gc.ca/pn-np/yt/kluane/activ/activ1/activ1bix_e.asp; Topo map: Kloo Lake 115 A/13*) This trail follows an old mining road into Sugden (Ferguson) Creek. It has a rocky surface, and there are good wildlife viewing opportunities in the Alsek valley. There are some creek crossings. Towards the end of the trail, you'll find the remains of a former horse camp and some old mining cabins.

MUSH LAKE ROAD (*Distance: 45km, 27.8 miles, round trip; Trailhead: 55km, 34 miles, south of Haines Junction on the Haines Rd; www.pc.gc.ca/pn-np/yt/kluane/activ/activ1/activ1bii_e.asp; Topo map: Mush Lake 115 A/6*) This is a fairly flat route along an old road that's still open to 4x4 traffic. Moose, black bear and waterfowl are commonly seen. There's a primitive campsite at Dalton Creek but it is not recommended you sleep here as bears are active in the area. There's a better campsite at the end of the trail, facing the lake; it has outhouses, a food cache and a fire pit. Remember that if you're camping in the park overnight, you need a permit (see page 103).

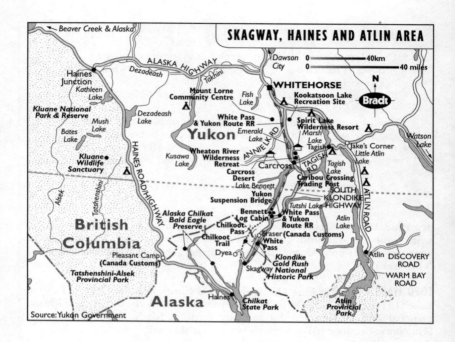

Source: Yukon Government

6

Skagway and the South Klondike Highway (plus Haines and Atlin)

From 1897 to 1898, Skagway's previously silent beaches swarmed, shrieked and scuttled with life as hundreds, then thousands of stampeders disembarked from ships and prepared to travel to the Yukon interior. Many of them were to join the great line of dreamers that trailed up the steep face of the snowy Chilkoot, creating the most abiding image of the Klondike gold rush.

Today, the steamers and their hopeful human cargo are long gone, and Skagway's tourism is dominated instead by crowds of the cruise-ship kind, who drop in here for a day to soak in the gripping gold-rush stories. But there's more to this area than its heartrending tales of triumph and tragedy. A short jaunt over the water, Haines is a picturesque haven for artists, photographers, wildlife watchers and outdoors types, while sleepy little Atlin, on the edge of Atlin Lake over in BC, basks in its own stunning surrounds. The roads that lead north into the Yukon from all three of these towns are simply fantastic – they're all paved and in good condition, yet the glacier-clad mountains that dazzle above glittering blue lakes create a backdrop that makes it hard to focus on the road.

SKAGWAY

In summer, Skagway is terrifically touristy: some days as many as five gargantuan cruise ships dock at the end of the main street and disgorge up to 9,000 dollar-wielding, ice-cream consuming passengers onto this tiny town. Still, Skagway remains a quaint enough place, and if you stay into the evening (when the cruise-ship passengers climb back aboard their floating behemoths and motor on), or visit slightly outside the main season, you'll have the place almost to yourself. It's worth a visit despite the crowds – Skagway's gold-rush history is packed with rattling good yarns, and there's plenty to keep the most irksome of visitors busy, from wildlife cruises to trips on the White Pass and Yukon Route railway to fabulous biking and hiking opportunities.

Note that most of the attractions operate in the summer season only. Be aware, too, that Skagway is in the USA: if you're dialling from Canada, you'll need to use the international dialling code +1, and its clocks are an hour behind the Canadians'.

HISTORY

The town of Skagway at this period of its existence was about the roughest place in the world. The population increased every day; gambling hells, dance halls and variety theatres were in full swing…

Robbery and murder were daily occurrences; many people came there with money, and next morning had not enough to get a meal having been robbed or cheated out of their last cent. Shots were exchanged on the streets in broad daylight,

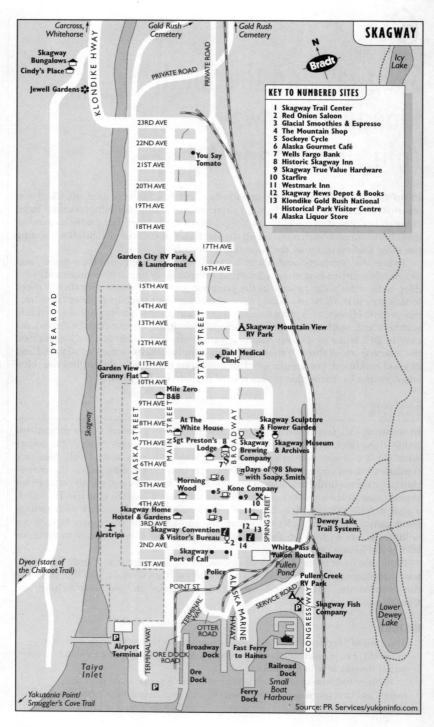

SKAGWAY

KEY TO NUMBERED SITES

1 Skagway Trail Center
2 Red Onion Saloon
3 Glacial Smoothies & Espresso
4 The Mountain Shop
5 Sockeye Cycle
6 Alaska Gourmet Café
7 Wells Fargo Bank
8 Historic Skagway Inn
9 Skagway True Value Hardware
10 Starfire
11 Westmark Inn
12 Skagway News Depot & Books
13 Klondike Gold Rush National
   Historical Park Visitor Centre
14 Alaska Liquor Store

Carcross, Whitehorse

Gold Rush Cemetery

Gold Rush Cemetery

Icy Lake

Skagway Bungalows
Cindy's Place
Jewell Gardens

KLONDIKE HWY

PRIVATE ROAD

PRIVATE ROAD

23RD AVE
22ND AVE
21ST AVE
20TH AVE
19TH AVE
18TH AVE

You Say Tomato

17TH AVE
16TH AVE

Garden City RV Park & Laundromat

15TH AVE
14TH AVE
13TH AVE
12TH AVE
11TH AVE

DYEA ROAD

Skagway

STATE STREET

Skagway Mountain View RV Park

Dahl Medical Clinic

Garden View Granny Flat

10TH AVE

Mile Zero B&B

9TH AVE
8TH AVE

At The White House

7TH AVE

Sgt Preston's Lodge

6TH AVE

5TH AVE

ALASKA STREET

MAIN STREET

BROADWAY

Skagway Sculpture & Flower Garden

Skagway Brewing Company

Skagway Museum & Archives

Days of '98 Show with Soapy Smith

Morning Wood

Kone Company

4TH AVE

Skagway Home Hostel & Gardens

3RD AVE

Airstrips

Skagway Convention & Visitor's Bureau

2ND AVE

Skagway Port of Call

1ST AVE

Police

POINT ST

SPRING STREET

Dewey Lake Trail System

White Pass & Yukon Route Railway

Pullen Pond

Pullen Creek RV Park

Skagway Fish Company

Lower Dewey Lake

ALASKA MARINE HWY

SERVICE ROAD

CONGRESS WAY

Dyea (start of the Chilkoot Trail)

Airport Terminal

TERMINAL WAY

ORE DOCK ROAD

OTTER ROAD

Broadway Dock

Ore Dock

Fast Ferry to Haines

Ferry Dock

Railroad Dock

Small Boat Harbour

Taiya Inlet

Yakutania Point/ Smuggler's Cove Trail

Source: PR Services/yukoninfo.com

and enraged Klondykers pursued the scoundrels of Soapy Smith's gang to get even with them. At night the crash of bands, shouts of 'Murder!', [and] cries for help mingled with the cracked voices of the singers in the variety halls.

So wrote Sam Steele, the superintendent who headed up the Yukon's division of the North West Mounted Police during the gold-rush years, in his memoirs *Forty Years in Canada*.

Skagway's townsite had been claimed well before the gold rush by a retired seaman named William Moore and he had named his new dominion for himself: Mooresville. Moore had been among William Ogilvie's party surveying the routes over the Coast Mountains in 1887 (see *George Dawson and the geological survey of Canada*, page 178); while Ogilive and company had gone over the Chilkoot Pass, Moore had surveyed the White Pass, and it was he who named it for the Canadian Minister of the Interior, Thomas White. As chance would have it, his Tlingit guide had been none other than Skookum Jim, one of the trio who eventually struck gold in Rabbit Creek (see page 166). Moore had concluded that when, one day, large quantities of gold were inevitably found in the Yukon interior, it would be this way that the masses would travel. He therefore claimed a 0.65km² (160-acre) homestead, built a saw mill, a wharf and a cabin, and sat and waited for the rush. When it came, however, the masses stampeded straight over his townsite, changed its name, and even forced him out of his own home – though Moore ended his days a wealthy man when a court awarded him a quarter of his Skagway's worth.

News of the Klondike gold rush broke in the outside world on 14 July 1897 (see pages 166–7). Immediately, gold fever rampaged through western America, then spread further afield – and it was to Skagway that most of the prospectors swarmed, arriving on steamers from America's west coast. The first ship docked on 29 July 1897, just 15 days after the momentous arrival of the *Excelsior* in San Francisco. The beach became heaped with gear as entire flotillas arrived laden with thousands of men and their chaotic piles of cargo. Within a year, Moore's sleepy little townsite had a population of 8,000.

These stampeders, for the most part, had little idea of what they were heading to. Neither did many of them know that their troubles would start so soon for, unlike in Canada, where the North West Mounted Police had a strict regard for order, Skagway was governed by criminality – and in particular by a colourful conman named Jefferson 'Soapy' Smith. His nickname came from sleight of hand scam he'd operated across the western United States: he'd set up a stall, wrap some bars of soap in paper money plus plain paper, and others just in plain paper, then sell them for a dollar: needless to say, only members of Soapy's own gang ever won the money-wrapped bars.

Soapy's mob roamed the town, some dressed as gentlemen, others as ruffians, and between them they inveigled their way into the newcomers' trust before relieving them of their cash. Most famous of Soapy's swindles was his fake telegraph operation (there was no telegraph in Skagway until 1901). Newly arrived prospectors paid $5 to send a telegraph home – and were then invited by friendly faces to join them in a game of poker. It was rigged, of course.

Soapy Smith finally met his end on a Skagway pier on 8 July 1898, in a shoot-out with vigilante Frank Reid. Reid, too, died of his injuries: 'He died for the honor of Skagway,' his tombstone reads. But it's Soapy whose memory is celebrated today with a wake in Skagway's Eagles Hall each 8 July, while visitors to the town flock to visit both men's graves in the Gold Rush Cemetery (see page 126).

If they survived their encounters with Soapy Smith, stampeders left the coast to climb either the Chilkoot or the White Pass. These trails ended at a series of lakes

A TON OF GOODS

There wasn't a specific list of mandatory items that the stampeders had to carry to the Canadian goldfields; however, various companies published their own suggestions. The following gear list was recommended by the Northern Pacific railroad company in the *Chicago Record's Book for Gold Seekers*, 1897.

150lbs bacon
400lbs flour
25lbs rolled oats
125lbs beans
10lbs tea
10lbs coffee
25lbs sugar
25lbs dried potatoes
2lbs dried onions
15lbs salt
1lb pepper
75lbs dried fruits
8lbs baking powder
2lbs soda
½lb evaporated vinegar
12oz compressed soup
1 can mustard
1 tin matches (for 4 men)
Stove for 4 men
Gold pan for each
Set granite buckets
Large bucket
Knife, fork, spoon, cup & plate
Frying pan
Coffee & teapot
Scythe stone
2 picks & 1 shovel
1 whipsaw
Pack strap

2 axes for 4 men & 1 extra handle
6 eight-inch files & 2 taper files for the party
Draw knife, brace & bits, jack plane, & hammer for party
200ft ³/₈-inch rope
8lbs of pitch & 5lbs of oakum for 4 men
Nails, 5lbs each of 6, 8, 10 & 12 penny, for 4 men
Tent, 10x12ft for 4 men
Canvas for wrapping
2 oil blankets to each boat
5yds of mosquito netting for each man
3 suits of heavy underwear
1 heavy mackinaw coat
2 pairs heavy machinaw trousers
1 heavy rubber-lined coat
1 dozen heavy wool socks
½ dozen heavy wool mittens
2 heavy overshirts
2 pairs heavy snagproof rubber boots
2 pairs shoes
4 pairs blankets (for 2 men)
4 towels
2 pairs overalls
1 suit oil clothing
Several changes of summer clothing
Small assortment of medicines

that connected to the Yukon River – and to Dawson City beyond. Both the Chilkoot and White Pass made for terrible going in the winter of 1897–98. Due to fear of famine in Dawson, the Canadian authorities insisted that stampeders crossing the international border carry a ton of supplies, which they deduced should be sufficient to last them a year (see *A ton of goods*, above).

The Chilkoot Trail (now maintained by the US National Parks Service and Parks Canada as a fantastic hiking trail – see pages 233–9) was the shorter of the two, but the last haul to the summit was so devilishly steep that pack animals couldn't make it: those who couldn't afford to hire packers had to make 30 or 40 journeys on foot – taking around three months – to ferry their goods past the Mounties who checked each traveller's outfit at the summit.

The White Pass (over which the railway now runs) had an incline sufficiently gentle that packhorses could climb it – but almost all of the 3,000 animals taken on the trail perished. Many of them were pushed to their deaths in 'Dead Horse Gulch', which is now spanned by the highest cantilever bridge of the White Pass and Yukon Route railway. Jack London went via the Chilkoot; however, he heard stories of the White Pass that enabled him to write a vivid description of this awful journey:

> The horses died like mosquitoes in the first frost, and from Skaguay to Bennett they rotted in heaps. They died at the Rocks, they were poisoned at the Summit, and they starved at the Lakes; they fell off the trail, what there was of it, or they went through it; in the river they drowned under their loads, or were smashed to pieces against the boulders; they snapped their legs in the crevices and broke their backs falling backwards with their packs; in the sloughs they sank from sight or smothered in the slime, and they were disembowelled in the bogs where the corduroy logs turned end up in the mud; men shot them, worked them to death, and when they were gone, went back to the beach and bought more. Some did not bother to shoot them, stripping the saddles off and the shoes and leaving them where they fell. Their hearts turned to stone – those which did not break – and they became beasts, the men on Dead Horse Trail.
>
> From 'Which Make Men Remember' by Jack London

The agony ended in July 1900, when the White Pass and Yukon Route railway was completed between Skagway and Whitehorse. From this point on, the railway became the principal means of travel to the Yukon interior until the South Klondike Highway was completed in 1979. As the gold rush dropped off, so did Skagway's population. Just 3,000 people lived here at the time of the 1900 census, and that number declined to 500 in the following 20 years. There was a brief hiatus again in 1942, when thousands of troops charged with supplying the construction of the Alaska Highway were stationed in Skagway.

Today, Skagway has a permanent population of around 800, but each summer it sees a stampede of the 21st-century kind: annual cruise-ship passenger numbers reach a staggering 800,000. Still, despite its swarms – and its Disneyesque 'Klondikeland' flavour – Skagway retains a certain charm. And if the souvenir shops and hiking

LORD AVONMORE'S UNSUCCESSFUL ADVENTURE

The Chilkoot Trail and White Pass routes weren't the only ways to the Klondike. Some tried to travel to Dawson from Prince William Sound and over the Valdez Glacier, while a few misguided British and Canadian patriots opted for all-Canadian routes, such as the Edmonton Trail. Many who chose this route took an agonizing two years to reach the Klondike. By the time they arrived, most of the gold was gone – as was their patriotic spirit.

One party intent on walking the Edmonton Trail was that of English peer Lord Avonmore. He arrived in Edmonton with 5,000kg of supplies, including 5kg of toilet paper. However, his entourage's troubles were such that they never even started on the trail. Pierre Berton explains in The Klondike Fever:

> One of the party, a Captain Alleyne, died of pneumonia contracted in the twenty-below weather. Another, a Dr Hoops, sprained his ankle and had scarcely recovered from this misadventure when he stumbled across a dog sleigh and cracked his ribs. A colonel in the party meanwhile broke his arm, while a Captain Powell froze his feet so badly that he died. A Captain O'Brien assumed leadership of the group and, as his first official act, arrested a compatriot, a Mr Bannerman, on a charge of embezzlement. Before he could pull things together, however, he was himself jailed for trying to stab his manservant, and the expedition tottered to a standstill.

A well-to-do Chicago woman, 32-year-old Mrs Martha Purdy, was bored of society and hungry for adventure. When she and her husband William Purdy heard of the wealth to be won in the Klondike, they decided to head there together with her brother George Munger. But just before they left Purdy abandoned the expedition. Martha responded by abandoning their marriage. She left her two young sons with her mother in Kansas, then she and George boarded a ship for Skagway.

They chose to travel to the Klondike via the Chilkoot Pass and had sufficient money to pay packers to carry their several tons of gear. Martha was not without her burdens, however: she hiked in a high buckram collar, a corset, a long corduroy skirt and full bloomers. When, eventually, she fell into a crevice and cut herself, she sat down and cried.

'For God's sake, Polly, buck up and be a man. Have some style and move on!' her brother retorted.

The pair made it to Dawson, and both staked claims. But now Martha found she was pregnant by the husband who had deserted her. Too poor to pay for a hospital bed, she gave birth in a log cabin on a hill above Lousetown in January 1899 (for more on Lousetown see The 'soiled doves' of Dawson, page 175). And then her father turned up and took her and the baby home.

Martha agreed to go on the condition that she'd be allowed to return should her claim, which George would manage in her absence, produce more than $10,000 in gold. This it did, and so in 1900 she returned to the Yukon, where she managed both her own mining camp and a saw mill (I'm not sure what happened to the baby – possibly Martha's mother was lumbered with a third). The men didn't like having a female boss; some went so far as to quit. But Martha pressed on, became a successful businesswoman, and in 1904 married attorney George Black who rose to be Commissioner of the Yukon Territory.

Even as First Lady of the Yukon, Mrs Black liked to court controversy and, according to Laura Berton in her book I Married the Klondike, her speech was well punctuated with hells and damns. When her husband left Dawson for Britain to fight in World War I, Mrs Black went with him. One of the generals is said to have told her that the ships crossing the Atlantic were only for men. She retorted that she'd crossed the Chilkoot Pass with several thousand men for company, and wasn't remotely concerned about crossing the Atlantic with several thousand more. Once in England, she lectured energetically about the Yukon to raise money for the war effort, and was made a Fellow of the Royal Geographical Society for her work collecting Yukon wildflowers.

The Blacks returned to Canada after the war, and George Black was elected a member of the Canadian parliament in Ottawa. When in 1935 ill health prevented him returning to parliament, Martha ran as the candidate for the Yukon, and was elected. She was the second woman ever to become a Canadian MP. She died in Whitehorse in 1957, aged 91.

opportunities aren't enough to impress you, get this for a claim to fame: on 4 July 2008, Skagway entered the *Guinness Book of World Records* for the most people tossing eggs. A sensational 1,162 people participated in this shell-shattering feat.

GETTING THERE

By sea The great majority of visitors to Skagway come on **cruise ships** (see page 24 for a list of cruise lines serving Skagway). They dock right at the end of the main street – which looks frankly bizarre. Alternatively the **Alaska Marine Highway**

top   Broken down and snowed under in Inuvik (PE) pages 202–14

above left & right   The sourtoe cocktail is served up in Dawson's Downtown Hotel — it's a shot of Yukon
                      Jack whiskey liqueur garnished with a genuine, severed human toe (both PE) page 179–80

below & inset   Percy DeWolfe, the 'iron man of the north', delivered the mail between Dawson City
                      and Eagle from 1910 to 1949 — a memorial mail race is still held in his honour
                      (main pic YA/AV, inset YA/CMT) page 188

top   **Inuvik has a strong Gwich'in and Inuvialuit population** (SW) pages 202–14

left   **Tuktoyaktuk's cemetery looks out over the Arctic Ocean** (PE) pages 214–16

below left   **Many of Dawson City's historic buildings still stand, and the streets are lined with wooden boardwalks rather than pavement** (PE) pages 165–89

below   **Inuvik's average annual temperature is −10°C (15°F)** (PE) pages 202–14

right   Lake Bennett with its pretty wooden church is a welcome sight at the end of the Chilkoot Trail (SW) pages 233–9

below   In Skagway, mighty cruise liners dock just at the end of the main street (SW) pages 115–26

bottom   Whitehorse, which sits on the banks of the Yukon River, was named by the gold rush stampeders for foaming rapids that looked like the manes of white horses (YG) pages 51–76

above left   Musk oxen have inhabited North America for at least 150,000 years (SW) page 9

above right   The pure-white Dall sheep is the most prolific subspecies of thinhorn sheep in the Yukon (SW) page 10

left   A least chipmunk burrows out from the snow (SW) page 11

below left   The Alaska Yukon moose is the largest deer in the world (SW) page 9

below right   The arctic ground squirrel is the only mammal known to let its body temperature drop below freezing during hibernation (PE) page 11

top   Porcupines keep Yukon vets busy in summer when inquisitive dogs sometimes take a sniff too close (SW) page 11

above   For thousands of years, the Yukon's First Nations people have depended on caribou for food and clothing (MN/FLPA) page 7

right   There are around 4,500 wolves in the Yukon; they are more abundant around large populations of moose (SW) page 10

(*Skagway office* ✆ *907 983 2229, Haines office* ✆ *907 766 2113, Juneau central reservations office* ✆ *907 465 3941, toll-free:* ✆ *1 800 642 0066; www.ferryalaska.com*) runs ferries connecting Skagway to Haines and Juneau, and from there to its entire system from Bellingham in Washington State along Alaska's Inside Passage and across to the Aleutian Islands. A passenger fare from Haines to Skagway is US$31 plus US$31 for a small vehicle; Juneau to Skagway is US$50 with vehicles starting from US$63; to go the whole way from Bellingham to Skagway costs US$363 per person with vehicles from US$478.

Haines–Skagway Fast Ferry (*142 Beach Rd, Haines;* ✆ *907 766 2100, toll-free:* ✆ *1 888 766 2103;* e *reservations@chilkatcruises.com; www.hainesskagwayfastferry.com*) runs between Haines and Skagway up to seven times a day from mid-May to late September. Adults US$38 one way, US$65 return, children US$18 one way, US$34 return. The journey takes 40 minutes. Note that this is a passenger ferry only; if you're travelling with a vehicle, you'll need to take the less frequent Alaska Marine Highway.

By rail The historic **White Pass and Yukon Route railway** runs between Skagway and Carcross in the summer. See pages 70–1 and 126.

By air Skagway is a 45-minute light aircraft flight from Juneau. There's no jet service to Skagway – large aeroplanes can't land – and there are no direct flights from Anchorage to Skagway. **Air Excursions** (✆ *907 697 2375, toll-free:* ✆ *1 800 3542479;* e *airex@ptialaska.net; www.airexcursions.com*) and **Wings of Alaska** (✆ *907 789 0790;* e *info@wingsofalaska.com; www.wingsofalaska.com*) both connect from Juneau to Skagway daily. Cautious spenders take note: there's a dollar difference in the ticket price. Air Excursions charges US$120 one-way while a ticket with Wings of Alaska costs US$119.

By road Skagway is 180km (110 miles) south of the Alaska Highway via the South Klondike Highway. You can rent RVs and cars in Skagway from the following companies. Note that all are seasonal apart from Sourdough Vehicle & Bicycle Rentals, which is open year round.

🚗 **Alaska Motorhome Rentals** 246 12th Av; ✆ 907 983 3333, toll-free: ✆ 1 800 254 9929; e alaskarv@aol.com; www.alaskarv.com

🚗 **Avis Rent A Car** Westmark Inn, 3rd Av & Spring St; ✆ 907 966 2404 mid-Sep to mid-May, 907 983 2247 mid-May to mid-Sep; www.avis.com

🚗 **Sourdough Vehicle & Bicycle Rentals** 351 6th Av; ✆ 907 983 2523, cell: 907 209 5026; e sourdoughrental@yahoo.com; www.geocities.com/sourdoughcarrentals

🚗 **USA RV Rentals** 12th & Broadway; ✆ 250 814 0253, toll-free: ✆ USA: 1 866 814 0253, UK & Germany: ✆ 800 4267 4267; www.usarvrentals.com

Yukon Alaska Tourist Tours (✆ *867 668 5944, ticket office:* ✆ *867 668 4414 May–Sep only; www.yukonalaskatouristtours.com; US$40–55*) offers a **bus** connection between Skagway and Whitehorse in the summer.

GETTING AROUND The SMART (Skagway Municipal and Regional Transit) provides a **shuttle bus** service that connects the dock to the town for $2, or $5 for an all-day pass.

TOURIST INFORMATION
🔲 **Skagway Convention & Visitor's Bureau** 2nd Av & Broadway; ✆ 907 983 2854; info@skagway.com; www.skagway.com; 🕐 8am–5pm daily May–Sep with longer hrs if the cruise ships are still in town, 8am–5pm Mon–Fri in winter.

Klondike Gold Rush National Historical Park Visitor Centre Located in old White Pass & Yukon Route depot at 2nd Av & Broadway; ✆ 907 983 2921; www.nps.gov/klgo. The park is divided in 2: firstly there's the Chilkoot Trail, & secondly there is a number of historic buildings downtown such as the **Mascot Saloon** (3rd & Broadway; ⊕ early May to mid-Sep 8am–6pm daily) & the **Moore House & Cabin** (5th & Spring St; ⊕ early May to mid-Sep 10am–5pm daily). The visitor centre hosts 45min ranger presentations daily at 10am, summer only. You can also watch a 30min film about the gold rush, 8am, 9am, 11am, noon, 1pm, 2pm, 3pm, 4pm, 5pm. There is also a program of evening events.

Skagway Trail Center Broadway, between 1st & 2nd Avs; ✆ 907 983 9234; ⊕ 8.30am–4.30pm daily in summer. The Trail Center provides information on the Chilkoot Trail & issues permits. See pages 233–9 for more information on hiking the Chilkoot.

LOCAL TOUR OPERATORS These tours are all seasonal, operating in the summer only.

Alaska Fjordlines ✆ toll-free: ✆ 1 800 320 0146; e info@alaskafjordlines.com; www.alaskafjordlines.com. Operates a day cruise from Skagway to Juneau; includes sightseeing bus tour of Juneau & lunch.

Alaska Icefield Expeditions ✆ 907 983 2299; e info@akdogtour.com; www.akdogtour.com. Flies guests by helicopter to Denver glacier where they embark on a summer dogsled adventure, with the opportunity to mush their own team. Tours last 2hrs, or you can stay overnight in a hut on the glacier.

Alaska Sled Dog Adventures ✆ 907 983 4444; e service@alaskaexcursions.com; www.alaskasleddog.com. Summer dogsled tours on wheeled carts along a woodland trail. Excursion lasts 2hrs 45mins.

Chilkoot Charters 340 7th Av; ✆ 907 983 3400, toll-free: ✆ 877 983 3400; e chilkoot@chilkootcharters.com; www.chilkootcharters.com. Bus tours, bus & rail combos, & fishing charters for groups of 13–25 passengers per guide.

Chilkoot Horseback Adventure ✆ 907 983 4444; www.chilkoothorseback.com. Offers summer trail rides out of its ranch at Dyea; tours last 3½hrs including van transport from Skagway.

Choctaw Charters Fishing Small Boat Harbor; ✆ summer: 907 612 0087, winter: 830 997 7799; e captmike@choctawcharters.com; http://fishing.eskagway.com. Half-day fishing trips & wildlife excursions in Taiya Inlet.

Discover Skagway Tours ✆ 907 983 2134, toll-free: ✆ 866 983 8687, cell: 954 292 0161; e info@discoverskagway.com; www.discoverskagway.com. Small independent company whose tours last 2½–5hrs & take in attractions including Jewell Gardens, White Pass Summit, the Gold Rush Cemetery & the Days of '98 Show.

Dockside Charters Small Boat Harbor; ✆ 907 983 3625, toll-free: ✆ 1 877 983 3625, cell: 907 209 9668; e fishing@skagwayfishing.com; www.skagwayfishing.com. Half-day & full-day salmon fishing, full-day halibut fishing plus wildlife tours.

Dyea Dave's Shuttle & Tours ✆ 907 209 5031; e dyeadave@msn.com; www.dyeadavetours.com. Dave McClelland offers van tours of Skagway & surrounding sights, plus the Klondike Highway into the Yukon.

Fat Salmon Charters Slip A5 in Small Boat Harbor; ✆ 907 209 7335; e fatsalmoncharters@yahoo.com; www.fatsalmoncharters.com. Half-day & full-day salmon fishing & wildlife cruises.

Frontier Excursions 1602 State St; ✆ 907 983 2512, toll-free: ✆ 1 877 983 2512; e tours@frontierexcursions.com; www.frontierexcursions.com. Offers half-day & day van trips around Skagway & into the Yukon, plus a shuttle service to the Chilkoot trailhead at Dyea.

Gray Line Skagway Located in the Westmark Inn — see page 124; ✆ 907 983 2241; e glainfo@hollandamerica.com; www.graylinealaska.com. White Pass & Yukon Route railway tickets, Glacier Bay packages, helicopter & dog mushing adventures, Haines Eagle Preserve jet boat & float adventures, plus local sightseeing.

Klondike Gold Dredge Tour Mile 1.7 Klondike Highway, ✆ 907 983 3175; e info@klondikegolddredge.com; www.klondikegolddredge.com. The dredge was transported from the Klondike & reconstructed on the shores of the Skagway River. A variety of excursions mixing tours of the town & the railway with gold-panning & dredge visits are on offer. The Gold Rush Brewery is also on site for local beer, Denali wine & food — there's a deck with a river & glacier view.

Klondike Tours 270 Broadway; ✆ 907 983 2075, toll-free: ✆ 1 866 983 2075; e klondiketours@yahoo.com; www.klondiketours.com. Van tours, flightseeing, summer dogsledding (with wheeled carts), rafting & wildlife-viewing tours.

M&M Tours 2nd Av & Spring St plus sales booths near the cruise-ship docks; ☎ 907 983 3900, toll-free: ☎ 1 866 983 3900; e info@skagwayadventures.com; www.skagwayadventures.com. M&M is a broker for various operators, & sells a huge number of trips departing from Skagway from wildlife cruises to horseback riding to flightseeing & van tours.

McCormick Charters Small Boat Harbor; ☎ 907 612 0345; e captain@mccormickcharters.com; www.mccormickcharters.com. Half-day & full-day salmon-fishing & wildlife tours.

Mountain Flying Service Skagway Airport Terminal; ☎ 907 766 3007, toll-free: ☎ 1 800 954 8747; e mtnfly@yahoo.com; www.flyglacierbay.com. Flightseeing over Glacier Bay as well as drop-offs & pick-ups for mountaineers & skiers.

Packer Expeditions Mountain Shop, 351 4th Av; ☎ 907 983 2544; e packer@aptalaska.net; www.packerexpeditions.com. Heli-hiking, glacier hiking, Chilkoot Trail & kayaking trips.

Princess Tours 95 Broadway; ☎ summer: 907 983 2895, winter: 907 463 3900; e skagwaylogistics@princesstours.com; www.princess.com. Mega cruise-ship company's touring arm offers pretty much every kind of trip you can think of.

Skaguay Tour Company 275 7th Av; ☎ 907 983 2168, toll-free: ☎ 1 866 983 2168; e troberts@aptalaska.net; www.skagwaytourco.com. City, White Pass summit & 'Yukon Adventure' van tours last 1½–3½hrs.

Skagway Classic Cars 2 Liarsville Rd; ☎ 907 983 2886, cell: 907 723 0594; akclassic@hotmail.com;

www.skagwayclassiccars.com. Tours of Skagway attractions in chauffeur-driven vintage cars.

Skagway Float Tours ☎ 907 983 3688; e skagwayfloat@aol.com; www.skagwayfloat.com. Gentle floating trips on inflatable rafts on the Taiya River, or hike & float combinations that take in a stretch of the Chilkoot Trail.

Skagway Street Car Company 270 2nd Av; ☎ 907 983 2908; e info@skagwaystreetcar.com; www.skagwaystreetcar.com. Climb aboard the bright-yellow 1927 sightseeing bus to view Skagway's sights.

Sockeye Cycle 381 5th Av; ☎ 907 983 2851; e sockeye@cyclealaska.com; www.cyclealaska.com; ⏱ May–Sep 9am–6pm daily. Bicycle & tandem rentals & repairs as well as guided bicycle tours lasting from 3 hrs to 10 days.

Southeast Tours 250 2nd Alleyway; ☎ 907 983 2990; e setours@charter.net; www.southeasttours.com. Day & half-day tours around Skagway & into the Yukon; trips include van tours, horseback-riding excursions, & a Chilkoot hike & float trip.

Temsco Helicopters ☎ 907 983 2900, toll-free: ☎ 1 866 683 2900; info@temscoair.com; www.temscoair.com. Helicopter glacier & icefields flightseeing.

Yukon Jeep Klondike Adventure Skagway Mountain View RV Park, 12th Av & Broadway; ☎ 907 983 3333, toll-free: ☎ 1 800 323 5757; e info@bestofalaskatravel.com; www.bestofalaskatravel.com. 4x4 jeep adventures last 5–5½hrs.

WHERE TO STAY
The following are open year round unless otherwise specified.

⌂ **Chilkoot Trail Outpost** (8 cabins) Km 11, mile 7 Dyea Rd; ☎ 907 983 3799; e info@chilkoottrailoutpost.com; www.chilkoottrailoutpost.com; ⏱ May–Sep. Log cabins have fridge, microwave & private bathroom; b/fast is served in the main lodge & there's a nightly campfire. Wheelchair friendly & wireless internet. Bicycle loan included in price; hiking on the Chilkoot Trail, whose trailhead is half a mile away, is a popular activity. Activity packages also available. $$$$–$$$$$

⌂ **The Historic Skagway Inn B&B** (10 rooms) Broadway & 7th Av; ☎ 907 983 2289, toll-free: ☎ 1 888 752 4929; e reservations@skagwayinn.com; wwwskagwayinn.com; ⏱ Mar–Oct. This place has a pleasant atmosphere, with 'Victorian-style' furnishings (think frills) & a garden filled with flowers. There's wireless internet, & they serve up a hearty cooked b/fast. $$$ (shared bath) $$$$$ (private bath)

⌂ **At the White House B&B** (10 rooms) 475 8th Av – cnr of Main St; ☎ 907 983 9000; e whitehse@aptalaska.net; www.atthewhitehouse.com. Comfortable B&B with all mod cons & wireless internet, & a substantial self-service b/fast. $$$–$$$$

⌂ **Garden View Granny Flat** 10th Av & Alaska, ☎ 907 983 2127, cell: 907 612 0814; www.alaskagrannyflat.com. Private apartment with 1 queen & 1 single bed, plus wireless internet, satellite TV, DVD & the rest. Guests are welcome to help themselves to fruit growing in the garden. $$$–$$$$

⌂ **Sgt Preston's Lodge** (40 rooms) 370 6th Av (behind the bank & post office, between Broadway & State); ☎ 907 983 2521, toll-free: ☎ 1 866 983 2521; e sgtprestons@eskagway.com; www.sgt-prestonslodgeskagway.com. All rooms have private bathroom; there's wireless internet. This used to be an army barracks during World War II & the building of the Alaska Highway. $$$–$$$$

6

🏠 **Skagway Bungalows** (2 cabins) Km 1.6, mile 1 Dyea Rd; 📞 907 983 2986, cell: 907 983 4608; e saldi@aptalaska.net; www.aptalaska.net/~saldi/; ⏰ Apr–Oct. Each cabin has microwave, fridge, bathroom & private deck. $$$–$$$$

🏠 **Westmark Inn** (151 rooms) 3rd Av & Spring St; 📞 907 983 6000, toll-free: 📞 1 800 544 0970; e khunt@hollandamerica.com; www.westmarkhotels.com; ⏰ mid-May to mid-Sep. Reliable member of the Westmark chain, part of the Holland America empire. The Westmark's Chilkoot Dining Room serves b/fast & dinner. $$$–$$$$

🏠 **Cindy's Place B&B** (3 cabins) Located 3km (2 miles) from downtown Skagway on Dyea Rd — courtesy transfer from downtown provided; 📞 907 983 2674, toll-free: 📞 1 800 831 8095; e croland@alaska.net; www.alaska.net/~croland; ⏰ May–Sep. Quiet setting & all mod cons. $$–$$$$

🏠 **Mile Zero Bed & Breakfast** (7 rooms) Main St & 9th Av; 📞 907 983 3045; e milezero@starband.net; www.mile-zero.com. Convenient downtown location. Wheelchair friendly. All rooms have private bath & porch, plus wireless internet. $$–$$$$

🏠 **Morning Wood Hotel** (8 rooms) 444 4th St; 📞 907 983 2200. Rooms are above the pizza restaurant & bar, & the establishment markets itself as suitable for those who enjoy nightlife... $$

🏠 **Skagway Home Hostel & Gardens** (1 mixed & 2 single-gender dorms) 456 3rd Av; 📞 907 983 2131; www.skagwayhostel.com. This family-style house has a relaxed & welcoming atmosphere, with kitchen, laundry & bikes. There's an honesty jar for food from the fridge; dinner is served each evening ($5 — free if you cook). Guests are expected to help with small household chores. Full kitchen, free internet & free veggies from the garden. No alcohol, smoking or pets. $

RV parks and campgrounds

⚑ **Dyea Campground** (22 sites) Located on the banks of the Taiya River off a dirt road off the Skagway–Dyea road, just before the Chilkoot trailhead; 📞 907 983 2921; www.nps.gov/archive/klgo/dyea_campground.htm. Managed by the National Park Service, the campground is serviced (& charges a fee via self-registration) from Memorial Day to Labor Day. After that it's open until the snow falls, free of charge. Has outhouses, picnic tables & bear-resistant containers. No hook-ups. $

⚑ **Garden City RV Park & Laundromat** (100 sites with full & partial hook-ups) State St between 15th & 17th; 📞 907 983 2378, toll-free: 📞 866 983 2378;

e gcrv@aptalaska.net; ⏰ summer only. Tours, cable TV & internet. $

⚑ **Pullen Creek RV Park** (34 sites) 📞 907 983 2768, toll-free: 📞 1 800 936 3731; www.pullencreekrv.com; ⏰ 15 Apr–15 Sep. Located right on the waterfront next to the Alaska State Ferry Dock, all sites have 30 amp power & water. $

⚑ **Skagway Mountain View RV Park** (187 sites) 12th Av & Broadway; 📞 907 983 3333, toll-free: 📞 1 888 778 7700; e info@bestofalaskatravel.com; www.bestofalaskatravel.com; ⏰ May–Sep. Full hook-up, electric & water only, & dry sites, plus local tour desk & wireless internet. $

✕ **WHERE TO EAT** There are many restaurants in Skagway, and a gentle amble along the town's few main streets will allow you to peer in the windows and look at the menus. I'm just listing a few:

Restaurants

✕ **Alaska Gourmet Café** 344 5th Av; 📞 907 983 2448; www.akgourmet.com; ⏰ 6am–10pm daily. Main dishes include sockeye salmon fillet & steak, plus there are sandwiches, soups & chowders, & cakes, all homemade. $$$

✕ **Skagway Fish Company** 201 Congress Way; 📞 907 983 3474; e sfcalaska@hotmail.com; ⏰ May–Sep. Specializing in seafood chowder, fish & chips, & king crab, this restaurant gets good reviews. $$–$$$$

Cafés

🍴 **Glacial Smoothies & Espresso** 3rd Av just off Broadway; 📞 907 983 3223; ⏰ 6am–6pm Sun–Thu,

✕ **Olivia's** The Historic Skagway Inn, Broadway & 7th Av; 📞 907 983 2289, toll-free: 📞 1 888 752 4929; e reservations@skagwayinn.com; wwwskagwayinn.com; ⏰ mid-May to mid-Sep 10am–6pm daily. Light meals, sandwiches & salads, featuring produce from the hotel's vegetable garden. $$

✕ **Starfire** 4th & Spring St; 📞 907 983 3663; ⏰ 15–30 Apr 4pm–10pm daily, beginning May–1st week Oct 11am–10pm daily. Serves up tasty Thai. $$

6am–4pm Fri–Sat. Good sandwiches, bagels, cakes, ice cream & so on, plus internet access. $–$$

Kone Kompany 5th & Broadway; ☎ 907 983 3439, toll-free: ☎ 1 800 664 2370; www.konekompany.com; ⊕ Mar–Oct 10am–9pm. Great for ice cream & fudge. **$**

ENTERTAINMENT AND NIGHTLIFE It's worth noting that most of the cruise-ship passengers dissolve into the night – their ships dock here for one day only – so the summer evenings are considerably more peaceful than the days.

☞ **The Days of 98 Show with Soapy Smith** Eagles Hall, 6th Av & Broadway; ☎ summer: 907 983 2545, winter: 808 328 9132; e info@thedaysof98show.com; www.thedaysof98show.com; shows ⊕ mid-May to mid-Sep 10.30am, 12.30pm, 2.30pm & 8pm daily. Incredibly, this show has been running since 1925, when Princess Steamships first brought passengers to Skagway & the locals decided to take to the stage to raise money for their hockey team.

♀ **Red Onion Saloon** 2nd Av & Broadway; ☎ 907 983 2222; e redonion@aptalaska.net; www.redonion1898.com; ⊕ Apr–Oct from 10am daily. Established in 1898, this was once a brothel. It's now a squeaky-clean tourist bar that plays on its risqué past. There's a food menu (**$–$$**). Pizzas have names such as 'Shady Lady', sandwiches

include Strumpet Roast Beef & Turkey Trollop, & there are also wings, nachos, soups & salads. 'Madams' offer tours upstairs & relate saucy tales: take, for example, the 10 dolls that the establishment used to keep behind the bar representing its 10 working girls. When a man requested time with one of the girls, her doll was laid on its back to indicate that its corresponding number was busy.

☐ **Skagway Brewing Co** 7th Av & Broadway; ☎ 907 983 2739; www.skagwaybrewing.com; ⊕ summer: from 10am, winter: from 4pm. Specializes in local & guest beers, plus there's a decent menu featuring salmon, halibut, sandwiches & salads (**$$–$$$**). The brewing company has been running since 1897.

SHOPPING Skagway's main streets are quite literally lined with shops to tempt in the summer tourists, selling clothing, jewellery, arts and crafts, souvenirs and pretty much anything else that can be squeezed onto a cruise ship at the end of a day's shore excursion. Those listed below are a few practical stores that stand apart.

Skaguay News Depot & Books 264 Broadway; ☎ 907 983 3354; www.skaguaybooks.com. Books, maps, magazines & newspapers.

Outdoors gear

The Mountain Shop 355 4th Av; ☎ 907 983 2544; e packer@aptalaska.net; www.packerexpeditions.com; ⊕ 9am–8pm daily. Sells backpacks, sleeping bags, tents, mountaineering &

cycling gear, & clothing, plus there's gear to rent – tents, backpacks, snowshoes & so on. **Skagway True Value Hardware** 400 Broadway; ☎ 907 983 2233. Stocks camping & fishing gear.

Groceries **Fairway Market** (*377 State St;* ☎ *907 983 3220*) sells groceries & over-the-counter medications while **You Say Tomato** (*2075 State St;* ☎ *907 983 2784*) specializes in organic food & bakery items. The **liquor store** is at 2nd Avenue and Broadway (☎ *907 983 3888*).

OTHER PRACTICALITIES

Police 79 State St; ☎ 907 983 2232
Medical Dahl Memorial Clinic; 310 11th Av; ☎ 907 983 2255; ⊕ 9am–5pm Mon, Tue, Thu, Fri, 9am–noon Wed
Post office 640 Broadway; ☎ 907 983 2330
Bank Wells Fargo Bank, 6th Av & Broadway; ☎ 907 983 2264

Internet Skagway Port of Call (2nd Av & State St; ☎ 907 983 3398) & Glacial Smoothies & Espresso (see page 124).
Laundry At Garden City RV Park & Laundromat, State St between 15th & 17th; ☎ 907 983 2378; ⊕ summer only 7am–9pm daily

6

WHAT TO SEE AND DO The **Skagway Museum & Archives** (*700 Spring St;* ✆ *907 983 2420;* e *info@skagwaymuseum.com; www.skagwaymuseum.com – website under construction at the time of writing; US$2 adults, US$1 children;* ⊕ *May–Sep 9am–5pm Mon–Fri, 10am–5pm Sat, 10am–3pm Sun*) displays historical artefacts from Tlingit times to the present day.

The **Gold Rush Cemetery** (*located about 3km, 2 miles from the docks – just follow Alaska St to the north*) is quite interesting for a brief stroll. The most famous graves are those of Soapy Smith and his nemesis Frank Reid (see page 117) but many other Klondike dreams were buried here, too.

The **White Pass and Yukon Route railway** (*231 2nd Av – cnr of Spring St; toll-free:* ✆ *1 800 343 7373;* e *info@whitepass.net; www.wpyr.com*) has a three-hour round-trip from Skagway to the White Pass summit, as well as Skagway–Carcross train/bus day trips, and other variatons. See page 71 for information on the railway's history.

Flowers may not be the first thing you think of when musing on Alaska, but Skagway has long been known for its gardens (for many years, the town held the record for America's largest dahlia). **Jewell Gardens** (*km 1.8, mile 1.1 Klondike Highway;* ✆ *907 983 2111;* e *info@jewellgardens.com; www.jewellgardens.com; adults $12, children $6, transportation from downtown $6;* ⊕ *May–Sep 9am–5pm daily*) offers guided and self-guided tours, plus a chance to try your lips at glassblowing in its dedicated studio. The **Skagway Sculpture & Flower Garden** (*Spring St between 7th & 8th;* ✆ *907 983 3311;* e *drbobwhite@gci.net; www.skagwaysculptureandflowergarden.org;* ⊕ *May–Sep 9am–5pm*) is more about the sculptures than the flowers – there are 29 bronze pieces, including a life-size grizzly, created by American artists. The gift shop stocks a variety of paintings.

Hiking The big one is the **Chilkoot**: its 52km (32 miles) take most people three or four days – see pages 233–9. There are plenty of shorter trails around Skagway, however. The **SEAtrails website** (*www.seatrails.org*) gives details of 75 hiking, biking and canoe/kayak trails and routes from 19 southeast Alaska communities, including Skagway. Skagway options include the 16km (10-mile) round-trip **Denver Glacier Trail**, which starts a few miles along the railway tracks; and the easier 8km (5-mile) **Lower Lake**, 9.7km (6-mile) **Upper Dewey Lake** and 13km (8-mile) **Devil's Punchbowl trails** (the trailhead for all three is just behind the White Pass and Yukon Route terminus – walk to the end of 2nd Avenue and then 150m (165yds) north – that's to say away from the docks). There's also the **Yakutania Point/Smuggler's Cove Trail**, which starts on the far side of the Taiya Inlet bridge (with your back to the docks, facing downtown Skagway, turn left to walk along Terminal Way and across the parking lot and you'll find it). If you're not close to a computer, just ask at the visitor centre for directions.

SKAGWAY TO CARCROSS

The **South Klondike Highway**, which leads north from Skagway, is a sensationally pretty road that climbs high into the hills where alpine lakes litter the landscape, and then drops down into the Yukon amid impressive panoramas.

Note that the mile and kilometre markers given below are the distances from Skagway.

KM II, MILE 7: US CUSTOMS AND INTERNATIONAL BORDER (✆ *immigration: 907 983 3144, customs: 907 983 2325;* ⊕ *24hrs daily year round*) Everyone entering the US from Canada must present their passport or other accepted ID and visa if required. Note that from June 2009 US citizens re-entering the United States by air, land or sea must present either a passport or NEXUS card.

KM 37, MILE 23: CANADA BORDER SERVICES AT FRASER (☎ *867 667 3943;* ⊕ *1 Apr–31 Oct 24hrs, 1 Nov–31 Mar 8am–midnight*) All those entering Canada from the US must present required documentation; note that you can't cross during the night in winter, and that Yukon time is one hour ahead of Alaska time.

KM 44, MILE 27: LOG CABIN This is where the Chilkoot's cut-off trail meets the highway. See page 234.

KM 47, MILE 29: YUKON SUSPENSION BRIDGE (☎ *604 628 5660;* ⒠ *info@ yukonsuspensionbridge.com; www.yukonsuspensionbridge.com; $18.50 adults, $17 seniors, $13 children up to age 12;* ⊕ *beginning May–end Sep 9am–5pm daily*) To me it seems a bit odd to build a bridge just so you can charge tourists to walk across but I dare say some people like it; apparently the views are good. There's a three-dimensional interpretive map you can wander round as well, plus a café.

TUTSHI LAKE The lake lies to the east of this part of the highway. It's good for lake trout and grayling – but remember, you are in BC, and so must have a BC fishing licence if you're to take any.

KM 80, MILE 50: BC–YUKON BORDER There's a pullout here: look to the mountains to the west and you may see Dall sheep and mountain goats.

CARCROSS *(km 105, mile 65)*

Established in 1899 as a maintenance station and connection point for the White Pass and Yukon Route railway, Carcross was at first called Caribou Crossing, as this was the spot where the local caribou herd crossed the narrows of the lakes. In 1904, however, the name was changed to Carcross at the behest of Bishop Bompas, who headed up the Anglican mission here: he requested the change because there were various Canadian towns called Caribou Crossing, and his mail kept going astray.

Carcross and Tagish both fall within Whitehorse's commuter belt – plenty of people who prefer the rural life drive into work from here – but Carcross's position as the northernmost stop of the White Pass and Yukon Route railway turns it into a tourist hub in the summer. Carcross has a population of around 450; about half of those belong to the Carcross/Tagish First Nation.

GETTING THERE Carcross is 71km (44 miles) south of Whitehorse on the South Klondike Highway.

By bus Greyhound Canada (*2191 Second Av;* ☎ *867 667 2223; www.greyhound.ca;* ⊕ *9am–5pm Mon–Fri*) offers a limited schedule of drop-offs and pick-ups at Carcross, though there is no ticket office or facilities. Tickets range from $4 one-way if bought 21 days in advance, to $10.70 for a fully flexible fare.

TOURIST INFORMATION There's a good government **visitor centre** at Carcross (*Old Train Depot;* ☎ *867 821 4331;* ⒠ *vic.carcross@gov.yk.ca;* ⊕ *mid-May to mid-Sep 8am–8pm daily, 2nd week of May & 3rd week of Sep 10am–6pm daily*) Leaflets include a walking tour of Carcross's historic buildings and information on the traditional culture and heritage of the Carcross/Tagish First Nation.

⌂ WHERE TO STAY

⌂ **Fox Hollow B&B** (1 room) Cnr of Fox & Tagish Sts; ☎ 867 821 3369; ⒠ foxhollowbb@yahoo.com; www.yukonalaska.com/foxhollow; ⊕ mid-May to mid-Sep. Basic accommodation (there's cold running

water only & to take a shower you have to walk 2 blocks to the Montana RV Park) this nonetheless has a convenient location & a good price. $$
⚊ Montana Services & RV Park (25 sites) ✆ 867 821 3708; e rvpark@montanarvpark.ca; www.montanarvpark.ca. RV sites have electricity, &

there's a sewage dump. Other features include laundry facilities, internet & mountain bike hire, plus a general store & restaurant. $
⚊ Carcross Territorial Campground (12 sites) Government campground; see page 35.

SHOPPING **Matthew Watson General Store** (✆ summer: 867 821 3501, winter: 250 860 1293; e mattwat@shaw.ca – winter only; ⏲ 15 May–30 Sep) is the oldest operating store in the Yukon. It's a surprisingly funky little place selling souvenirs and general paraphernalia. The **Carcross Barracks** (✆ 867 821 4372; e barracks@klondiker.com; www.carcrossbarracks.com) was constructed in 1920 as a private house by Johnny Williams, a foreman on the White Pass and Yukon Route railway. Williams used local logs but, as the gold-rush stampeders had cut down all the large trees to build their boats some years earlier, he had to use small ones. The building later became an RCMP barracks. Now it's a shop selling locally created jewellery, arts and crafts.

OTHER PRACTICALITIES The Carcross **RCMP** is on ✆ 867 821 5555 and the **health centre** is on ✆ 867 821 4444.

WHAT TO SEE AND DO The main attraction of Carcross is that it's a terminus for the **White Pass and Yukon Route railway**; you can ride the train to Skagway and back from here. There's a cairn to mark the place where the crew building the railway from the south met the crew coming from the north; see page 71. There are also a couple of pretty wooden churches, plus the remains of the sternwheeler *SS Tutshi*, which used to carry tourists and miners to Atlin in the first half of the 20th century; it was a historic site until it burned down in 1990. The shore of Lake Bennett is sandy and good for sunbathing and swimming in fine weather.

TAGISH AND THE TAGISH ROAD

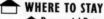

⌂ WHERE TO STAY

⌂ **Dunroamin' Retreat** (1 cabin, sleeps up to 4) Crag Lake, 14km, 9 miles from Carcross on the Tagish Rd, or 40km, 25 miles from Jake's Corner; ✆ 867 821 3492; e relax@dunroaminretreat.com; www.dunroaminretreat.com. An arts-&-crafts based wellness retreat. Workshops include photography, journal making & writing, & glassworks, & last from half a day, plus there's hiking, snowshoeing & the rest. B&B $$$

⌂ **Tagish Cabins B&B & Tours** (2 cabins, each sleep up to 4, plus campground for tents) Lot 1065 Tagish Estates, ✆ 867 399 3040, toll-free: ✆ 1 866 660 4629; e info@tagish-cabins.com; www.tagish-cabins.com. Each cabin has 2 bedrooms, kitchen with propane stove & fridge-freezer, living room with wood stove, porch & barbecue; there's a separate shower house & bathroom. Fishing, canoe & kayak tours & rentals also available. Cabins $$, tent sites $

Tagish Stores, Café, Motel & RV Park (5 motel rooms, 8 RV sites with power) Km 22, mile 14 Tagish Rd; ✆ 867 399 3032; e kurt.gantner@ yukontagishstores.com; www.yukontagishstores.com. Downtown Tagish is all tied up in one neat establishment. Not only is this the motel & RV park, it's also the village's general store, restaurant & post office (*official post office hrs are Mon, Wed & Fri afternoons, but at other times just ask at the store,* ⊕ *9am–6pm Wed–Mon, closed Tue*), plus they rent mountain bikes & snowmobiles. Motel rooms $$, RV sites $

WHAT TO SEE AND DO

Tagish Bridge Recreation Site (*Km 21, mile 13 Tagish Rd*) Tagish Bridge is a popular fishing spot, and also a good place from which to watch and photograph migrating swans in spring and fall – hundreds of swans sometimes gather here.

FROM CARCROSS TO THE ALASKA HIGHWAY

KM 107, MILE 66: CARCROSS DESERT They say this is the world's smallest desert, though real desert buffs will tell you that it's not a desert at all, but merely a series of sand dunes that once formed the bed of a glacial lake. Whatever they are, they seem a little quirky amid the lush surroundings of the Yukon's southern lakes. They are popular with local ATV and snowboard enthusiasts.

KM 109, MILE 68: CARIBOU CROSSING TRADING POST (✆ *867 821 4055;* e *marilyn@ cariboucrossing.ca; www.cariboucrossing.ca;* ⊕ *May–Sep 9am–4.30pm daily*) This is a very touristy conglomeration comprising a large gift shop, gold-panning, husky cart rides (you may get to meet the puppies), mini-golf, and a small 'wildlife museum'. There's also a Caribou Café selling soups, sandwiches, ice cream and bakery items, and a chicken barbecue (predominantly for large groups) from 11.30am to 1.30pm – you need to book ahead for the barbecue. **Tlingit Tours** (✆ *867 821 4113;* e *andycorinne@northwestel.net; www.atvyukon.ca*) operates ATV trips out of Caribou Crossing.

KM 115, MILE 72: SPIRIT LAKE WILDERNESS RESORT (✆ *867 821 4337, toll-free:* ✆ *1 866 739 8566;* e *info@spiritlakeyukon.com; www.spiritlakeyukon.com;* ⊕ *May–Sep 9am–4.30pm daily*) Rather more directly on the highway than the photos on its website and brochures suggest, Spirit Lake offers horseback riding (hour, half-day and full-day tours), guided fishing, and occasional themed vacations. Accommodation is in a 'log-style motel' with electricity and en-suite bathroom

TAGISH ELVIS

Gilbert Nelles grew up in Whitehorse and was working as a chef until, one day, he was struck by beams of light from a passing UFO. In a moment, Gilbert the chef disappeared and his body became inhabited instead by a reincarnation of The King.

Nelles changed his name legally to Elvis Aaron Presley, and became known as 'Tagish Elvis' as he gave a number of impromptu concerts in locations about the town. He released two albums *Elvis Presley Still Living* (1996) and *Elvis Presley Armageddon Angel* (2003). In 2003, local filmmaker Adam Green released a 45-minute documentary, *The Elvis Project: A Yukon Road Documentary*, which tells Tagish Elvis's story and follows him and his band, the Armageddon Angels, on tour round the Yukon communities of Ross River, Mayo, Dawson City, Carmacks and Whitehorse.

Tagish Elvis now lives in Ross River, but sticks with the Tagish moniker. In 2005, he ran for the leadership of the Yukon Liberal Party. He came in fourth place, with five votes.

($$$), cabins with no power or water but use of communal shower house ($$), slightly cheaper cottage rooms ($$), and RV and tenting ($).

KM 117, MILE 73: EMERALD LAKE You don't really need a guidebook writer to point this out. When you see the colour of this lake, you'll pull over and grab your camera whether I recommend it or not. But I can, perhaps, add depth to your photography session by telling you that the colour is created by sunlight reflecting off a white layer of 'marl' – a calcium carbonate clay formed when dissolving limestone reacts with calcium in the water – on the lake bed.

KM 140, MILE 87: ANNIE LAKE ROAD Annie Lake Road is the centre of the **Hamlet of Mount Lorne**, which stretches from just south of the junction of the Alaska and Klondike Highways to south of Bear Creek; it covers an area of 245km² (94.5 square miles) and has a population of just under 400.

The **Annie Lake Golf Club** (*km 3, mile 1.8 Annie Lake Rd, contact Lorne Mountain Community Centre, km 1 Annie Lake Rd;* ↘ *867 667 7083;* e *lmca@ northwestel.net; http://mountlorne.yk.net/golf.html; $2 – you just drop your money in the box;* ☺ *May–Sep 24hrs daily*) has wonderful views to compensate the rather rough terrain on which its 18 holes sit. The Lorne Mountain Community Centre also maintains 12km (8 miles) of **ski trails** in winter. You should drop $2 in the donation box at the trailhead. Ask at the Community Centre for more information. Plus the **Carbon Hill Sled Dog Race** (30-mile and 10-mile dogsled race, 30-mile and 6-mile skijor, and kids' races) is run by the Community Centre each February.

Wheaton River Wilderness Retreat (*1 guest cabin; Annie Lake Rd;* ↘ *867 332 3456 or 867 668 2997;* e *info@wheatonriver.net; www.wheatonriver.net; $$$*) has a rustic location with good hiking, skiing and snowshoeing opportunities, and both Annie Lake and the Upper Wheaton River close by for paddling enthusiasts. The cabin has a propane stove, kerosene lamps, and a wood stove. 'Facilities' are of the outhouse kind.

KM 142, MILE 88: ROBINSON ROADHOUSE Robinson was a flag station of the White Pass and Yukon Route railway. In 1906 a mini gold rush stampeded to the Wheaton River district, just west of here: 500 claims were staked in just three months, and Robinson was surveyed as a potential townsite. But then the boom fizzled out, and Robinson remained a one-roadhouse wonder.

KM 146, MILE 90: MOUNT LORNE AURORA B&B AND CABIN RENTALS (*3 rooms;* ↘ *867 456 2729;* e *klondikesunsnow@yahoo.ca; www.yukonrecreation.com; $$*) Bed and breakfast, ATV tours, canoe rentals and RV rentals in summer; aurora and activity packages in winter. Close to Annie Lake Golf Course and Kookatsoon Lake.

KM 152, MILE 94: KOOKATSOON LAKE RECREATION SITE The lake has a sandy shore and the water is often warm enough for swimming. There are picnic tables and firepits, too.

HAINES

Haines is a friendly town with a spectacular location: it's perched beneath glacier-covered mountains on the upper arm of the Lynn Canal. Its population, at 2,500, is larger by far than Skagway's yet, as an endless stream of cruise ships doesn't park at the end of its main street each summer, it retains a more laid-back feel. It's an excellent spot for wildlife viewing and outdoors activities – and also attracts an artistic contingent whose work enlivens galleries and shops across town.

HAINES HIGHWAY OR HAINES ROAD?

It's the same thing. Alaskans seem to prefer the word highway, while the Canadians appear to opt for road. I've, rather inconsistently, used 'Highway' in street addresses referring to Haines, as that is how the locals do it, and 'Road' in the Kluane chapter of this guidebook for the very same reason.

HISTORY The first settlers here were the Chilkat Tlingits: the natural abundance of the area meant that they didn't need to spend all their time hunting and fishing, and so they developed sophisticated crafts and wood-carving traditions, and a trade network that stretched far to the north. The first Russian ship arrived in the mid-1700s following the discovery of furs in the area by Bering's crew in 1741; soon a fur trade was established between Russians and Tlingits. Jack Dalton came in 1892 and created his Dalton Trail toll road from one of the traditional trading routes. This became the Haines Highway during World War II. See pages 101–2.

Fort William H Seward was built in 1902 as a result of an ongoing border dispute between the USA and Canada – it was the first permanent army post in Alaska. The fort was decommissioned in 1947, and bought by a group of war veterans who wanted to establish a creative community here; still today Fort Seward is home to art galleries, restaurants and hotels.

GETTING THERE

By road Haines is 235km (146 miles) from Haines Junction in the Yukon, down the Haines Highway. It takes 3–3½ hours to drive (or 5 hours from Whitehorse if you put your foot down and don't stop) – and is yet another stunningly scenic route that hugs the Kluane Wildlife Sanctuary, Tatshenshini–Alsek Park, and Alaska Chilkat Bald Eagle Preseve. The circular route Skagway–Whitehorse–Haines Junction–Haines–Skagway is a popular road trip, sometimes called the 'Golden Circle'. Note that the Haines–Skagway section has to be 'driven' by ferry.

If you travel to or from Haines by road, you will need to cross the international border, which lies 65km (40 miles) north of the town, and present a passport or other accepted ID. From June 2009 US citizens re-entering the United States by air, land or sea must present either a passport or NEXUS card.

By air Wings of Alaska (*1 Airport Rd;* ✆ *907 766 2030;* e *info@wingsofwlaska.com; www.wingsofalaska.com*) runs a daily scheduled service connecting Haines to Juneau (US$109 one-way). **Air Excursions** (✆ *907 697 2375, toll-free:* ✆ *1 800 3542479;* e *airex@ptialaska.net; www.airexcursions.com*) also operates the Juneau–Haines route (US$105).

By sea Haines is an easy hop across the water from Skagway on the **Alaska Marine Highway** (for details see pages 120–1) but the schedule may not be to your liking – ferries tend to leave at 7am or in the early evening and don't go every day. The **Haines–Skagway Fast Ferry** (see page 121) is more convenient, but is for foot passengers only. It operates from the pier on Beach Road.

GETTING AROUND

Vehicle rentals Avis has a desk at the **Hotel Halsingland**, see page 134. **Eagle's Nest Motel, Lynn View Lodge, Beach Roadhouse** and **Captain's Choice Motel** also offer rentals, see *Where to stay*, pages 134–6.

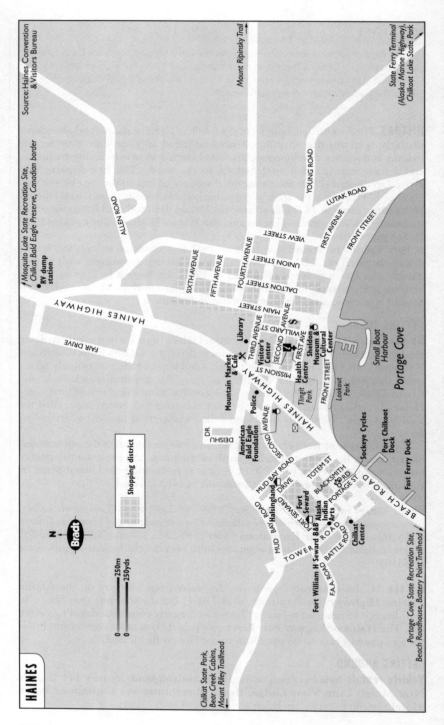

HAINES

Source: Haines Convention & Visitors Bureau

Mosquito Lake State Recreation Site,
Chilkat Bald Eagle Preserve, Canadian border
RV dump station

ALLEN ROAD

HAINES HIGHWAY

FAIR DRIVE

SIXTH AVENUE

FIFTH AVENUE

FOURTH AVENUE

UNION STREET

VIEW STREET

DALTON STREET

FIRST AVENUE

LUTAK ROAD

YOUNG ROAD

FRONT STREET

Mount Ripinsky Trail

State Ferry Terminal
(Alaska Marine Highway),
Chilkoot Lake State Park

Library

Visitor's Center

Mountain Market & Café

THIRD AVENUE

SECOND AVENUE

WILLARD ST

MISSION ST

MAIN STREET

Health Centre

FIRST AVE

Sheldon Museum & Cultural Centre

FRONT STREET

Small Boat Harbour

Portage Cove

Lookout Park

Police

American Bald Eagle Foundation

DEISHU DR

HAINES HIGHWAY

SECOND AVENUE

Tlingit Park

Sockeye Cycles

Port Chilkoot Dock

Fast Ferry Dock

MUD BAY ROAD

Halsingland DRIVE

MUD BAY ROAD

TOWER ROAD

FORT SEWARD ROAD

TOTEM ST

BLACKSMITH ST

PORTAGE ST

BEACH ROAD

Fort Seward

Alaska Indian Arts

Fort William H Seward B&B

F.A.A. ROAD

BATTLE ROAD

Chilkat Center

Chilkat State Park,
Bear Creek Cabins,
Mount Riley Trailhead

Portage Cove State Recreation Site,
Beach Roadhouse, Battery Point Trailhead

Shopping district

N

Bradt

250m
250yds
0

132

Bicycles **Sockeye Cycle** (*24 Portage St in Fort Seward, half a block uphill from the Port Chilkoot Cruise Ship Dock;* ☎ *907 766 2869, toll-free:* ☎ *877 292 4154;* e *sockeye@ cyclealaska.com; www.cyclealaska.com; office* ⊕ *year round, bicycle mechanic & rentals available Apr–Sep Mon–Sat*) offers bicycle rentals, repairs and tours.

Fly-ins and flightseeing **Mountain Flying Service** (*132 Second Av S,* ☎ *907 766 3007, toll-free:* ☎ *1 800 954 8747;* e *mtnfly@yahoo.com; www.flyglacierbay.com*) and **Fly Drake** (☎ *907 314 0675;* e *drake@flydrake.com; www.flydrake.com*) offer charter flights including flightseeing and climbing/ski transport.

TOURIST INFORMATION

🛈 **Haines Visitor Center** 122 Second Av; ☎ 907 766 2234, toll-free: ☎ 1 800 458 3579; e hcvb@haines.ak.us; www.haines.ak.us; ⊕ summer: 8am–6pm Mon–Fri, 9am–5pm Sat–Sun, winter: 8am–5pm Mon–Fri. The visitor centre publishes a useful vacation planner with extensive listings; you can pick up a hard copy or download the electronic version from its website. 🛈 **State Parks Ranger Station** 259 Main St, Room 25; ☎ 907 766 2292

TOUR OPERATORS

Alaska Fjordlines Toll-free: ☎ 1 800 320 0146; e info@alaskafjordlines.com; www.alaskafjordlines.com. Day cruise from Haines to Juneau; includes sightseeing bus tour of Juneau & lunch.

Alaska Heli-Skiing & Alaska Guide School ☎ 907 767 5745; e seadog@alaskaheliskiing.com; www.alaskaheliskiing.com. Backcountry skiing & snowboarding plus courses in avalanche, crevasse & helicopter rescue, & wilderness first aid.

Alaska Mountain Guides & Climbing School ☎ 907 766 3396, toll-free: ☎ 1 800 766 3396; e info@ alaskamountainguides.com; www.alaskamountainguides.com. Tours & courses in mountaineering, rock climbing, ice climbing, sea kayaking, back-country skiing, helicopter skiing & snowboarding, wilderness leadership courses...the list goes on.

Alaska Nature Tours 109 Second Av; ☎ 907 766 2876; e antops@mac.com; www.alaskanaturetours.net. Together with sister company **Alaska Backcountry Outfitter** (*210 Main St*), Alaska Nature Tours offers wildlife viewing, guided hikes, cross-country skiing & equipment, & clothing rentals & sales.

Chilkat Lake Tours 1069 Haines Hwy; ☎ 907 766 3779; e chilkoottours@aptalaska.net; www.alaskaeagletours.com. Fishing & wildlife watching from Eagle's Nest Motel owners, see page 134.

Chilkat River Adventures 842 Main St; ☎ 907 766 2050, toll-free: ☎ 1 800 478 9827; e riveradventures@aptalaska.net; www.jetboatalaska.com. Jetboat tours in the Bald Eagle Preserve.

ALASKA CHILKAT BALD EAGLE PRESERVE

The preserve was created in 1982 to protect the world's largest concentration of bald eagles. It covers 195km² (48,000 acres) just to the north of Haines, and is the year-round home of 200–400 birds. During the fall congregation, from October to February, more than 3,000 eagles gather here. For those who don't want to venture far from their vehicles, km 30–40 (miles 19–25) of the Haines Highway are great for spotting bald eagles; pullouts from the road have been constructed at those points where the view is best. For more information on the Alaska Chilkat Bald Eagle Preserve, ask at the **American Bald Eagle Foundation** (*113 Haines Hwy;* ☎ *907 766 3094;* e *info@baldeagles.org; www.baldeagles.org;* ⊕ *daily in summer & by appointment in winter*), which houses a museum dedicated to bald eagles and provides practical information on viewing birds in the preserve.

Each November, the Bald Eagle Foundation hosts the **Alaska Bald Eagle Festival** (*www.baldeaglefestival.org*). Activities include workshops, wildlife presentations, guided eagle viewing in the preserve, art and photography.

Driftwood Charters ☎ 907 766 3810; e driftwood@aptalaka.net. Salmon & halibut fishing, wildlife & photography tours.

Eagle Preserve Floats 170 Sawmill Rd; ☎ 907 766 2491; e raftalaska@chilkatguides.com; www.raftalaska.com. Day & multi-day rafting trips.

The Expedition Broker 219 Main St; ☎ 907 766 3977/209 1320, toll-free: ☎ 1 877 406 1320; e travel@expeditionbroker.com; www.expeditionbroker.com. Does what it says on the tin — it's an agency that sells paddling, fishing, skiing, climbing & so on expeditions in southeast Alaska & beyond.

First Out, Last In Yacht Adventures Km 5, mile 3 Haines Hwy; ☎ 907 766 2854, toll-free: ☎ 1 877 881 2854, cell: 907 314 0854; e loomis@ aptalaska.net; www.firstoutlastin.com. 5- to 8-day liveaboard cruises featuring whale watching, glaciers & fishing.

Glacier Valley Adventures ☎ 907 767 5522/766 2334; e glaciervalley@aptalaska.net; www.glaciervalleyadventures.net. Gold mine camp on a wilderness river offers adventure packages including raft trips, glacier hikes & gold prospecting. Fly or boat in only — daily departures from Haines & Skagway in summer. Accommodation available in rustic cabins.

Hart's Fishing Charters ☎ 907 766 2683; e footloose@aptalaska.net;

www.hartsalaskafishing.com. Half- & full-day halibut- & salmon-fishing trips.

Keet Gooshi Tours 32 Helms Loop; ☎ 907 766 2168, toll-free: ☎ 1 877 776 2168; e info@ keetgooshi.com; www.keetgooshi.com. Tour of Tlingit village of Klukwan, in the Bald Eagle Preserve.

Rainbow Glacier Adventures ☎ 907 766 3576; e joeorga@hotmail.com; www.joeordonez.com. Wildlife watching, kayaking, biking, hiking, van, boat & flightseeing trips.

Sheltered Harbor Shuttle & Tours (see A Sheltered Harbor B&B for contact details, page 135) Runs Haines tours of 1½ to 3hrs.

Sockeye Cycle (See page 133) Operates bike tours.

Southeast Alaska Backcountry Adventures 10 Inlet Dr; ☎ 907 314 0445, toll-free: ☎ 1 877 617 3418; e skiseaba@gmail.com; www.skiseaba.com. Guided heliskiing & snow cat skiing in winter, plus fishing in summer.

Takshanuk Mountain Trail Km 11, mile 7 Lutak Rd; ☎ 907 766 3179, cell: 540 230 2304; e takshanuktrail2@yahoo.com; www.takshanuktrail.com. Drive your own 'Kawasaki mule' along a scenic trail. Tours last 3hrs beginning 9am, 1pm & 4pm.

Travel Connection 115 Second Av; ☎ 907 766 2681, toll-free: ☎ 1 800 572 8006; e randa@ alaska4you.com; www.alaska4you.com. Customized tours in the Haines area & across Alaska.

WHERE TO STAY
Hotels and motels

Captain's Choice Motel (39 rooms) 108 Second Av; ☎ 907 766 3111, toll-free: ☎ 1 800 478 2345; e capchoice@usa.net; www.capchoice.com. Downtown location; tours & car rentals also offered. $$$

Eagle's Nest Motel (13 rooms) Km 1.6, mile 1 Haines Hwy; ☎ 907 766 2891, toll-free: ☎ 1 800 354 6009; e eaglesnest@aptalaska.net; www.alaskaeagletours.com. Also offers car rentals. $$$

Thunderbird Motel (20 rooms) 216 Dalton St; ☎ 907 766 2131, toll-free: ☎ 1 800 327 2556; e mbr@thunderbird-motel.com; www.thunderbird-motel.com. $$$

Fort Seward Lodge (10 rooms) 39 Mud Bay Rd; ☎ 907 766 2009, toll-free: ☎ 1 877 617 3418;

e fortseward@gmail.com; www.ftsewardlodge.com; ⏰ Feb–Oct. Free Wi-Fi. Also runs a backcountry skiing operation in winter. $$–$$$

Hotel Halsingland (50 rooms) 13 Fort Seward Dr; ☎ 907 766 2000, toll-free: ☎ 1 800 542 6363; e reservations@hotelhalsingland.com; www.hotelhalsingland.com; ⏰ mid-Apr to mid-Oct plus the week of the Eagle Festival. A pleasant historical building in Fort Seward with full dining service & the rest. $$–$$$

Mountain View (9 rooms) 57 Mud Bay Rd — cnr of Second Av; ☎ 907 766 2900, toll-free: ☎ 1 800 478 2902; e lodgings@mtviewinn.net; www.mtviewinn.net. Free Wi-Fi. $$–$$$

Bed and breakfasts

Bear Lodge B&B (4 rooms) Km 14, mile 8.7 Lutak Rd; ☎ May–Sep: 907 766 2436, year round: 812 371 5507; e hainesbearlodge@hotmail.com; www.bearlodgebb.com; ⏰ May to mid-Sep. Custom built as a guest lodge in 2004, Bear Lodge

overlooks the north end of the Inside Passage. Eagles & bears are commonly seen. It's 14km (9 miles) from downtown Haines, & 5km (3 miles) from the ferry terminal. $$$$

⌂ **Tanani Bay B&B** (1 room) 46 Dolphin St; ☏ 907 766 3750; ℮ tananibay@aptalaska.net; www.tananibaybnb.com. $$$$

⌂ **Fort William H Seward B&B** (7 rooms) House 1 Fort Seward Dr; ☏ 907 766 2856, toll-free: ☏ 1 800 615 6676; ℮ fortseward@yahoo.com; www.fortsewardalaska.com; ⏲ Easter to mid-Oct. $$$–$$$$

⌂ **Lynn View Lodge and Cabins** (3 bedrooms, 2 cabins) Km 5.6, mile 3.5 Lutak Rd; ☏ 907 766 3713; ℮ info@lynnviewlodge.com; www.lynnviewlodge.com. Also rents cars. $$$–$$$$

⌂ **A Sheltered Harbor B&B** (5 rooms) 57 Beach Rd; ☏ summer: 907 766 2741, winter: 616 780 1128/269 367 4561; ℮ asheltered@yahoo.com; www.sheltered-harbor.com. $$$

⌂ **Chilkat Eagle B&B Inn** (4 rooms) 67 Soap Suds Alley; ☏ 907 766 2763; ℮ dave@eagle-bb.com; www.eagle-bb.com. Located within Fort Seward National Historic Landmark, the B&B also offers van tours & kayak rental & tours. $$$

Apartments, lodges and cabins

⌂ **Alaska Eagle View Lodge** (4 rooms) Km 41, mile 25.5 Haines Hwy; ☏ 907 766 2855; ℮ miles1@starband.net; www.eagleviewalaska.com. Log house in the heart of the Chilkat Bald Eagle preserve, a 30min drive from Haines. Guests rent the whole house for a minimum of 3 nights. $$$$–$$$$$

⌂ **Fort Seward Condos** (4 rooms) 4 Fort Seward Dr; ☏ 907 766 2708; fscondos@aptalaska.net; www.fortsewardcondos.com. 1- & 2-bedroom fully furnished suites. $$$$

⌂ **Raven's Ridge** (1 room) 1 Ridge Rd; ☏ 907 336 1575, cell: 775 750 1619; ℮ dgeasan@gmail.com. Secluded location 5mins' south of Haines with views of Lynn Canal, Rainbow Glacier & the Chilkat Range. $$$$

⌂ **River House** (2 rooms) 84 River Rd; ☏ 907 766 3849; ℮ info@riverhousehaines.com; www.riverhousehaines.com. Independent cottage at the mouth of the Chilkat River – can rent upper & lower units separately or together. $$$–$$$$

⌂ **Mountain Greenery Chalet** (2 rooms, sleeps 6 with sofa bed) Km 44, mile 27 Haines Hwy; ☏ May–Nov: 907 767 5476, Dec–Apr: 941 371 3221; ℮ mountaingreenerychalet@yahoo.com; www.mountaingreenerychalet.com; ⏲ Apr–Nov. Newly built chalet with full kitchen, wood stove & modern heating within the Tongass National Forest & the National Bald Eagle Preserve. The chalet is let as a whole; you can't just book 1 room. $$$–$$$$

⌂ **Summer Inn B&B** (5 rooms) 117 Second Av; ☏ 907 766 2970; ℮ innkeeper@summerinnbnb.com; www.summerinnbnb.com. Attractive historical house with downtown location. $$$

⌂ **K J Tucker's Farm B&B** (3 rooms plus 1 private cabin) Km 42, mile 26 Haines Hwy; ☏ 907 767 5490; ℮ kjtuckers@gmail.com; www.kjtuckers.com. Peaceful retreat located on 14ha (35 acres) overlooking Klehini River. $$–$$$$$

⌂ **Alaska Guardhouse** (3 rooms) ☏ 907 766 2566, toll-free: ☏ 1 866 290 7445; ℮ info@alaskaguardhouse.com; www.alaskaguardhouse.com. Historical house located in Fort Seward, 1 block from the waterfront & a 10min walk from downtown. $$–$$$

⌂ **A Quiet Place B&B** (2 rooms) 116 Bear Trail Lane; ☏ 907 766 2695/303 7244; ℮ gdhess@aptalaska.net. Located 1.6km (1 mile) out of town. $$

⌂ **Beach Roadhouse** (2 cabins & 4 rooms) Located 1.6km (1 mile) along Beach Rd at Battery Point trailhead; ☏ 907 766 3060, toll-free: ☏ 1 866 736 3060; ℮ frontdesk@beachroadhouse.com; www.beachroadhouse.com; ⏲ Feb to mid-Nov. Also has an SUV for rent. $$$–$$$$

⌂ **Bear Den Suite** (1 room) 8½ Main St; ☏ Apr–Oct: 907 766 2117, Nov–Mar: 520 289 6198/883 3122; ℮ alaskabearden@hotmail.com; www.alaskabearden.com. Located by Haines Marina, this 1-bedroom apt (sleeps 4 with fold-out couch) is part of a complex including a gift shop & restaurant. It has Wi-Fi & all modern amenities. 2 nights minimum stay. $$$

⌂ **Cherry House** (1 room) Located in Fort Seward between Portage St & Soap Suds Alley; ☏ 907 766 3440; ℮ thecherryhouse@yahoo.com; www.thecherryhouse.com. $$$

⌂ **Su Casa** (studio apt) Lentnikof Estates, Lot 14, View Point Rd; ☏ summer: 907 766 3143, winter: 760 446 4483; ℮ sucasa@majorproduction.net; www.majorproduction.net/lentnikof/sucasa. Located 10km (6 miles) south of town. 2 nights minimum. $$$

⌂ **The Attic** (2 rooms) 115B Second Av S; ☏ 907 766 2681; ℮ randa@alaska4you.com; www.theatticinhaines.com. 2nd-floor apt with private deck & downtown location. $$$–$$$$

⌂ **Bear Creek Cabins** Km 2.5, mile 1.5, Small Tracts Rd; ☏ 907 766 2259; ℮ bearcreekcabin@yahoo.com;

www.bearcreekcabinsalaska.com; ☀ summer only. Backpackers' hostel 1.6km (1 mile) from downtown Haines near the Mt Riley & Mt Ripinski trailheads. Has dorms, family cabins & private cabins. Shared bathroom & kitchen facilities. $

Campgrounds and RV parks

🏕 **Chilkat State Park** (32 pull-through sites, 3 tent sites) 13km (8 miles) south of Haines on Mud Bay Rd; ☀ mid-May to mid-Sep. There's a log cabin interpretive centre, plus fishing, hiking & glacier views. $

🏕 **Chilkoot State Park** (32 sites) 16km (10 miles) north of Haines off Lutak Rd; ☀ mid-May to mid-Sep. Lake views, fishing & boat launch. $

🏕 **Haines Hitch-Up RV Park** (92 sites) Intersection of Haines Hwy & Main St; ☎ 907 766 2882; e info@hitchuprv.com; www.hitchuprv.com; ☀ mid-May to mid-Sep. Amenities include 50 amp sites, cable TV, wireless internet, laundry, showers, gift shop, tour info & ticket sales. $

🏕 **Mosquito Lake State Recreation Site** (7 sites) Km 44, mile 27 Haines Hwy (turn off onto Mosquito Lake Rd) $

🏕 **Oceanside RV Park** 14 Front St – cnr of Main St; ☎ 907 766 2437; e greatview@oceansiderv.com; www.oceansiderv.com; ☀ year round. Downtown waterfront location with full hook-ups & amenities. $

🏕 **Port Chilkoot Camper Park** 13 Fort Seward Dr; ☎ 907 766 2000, toll-free: ☎ 1 800 542 6363; e reservations@hotelhalsingland.com; www.hotelhalsingland.com; ☀ summer only. Managed by Hotel Halsingland, there are RV hook-ups & tenting, showers & laundry, & views over the Lynn Canal. $

🏕 **Portage Cove State Recreation Site** Located 1.6km (1 mile) south of Haines on Beach Rd; ☀ mid-May to 1 Sep. Tent camping for backpackers & cyclists only; no overnight parking. $

✗ WHERE TO EAT

✗ **Fort Seward Lodge** 39 Mud Bay Rd; ☎ 907 766 2009, toll-free: ☎ 1 800 478 7772; e fortseward@gmail.com; www.ftsewardlodge.com. Steak & seafood, burgers & wings, & fresh crab in season (mid-Jun to mid-Aug). $$–$$$$

✗ **The Lighthouse** 101 Front St; ☎ 907 766 2442; ☀ summer: 6am–11pm daily, winter: 11am–2pm, 4pm–8pm daily. A wide-ranging menu from pancakes & eggs for breakfast to burgers, pita sandwiches, pasta, steaks, halibut & salmon later in the day, all dished up with fantastic waterfront views. $$–$$$

✗ **Fireweed Restaurant** Bldg 37 Blacksmith Rd, Fort Seward, ☎ 907 766 3838; ☀ May–Aug 11.30am–3pm & 4.30pm–9pm Wed–Sat, Apr & Sep dinner only. This popular restaurant is tiny, so be prepared for a squeeze. It serves up pizza, pasta, fish & salads. $$

✗ **Mountain Market & Café** 151 Third Av; ☎ 907 766 3340; e mountain_market@yahoo.com. Sandwiches, wraps, baked goods, & so on. $

SHOPPING Haines has around 20 galleries and gift shops selling local artists' work from paintings to pottery to jewellery and carvings. Ask at the visitor centre for a shopping brochure. Look out especially for **Alaska Indian Arts** (*13 Fort Seward Dr;* ☎ *907 766 2160;* e *mail@alaskaindianarts.com; www.alaskaindianarts.com*) for carving and silkscreen prints – you can even order your own totem pole.

OTHER PRACTICALITIES

First National Bank Alaska 23 Main St; ☎ 907 766 6100

Police 215 Haines Hwy; ☎ 907 766 2121

Health Centre 131 First Av N; ☎ 907 766 6300

Post office 55 Haines Hwy, between Second Av & Mud Bay Rd; ☎ 907 766 2930

There's free **internet access** at **Haines Borough Public Library** (*111 Third Av;* ☎ *907 766 2545;* e *haineslibrary@aptalaska.net; www.haineslibrary.org*).

WHAT TO SEE The main cultural draw is the **Sheldon Museum & Cultural Center** (*11 Main St;* ☎ *907 766 2366;* e *museumdirector@aptalaska.net; www.sheldonmuseum.org; adults $3, children aged 12 & under free;* ☀ *summer: 10am–5pm*

Mon–Fri, 1pm–4pm Sat–Sun, winter: 1pm–4pm Mon–Sat, closed Sun), which houses artifacts and displays relating to the area's people and history. Also try the **Chilkat Dancers Storytelling Theater** (*Fort Seward Parade Grounds;* ☏ *907 766 2540; www.tresham.com/show*). The **Tsirku Canning Company Museum** (*Fifth & Main St;* ☏ *907 766 3474;* e *tsirku@cannerytour.com; www.cannerytour.com; adults $10, children aged 12 & under free;* ☉ *mid-May to mid-Sep, tours last 1hr & times vary so call for the current schedule*) demonstrates the operation of a restored 1920s' salmon canning line. Rather more quirky is the **Hammer Museum** (*108 Main St;* ☏ *907 766 2374;* e *hammermuseum@aptalaska.net; www.hammermuseum.org; adults $3, children aged 12 & under free;* ☉ *summer only 10am–5pm Mon–Fri*) which has collected more than 1,500 hammers (well, haven't you?).

For wildlife enthusiasts, there's the **American Bald Eagle Foundation Museum** (see page 133) and **Kroschel Films Wildlife Center** (*km 3, mile 1.8 Mosquito Lake Rd;* ☏ *907 767 5464;* e *kroschelfilms@aptalaska.net; www.kroschelfilms.com*) which runs 1½-hour tours (*$30, children aged 5 & under free; call ahead for times*) during which you'll see 15 species of wildlife including grizzly bear, moose lynx, fox, wolverine and porcupine. Pick up a copy of the *Haines Wildlife Viewing Guide* from the visitor centre, or download it from www.haines.ak.us/hainesweb/tripplanning/viewingguide.pdf. Bird watchers should also grab a copy of *Birds of the Chilkat Valley: A Checklist* (*www.haines.ak.us/hainesweb/tripplanning/birds.pdf*).

Golfers can play nine holes at the **Valley of the Eagles Golf Links & Driving Range** (*km 2, mile 1.5 Haines Hwy;* ☏ *907 766 2401 or 907 314 0760;* e *snjones@ aptalaska.net; www.hainesgolf.com; $20 per round with discounts for multiple rounds, $30 day pass, equipment rental available;* ☉ *summer only 3am–10pm*). Look out for bear and moose tracks as you putt.

For **short walks**, take a stroll around the docks at the small boat harbour, or around the historic area of Fort Seward – the visitor centre has a Fort Seward walking tour brochure. Haines is a haven for hikers in summer, and for skiers in winter. Pick up a copy of the *Haines is for Hikers* brochure from the visitor centre. **Seduction Point Hiking Trail** runs over beach and through the forest, and rewards walkers with views of the Davidson Glacier. It's a 22km (14-mile) round trip. Other popular hikes include **Mount Ripinsky** and **Mount Riley**.

ATLIN AND THE ATLIN ROAD

About half of the Atlin Road is in the Yukon; it starts just south of the Tagish Road intersection at Jake's Corner on the Alaska Highway and heads south, crossing the Yukon–BC border before finishing up in the spectacular little town of Atlin (population: 450), which attracts writers and artists alongside outdoors enthusiasts. Almost the entire road follows the shore of Tagish and Atlin Lakes making for – dare I say it? – yet another remarkably scenic drive.

TOURIST INFORMATION The **Atlin Historical Museum and Visitor Information Centre** (*Third St & Trainor Av;* ☏ *250 651 7522; museum $2.50 adults, $2 seniors, $1 children;* ☉ *May–early Sep 10am–1pm, 2pm–5pm daily*) is a good source of information. The Atlin Historical Society, which runs the museum and information kiosk, also offers a walking tour of the town (by donation and by appointment). It includes the *MV Tarahne*, a partially restored lake steamer that was in operation from 1916 to 1936.

TOUR OPERATORS

Gary Hill Lake Trout Fishing ☏ 250 651 7553; e info@gary-hill.com; www.gary-hill.com/lake-trout-guide. Fishing on Atlin Lake.

Klondike Heliskiing ☏ summer: 604 932 5327, winter: 250 651 2200/7546; e heliski@tirol.com; www.atlinheliski.com. Gives its clients 45 heli-ski runs (from a choice of around 300), plus basic room & board for roughly $7,000 per week.

Sidka Tours 12km (7.5 miles) south on Warm Bay Rd (just above the glacier lookout); ☎ 250 651 7691; e sidkatours@atlin.net; www.glacierviewcabins.ca. Evening wildlife viewing by canoe – the tour lasts about 4hrs, 6pm–10pm, & includes a campfire BBQ. All ages welcome & no previous canoeing experience required. $50 pp includes canoe, guide & BBQ. Also rents canoes ($25 per day) & sea kayaks (sgl $35, dbl $49 per day).

🏠 WHERE TO STAY

🏠 **Brooklands Wilderness Camp** (3 cabins) ☎ 250 651 7716; e gpiwowar@northwestel.net; www.piwoweb.com/brooklan/index.htm; ⊕ late May–Oct. Lakeside cabin rentals from a family that's lived in the area since 1912. Cabins come with full housekeeping; you just need to bring your food. There's no road access – they'll collect you by boat. Each cabin sleeps 3, & comes complete with a fishing boat. $$$$$ (inc boat & fuel)

🏠 **Brewery Bay Chalet** (8 suites) McBride Bd; ☎ 250 651 0040; e thechalet@ brewerybay.infosathse.com; www.brewerybay.infosathse.com. 2-bedroom suites with sitting rooms & kitchenettes have downtown location overlooking Atlin Lake. Wireless internet $5 per day. $$$

🏠 **Glacier View Cabins** (3 cabins) 12km (7.5 miles) south on Warm Bay Rd (just above the glacier lookout); ☎ 250 651 7691; sidkatours@atlin.net; www.glacierviewcabins.ca. Run by the same people as Sidka Tours (see above), there's 1 large & 2 small log cabins; all are located on a hill overlooking Atlin Lake & the Juneau Icefield. The large cabin has 2 bedrooms each with queen-size bed, full kitchen, dining/living room, bathroom & large balcony with propane BBQ, plus big 2nd-floor room with armchairs, DVD, TV & a further single bed (additional foamies are provided for larger groups) & a balcony with a view. Small cabins have 1 bedroom with queen-size bed plus kitchen/living room, & either a cot or bunk, so both can sleep 3. The small cabins share a shower house. $$–$$$

🏠 **Moore House B&B** (2 rooms plus a sitting room with sofa bed) 69 Monarch Mountain Rd, 4km (2½ miles) south of Atlin; ☎ 250 651 0015, toll-free: ☎ 1 877 399 2665; e info@discoveratlin.com; www.discoveratlin.com. An attractive log house situated amid private woodlands. Shared bathroom; wireless internet. $$–$$$

🏠 **Little Atlin Lodge** (2 cabins, 1 sleeps 6, the other sleeps 5) Km 6, mile 4, Atlin Rd; ☎ 867 399 7777, cell: 867 332 1677; e yukon@ littleatlinlodge.com; www.littleatlinlodge.com. Wilderness lodge just south of the Alaska Highway & an hour's drive from Whitehorse. Each cabin has complete kitchen & bathroom with electricity & running water. Activities include hiking, canoeing, fishing, ice fishing, snowshoeing & cross-country skiing. Horseback riding, rafting, heliskiing, dog mushing & snowmobiling can be arranged. $$

🏠 **Minto View Cabins** (2 cabins) Km 62, mile 38 Atlin Rd – 30km (18 miles) north of Atlin; ☎ 250 651 2253/250 483 3733; e mintoview@hughes.net; www.atlinmintoviewcabins.com; ⊕ 1 May–end Sep. 1 cabin sleeps 4–6 with kitchen & shower, the other sleeps 2 & has basic amenities. Walking & photography tours are also available. $–$$

Campgrounds **Snafu Lake** (*4 sites, km 26, mile 16 Atlin Rd*) and **Tarfu Lake** (*4 sites, km 32.6, mile 20 Atlin Rd*) are both Yukon government campgrounds, see page 35. **Norseman Adventures RV Park** (*20 sites; First St;* ☎ *250 651 7535;* ⊕ *summer only;* $) has RV sites with power, showers, laundry and so on – plus mind-boggling lake views.

The following campgrounds around Atlin have no power or water, and are free of charge: **Pine Creek Campground** (*Warm Bay Rd*); **Palmer Lake Campground** (*20km, 12 miles, south of Atlin on the east side of Warm Bay Rd*); **Warm Bay Campground** (*24km, 15 miles, south of Atlin on Warm Bay Rd*); **Grotto Campground** (*27km, 17 miles, south of Atlin on Warm Bay Rd*); **Surprise Lake Campground** (*17km, 11 miles, east of Atlin, across the Pine Creek bridge, along the shore of Surprise Lake*); **McDonald Lakes Campground** (*Fourth of July Rd, north of Atlin*).

✗ WHERE TO EAT
The **Pine Tree Restaurant** (*Third St & Discovery Av;* ☎ *250 651 7781;* ⊕ *11am–8pm daily;* $$) serves fish and chips, pizza and so on. Newly opened

at the time of writing is the upstairs restaurant at the **Atlin Inn** (*First St;* ✆ *250 651 7546;* ⊕ *summer only 8am–4pm daily;* **$$**). The menu includes full breakfast, plus simple lunch dishes such as burgers and chicken sandwiches, and there are wonderful lake views.

OTHER PRACTICALITIES The **RCMP** is on ✆ 250 651 7511; the **health centre** is on ✆ 250 651 7677.

WHAT TO SEE AND DO The **Atlin Historical Museum** (*Third St & Trainor Av;* ✆ *250 651 7522; $2.50 adults, $2 seniors, $1 children;* ⊕ *May–early Sep 10am–1pm, 2pm–5pm daily*) displays artefacts from the town's past. The Atlin Historical Society, which runs the museum and information kiosk, also offers a walking tour of the town (by donation and by appointment, see above). The Historical Society also owns Atlin's old courthouse, where the **Artists' Courthouse Gallery** sets up shop each summer (⊕ *Jun–Aug 11am–5pm Thu–Mon*), providing an outlet for local artists to sell direct to visitors.

Hikers, anglers and watersports enthusiasts might want to head into **Atlin Provincial Park**, which lies to the south of the town, though access is by boat or float plane only. Atlin Lake is popular for kayaking and canoeing but stay close to shore: high winds are common. Hikers embarking on multi-day trips should be self-sufficient and experienced in backcountry travel as there is no support. Go to www.env.gov.bc.ca/bcparks/explore/parkpgs/atlin/ for more information. You need to pay a fee if you're going to camp in the park – go to www.env.gov.bc.ca/bcparks/fees/fees.html. Closer to town, in winter, the **Atlin Ski Club** (✆ *Hein de Vries on 250 651 2480 or go to www.atlinskiclub.org*) maintains a few groomed trails.

The **Atlin Arts & Music Festival** (*www.atlinfestival.ca*) takes place in July each year featuring workshops, exhibitions and performances.

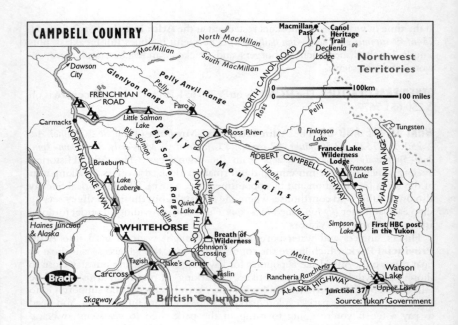

CAMPBELL COUNTRY

Macmillan Pass
Canol Heritage Trail
Dechenla Lodge
Northwest Territories

North MacMillan
South MacMillan
MacMillan
Pelly

Dawson City
Glenlyon Range
Pelly Anvil Range
NORTH CANOL ROAD
Ross
100km
100 miles

FRENCHMAN ROAD
Faro
Pelly
Finlayson Lake
Tungsten

Carmacks
Little Salmon Lake
Ross River
Frances Lake Wilderness Lodge
Frances Lake

Braeburn
Big Salmon
Pelly Mountains
ROBERT CAMPBELL HIGHWAY
NAHANNI RANGE ROAD

Lake Laberge
Big Salmon Range
SOUTH CANOL ROAD
Nisutlin
Hoole
Liard
Frances
Hyland

Haines Junction & Alaska
Teslin
Quiet Lake
Simpson Lake
First HBC post in the Yukon

WHITEHORSE
Breath of Wilderness
Johnson's Crossing

N
Tagish
Jake's Corner
Meister
Watson Lake

Bradt
Carcross
Teslin
Rancheria Rancheria
Upper Liard

Skagway
ALASKA HIGHWAY
Junction 37

British Columbia
Source: Yukon Government

7

Campbell Country

This is the great swathe of southeast Yukon, intersected by the rough Campbell Highway and the even rougher Canol Road. It's an area with little human habitation and few services – but those with an adventurous spirit and a robust set of wheels will find an extensive natural beauty almost untouched by the hand of man. For travellers from the south heading towards Dawson, or vice versa: the Campbell Highway–Klondike Highway route is marginally shorter in distance than going via Whitehorse on the Alaska Highway. It is also slower, however, as the alternative, and more popular, route is paved.

THE CAMPBELL HIGHWAY

Its full name is the Robert Campbell Highway, and it's named for the first white man to explore the Yukon (see box pages 142–3). The road is wild and wonderful; while most visitors to the Yukon don't come this way, many of those who do recall the drive as one of the highlights of their trip. To start with the route is flanked by poplar trees; then, as it climbs, travellers are rewarded with mountain panoramas. The burn areas are particularly pretty as the trees have no leaves to obscure the view and, in summer, fireweed blooms pink. The highway is known for its rich concentration of wildlife.

Personally I find it difficult to write with unreserved enthusiasm about the Campbell Highway, as the only time I've driven along it I lost control of the steering of the truck I was driving just by the Finlayson airstrip (the police thought it was simply a case of catching some soft gravel), fishtailed, overcorrected, and ended up rolling the vehicle in the ditch. I walked out of it with just a cut lip (the truck was not so lucky) but still, my memories of the drive are somewhat marred! Others have told me that they've found the Campbell Highway to be glorious, however, so please don't let my inability to keep a vehicle the right way up affect your plans.

On a practical note: although some maps and guides show a gas station in Faro, at the time of writing there is none. It burned down in September 2007 and the gas companies have, so far, been unwilling to rebuild. Agreement may one day be reached and a new gas station opened: ask the locals about the current situation. Assuming Faro still has no gas, you need to fill up at Ross River (and the service station there closes at 5.30pm or 6pm depending on the day – see page 146), as well as starting with a full tank from either Watson Lake or Carmacks. If you're going to detour up Nahanni Range Road or the Canol Road, you must carry extra gas. Be aware that both Nahanni Range Road and the Canol Road, in particular its northern section, are remote and little used. If you run into difficulties, you may have a long wait before another vehicle comes by.

Between Watson Lake and Ross River, the Campbell Highway is for the most part gravel and it is severely pot-holed in places. The majority of the stretch between Ross River and Carmacks is paved. Note that the term 'construction' does not carry the same connotations on these northern gravel roads as it does on smooth southern highways – here roadworks are piled with soft, fresh dirt which, in wet weather, can make for treacherous going.

KM 31, MILE 19: TOM CREEK WETLAND Follow a short (25m, 27yd) gravel road off the east side of the highway to a wetland area where you may see rusty blackbirds, common yellowthroats, ruby-crowned kinglets and violet-green swallows.

KM 35, MILE 22: TOM CREEK This creek is renowned for its grayling fishing.

ROBERT CAMPBELL

The man for whom the highway is named was a stalwart, strapping Scot with a yearning for adventure. In 1830, at the age of 22, he left his father and the sheep farm on which he had been raised, and sailed for Canada and employment with the Hudson's Bay Company.

Campbell's first position was as sub-manager on a farm that the Company had established in present-day Manitoba. Within a few years, however, George Simpson, the governor of the HBC's Northern and Southern Departments, had singled him out as a man with mettle, suitable to lead explorations to the west. He transferred him to the Mackenzie River District; in 1835 Campbell was put in charge of the Company's Fort Liard post in the present-day Northwest Territories (today the hamlet of Fort Liard is on the Liard Highway, and is home to around 500 people). Two years later, Campbell set out to establish a new trading post on Dease Lake (now in BC): the previous year, another Company man had been dispatched on the same mission but had retreated in terror when, allegedly, he and his men had run into the hostile Nahanni tribe. Campbell doubted his colleague's story, motivated his frightened men to venture into the territory, and was eventually able to prove to them that there had been no Indians – the original party's supplies were found where they'd dropped them and run, but they were untouched.

Over the years that followed, Campbell established cordial relations with the local tribes; he struck up a particularly strong rapport with a striking-looking Nahanni chieftainess. His relationship with Chief Trader Murdoch McPherson (for whom Fort McPherson is named, see page 201) was less amicable. Campbell viewed his countryman as a tight-fisted skinflint, and the miserly provisions that McPherson, who was in charge of the Mackenzie River District, apportioned to Campbell and his men resulted in near-starvation during consecutive winters – by the end of their first winter at the Dease Lake post, some were so emaciated that they could scarcely stand. It was only a visit from the well-supplied chieftainess that saved them.

In 1839, further instructions arrived from Governor Simpson: Campbell was to further his explorations into the country to the west, with a view to determining whether this region was suitable for a Hudson's Bay Company post. Campbell's happiness was compounded when he learnt that McPherson had taken a year's furlough, and that provisions were being dealt out by the more generous John Lee Lewes. And so, in May 1840, Campbell and his team set off up the Liard River. On 19 July, Campbell recorded in his journal that they reached 'a beautiful sheet of water which, in honour of Lady Simpson, I called Frances Lake.'

Campbell established Fort Frances on the shores of the lake. This was the first Hudson's Bay Company post in the present-day Yukon. He named the river that ran into Frances Lake the Frances River, and a lake to its east Simpson Lake (there's now a government campground there, see page 143).

KM 81, MILE 51: SIMPSON LAKE CAMPGROUND (10 sites) This government campground (see page 35) sits 1.5km (about a mile) off the highway, right on the shores of the picturesque lake, which is pleasant for swimming in warm weather. It takes about 1½ hours to drive here from Watson Lake. There's good fishing for grayling, northern pike and lake trout, and you may see nesting loons. This is good moose habitat, too.

KM 107, MILE 67: NAHANNI RANGE ROAD JUNCTION Nahanni Range Road runs 200km (125 miles) to a tungsten mine called, imaginatively enough, Tungsten, just over the border in the NWT. It's reputed to be scenically fantastic as it passes through the Logan Mountains, and there are good hiking opportunities and excellent grayling

From Frances Lake, Campbell continued his journey along the Finlayson River and Finlayson Lake, and he continued his naming spree, as well. The Finlayson River and Lake were named after Chief Factor Duncan Finlayson of the Hudson's Bay Company. From there he and his men portaged over to the Pelly River, which he christened for Sir John Henry Pelly, the London-based 'home governor' of the Hudson's Bay Company from 1822 to 1852. One of the tributaries to the Pelly, the Hoole River, he named after his colleague and interpreter Francis Hoole, an expert builder of birchbark canoes. The Lewes River was for Chief Factor Lewes; it's no longer called the Lewes, but this was once the stretch of the Yukon River between Marsh Lake and Fort Selkirk. Campbell also named the MacMillan River after Chief Factor McMillan (the spelling has changed over the years); Ross River after Chief Trader Donald Ross; and the Ketza River after Kitza, one of his most-trusted Indian hunters.

At this point Campbell was forced to turn back and to spend several years building up trade at the Frances Lake post; it wasn't until 1848 that he finally returned to the Pelly and established the post of Fort Selkirk (see page 160) – which he named for Thomas Douglas, the fifth Earl of Selkirk, who bought considerable shares in the HBC in the early 1800s in order to acquire land and create a colony for displaced Scottish crofters. The Fort Selkirk post was not a great success, however, and when in 1852 the post was ransacked by the Chilkat tribe, it was abandoned.

Chief Trader James Anderson, who took charge of the Mackenzie River District from 1851, harboured severe doubts about Campbell's business acumen and thought that the Selkirk post was unlikely ever to return sufficient profit. Faced with the closure of everything he had worked for, Campbell now embarked on perhaps the most extraordinary journey of his life. Desperate to talk in person with Governor Simpson, whom he hoped to persuade of the usefulness of Fort Selkirk, and unwilling to wait till the following spring, Campbell set out in November 1852 to snowshoe up the Mackenzie River and east to where Simpson was spending the winter near Montreal. He travelled more than 3,000 miles in a little more than three months. When he arrived, Simpson persuaded the doubtless exhausted and ranting Campbell to take a long-overdue furlough in Scotland.

Campbell's Yukon career was over – though he continued to work for the Hudson's Bay Company for a further 20 years. His belief in Fort Selkirk was finally vindicated after his death: a post was re-established there by the Hudson's Bay Company in 1938, and it continued to trade until 1950 when construction of the Klondike Highway resulted in the entire settlement moving to present-day Pelly Crossing.

Despite all the lakes and rivers that Campbell named for others, he himself wasn't so honoured until the Robert Campbell Highway, which follows the route of Campbell's early explorations along the Frances, Finlayson and Pelly Rivers, was built in 1966.

fishing in many of the creeks it crosses. Note, however, that the going is rough. The government maintains the road to km 134 (mile 83); after that its condition deteriorates further. There are no facilities or services, and passing traffic is infrequent. If you're planning to travel any distance down the road, you'll need to carry extra gas. There's a **government campsite** with ten sites at km 84 (mile 52).

KM 171, MILE 107: FRANCES LAKE CAMPGROUND (24 sites) Another pretty government campground (see page 35), about a three-hour drive from Watson Lake. Grayling, northern pike and lake trout can be fished from the lake; birders should look out for scoters, scaups and mergansers. In the summer, Martin and Andrea from Frances Lake Wilderness Lodge (below) collect their visitors from the boat ramp next to the campground.

Frances Lake Wilderness Lodge (5 cabins; owners Martin & Andrea Laternser are at Frances Lake Lodge Feb–Mar & Jun–Sep. During those times they are contactable by satellite phone ⟍ 780 628 5322 or radiophone 2M3180 on Murray channel, or the same number on McEvoy channel if Murray channel doesn't work – the best times for calling the radio phone are before 10am or after 5pm. Outside the winter & summer tourist seasons they can be reached via normal phone in Switzerland ⟍ +41 44 781 1920. Email is easier & more reliable during the tourist season, e info@franceslake.ca; www.franceslake.ca; $$$$$ inc full board, transport from boat ramp, guided excursions & unlimited use of canoes & kayaks, self-catering cabin also available, minimum stay 2 nights) In summer, the lodge is accessible by boat only; Martin fetches guests at a pre-arranged time (usually 5pm) from the boat ramp on Frances Lake, by the campground at km 171, mile 107. It's about a three-hour drive from Watson Lake. Note that while the lodge's website says that it takes seven hours to drive from Whitehorse, I think this is very optimistic, and assumes that you will make no stops at all along the way. If you're driving from Whitehorse, you'll have more fun if you take your time, and stay overnight either at Dawson Peaks on the Alaska Highway or one of the bed and breakfasts at the Watson Lake end of the Campbell Highway. Alternatively, you can fly in by float plane from Whitehorse. In winter, guests fly in by ski plane on fixed dates.

Frances Lake Lodge is by far the most delightful accommodation option in the area – indeed, it's the only reason many people come to this remote part of the Yukon. It's a supremely relaxing haven on the scenic Frances Lake, far from the world and its worries. Guests sleep in cabins that are rustic but full of character (I slept in an old A-frame that's been there since 1969). The cabins have no electricity or running water but there are wood stoves, oil lamps and flushing chemical toilets, plus an outhouse up the path. There's a shower house that guests share with water pumped up from the lake and heated, and a sauna.

Martin and Andrea bought the lodge in 2007. He is a glaciologist and she is a teacher by training; both are keen outdoors people and guide multi-day paddling (including the Liard and Dease rivers) and hiking trips from the lodge in summer; for the less energetic, there are gentle nature walks and short paddling outings. In winter there's skiing and snowshoeing; Martin and Andrea have plans to offer multi-day ski touring and cross-country ski trips – email to ask if these are in place yet. Guests eat dinner together each evening in the main lodge; there's also a lounge area in the main lodge with well-stocked bookcases that invite lazy afternoons.

KM 230, MILE 144: FINLAYSON LAKE There's a picnic area here, and interpretive boards that give information on the Finlayson caribou herd. Finlayson Lake, incidentally, lies on the Continental Divide, separating the watersheds of the Mackenzie and Yukon rivers.

KM 348, MILE 218: COFFEE LAKE This lake is popular for swimming, and is stocked with trout. It's a good picnic spot, and a great place for watching waterbirds.

KM 355, MILE 220: CANOL ROAD JUNCTION See pages 150–3 for information on the Canol Road.

ROSS RIVER Ross River (population: 337) lies 11km (7 miles) off the Campbell Highway. It is not a tourist hub; most visitors prefer to stay instead at Faro, 52km (32 miles) away. I hadn't planned on staying the night there – I had been advised it was a little rough around the edges – but following an altercation with the controls of the vehicle I was driving it was in Ross River that I found myself in search of a bed (and a policeman, and a nurse, but not all together). As is often the way when life defies one's plans, I found the warnings against Ross River to be groundless, and its people to be entirely charming and sympathetic. So I'll leave the lukewarm opinions to others: Ross River was kind to me.

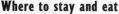

Where to stay and eat

🏠 **TND Motor Inn** (23 rooms, 11 kitchenette units) ☎ 867 969 2218. Has wireless internet. Don't expect glamorous accommodation here; however, the people are pleasant & the food in the restaurant (🕐 7am–7pm; $$) is good. The lounge is open 4pm–midnight. It may seem surprising, but the night I was in Ross River the hotel was totally booked out – if you're likely to

have to stay the night here while you wait for the gas station to open, it's a good idea to reserve your room ahead. $$–$$$

🏠 **Jackfish Lake Bed & Breakfast** (3 rooms, 2 sgl, 1 dbl) At junction of Canol Rd & Robert Campbell Hwy; ☎ 867 969 2260. Shared bathroom; guests can use deck, weights room, hot tub & internet computer. $$

DINOSAURS

Fossilized dinosaur prints were discovered at Ross River in the spring of 1999 – this was the first time evidence of dinosaurs had been found in the Yukon. Scientists subsequently located more than 200 footprints of four different kinds of animals that lived in this area 85 million years ago:

Carnosaurs were meat-eating dinosaurs that could grow to a terrifying 15m (50ft) in length. They had powerful tails to counterbalance their huge heads (complete with dagger-shaped teeth), short arms and long legs with clawed feet.

Hadrosaurs moved on all four legs and had massive beaks like a duck's. In the backs of their mouths, however, they had thousands of teeth for grinding the huge quantities of vegetable matter that they ate; this included rotting wood, whose fungi and bugs contained important nutrients. No prizes for guessing what their breath smelled like. Hadrosaurs are thought to have lived in herds; adults grew to around 10m (30ft) long.

Ornithomimus was an ostrich-like creature: it wasn't very big (a mere 4m, or 12ft, in length counting its long tail, and 2m or 7ft tall) but it was quick and cunning, and its guile allowed it to compete with heftier opponents for food.

The **Euoplocephalus** was covered in thick, spiky, armoured plates and had a horny beak. The only way to harm it was to flip it over and attack its soft belly. The euoplocephalus was vegetarian, but munched through sufficient plant matter to grow to the size of a small elephant – that's to say it was about 6m (20ft) long. Its best weapon was the 30kg (66lb) bony club at the end of its muscular tail, which it used to clobber those unfortunate dinosaurs that annoyed it.

And you thought grizzlies were scary?

Other practicalities

Ross River Service Centre (↘ *867 969 2212; ☉ 9am–noon, 1pm–6pm Mon–Fri, 9am–noon, 1pm–5.30pm Sat, Sun & holidays*) is the town's gas station; it's an important landmark as it's the only one between Watson Lake and Carmacks, and you won't make it between those two on a single tank. Obviously its hours mean that, unless you want to spend the night in Ross River (and Faro is the better option), you need to arrive here before 5.30pm or 6pm in order to fill up with fuel.

Dena General Store (↘ *867 969 2280*) is open ☉ 9.30am–5.30pm Monday–Friday and 10am–5pm Saturday to Sunday. It's closed over the holidays.

Unfortunately, I am able personally to vouch for the excellent service provided by both the **RCMP** (↘ *867 969 5555*) and the **health centre** (↘ *867 969 4444; e ross.river.hc@gov.yk.ca*) in Ross River.

What to see and do

Ross River Suspension Bridge At 182m (600ft) this footbridge is the longest suspension bridge in the Yukon. It was built in the 1940s as part of the Canol project. A 1.6km (one-mile) trail leads from the other side of the bridge to an abandoned First Nations village.

The **Ross River Drummers** are well known in the Yukon. They perform at the Ross River Cultural Exchange, which takes place in the last weekend of July call: ↘ 867 969 2279 for more information or check them out on YouTube: www.youtube.com/watch?v=aySJ6k00_Bs.

KM 365, MILE 227: LAPIE CANYON CAMPGROUND (18 sites) Government campground (see page 35) with access to pretty (if short) walking trails. The canyon is picturesque – keep an eye on the canyon walls for cliff-nesting birds, in particular ravens – and there's good trout fishing.

KM 415 + 3.5KM ON FARO ROAD (MILE 258 + 2.2): JOHNSON LAKE CAMPGROUND (15 sites) Another government campground (see page 35) with boat launch.

FARO Faro is a delightful little village (population: 375), which makes a genuine effort to welcome visitors. It lies 9km (5.5 miles) off the Campbell Highway; the junction is at km 415/mile 258. It has its own website at www.faroyukon.ca. Note that, at the time of writing, there is no gas station in the town.

History This makes a change: Faro was not named for a Hudson's Bay Company man but for the card game. I have been unable to find out why – maybe some cruel soul simply wanted to torment the ghost of the clean-living Robert Campbell. The town was first built in 1968 to support the local lead-zinc mine. It was destroyed by a forest fire the following year, however, and had to be entirely reconstructed. The mine – once the largest open lead-zinc mine in the world, a major contributor to the Yukon's economy and Faro's principal employer – closed in 1998 following decades of chequered ownership. The town's economy now relies in part on the clean-up of the old mine; additionally Faro is making a concerted effort to develop its tourism potential.

Tourist information and tour operators The excellent **Campbell Region Interpretive Centre** (*Kitza Av;* ↘ *summer: 867 994 2288, winter: 867 994 2728; e cric@faroyukon.ca; www.faroyukon.ca; ☉ Jun–Aug 8am–5pm daily, 2nd half of May & Sep 9am–5pm daily*) has friendly and knowledgeable staff and is packed full of information on Faro and its surroundings. There are also interesting interpretive displays about the mine and local wildlife. The interpretive centre hosts regular

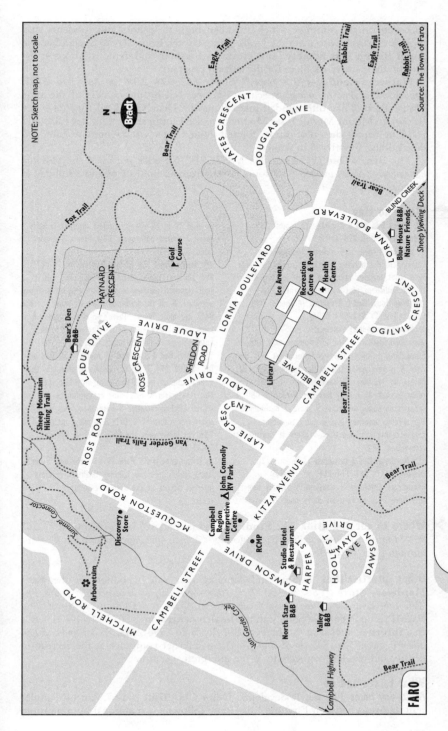

NOTE: Sketch map, not to scale.

Source: The Town of Faro

FARO

Eagle Trail

Rabbit Trail

Eagle Trail

Rabbit Trail

Bear Trail

YATES CRESCENT

DOUGLAS DRIVE

Bear Trail

Fox Trail

BLIND CREEK

LORNA BOULEVARD

Blue House B&B/
Nature Friends

Sheep Viewing Deck

Golf Course

MAYNARD CRESCENT

Ice Arena

LORNA BOULEVARD

Recreation
Centre & Pool

Health
Centre

Bear's Den
B&B

LADUE DRIVE

LADUE DRIVE

ROSE CRESCENT

SHELDON
ROAD

Library

BELLE AVE

CAMPBELL STREET

OGILVIE CRESCENT

Sheep Mountain
Hiking Trail

LADUE DRIVE

LADUE DRIVE

LAPIE CRESCENT

Bear Trail

ROSS ROAD

Van Gorder Falls Trail

Bear Trail

MCQUESTON ROAD

Campbell
Region
Interpretive
Centre

John Connolly
RV Park

KITZA AVENUE

Summer Connector

Discovery
Store

RCMP

Studio Hotel
& Restaurant

HARPER ST

HOOLE ST

MAYO AVE

DAWSON DRIVE

MITCHELL ROAD

Arboretum

CAMPBELL STREET

DAWSON DRIVE

North Star
B&B

Valley
B&B

Van Gorder Creek

Campbell Highway

Bear Trail

147

barbecues in the summer which are open both to visitors and residents, and provide a great way to meet the locals. Twice a week from May to September, the **Anvil Range Arts Society** hosts creative workshops and demonstrations at the interpretive centre; ask there for the current program.

Nature Friends (*440 Campbell St;* ✆ *867 994 2106 or 867 994 3102; naturefriends@yknet.ca; www.nfyukon.com*) is operated by the owners of the Blue House B&B. They offer guided hikes along the Dena Cho Trail (five days, see below), to Mount Mye or Rose Mountain to see Fannin sheep, plus day hikes and paddling trips – they rent canoes for self-guided trips. Cross-country skiing and dogsledding are offered in winter.

The Bear's Den (*517 Ladue Dr;* ✆ *867 994 2103;* e *the_bears_den_faro_yukon@ hotmail.com*) offers guided ATV tours lasting from an hour or two to a full day to overnight trips.

🏠 **Where to stay**

🏠 **Bear's Den Bed & Breakfast** (2 rooms) 517 Ladue Dr, ✆ 867 994 2103; e the_bears_den_faro_yukon@hotmail.com. Catering to the hunting & fishing crowd, the décor here tends towards taxidermy. Guest kitchen & shared bathroom, plus wireless internet. $$

🏠 **Blue House Bed & Breakfast** (4 rooms) 440 Campbell St; ✆ 867 994 2106; e bluehousebandb@yknet.ca; www.bluehousebandb.com; ⏰ summer only. This European-style house has wonderful views over the river & is very quiet: the owners make a point of having no TV. They do, however, have a guest living room, kitchen & laundry facilities, garden & BBQ. 1 room is en suite, the other 3 share 2 bathrooms. Has wireless internet, plus a guest computer. 3-course dinner available upon request at the time of reservation. $$

🏠 **Northstar Bed & Breakfast** (5 rooms) 130 Dawson Dr; ✆ 867 994 2243; e shaw@lincsat.com. Comfortable house with friendly owners who have lived in Faro for more than 30 years;

satellite TV in all rooms; wireless internet; laundry room; 2 shared bathrooms; BBQ, firepit & picnic table. $$

🏠 **Studio Hotel** (26 rooms) Dawson Dr; ✆ 867 994 3003; e studio_hotel@hotmail.com. This is your standard motel-style establishment; it's perfectly adequate, & all the bathrooms are en suite, but the B&Bs are more homey. There's wireless internet & some rooms have kitchenettes. The owner of the hotel also owns the Northstar B&B. $$

🏠 **Valley Bed & Breakfast** (5 rooms) 150 Dawson Dr; ✆ 867 994 2122; e valleybedandbreakfast@hotmail.com or info@faro-yt.ca; www.faro-yt.ca. This is a warm & welcoming establishment with shared kitchen facilities & bathrooms, plus sitting room with cable TV & DVD, & wireless internet. The B&B has views over the Pelly River & Tintina Trench. $$

Å **John Connolly RV Park** (9 RV hook-ups, 5 tent sites) Free showers & laundry facilities. Wireless internet access at the adjoining interpretive centre. $

✗ **Where to eat and drink** The **Studio Hotel** (see above) has a restaurant (✆ *867 994 3133;* ⏰ *7am–9pm daily;* $$) and lounge (⏰ *from 4pm daily*), which is a pleasant enough place to drink a couple of beers.

Other practicalities Fishing and camping gear can be bought at the **Faro Hardware Store** (✆ *867 994 3357;* ⏰ *10am–6pm daily or, as owner Mel Smith says, 'When the lights are on, we're open'*). There's an ATM in the Discovery Store. The **RCMP** is on ✆ *867 994 5555*, and the **health centre** on ✆ *867 994 4444*. There's free **internet access** at the library (*Bell Av;* ✆ *867 994 2684;* ⏰ *4.30pm–7.30pm Tue–Fri, noon–5pm Sat, closed Sun–Mon*), an internet computer at the recreation centre, and wireless connectivity at the interpretive centre.

What to see and do
Multi-day hikes The newly developed **Dena Cho Trail** is a 67.6km (41.7-mile) trail that runs between Faro and Ross River following a traditional hunting route

of the Kaska people. It offers spectacular views. Most people take three or four days to complete it; there are four warm-up cabins with wood stoves along the way, though hikers should carry tents to sleep in. In winter, it's possible to ski the Dena Cho Trail. The trail is still in the process of development at the time of writing, and not all signposts are installed. Ask at the Campbell Region Interpretive Centre in Faro (see pages 146–8) or the Town of Faro's office (867 994 2728; cao-faro@ faroyukon.ca) for further information.

An alternative multi-day trail leads up **Mount Mye**; this offers good opportunities to see Fannin sheep in summer. You can park in the lot on Blind Creek Road. The ascent can be made in one very long day, but the hike is better enjoyed over two or three days. Ask at the Campbell Region Interpretive Centre (see pages 146–8) for more information.

Nature Friends (see page 148) operates guided hikes on both the Dena Cho and Mount Mye trails.

Short hikes around Faro The Town of Faro has made an outstanding effort to create and mark an excellent network of hiking trails of varying lengths that will appeal to visitors. Pick up the Faro Trails leaflet at the interpretive centre; the leaflet features many more trails than those listed below.

Van Gorder Falls Trail (*Distance: 3.2km, 2 miles round trip; Trailhead: John Connolly RV park*) Download the leaflet on plants, wildlife and tracks to spot along the trail from www.environmentyukon.gov.yk.ca/pdf/vangorder.pdf or pick one up at the interpretive centre. The trail is named for Del Charles Van Gorder, who was a prospector and trapper in the area in the early 1900s.

Faro Arboretum Trail (*Distance: 1.2km, 0.75 miles loop; Trailhead: accessed from Mitchell Rd, the access rd from the Campbell Highway – the arboretum is 800m or half a mile after the turnoff to the town*) Showcases native plants and animals with interpretive panels and viewing decks. There's a trail connecting to the Van Gorder Falls Trail in summer.

Bear Trail (*Time: 3–3½hrs when combined with the Van Gorder Falls trail; Trailhead: trail runs between the Van Gorder Falls trail – a few hundred metres from the start – & Dawson Dr*) Loops around the town of Faro with good views over the Pelly River valley.

Rabbit Trail (*Distance: approx 3.5km, 2 miles; Trailhead: connects Blind Creek Road with Bear Trail & gives access onto the Dena Cho trail*) Gives good views across the Tintina Trench valley, and is a popular cross-country ski route in winter.

Wildlife viewing The broad valley of the Tintina Trench on which Faro sits is a natural corridor for wildlife. The spring and fall are particularly good times for naturalists to visit. Over a quarter of a million sandhill cranes migrate this way each year, as do tundra swans and Peregrine falcons. Chinook salmon spawn in Blind Creek in August. Pick up a copy of the leaflet *Viewing Wildlife in Faro* from the interpretive centre.

The land around Faro is also known for its Fannin sheep, a subspecies of thinhorn. There are only around 3,000 Fannin sheep in existence, and a herd of about 100 lives near the town. If you want to see the sheep in summer, you'll have to lace up your walking boots and hike up Mount Mye: they spend the months from June to October in the higher alpine area. Between November and May, however, they can be spotted from various points along Blind Creek Road. Note that this is a rough gravel road and is not recommended for RVs.

Sheep Mountain Viewing Deck Drive or walk 5.5km (3½ miles) out of Faro along Blind Creek Road to a pullout, from which a short trail leads to a viewing platform.

Mount Mye Sheep Centre This lies 2km (1.2 miles) further along Blind Creek Road from the Sheep Mountain Viewing Deck. Keep left at the fork and you'll come to a viewing cabin, which offers interpretive panels and an excellent vantage point.

Sheep Mineral Lick This is 11.5km (7 miles) along Blind Creek Road. Turn right at the fork onto Lower Blind Creek Road and, at the next junction, turn left onto an old mine road. You'll come to a trailhead and carpark. There's a pretty trail leading out of the car park and along the bottom of the bluff. You can often see Fannin sheep along the top edge of the bluff – they come here to lick minerals from the soil.

Each May, Faro hosts a **Crane and Sheep Viewing Festival**, which incorporates natural history talks and viewing tours.

Golf Faro has a nine-hole 'urban' golf course (☎ *867 994 2640; farogolfclub@hotmail.com; 9 holes cost $9, club rentals $7.50, golf cart rentals $20*), which weaves slightly strangely across the town's green spaces, and even hosts an open tournament each July.

Recreation centre and pool Faro has a 15m pool, open summer only, curling rink, open winter only, indoor ice arena, squash court and weights room (*Bell Av;* ☎ *867 994 2375;* ⊕ *generally afternoons & evenings Tue–Sat but call for current hrs*). There's also an internet computer here.

KM 420, MILE 261: FISHEYE LAKE There's a boat ramp, picnic facilities, and excellent fishing – the lake is stocked with rainbow trout and kokanee salmon. If the weather's warm – and you're feeling brave – you can swim here too. Birders: look out for diving ducks and loons.

KM 469, MILE 291: DRURY CREEK CAMPGROUND (10 sites) This government campground (see page 35) sits at the eastern end of Little Salmon Lake. There's good fishing for northern pike, grayling, lake trout and whitefish. In early summer Canada geese, Bonaparte, mew and herring gulls, lesser scaup, northern pintail and long-tailed ducks gather here.

KM 502, MILE 312: LITTLE SALMON LAKE CAMPGROUND (15 sites) Again, a government campground (see page 35) with boat launch and fishing for lake trout, grayling and northern pike. Listen for the call of the common loon.

KM 543, MILE 338: ACCESS ROAD TO FRENCHMAN LAKE, NUNATAK AND TATCHUN LAKE CAMPGROUNDS (10 sites, 10 sites, 20 sites) These three government sites (see page 35) lie 8km (5 miles), 15km (9.3 miles) and 41km (25.3 miles) along Frenchman Road respectively. Frenchman Road is a through road that joins the Klondike Highway – Tatchun Lake is nearer to the Klondike Highway junction than the Campbell – but note that after Frenchman Lake the road can get a little ropey.

THE CANOL ROAD

Let's cut to the chase: the Canol (which is short for Canadian Oil) project was not a success. It was dreamed up by the American government in the early 1940s: on 7 December 1941 the Japanese had attacked Pearl Harbor, sparking real fear of an invasion of America via its westernmost territories. The Alaska Highway was rapidly constructed in 1942 in order to supply defences on Alaska's coast (see pages 77–9).

The Canol pipeline, which would channel oil from the existing oilfields at Norman Wells in Canada's Northwest Territories to Whitehorse, was intended to provide a safe source of fuel to Alaska-bound aeroplanes, and to those of the lend-lease program, as well as to traffic on the Alaska Highway. The Canol Road was built as a tote road, to supply the pipeline that would supply the trucks and planes that would supply the Alaska defences.

The project was never meant to be easy. Take this ad that was posted in the Edmonton hiring office of Bechtel-Price-Callahan, the conglomeration of US contractors responsible for the pipeline's construction:

June 15 42

THIS IS NO PICNIC

Working and living conditions on this job are as difficult as those encountered on any construction job ever done in the United States or foreign territory. Men hired for this job will be required to work and live under the most extreme conditions imaginable. Temperature will range from 90° above zero to 70° below zero. Men will have to fight swamps, rivers, ice and cold. Mosquitos, flies, and gnats will not only be annoying but will cause bodily harm. If you are not prepared to work under these and similar conditions, DO NOT APPLY.

But, as nobody had ever built an oil pipeline through such northerly terrain before, nobody quite knew just how difficult it would be – nor that the pipeline with its surrounding roads, air strips and communications network would cost more than five times the original estimate. The bill came in at US$135 million, considered a staggering sum in the 1940s. The US Army was later accused of having squandered taxpayers' money. To make matters worse, after completion the pipeline was operational for just 11 months, from April 1944 to March 1945.

The rusting paraphernalia that remained was never properly cleared up. Even today, you can drive the Canol Road – declared a National Historic Site in 1990 – and find slowly oxidizing vehicles that pay crumbling testament to this heroic endeavour that, ultimately, failed.

PRACTICALITIES The Canol Road runs from Johnson's Crossing on the Alaska Highway (see page 90) to MacMillan Pass on the NWT border. After MacMillan pass, the route is impassable by vehicles and becomes the Canol Heritage Trail (see page 153). The road intersects the Campbell Highway at Ross River. The section north of Ross River is known as the North Canol Road (232km, 144 miles) and the section south of Ross River is the South Canol Road (230km, 142 miles). The Campbell Region Interpretive Centre in Faro (see pages 146–8) has leaflets on both the north and south sections of the road detailing points of interest along the way.

The Canol Road is unpaved throughout, and it can be very rough. There are no services along the road except at Ross River and Johnson's Crossing. While the South Canol Road should be navigable for most vehicles except large RVs, you will probably want a 4x4 vehicle for the North Canol Road; ask locals for advice on current conditions. To access the North Canol Road you'll need to take the government car ferry across the Pelly River at Ross River. It runs 8am–noon and 1pm–5pm in the summer. The Canol Road – both north and south sections – is closed in winter.

Sockeye Cycle (*381 Fifth Av, Skagway;* ☏ *907 983 2851;* e *sockeye@ cyclealaska.com; www.cyclealaska.com*) runs an 11-day guided cycle trip along the Canol Road each year, starting and finishing in Skagway, Alaska.

Campbell Country **THE CANOL ROAD**

7

SOUTH CANOL ROAD The southern section of the road runs between Johnson's Crossing on the Alaska Highway and Ross River. It's peppered with pristine lakes and rivers that make a fisherman's paradise. The section north of Quiet Lake is particularly exquisite as it follows the Rose and Lapie rivers and lakes.

Km 6.5, mile 4: Breath Of Wilderness (⟍ *403 997 3824;* e *info@ breathofwilderness.com; www.breathofwilderness.com;* $$$) Claudia Huber and Matthias Liniger have a cabin for rent; it sleeps up to four people. They also offer canoeing, hiking, mountain biking and fishing tours in summer, and snowshoeing, ice fishing, igloo building and snowmobiling in winter. Price includes use of canoes, fishing gear, mountain bikes and snowshoes, and instruction in igloo building. Guided canoeing, hiking, snowmobiling and dogsledding trips cost extra.

Km 68, mile 42: Nisutlin River Recreation Site This is an unmaintained campground, and the place to put in for the paddle to Teslin Lake (see page 90). Keep an eye out for moose, bears, beavers and bald eagles, as well as Trumpeter swans in the wetlands.

Km 77, mile 48: Quiet Lake Campground (20 sites) There are two government campgrounds (see page 35) on Quiet Lake; this is the more southerly. It's a good spot from which to embark on a wildlife safari by boat or canoe: mink, moose and coyote may be seen along the lake's shore.

Km 99, mile 61: Quiet Lake Recreation Site (10 sites) This is the more northerly of the two government campgrounds on Quiet Lake, and the spot from which canoeists put in to paddle the Big Salmon River. See pages 247–50 for a detailed route description of this trip. Salmon spawn here during August and September; look out for feeding bears.

Km 161, mile 99: Groundhog Creek There's an old mining road running along this creek. It leads to Seagull Lakes, which are reputed to offer good grayling fishing.

Km 163, mile 101: Lapie Lakes These lakes are a wonderful spot for a peaceful jaunt in a canoe. Watch out for moose grazing on the shore, as well as waterfowl and arctic terns. There's an unmaintained campground here, and a short walking trail to the Ian H Thomson Falls. Disused mining roads around the lakes make for good hiking and mountain biking. Lapie was an Iroquois Indian canoeist who travelled with Robert Campbell – but the river and lakes were named not by Campbell but by George Dawson (see page 178) when he made his geological survey of Canada in 1887.

Km 213, mile 132: Lapie River Stroll the short trail from the bridge to the small Lapie Canyon. You can sometimes see Stone sheep on the mountains to the west.

NORTH CANOL ROAD The northern section of the Canol Road is more rugged still than the south. In wet weather the road is very slippery and in places it floods. The brave will tell you that the scenery makes up for the hairy driving conditions, however. The lack of vehicles and breathtaking scenery make the North Canol an appealing route for cyclists – as long as they're equipped to be wholly self-sufficient. The road passes beneath the dramatic Itsi Range and Hess Mountains; rusting vehicles, dumped by the US Army when the Canol project failed, still lie in heaps to the side of the road and add a historical touch. Note that any crumbling bits of metal you find are protected by law as heritage artefacts.

Distances shown are from the Alaska Highway junction.

Km 324, mile 200: Dragon Lake This lake has a good reputation for plentiful jackfish, trout and grayling, plus there's an unmaintained campsite.

Km 343, mile 213: Sheldon Lake The sandy shore makes this a good spot to camp.

Km 413, mile 255: South MacMillan River This waterway is popular with intermediate whitewater paddlers.

CANOL HERITAGE TRAIL This is a beautiful but extreme hike, considered to be one of the most challenging in Canada, with dangerous river crossings and no facilities or support. It stretches 355km (219 miles) from the Yukon–Northwest Territories border through the Mackenzie Mountains to Norman Wells. It follows the former route of the Canol pipeline, and historical artefacts lie along the way. It's reckoned to take around three weeks to complete though some have done it in two.

There are various landing strips where food drops can be deposited by small planes; most hikers arrange for two or three food drops. The western sections of the trail make for good mountain biking. The trail is not recommended for winter travel. Go to www.normanwells.com/visit/canol_trail.html for more information, and contact the Norman Wells Historical Centre (*23 Mackenzie Dr; Norman Wells;* ↘ *867 587 2415*) and ask for a copy of their *Hiker's Guide to the Canol Heritage Trail*. You should tell the RCMP in either Norman Wells or Ross River about your trip plans before setting out, and report back to them when you've finished.

If that all sounds a bit much, but you'd still like to hike around the southwestern end of the trail, look into staying at **Dechenla Lodge** (↘ *867 667 2639;* e *j_barichello@hotmail.com or bgale@northwestel.net; www.dechenla.ca;* $$$$ *per day inc all meals & guided hiking/biking*) which sits at the beginning of the Canol Heritage Trail, just over the border in the Northwest Territories. I've heard great things about the lodge, which has seven guest cabins and, apparently, excellent food and outstanding views. The owners offer guided nature hikes and multi-day biking/hiking packages; the packages generally last a week. However, it's only open in July and August and tends to book up a long way in advance. If the road sounds too terrifying, you can fly in from Whitehorse ($800–900 return).

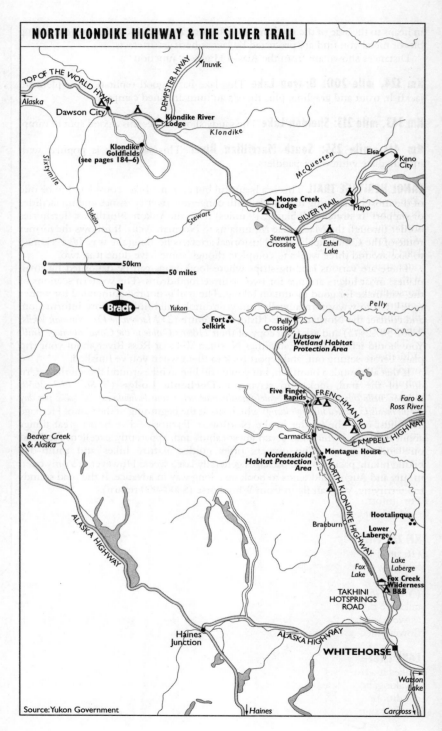

NORTH KLONDIKE HIGHWAY & THE SILVER TRAIL

TOP OF THE WORLD HWY

DEMPSTER HWY

Inuvik

Alaska

Dawson City

Klondike River Lodge

Klondike

Klondike Goldfields (see pages 184–6)

Sixtymile

Elsa

Keno City

McQuesten

Moose Creek Lodge

Stewart

SILVER TRAIL

Mayo

Yukon

Stewart Crossing

Ethel Lake

0   50km
0   50 miles

N

Bradt

Yukon

Fort Selkirk

Pelly Crossing

Pelly

Llutsaw Wetland Habitat Protection Area

Five Finger Rapids

FRENCHMAN RD

Faro & Ross River

Carmacks

CAMPBELL HIGHWAY

Nordenskiold Habitat Protection Area

Montague House

Hootalinqua

Braeburn

Lower Laberge

NORTH KLONDIKE HIGHWAY

ALASKA HIGHWAY

Fox Lake

Lake Laberge

Fox Creek Wilderness B&B

TAKHINI HOTSPRINGS ROAD

Beaver Creek & Alaska

Haines Junction

ALASKA HIGHWAY

WHITEHORSE

Watson Lake

Source: Yukon Government

Haines

Carcross

8

The North Klondike Highway and the Silver Trail

The road may date only from the 1950s, but this is an area rich with history. The North Klondike Highway takes travellers firstly from Whitehorse to Lake Laberge, immortalized by Robert Service and his poem 'The Cremation of Sam McGee' whose famous furnace is created from the remains of a derelict sternwheeler on the lake. It follows sections of the Yukon River, including the Five Finger Rapids that once struck terror into the hearts of shipping captains, and now provide tourists with a picturesque photo op. And it was this way that passengers travelled by horse-drawn sleigh on the winter Overland Trail for the first half of the 20th century. To the northeast, Mayo and Keno were once bustling mining towns. Now the mines are, for the most part, silent – but the disused mining roads create fabulous hiking and biking trails through a little-visited but spectacular landscape.

The Overland Trail and river traffic both stuttered to a halt when the Whitehorse–Mayo road was completed in 1953. The onward route to Dawson was originally a minor spur that opened two years later. Over the years the road was rebuilt, rerouted and renamed – and, as on all Yukon highways, there's some discrepancy with the mile and kilometre markers. Some residents and businesses still refer to their location by the original Mayo Road markers; others measure their position from the start of the Klondike Highway in Skagway. In this chapter, I've chosen the latter system. Given that I'm writing about the Yukon, which is full of opinionated folk, I can be sure that not everyone will agree with my choice.

WHITEHORSE TO CARMACKS

For information on the Takhini Hot Springs, Sundog Retreat, and other establishments close to the city of Whitehorse, see *Chapter 3: Whitehorse*.

KM 225, MILE 140: ACCESS ROAD TO LAKE LABERGE CAMPGROUND The campground (16 sites) is one of the Yukon's most popular. It's located 2.9km (1.8 miles) off the highway, and gets very busy with weekending Whitehorse folk in summer.

Before you come to the campground you'll pass the delightful **Mom's Bakery** (\ *867 456 4010*; e *momsbakery30@hotmail.com*), which comes complete with a talkative macaw parrot and serves up home-baked pies, cakes and cinnamon buns, as well as superlative halibut chowder and bison chilli. You can eat on the pretty, flower-filled terrace if the weather's fine.

LAKE LABERGE Lake Laberge's (pronounced La-BARGE) proximity to Whitehorse makes it a hugely popular fishing and boating retreat. Be aware when canoeing or kayaking, however, that winds can blow up on the lake without warning and render conditions treacherous. Stay close to shore at all times and come off the water at the first sign of wind.

There are a few accommodation options along the lake's shores beyond the government campground.

Where to stay

Fox Bay Retreat Km 8, mile 5 Fox Creek Rd; ☏ 867 668 4899; e info@foxbayretreat.com; www.foxbayretreat.com. Owned by Whitehorse-based Kanoe People (see page 25), the retreat consists of several rustic cabins (propane lighting, woodstove, communal washhouse & wood-heated sauna) of varying sizes. All cabin rentals include transfer to & from Whitehorse; canoes, kayaks, snowshoes & snowmobiles are available for an extra fee. Summer & winter activity packages are also offered – see website for details. Reservations must be made in advance. $$$

The Lodge at Lake Laberge (1 guest room, 1 guest cabin) Km 1.9, mile 1.2 Fossil Point Rd – between Lot 99 & Spirit of the North, Fossil Point Rd is on the left off Deep Creek Rd, just before the Lake Laberge campground; ☏ 867 633 2747; e janet@lakelaberge.ca; www.lakelaberge.ca. This comfortable lodge features extensive views & all mod cons – it's a good option if electricity & en-suite bathrooms are important to you. Evening meal available if booked 24hrs in advance. $$$

Spirit of the North (1 log cabin sleeps 2) ☏ 867 456 4339, toll-free: ☏ 1 888 633 4610; e rob.spiritnorth@yahoo.com; www.spiritnorth.yk.ca. Use of a canoe is included in the rental price. Spirit of the North also offers guided fishing trips, canoe, kayak & boat tours. $$

KM 229, MILE 142 (+ 5KM/3 MILES OF PRIVATE ROAD): FOX CREEK WILDERNESS B&B (*2 rooms;* ☏ *867 668 2220;* e *joelinda@foxcreekwild.com; www.foxcreekwild.com;* $$$) Quality bed and breakfast in a charming log building, just 52km (32 miles) from Whitehorse but with a full wilderness setting. Dinner is available if pre-booked.

KM 248, MILE 154: FOX LAKE CAMPGROUND (33 sites) Again, this is very busy on summer weekends with local fishing enthusiasts. There's room for boat and trailer parking, and there's a boat launch. See page 35 for government campground regulations.

KM 272, MILE 167: FOX LAKE BURN There's a 200m (650ft) trail here with interpretive boards about the importance of forest fires.

KM 273–340, MILE 171–212: BRAEBURN ELK HERD The herd numbers around 100 animals, which are frequently seen by highway travellers.

KM 281, MILE 175: BRAEBURN LODGE (☏ *867 456 2867;* ⏱ *7am–1am;* $–$$) For anyone with functioning taste buds, this is a must-stop. The cinnamon buns are legendary and outlandishly large (many Yukon establishments advertise their cinnamon buns but this is *the* place to buy them), and the rest of the menu – soups, burgers and so on – is excellent. The proprietor is a good ole Yukoner and a charming conversationalist. There's gas here, too.

KM 308, MILE 191: TWIN LAKES CAMPGROUND The lakes are pretty and provide a good swimming hole for hardy humans and stocked fish.

KM 320, MILE 199: NORDENSKIOLD HABITAT PROTECTION AREA These wetlands are a good spot for viewing waterfowl, and are also popular with moose, muskrat, beaver, mink and fox.

KM 322, MILE 200: MONTAGUE HOUSE Quite interesting for a quick leg stretch, Montague House was one of many roadhouses built along the Overland Trail (see *The Overland Trail*, page 157). Although the two remaining log cabins are now *sans*

In the years that followed the Klondike gold rush, people travelled between Dawson and Whitehorse by riverboat – in the summer. In the winter, however, the river was frozen and, though a few vigorous souls followed its route with their dog teams, an alternative, more accessible, form of transport was needed.

In 1902 the Yukon government contracted the White Pass and Yukon Route to build a winter road between Whitehorse and Dawson. The company was also awarded the mail contract, and used horse-drawn sleighs to ferry passengers, luggage and mail along its new 530km (330-mile) trail.

The stages travelled from 6am to 6pm; the journey took around five days and cost a hefty $125 with accommodation ($1) and meals ($1.50) on top. There were roadhouses every 30–50km (roughly 20–30 miles) and the stages stopped two or three times a day to change the horses: the company employed around 275 horses each season. The service generally ran three times a week except in March, when businesspeople were keen to travel to Dawson before river ice broke and the sternwheeler season began; then there was often a daily departure. There's a lovely description of travelling the Overland Trail – sometimes called the Dawson Trail – in Laura Berton's book *I Married the Klondike*.

A 112km (70-mile) section of the historic Overland Trail, from Tahkini Crossing near Whitehorse to Braeburn Lodge, is now maintained for hiking, horseback riding, mountain biking, ATVing, backcountry skiing and snowmobiling as part of the Trans Canada Trail (*www.tctrail.ca*).

roof and somewhat lurching, they still stand in sufficiently good order to get an idea of the set-up. The original Montague House was built on the other side of the current highway (which then, of course, did not exist) but it burned down and this replacement was constructed in 1915. The ground floor consisted of a kitchen and eating area; the bedrooms were upstairs. The inside of the building was lined with cheesecloth, partly to lighten the dark interior, and partly so that dirt couldn't fall from the logs into the rooms. The roadhouse was used until the 1950s.

CARMACKS

At the confluence of the Yukon and Nordenskiold rivers, the spot on which Carmacks (*km 357, mile 222 Klondike Highway*) now sits was traditionally a Northern Tutchone fish camp to which the southern Chilkats came to trade. In 1893 George Carmack (he who would later discover the Klondike's gold – see pages 165–6) set up a small trading post at the camp, and it became known as Carmack's Landing. The name change began as a punctuation mistake on a signpost.

Carmacks sat on the river route of the summer sternwheelers, and on the winter route of the Overland Trail. A roadhouse was built in 1903, and it became the heartbeat of this growing community until, in 1953, the road to Mayo was completed and roadhouses fell out of demand.

Today Carmacks has a population of around 400; the Little Salmon/Carmacks First Nation makes up about 70% of the population.

TOURIST INFORMATION AND TOUR OPERATORS There's a **visitor centre** in the village's old telegraph station (*109 River Rd;* ☏ *867 863 6330;* ⊕ *mid-May to 1 Sep*) plus an unstaffed visitor information point at a pull-out on the highway (*35500 North Klondike Highway*). Outside the summer season, contact the **Village of Carmacks office** (☏ *867 863 6271;* e *carmacks@northwestel.net; www.carmacks.ca*).

The North Klondike Highway and the Silver Trail **CARMACKS**

8

Canadian Wilderness Travel (*137 Guder Dr;* ☎ *867 863 5404, toll-free:* ☎ *1 877 863 5408;* e *info@canwild.com; www.canwild.com*) offers guided hiking, canoeing and northern lights viewing tours, both day and multi-day, plus canoe rentals. They also have a wilderness log cabin for rent, see below.

🏠 WHERE TO STAY AND EAT

🏠 **Hotel Carmacks** (22 rooms, 10 cabins, 15 RV sites with full hook-up) ☎ 867 863 5221; e info@hotelcarmacks.com; www.hotelcarmacks.com; ⊕ hotel open year round, cabins open summer only. The hotel rooms are clean & comfortable, & the cabins have electricity & bathroom. Wireless internet is free. The Gold Panner Restaurant is part of the Hotel Carmacks complex. Hotel rooms $$$, cabins $$, RV sites $

🏠 **Mukluk Manor B&B** (3 suites) Lot 151 Guder Dr; ☎ 867 863 5232; e ldesroches@ northwestel.net. Suites are like mini-apts with separate entrances & private bathrooms. They have satellite TV, DVD, kitchenettes & wireless internet, plus outdoor sitting area. $$$

🏠 **Canadian Wilderness Travel** (Details above) Rural log cabin for rent 4km (2.5 miles) outside Carmacks. It can sleep up to 4 people, & makes a good, quiet base for hiking, mountain biking & fishing in summer & skiing, snowshoeing & aurora viewing in winter. $$$

🏠 **The Coal Mine Campground** Km 359, mile 223 (located 1.6km, 1 mile north of Carmacks on the Klondike Highway); ☎ 867 863 6363; e coalminecampgroundcarmacks@yahoo.ca. Pleasant, privately owned campground on the banks of the Yukon River & a popular place for canoeists to put in & take out. There are showers, laundry, bicycle rentals & cabin rentals, plus a hamburger & ice cream restaurant. $

OTHER PRACTICALITIES The **Tatchun Centre, General Store & Gas Bar** (☎ *867 863 6171;* e *info@hotelcarmacks.com; www.hotelcarmacks.com;* ⊕ *summer: 7am–11pm, winter: 8am–10pm daily*) sells gas, groceries, bakery goods, hunting and fishing licences, and fishing gear.

The **RCMP** is on ☎ 867 863 5555; the **health centre** is on ☎ 867 863 4444. There's **internet access** at the library, and sometimes at the college. There is no cell phone coverage in Carmacks, nor is there a bank.

WHAT TO SEE AND DO The **Tagé Cho Hudän Interpretive Centre** (*located just north of the Yukon River bridge in Carmacks;* ☎ *867 863 5830;* e *tagechohudan@ northwestel.net; admission free;* ⊕ *mid-May to mid-Sep 9am–6pm daily & by appointment in the off-season –* ☎ *867 863 5576 ext 252*) is a great place to visit, and makes a good highway break even if you're not planning to stop long in Carmacks. It houses engaging displays featuring the Northern Tutchone people and their way of life. My favourite exhibit is the 'Lady's Walking Stick: Made to Kill Bears'. The idea was that when a lady went for a walk in the wilderness she would take with her a long, speared stick. Should a bear happen to charge, she would straddle the stick, digging one end into the ground behind her so that the speared end pointed up and forwards – as the bear lunged to maul her, it would spear itself through the chest. Hopefully.

The **Carmacks Roadhouse** (*on River Rd by the Nordenskiold River bridge*) has been restored for visitors; originally built in 1903, it once had 12 rooms and a stable block.

There are a few good **walking** options in Carmacks. A boardwalk runs along the riverfront and makes a pleasant stroll; it's wheelchair-accessible, and there are benches and a gazebo for those who want to sit and stare. There's also a short walking trail at the Tagé Cho Hudän Interpretive Centre (see above), which weaves through First Nations cultural displays. Alternatively, pick up a *Carmacks Historical Buildings Walking Tour* leaflet from one of the visitor centres to take a self-guided tour of Carmacks's historic buildings.

Coal Lake is a good swimming and picnicking destination; the trail is marked with the trailhead on the right of the Klondike Highway, just before the road crosses the Yukon River bridge as it heads north. The trail follows the riverbank then climbs to the picturesque lake. It's about 2km (1.2 miles) each way. You can also walk along the Nordenskiold ridge, where you'll see First Nations spirit houses; the ridge runs between the Yukon and Nordenskiold rivers, from the Carmacks Roadhouse to the Klondike Highway.

CARMACKS TO STEWART CROSSING

KM 358, MILE 223: CAMPBELL HIGHWAY JUNCTION See pages 141–50 for information on the Campbell Highway.

KM 380, MILE 237: FIVE FINGER RAPIDS These rapids were once notorious for dashing the hopes of prospective goldminers, and for provoking clammy night-time sweats among riverboat captains. Now the sternwheelers are no more, and the Five Finger Rapids are best-known as a tourists' photo stop. There's a pull-out from the highway, and interpretive panels explain the area's local history as well as the hair-raising role the rapids played in Yukon River travel across the years. You can walk down the long staircase and along a trail to the river – it takes about 45 minutes for the round trip.

KM 382, MILE 239 TATCHUN CREEK CAMPSITE (12 sites). See page 35.

KM 383, MILE 240: TURN-OFF TO FRENCHMAN ROAD Access to Tatchun Creek, Nanatak and Frenchman Lake government campgrounds. Frenchman Road connects to the Campbell Highway; see page 141.

KM 442, MILE 276: LLUTSAW WETLAND HABITAT PROTECTION AREA Like Nordenskiold, this small wetland area flanks the highway, on its southeastern side this time. It's an important place for duck staging and nesting.

KM 449, MILE 281: TTHE NDU LAKE Look out for American coots, geese and ducks, and, in spring and autumn, sandhill cranes that migrate overhead.

KM 458, MILE 286: MEADOW LAKE This is interesting because it is an athalassic, or salty, lake – there are several in this area.

KM 463, MILE 286: PELLY CROSSING This community of fewer than 300 is the base for the Selkirk First Nation, which moved from its traditional centre at Fort Selkirk (see *Fort Selkirk*, page 160) when the highway was built. There's a chance that Pelly Crossing might develop its ecotourism potential in the future, given its location close to well-populated wetlands and wildlife protection areas, but there's not much on offer as yet.

Big Jonathon House Heritage Centre (*next to the gas station/general store,* ✆ *867 537 3150; admission by donation;* ⊕ *mid-May to mid-Sep 9am–7pm daily*) has information on the Northern Tutchone people and their traditional lifestyle. It's briefly interesting but the Tagé Cho Hudän Interpretive Centre in Carmacks has more life about it. The original house was built by Big Jonathon at Fort Selkirk but was taken down as a mark of respect when he died. This smaller replica was later built at Pelly Crossing as a heritage centre. The **Selkirk Centre** (*6 rooms;* ✆ *867 537 3031; store & gas station* ⊕ *9am–7pm daily;* $$$) is the gas station, well-provisioned grocery store, post office, motel, bank and laundry. There's wireless internet here, free with the rooms or $6 an hour for drop-ins. There's also a **campground**, opposite the Selkirk Centre on the river, open year round and free of charge.

People inhabited the Fort Selkirk site, which sits at the confluence of the Yukon and Pelly rivers, for many thousands of years: stone tools dating back 8,000 to 10,000 years have been discovered here. The Northern Tutchone people used this flat piece of land as a base camp for hunting and fishing, and the Chilkats, a Tlingit tribe from the Alaska coast, used to travel here over their traditional trading trail. This was the same trail that Jack Dalton developed in the early 1890s (see pages 101–2), which served as an alternative to the Chilkoot Trail–Yukon River route from the coast to the interior. Today, the Haines Road follows a part of that same route.

Robert Campbell established a Hudson's Bay Company trading post at Fort Selkirk in 1848 (see pages 142–3). By trading with the Northern Tutchone people, he disrupted the Chilkat people's traditional economic activities. The Chilkat responded by ransacking the Hudson's Bay Company post and putting paid to Campbell's Yukon ambitions.

In 1892, however, Arthur Harper (see page 17) succeeded in establishing a trading post here; other stores followed including a reincarnation of the Hudson's Bay Company post in 1938. Anglican and Roman Catholic missionaries set up home at Fort Selkirk from the early 1890s; the military arrived in 1898 – they were to make sure the tens of thousands of Americans stampeding to the Klondike appreciated Canadian sovereignty – and constructed 11 log buildings together with a parade square. The soldiers were based here for less than a year but the North West Mounted Police, who also made their first appearance at Fort Selkirk in 1898, stayed longer.

Fort Selkirk grew into a flourishing, permanent community shared by the Selkirk First Nation and white settlers. But when, in the 1950s, the Klondike Highway was built, its inhabitants relocated to Pelly Crossing.

More than 30 buildings in Fort Selkirk still stand, and have been restored by the Yukon government's Heritage Branch and the Selkirk First Nation. The settlement is inaccessible by road but is a requisite stop for canoeists paddling this part of the Yukon River, and is also visited by the Great River Journey boats (see page 25). At the time of writing, there are no day trips running to Fort Selkirk from any of the highway communities.

Fort Selkirk has a great campsite – free of charge – with picnic tables, a kitchen shelter, firewood, outhouses and a water pump. Sometimes First Nations guides are around to talk about their people's traditions, and to tell stories. There's also a lot of information at www.virtualmuseum.ca/Exhibitions/FortSelkirk.

Should you encounter an emergency in the Pelly Crossing area, the **RCMP** is on ☎ 867 537 5555 and the **health centre** is on ☎ 867 537 4444.

KM 523, MILE 323 + 24KM, 15 MILES ON ETHEL LAKE RD: ETHEL LAKE CAMPGROUND (12 sites) There's fishing in the lake for northern pike and lake trout. It's also popular with moose – and with those humans who make it out here, for this is a particularly beautiful spot. It's a government campground; see page 35.

KM 534, MILE 330: STEWART CROSSING There's a **visitor information** cabin on the highway, with information on the Silver Trail. It's a funny little hut with a roof that looks as though it were created by an origami master. On the other side of the road is **Whispering Willows Restaurant & RV Park** (*32 RV hook-ups with power & water plus additional space for tents*, $; ☎ *867 996 2130*; e *whispering.willows@ hotmail.com*), which has a pleasant log cabin building with a friendly owner, right next to the river. There's a licensed restaurant ($$) serving breakfast, lunch and dinner – the menu features steak sandwiches, pork chops, salads and so on – plus an outdoor terrace & free Wi-Fi. There's a gas station next door.

THE SILVER TRAIL

Oh crikey, what can I say? This is yet another stunning stretch of road. It leads to the town of Mayo which, with its population of around 400, is a positive metropolis when compared to neighbouring Keno, which has a mere 20 inhabitants.

Keno wasn't always so small, though. As the road's name suggests, it was silver mining that led to this area's development. The first silver claim was recorded near present-day Elsa in 1903, and when substantial silver deposits were struck on Keno Hill in 1919, the real rush began. By 1989, when the mine at Elsa finally closed, the area had produced over 213 million ounces of silver, 710 million pounds of lead, and 436 million pounds of zinc.

Today, some placer mining and mineral exploration continues. Additionally, a growing tourist trade caters to wilderness enthusiasts: the land around the Silver Trail is little trodden but scenically fantastic offering outstanding hiking, while its Wind, Snake and Bonnet Plume rivers are reckoned to offer some of the best paddling in all the Yukon.

Note that distances in this chapter are measured from the junction with the Klondike Highway (at km 531, mile 331).

KM 4–16, MILES 2–10 Keep an eye out for moose, especially in spring: this is a popular calving area, and has been designated a no-hunting zone.

KM 103, MILE 6: DEVIL'S ELBOW There's a nice, short walk here (750m or about 800yds) with interpretive panels. You may see moose and waterfowl. The trail starts in the parking area south of the road.

KM 51, MILE 32: MAYO Mayo (km 51, mile 32) is a pleasant little place laid out on a nice, simple grid. The First Nation of Na-Cho Nyak Dun make up 60% to 70% of the community.

Tourist information and support

7 Binet House Interpretive Centre 304 Second Av, Mayo — cnr of Centre St; ☎ summer: 867 996 2926, off-season: 867 996 2317; e mayo@ northwestel.net; www.yukonweb.com/community/ mayo; ⊕ Jun–Aug 10am–6pm daily.

7 Black Sheep Aviation ☎ 867 668 7761; e blacksheep@northwestel.net; www.flyblacksheep.ca. Black Sheep has a satellite base in Mayo offering float plane support for hikers, canoeists & anglers.

Where to stay

⌂ **Bedrock Motel** (12 rooms plus 10 RV sites, 3 with full hook-up, 7 with electricity only) Located on the edge of town on the road to Keno; ☎ 867 996 2290; e bedrock@northwestel.net; www.bedrockmotel.com. The rooms are spacious & there's a good communal area. Has wireless internet. It's a little way out of 'downtown', though. $$$

⌂ **North Star Motel** (9 rooms) Cnr of Centre St & Fourth Av; ☎ 867 996 2231; e bs.menelon@ northwestel.net; www.kenocity.info/motel.html. This is

a delightful flower-bedecked bungalow. All rooms have a kitchen with fridge, stove, microwave & satellite TV. There's wireless internet & a licensed bar as well. $$

⋏ **Five Mile Lake Campground** (20 sites) Km 57, mile 35 Silver Trail Highway. The campground occupies a beautiful site 8km (5 miles) out of town towards Keno — the lake is truly idyllic & there are swimming platforms for real lunatics. It's a government site — see page 35. There's a walking trail round the lake; the wetland here is

Three of the Yukon's most picturesque paddling adventures – the Wind River, the Snake River, and the Bonnet Plume River – lie within this area. They're all tributaries of the Peel River, and are known for their superb scenery and wildlife-viewing opportunities. The Wind is the easiest of the three, then the Snake; for the Bonnet Plume you'll need good whitewater skills. They're not cheap trips as they all require a fly-in. Consult a specialist operator for more information; see pages 24–6.

particularly productive in early summer. You may see mule deer on the hillsides.

⚠ Gordon Park and McIntyre Park campgrounds (8 sites each) On the southern side of Mayo, they are free of charge.

Hiking Popular hikes include **Mount Haldane**: turn off the highway at km 76 (mile 47) and there's a 3.5km (2-mile) road to the trailhead. The hike to the summit – from which you'll be rewarded with amazing views assuming the weather is fine – and back usually takes around six hours. The Binet House Interpretive Centre in Mayo has a trail guide. For an easier stroll try the 3.6km (2.2-mile) **Prince of Wales Trail** – a section of the Trans Canada Trail – which starts at Binet House.

The really energetic might like to lace up their shoes for the **Mayo Midnight Marathon**, run on 21 June each year. There are also half marathons and 10km (6-mile) races. For more information contact Cheryl Klippert (↘ *867 996 2368;* e *stephron@northwestel.net*).

KM 97, MILE 60: ELSA Once a privately owned mining town, Elsa is now uninhabited apart from caretakers, and most of its buildings have been dismantled.

KM III, MILE 70: KENO CITY Forget the word 'city'. Keno is a tiny village but it makes up for its diminutive size with a big character. Placer miners rub up against newly arrived artists – Keno has recently started to attract creative types; visit for example the **Blue Roof Studio** (↘ *867 995 2892;* e *insa@polarcom.com*) for handmade jewellery, photographs, cards and so on – and one or two old-timers who've been here so long they probably couldn't move if they wanted to. The surrounding countryside is known not only for its rich mineral deposits but for its fabulous hiking – disued mining roads make great trails. For visitors, it's a real off-the-beaten-track destination in a region that's hardly on the global main road. It's a lovely place just to kick back and commune with nature for a few days. A word of warning though: bring your own groceries. There's no store in Keno. Oh yes, and the road, which is paved from the Klondike Highway, turns to gravel between Mayo and Keno. It's generally well-maintained but can be rougher than a grizzly bear's breath after bad weather.

The main non-wilderness attraction is the genuinely interesting **Keno City Mining Museum** (↘ *867 995 3103;* e *yvonne@northwestel.net; www.kenocity.info/ museum.htm; adults $3.50, seniors $2.50, children under 12 free;* ⊕ *Jun–end Aug 10am–6pm daily*). The **Corp & Ryan Snackbar** is also here. Next to the museum is the **Keno City Alpine Interpretive Centre & Hiking Information**. One of Keno's most popular walks is up Keno Hill (a good spot for seeing some of the Yukon's 90 butterfly species) to the signpost that indicates the distance from Keno to Helsinki, Haifa and about 20 destinations more.

Where to stay

🏠 **Keno Cabins B&B** (2 cabins each sleeping up to 4 people) It's the first house on the left as you come into the village; ☎ 867 995 2892; e insa@ polarcom.com; www.kenocity.info/cabins.htm. Each comfortable cabin has fridge, electric or propane stove, & TV. I cabin has indoor plumbing, the other uses an outhouse & water barrel. Showers are available in Keno Community Club's washhouse across the street. $$–$$$

⚔ **Keno City Campground** (12 sites) By Lightning Creek; ☎ 867 995 3103; e yvonne@ northwestel.net. There's a gazebo with woodstove, firewood & water. $

STEWART CROSSING TO DAWSON

KM 559, MILE 335: MOOSE CREEK LODGE (*3 cabins;* ☎ *867 996 2550;* ☉ *May–Sep;* $$) A lovely spot just over the road from the Moose Creek campground (below) with rustic cabins – they have propane lamps and no running water but there's a shower house. No internet. There's also an atmospheric little souvenir shop (T-shirts, books, handpainted gold pans, etc) and café/restaurant (**$–$$**) in the main log building. It's a good place for a coffee-and-cake break, or for a more substantial meal, even if you don't want to stop for the night.

KM 559, MILE 345: MOOSE CREEK CAMPGROUND (36 sites) Government campground, see page 35. There's a 2.5km (1.5-mile) interpretive loop trail to Stewart River.

KM 655, MILE 409: TINTINA TRENCH VIEWPOINT This an important corridor for migrating birds.

KM 675, MILE 416: DEMPSTER CORNER This is the junction with the Dempster Highway, see pages 191–202. The **Klondike River Lodge** (*10 rooms, 10 RV sites with full hook-up, 27 RV sites with power & water;* ☎ *867 993 6892; rooms* $$, *RV sites* $) is right on the corner. The rooms are all twins with single beds. Internet access is via a guest computer in the lounge. There's nothing the matter with the lodge – it's a perfectly good place to spend the night if you're in a hurry to hoon up the Dempster, and the people are friendly – but you'll find accommodation options with greater character and more exciting surroundings in Dawson, 40km (25 miles) along the road. There's also gas plus a licensed mechanic here as well as tyres and repairs, a restaurant and a shop (☉ *summer 6am–10pm, call for winter hrs*).

KM 697, MILE 430: KLONDIKE RIVER CAMPGROUND (38 sites) Government campground. Yet another pleasant wooded site, of the kind the government campgrounds favour. There's a 1.7km (1-mile) interpretive trail loop.

For information on the Klondike Highway from here to Dawson City, see *Chapter 9: Dawson City*.

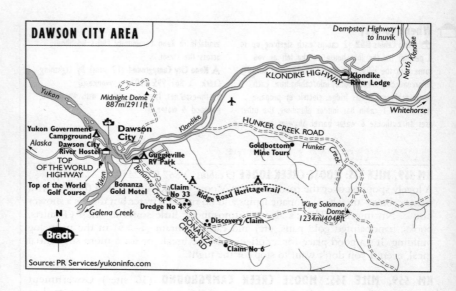

DAWSON CITY AREA

Dempster Highway ↑
to Inuvik

North Klondike

KLONDIKE HIGHWAY

Klondike
River Lodge

Whitehorse

Yukon

Midnight Dome
887m/2911ft

Klondike

HUNKER CREEK ROAD

Hunker Creek

Yukon Government
Campground
Alaska
Dawson City
River Hostel
TOP
OF THE WORLD
HIGHWAY
Top of the World
Golf Course

Dawson
City

Guggieville
RV Park

Goldbottom
Mine Tours

Bonanza
Gold Motel

Claim
No 33

Ridge Road HeritageTrail

King Solomon
Dome
1234m/4048ft

Dredge No 4

Galena Creek

Discovery Claim

N

Bradt

Claim No 6

Source: PR Services/yukoninfo.com

9

Dawson City

It could so easily be awful. This town that sprung up in a swampy moose pasture to house the stampeders to the Klondike gold rush seems at first glance to be a one-story wonder, and to cling to the past. It still has wooden boardwalks instead of pavements. The houses are all low-rise weatherboard, built in the traditional style. The names of the restaurants and businesses claw onto Dawson's fleeting days of fame – there's a Klondike Kate's restaurant, a Jack London Grill, and a Diamond Tooth Gertie's dance hall. In the summer, tourists pan for gold, watch the dance girls doing their thing, and follow students with summer jobs dressed up in period costume round the buildings of the gold-rush days.

Strangely, however, Dawson has totally failed to turn itself into some kind of Klondike version of Disneyland, despite what seem to be its very best efforts. Instead, it's utterly enchanting – a remote, laid-back jewel of a village with a real Wild West, bordertown vibe. The secret of its success, I think, lies with the people that live there today. They keep Dawson not quite polished enough for a theme park: piles of junk lie stacked on those historic porches alongside heaps of moose antlers, and too many of the old buildings are boarded up, lurching and crumbling for this to feel like Klondikeworld or Goldrushland. Dawson now has fewer than 2,000 permanent residents but they're creative, resourceful people (and generally opinionated to boot). It enjoys an astonishingly full cultural calendar for a town so small, with musicians and artists flying in to perform from far and wide, plus artist and writer in residence programs.

But the real point, I think, is this: everyone living in Dawson genuinely wants to be there. You don't end up in a shrunken town a couple of hundred miles from the Arctic Circle by accident. And because of the people who've made their way here, have loved what they found, and so have stayed, Dawson is a town that thrums not just with its dazzling past but with its gloriously eccentric present.

HISTORY

One summer's day in 1896, an American named George Carmack was drying salmon on the banks of the Klondike River with his Indian wife's brothers, Skookum Jim and Tagish Charlie. Carmack wasn't much interested in gold; he lived quietly with his wife's people and the other white men looked down on him. As Carmack and his companions worked, a miner named Robert Henderson poled by in his boat. He'd staked a claim on nearby Gold Bottom Creek and he told Carmack he reckoned its prospects were good. Carmack suggested that he and his brothers-in-law might join Henderson for a little gold panning once they had the fish in.

'There's a chance for you George, but I don't want any damn Siwashes staking on that creek,' Henderson is said to have replied. And so Robert Henderson blew his fortune.

The three men finished their work with the fish and moved on to Rabbit Creek (soon to be renamed Bonanza) rather than Gold Bottom. There, on 16 August 1896, they found thick flakes of gold between the rocks – it was later described as lying like cheese in a sandwich. The following morning, they staked their claims (the Monday closest to 17 August is to this day celebrated with a public holiday in the Yukon). An unwritten miners' code dictated that they should tell Henderson what they'd found – Carmack had apparently promised to tell the other miner if he found good prospects, in any case – but, offended by his earlier remark, they didn't. Instead, Carmack travelled to Fortymile, an existing prospectors' settlement near the Alaska border, to record his and his companions' claims. On his way to the recorder's office, he strolled into Bill McPhee's saloon and told the men there of his find.

The miners in the saloon were derisive: Siwash George, as they called him, wasn't much of a prospector, and neither was he known for telling the truth. Carmack tipped his nuggets onto the counter – and in a moment, the room's atmosphere became charged with excitement. Each creek's gold is slightly different and these experienced prospectors knew they'd never seen the likes of this before. Overnight, the camp of Fortymile became a ghost town as its inhabitants propelled themselves up the Yukon River towards the Klondike. It wasn't until about three weeks later, when jubilant miners from Fortymile were crawling all over the Klondike's creeks, that three men wandered into Henderson's less profitable camp and broke to him the news from which he would never recover.

One of those that rushed to the Klondike did not have prospecting on his mind, however. Joe Ladue had climbed over the Chilkoot (see pages 233–9) in 1881 and had been in the north ever since; he'd joined forces with McQuesten, Harper and Mayo (see page 171) in their trading operation in 1883. Ten years later, the four partners had set up a new trading post at the mouth of the Sixtymile River; they'd named it Ogilvie for William Ogilvie, a government surveyor who had drawn in the boundary between Alaska and Canada and would become Commissioner of the Yukon in 1898. In addition to the trading post, Ladue had built a sawmill at Ogilvie to supply miners with wood for their sluice boxes.

When Carmack and company's discovery sparked the rush to the Klondike, Ladue realized the stampeders would need lumber for their sluice boxes as well as homes to live in, and buildings in which to base their new businesses. And so he went there, and on 28 August 1896 he staked out a townsite on the boggy, flat land at the confluence of the Klondike and Yukon rivers, which had until now been a summer fish camp of the Tr'ondëk Hwëch'in First Nation people (displaced by the miners, they were forced to move downriver to create the village of Moosehide). Ladue named his new domain Dawson City after George M Dawson, a geologist who had explored and mapped the area ten years previously (see *George Dawson and the geological survey of Canada*, page 178). He then returned to Ogilvie, loaded his sawmill and all his lumber onto a raft, and floated it downriver to Dawson.

Immediately, demand surged for Ladue's lumber: the miners needed sluice boxes. The lots of land, priced at $5 to $25 that winter, didn't sell well at first – most of the miners lived in tents. But Ladue had discovered his own streak of paydirt: at the peak of the gold rush in 1898, Front Street lots would sell for $40,000.

THE OUTSIDE RUSHES IN All through the winter of 1896–97 the miners toiled on their claims in tortuous temperatures, building fires to melt the permafrost. As the ground thawed, they dug out the gold-bearing gravel and piled it in great frozen mounds. When the weather warmed in spring, they used the running water of the creeks to sluice the pay dirt and extract their gold (see *How does a sluice box work?*, page 186). Meanwhile, the outside world knew nothing of the fortunes that were being shovelled from the ground in the Canadian sub-Arctic. The ice on the Yukon River was frozen: nobody could get out, none could come in. Government surveyor William Ogilvie did try to send messages by dogsled to his superiors in Ottawa to warn them of the furore that would soon descend but they ignored him.

Then, in mid-May 1897, the ice on the Yukon River broke. A few grizzled miners packed their nuggets and gold flakes into battered bags and boxes, headed downriver to St Michael, and from there by steamer to Seattle and San Francisco. Among them were Clarence and Ethel Berry. Clarence had been working as a bartender in Bill McPhee's Fortymile saloon that momentous evening when Carmack had sauntered in with his gold. The Berrys had rushed to the Klondike and staked a highly lucrative claim; it's said that when Ethel wanted housekeeping money, she just walked out to the yard, bashed the frozen pile of paydirt with a stick, and helped herself to a couple of nuggets. As she and her husband sailed for civilization they were dressed in rags, but carried gold worth $130,000.

The *Excelsior* docked in San Francisco on 14 July 1897. America was at the time in the grips of depression and when a weary public saw the cargo that her passengers had hauled from the Klondike, its imagination was set ablaze. By the time the *Portland*, also from St Michael, arrived in Seattle three days later, 5,000 people crowded the docks to gaze – and Klondike fever swept the city.

'GOLD! GOLD! GOLD! GOLD!' shrieked the headline of the *Seattle Post Intelligencer* on 17 July 1897. 'Sixty-Eight Rich Men on the Steamer Portland. Stacks of yellow metal.'

'All that anyone hears at present is "Klondyke,"' the *Seattle Daily Times* reported six days later. 'It is impossible to escape it. It is talked in the morning; it is discussed at lunch; it demands attention at the dinner table; it is all one hears during the interval of his after-dinner smoke; and at night one dreams about mountains of yellow metal with nuggets as big as fire plugs.'

Storekeepers closed up shop, clerks resigned their posts, policemen left their beats and teachers abandoned their classrooms. Within weeks, thousands – including a young Jack London – had left home to find their fortunes in the Klondike.

It's reckoned that around 100,000 dreamers set out for the goldfields. Most were city folk and had no idea what they were heading to. Tens of thousands turned back before they reached their journey's end; many died.

MEANWHILE, BACK IN DAWSON CITY During the winter of 1897–98, food became scarce in Dawson. The cities on the Outside (as northerners referred to everywhere else), which were making great profits by supplying stampeders with their outfits, saw their businesses threatened. Not wanting their prospective customers to be put off their journeys by the inconvenient possibility of starving to death, they took action: various American Chambers of Commerce lobbied Congress who, in December 1897, agreed to spend $200,000 on a herd of reindeer to feed the Klondike.

It's generally agreed that the reindeer relief effort was one of the stranger episodes of a very peculiar time. An American delegation travelled to Norway where they bought 539 animals that were driven to the Klondike by a team of Laplanders, Finns and Norwegians. The expedition was not a success. Herdsmen and reindeer travelled by sea to Haines, which they reached in May 1898. From there they hiked over the Dalton Trail; it took them almost nine months of overland travel to reach Dawson. Ironically, many of the reindeer starved to death on the way, deprived of the lichen that constitutes their normal diet. By 27 January 1899, when the 'Klondike Relief Expedition' limped into Dawson, just 114 animals remained. The skeletal reindeer and their brightly dressed drivers (for the Laplanders wore their traditional garb) created a small sensation but by this time, in Dawson, nobody was much surprised by anything.

In any case, by the summer of 1898 fears of starvation had passed. Dawson City and its surrounding area had a population of 40,000 (and one milk cow that arrived to rapturous welcome that July). It had electricity, running water, telephones, theatres, dance halls and the latest fashions from Paris. But Dawson was never the lawless town that some imagined it to be for it was rigorously overseen by the North West Mounted Police. Handguns were forbidden (this was Canada, after all): as Pierre Berton points out in his book *The Klondike Fever*, had there ever been a Dan McGrew and a Malemute Saloon in Dawson, as Robert Service's fictional poem relates, there could never have been a shooting as the Mounties would have confiscated the revolvers before the duel began. Superintendent Sam Steele, who had overseen the stampede's crossing of the passes from Alaska, was in charge of the police in Dawson from autumn 1898. He instigated two main punishments for miscreants: the blue ticket – which was an instruction to leave town – and hard labour at the town's woodpile.

Despite all the hullaballoo, only a few hundred people found substantial quantities of gold in the creeks of the Klondike, and just a handful managed to hold on to their wealth. By the time the masses arrived, the good claims had gone; many turned round and headed straight back home. They were rich in stories, if not in gold, and they'd had enough of adventures.

AFTER THE STAMPEDE Dawson's gold rush didn't last. Just three years after the Klondike discovery, large quantities of gold dust were found at Nome, on Alaska's Bering Strait coast. Dawson fell quiet as the stampede swarmed west: 8,000 people left in August 1899 alone, and they continued to stream down the frozen Yukon River through the winter. By 1902, fewer than 5,000 people lived in Dawson, and the numbers dwindled further as the years progressed.

Dawson was diminished, but it never died. For when the individual miners with their gold pans and sluice boxes moved on, the corporate giants with their dredges took over – and changed the Klondike's landscape forever.

Steam-powered dredges chewed their way through the creeks of the Klondike, processing sand, gravel and gold with a speed and efficiency that no miner with a sluice box could ever hope for. They left behind them tremendous tailings that still today define the landscape around the Klondike creeks. In summer their appearance suggests that an outsized mole has been tunnelling beneath the surface; in winter they look like the toothpaste squeezed from giant's tube.

There were two main players in the dredging game: Arthur Treadgold, a Briton and a direct descendant of Sir Isaac Newton, who used his famous forebear's great discovery to lucrative effect (for more on gravity's use in gold-mining, see *How does a sluice box work?*, page 186), and Joe Boyle.

THE DAWSON NUGGETS AND THE STANLEY CUP

The installation of Canadian Number 1 dredge wasn't the only audacious enterprise that Joe Boyle entered into in 1905. The same year, he challenged the Ottawa Silver Seven for the Stanley Cup. Boyle's hockey team, the Dawson Nuggets, endured an epic journey to Ottawa – it took them a month to get there travelling by dogsled, bicycle, ship and train. Delays meant that they arrived, exhausted, just the day before the game, which they lost with the most resounding defeat in the Cup's history. Dawson is still the smallest town ever to have challenged for the Stanley Cup.

Joe Boyle left the Yukon and his dredges in 1916 for the war in Europe. He was never to return – but his adventures grew bigger and bolder than ever before.

Boyle was a man of action, and it was frustrating for him that, at the age of 49, he was deemed too old to fight. He was, however, made an honorary lieutenant colonel in recognition of his contribution to the war effort in the form of his machine-gun battery. He had a serge uniform tailored, which he wore doggedly despite official displeasure. On each lapel, he pinned a Canadian maple leaf fashioned from glittering Klondike gold.

Boyle was desperate to be allowed to do something useful and, thanks to his social connections, he was eventually dispatched to Russia to sort out the country's chaotic railways. Boyle spoke no Russian and knew little of railways; he was, however, very good at getting things done. When fighting prevented food from leaving St Petersburg for Moscow, and the people were starving as a result, Boyle was charged with fixing the problem. He solved it in three days: he simply pushed those empty trains that were creating a bottleneck over the edge of the embankments.

His most famous escapades, though, took place in Romania. He saved a contingent of high-profile Romanian prisoners from near-certain execution by valiantly boarding their ship, and bribing, bluffing and engaging his own men to overcome the Bolshevik guards. And he fell passionately in love with Romania's queen. It's not known whether their mutual love was consummated (though it seems likely), but this was the one true and lasting relationship of Boyle's life. Sadly for him, Queen Marie decided that she was unable to commit and Boyle died a broken man in 1923, in Middlesex, England, at the age of 56.

Treadgold came to the Yukon in 1898 as a newspaper correspondent. He was a small, wiry, superior man. As the stampeders moved west to Alaska or just went home, Treadgold began to consolidate their abandoned claims. In 1901 the Canadian government granted him a concession to a large chunk of the Klondike goldfields, including timber and water rights. The locals howled but Treadgold continued to chase his dream and secured financial backing from the Guggenheim family under the auspices of the Yukon Gold Company.

Joe Boyle was a very different character. Big in both heart and body, he was an open-handed, breathtakingly ambitious man. He'd been in Victoria with his boxing partner, Frank Slavin (they had embarked on an exhibition tour), when he heard of the Klondike strike and was already on the White Pass in July 1897 when the news was just breaking in the rest of the world. For a few short months Boyle laboured with shovel and sluice box, but he had grander visions. And so, while the thousands were still teeming towards Dawson, Boyle went the other way – towards Ottawa where in 1900 the government granted him an eight-mile (13km) hydraulic concession.

In 1904 he established the Canadian Klondyke Mining Company, and built his first dredge, Canadian Number 1, the following year. It cost $200,000 to construct, and paid for itself in 60 days. Boyle went on to build three more dredges, each larger and more ridiculously ambitious than the last, and all powered by huge, snaking electricity cables (Dredge Number 4 can be toured in the summer, see page 186). Boyle had his naysayers, but even they soon had to admit that the gold was pouring through his giant, mechanized sluice boxes, and landing tidily in his coffers. Boyle's energy seemed to know no limits. He even diverted the Klondike River so that it would run over his concession, thawing the ground; with this and the installation of electric heaters along the dredges' routes, he was able to extend his mining season to ten months a year. For those ten months, the screaming drone of the dredge at work could be heard for miles, 24 hours a day.

Boyle was a controversial character; within a few years he had bought out Dawson's electricity, running water and telephone companies, and locals accused him of charging too much. But his massive personality and boundless drive always raised a good story (see *The Dawson Nuggets and the Stanley Cup*, page 168, and *Joe Boyle and his European escapades*, page 169).

When World War I broke out, Boyle financed and equipped a machine-gun unit of 50 men from the Klondike. He sailed for Europe, leaving the Canadian Klondyke Mining Company under the command of his son. Times, though, were tough, and in 1921 the company went bankrupt. Dredging continued in the Klondike, however, until 1966 when Arthur Treadgold's Yukon Consolidated Gold Corporation, which had bought out the Canadian Klondyke machines, shut down the last of its dredges.

A core of a couple of thousand residents continued to live in Dawson City, as they do today. The road connecting Dawson to the Whitehorse–Mayo highway was completed in 1955 (it later became the North Klondike Highway) while the Dempster Highway, which connects the North Klondike Highway just outside Dawson with Inuvik in the Northwest Territories, was opened in 1979. In the 1960s Dawson was declared a National Historic Site. Today its economy relies largely on summer tourism; about 8% of the workforce is employed in mining.

GETTING THERE

BY ROAD

From Whitehorse Dawson is 533km (331 miles) from Whitehorse on the North Klondike Highway. The road is paved all the way and is in good condition give or take the odd pot-hole. The journey takes about six hours.

From Alaska The Top of the World Highway is open in summer only; it's a chip-sealed road that connects Dawson to the Taylor Highway and Tok in Alaska. It's yet another sensationally scenic route that gives onto vast panoramas, and if you have wheels you should drive some of it, even if you don't have the remotest intention of actually entering Alaska. If you are crossing the border, it's open from 8am–8pm Alaska time and 9am–9pm Yukon time from mid-May to early October.

From the north The Dempster Highway connects the Klondike Highway 40km (25 miles) outside Dawson to Inuvik in the Northwest Territories. See pages 191–202.

BY BUS Buses connect Dawson with Whitehorse and Fairbanks during the summer only.

🚌 **Alaska/Yukon Trails** ☎ 1 800 770 7275 from Canada & US only (toll-free); e alaskashuttle@ yahoo.com; www.alaskashuttle.com. This shuttle runs between Whitehorse & Dawson from mid-May to mid-Sep, stopping at Braeburn Lodge & Carmacks *en route*. Leaves Whitehorse Sun, Tue, Fri & leaves Dawson Mon, Wed, Sat; US$149. There's also a Fairbanks–Dawson route taking in the Top of the World Highway. It leaves in both directions on Sun, Tue, Fri with stops at Delta Junction, Tok & Chicken; US$169.

BY AIR Air North (☎ 867 668 2228, toll-free: ☎ 1 800 661 0407; *www.flyairnorth.com*) connects Dawson to Whitehorse, Inuvik and Old Crow (*between 3 & 6 times a week, depending on the season – check the website or call for details*) and Fairbanks, Alaska (*3*

Some of the rivers and early mining camps in the Yukon are named as though they were mile markers – Fortymile, Sixtymile and Twelvemile, for example. They were given these names by three traders, Arthur Harper, Jack McQuesten, and Al Mayo, all of whom had arrived in the area more than two decades before the Klondike discovery, in 1873 (and who later joined forces with Joe Ladue, who staked the townsite of Dawson). The trio set up a string of trading posts along the Yukon River. The first of these was at Fort Reliance, just downstream from where Dawson City would later be built. The Fortymile River (which in turn gave its name to the miners' camp where Carmack recorded his Klondike claim) was so-called because it met the Yukon River forty miles downstream from the traders' base at Fort Reliance, the Twelvemile because it was twelve miles from Fort Reliance, and so on.

McQuesten, incidentally, was famous not only for his trading posts but for his homemade thermometer. In the days before the Klondike rush there were no mercury thermometers in this part of the world. Arthur Walden, who worked as a dog driver ferrying mail, freight and passengers between mining camps, recalled in his book *A Dog Puncher on the Yukon* that McQuesten, who was at the time running a trading post at the mining town of Circle City in Alaska, had assembled an effective alternative that served the whole community.

'This consisted of a set of vials fitted into a rack, one containing quicksilver, one the best whiskey in the country, one kerosene, and one Perry Davis's Pain-Killer. These congealed in the order mentioned, and a man starting on a journey started with a smile at frozen quicksilver, still went at whiskey, hesitated at the kerosene, and dived back into his cabin when the Pain-Killer lay down.'

---

times a week, summer only). Air North could well be my favourite airline in all the world, especially since the day when the steward – who I'd never clapped eyes on before – greeted me by name as I boarded. He knew both the other passengers as they were regulars, so I had to be Polly Evans, passenger number three and the only unknown face on the plane. Tickets cost around $130 one way between Whitehorse and Dawson, and $195 from Dawson to Inuvik.

Dawson's **airport** is 15km (9.3 miles) east of town on the North Klondike Highway. All hotels and bed and breakfasts will organize transfers.

BY RIVER It takes 10 days to three weeks to paddle the Yukon River from Whitehorse to Dawson.

BY DOGSLED A dog team will take a week or two to haul you between Dawson and Whitehorse, or Dawson and Fairbanks, on the Yukon Quest trail (Dawson is at the race's halfway point). Don't forget your mittens.

GETTING AROUND

Dawson City itself is small enough to navigate on foot, though you'll need transport if you're going to pan for gold in the creeks of the Klondike, or to visit Dredge Number 4.

CROSSING THE RIVER There's a free car ferry across the river during the summer months connecting downtown Dawson to West Dawson and the Top of the World Highway. It runs 24 hours a day, except for 5am–7am on Wednesdays, plus three 15-minute breaks each day for shift changes and refuelling. The crossing takes a little over five minutes, so what with loading and unloading the vehicles and turning round, it leaves each side every 15 to 20 minutes. There can be long queues in high season. In winter there's an ice road across the river. During the weeks of freeze-up and break-up, you have to decide which side of the river you're going to sit on, and stay there.

BIKE RENTAL Circle Cycle (*Seventh Av & King St;* ☎ *867 993 6270*) rents good-quality mountain bikes for $25 per day or $15 per half day, with special rates for longer rentals. There's a tandem if you're feeling harmonious. **Dawson City River Hostel & Tenting** also rents bikes. See page 178.

TOURIST INFORMATION

Jointly operated by Yukon Tourism and Parks Canada, the **Dawson City Yukon Visitor Information Centre** (*cnr of Front St & King St; Yukon Tourism:* ☎ *867 993 5566;* e *vic.dawsoncity.gov.yk.ca; www.travelyukon.com; Parks Canada:* ☎ *867 993 7200;* e *dawson.info @pc.gc.ca; www.pc.gc.ca/lhn-nhs/yt/dawson/index_e.asp;* ☉ *mid-May to mid-Sep 8am–8pm daily, early May & late Sep 10am–6pm*) offers a good supply of information and videos/DVDs. Parks Canada also operates a number of attractions in Dawson, including the museum, Dredge Number 4, and some really excellent walking tours of the town; see pages 187–8.

In the same building is the **Klondike Visitors' Association** (☎ *867 993 5575;* e *kva@dawson.net; www.dawsoncity.ca*), a non-profit organization that operates some Dawson attractions, and provides information on the town.

'DOING' THE KLONDIKE FOR PLEASURE

In July 1898, two unusually elegant creatures set up home in West Dawson. They were Mary Hitchcock and Edith Van Buren, society ladies from New York who had decided to 'do' the Klondike as a pleasure trip. To make their stay adequately comfortable, they brought with them 500kg of supplies including a portable bowling alley and an animatoscope that showed films.

Mary and Edith also started their journey with a parrot, two dozen pigeons, a pair of canaries and two Great Danes named Queen and Ivan, but not all these creatures completed the course, as Mary related in her account of their travels, *Two Women in the Klondike*. 'I've got some very bad news for you, Madam,' a porter told Mary during the voyage from San Francisco to St Michael.

'Not the dogs?' I cried in alarm.
'No Madam.'
'Nor the parrot?'
'No, Madam, but one of the canaries is dead. I did all I could for him, and left him two hours ago bright and lively, but returned to find the other mourning his mate, who was lying cold at the bottom of the cage. I'm very sorry, but as the two dozen pigeons are in perfect health, you must see that I have given great attention to your birds and animals.'

Queen never made it to the Klondike either. Having heard terrible tales from returned miners of the dangers their destination held for dogs, Edith sent hers back to San Francisco when the entourage docked at St Michael.

The tent that Mary and Edith had erected for them on the West Dawson riverbank covered 260m² (2,800 square ft).

The **Northwest Territories Dempster Delta Western Arctic Visitor Reception Centre** (*cnr of Front St & King St, opposite the Dawson City visitor centre;* ☏ *867 993 6167;* ☉ *mid-May to mid-Sep*) is a useful stop for those planning to drive the Dempster as it has up-to-date information on road conditions, as well as information on Inuvik and the NWT.

TOUR OPERATORS

Fishwheel Charter Services ☏ 867 993 6237; e fishwheel007@northwestel.net. 2hr river tours in the summer (tickets from the Gold Rush Campground, see page 178), plus custom dogsledding, snowmobiling & other tours in winter, run by a Han First Nation guide.
Gray Line Yukon 902 Front St; ☏ 867 993 5599, toll-free: ☏ 1 888 452 1737 (reservations); e glainfo@hollandamerica.com; www.graylineyukon.com. Part of the Holland America empire, Gray Line runs half-day & day trips around Dawson City, to the goldfields, along the Yukon River,

up a part of the Dempster Highway & to the Top of the World Golf Course.
Klondyke Jet Boat Tours Tickets from Dawson City Trading Post at 966 Front St; ☏ 604 852 7724, toll-free: ☏ 1 877 458 2628. Hour-long jetboat tours of the Yukon River for max 6 people; custom half-day or day trips can also be arranged.
Klondike Spirit Tickets from Triple J Hotel at Fifth Av & Queen St; ☏ 867 993 5323. 2hr paddlewheeler cruise down the Yukon River from 6pm to 8pm each evening in summer. Dinner optional.

CANOE RENTALS

Castlerock Canoe Dawson Trading Post, 966 Front St; ☏ 867 993 5316; e crocusbluff@yahoo.ca

Dawson City River Hostel & Tenting See page 178.

'People came during the morning from all parts to have a look at our wonderful tent, the fame of which seems to have gone far beyond Dawson,' Mary wrote.
They had trouble finding servants to match those back home.

'Isaacs, do try to keep the butter covered; here it is open again with all the dust and dirt falling into it, and you've been requested so many times to cover it.'
'See here, I wish you ladies would find something complimentary to say once in a while.'
'You must not be impertinent.'
'I'm not impertinent, I'm only just speakin' the truth; it's rather painful sometimes.'

With the help of the opinionated Isaacs, Mary and Edith gave their first dinner party on 7 August 1898. Mary recorded the event:

Under ordinary circumstances it would be bad form for a hostess to give her menu or refer to the food presented to guests, but I really must state how well we lived in that corner of the world where so many are supposed to be starving.
1st Anchovy on soda-biscuit.
2nd Mock-turtle soup.
3rd Roast moose and potato-balls.
4th Escalloped tomatoes, prepared so deliciously by E— that each one asked for a second helping.
5th Asparagus salad, for which I made the French dressing.
6th Peach ice-cream, and 'though I say it as I shouldn't,' for I made it, it was so good that all were helped twice and some thrice.
7th A very delicious cake made by Isaacs.
8th E—'s French-drip coffee – and all washed down by sparkling Moselle.

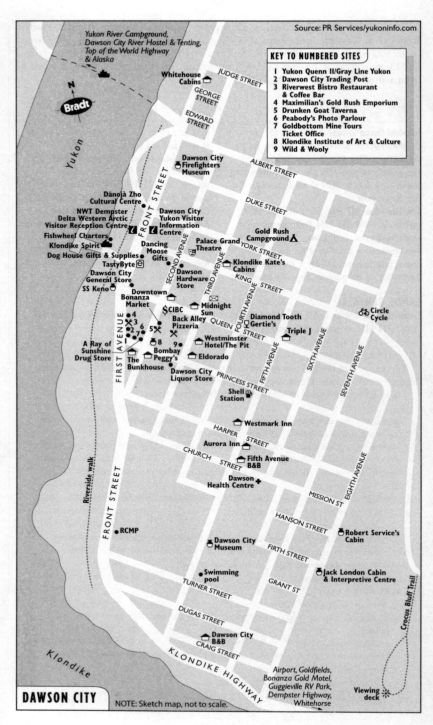

Source: PR Services/yukoninfo.com

Yukon River Campground,
Dawson City River Hostel & Tenting,
Top of the World Highway
& Alaska

N

Bradt

Yukon

JUDGE STREET

Whitehouse
Cabins

GEORGE
STREET

EDWARD
STREET

KEY TO NUMBERED SITES

1 Yukon Quenn II/Gray Line Yukon
2 Dawson City Trading Post
3 Riverwest Bistro Restaurant
   & Coffee Bar
4 Maximilian's Gold Rush Emporium
5 Drunken Goat Taverna
6 Peabody's Photo Parlour
7 Goldbottom Mine Tours
   Ticket Office
8 Klondike Institute of Art & Culture
9 Wild & Wooly

Dawson City
Firefighters
Museum

ALBERT STREET

FRONT STREET

DUKE STREET

Dänojà Zho
Cultural Centre

Dawson City
Yukon Visitor
Information
Centre

NWT Dempster
Delta Western Arctic
Visitor Reception Centre

Gold Rush
Campground

Fishwheel Charters

Klondike Spirit

Dog House Gifts & Supplies

Dancing
Moose
Gifts

Palace Grand
Theatre

YORK STREET

TastyByte

Dawson City
General Store

Dawson
Hardware
Store

SECOND AVENUE

Klondike Kate's
Cabins

THIRD AVENUE

KING STREET

SS Keno

Downtown
Bonanza
Market

FIRST AVENUE

CIBC

Midnight
Sun

FOURTH AVENUE

Circle
Cycle

Back Alley
Pizzeria

QUEEN STREET

Diamond Tooth
Gertie's

Triple J

FIFTH AVENUE

SIXTH AVENUE

SEVENTH AVENUE

A Ray of
Sunshine
Drug Store

Bombay
Peggy's

Westminster
Hotel/The Pit

The
Bunkhouse

Eldorado

Dawson City
Liquor Store

PRINCESS STREET

Shell
Station

Westmark Inn

HARPER STREET

Aurora Inn

CHURCH STREET

Fifth Avenue
B&B

EIGHTH AVENUE

Dawson
Health Centre

MISSION ST

HANSON STREET

Riverside walk

FRONT STREET

RCMP

Robert Service's
Cabin

Dawson City
Museum

FIRTH STREET

Swimming
pool

Jack London Cabin
& Interpretive Centre

GRANT ST

TURNER STREET

Crocus Bluff Trail

DUGAS STREET

Dawson City
B&B

CRAIG STREET

KLONDIKE HIGHWAY

Klondike

Airport, Goldfields,
Bonanza Gold Motel,
Guggieville RV Park,
Dempster Highway,
Whitehorse

Viewing
deck

DAWSON CITY

NOTE: Sketch map, not to scale.

BIKE RENTALS

Circle Cycle See page 172.

Dawson City River Hostel & Tenting See page 178.

WHERE TO STAY

HOTELS

🏠 **Eldorado Hotel** (45 rooms) 902 Third Av; ☎ 867 993 5451; e eldorado@yknet.ca; www.eldoradohotel.ca. The Eldorado has a wide range of rooms, from its basic annexe to large & comfortable dbl queen suites – but, to me, it seems over-priced. Free wireless internet. The Eldorado also operates the Yukon Hotel on Front St, a heritage building with kitchenettes. $$$–$$$$$

🏠 **Aurora Inn** (20 rooms) Fifth Av & Harper St; ☎ 867 993 6860; e aurorainn@aurorainn.ca; www.aurorainn.ca. Aurora Inn ties in first equal with Peggy's (below), in my opinion. It's very different in style. Owned by Europeans, the Aurora is all pine furniture & clean lines, & the rooms are large & airy. Free wireless internet access & guest computer. The Aurora's restaurant is also excellent, see page 179. $$$–$$$$

🏠 **Bombay Peggy's Victorian Inn & Pub** (10 rooms) Second Av & Princess St; ☎ 867 993 6969; e info@bombaypeggys.com; www.bombaypeggys.com. Peggy's has style. Calling itself 'the Yukon's only restored brothel' (Peggy was the original madam; the current proprietress is called Wendy), it's decorated in deep colours & glorious fabrics. This is probably the best hotel in town for those who like things lush, & the adjoining bar is Dawson's top choice for a drink. Wireless internet access. $$$–$$$$

🏠 **Westmark Inn** (177 rooms) Fifth Av & Harper St; ☎ 867 993 5542, toll-free: ☎ 1 800 544 0970; e wmidw-gm@hollandamerica.com; www.westmarkhotels.com; ⏰ mid-May to mid-Sep. Another good option, the Westmark is owned by Holland America so sees large numbers of cruise-ship passengers, but it's an efficient operation that handles the numbers well. The Dawson Westmark comprises various buildings; there's a nice sunny terrace adjoining the bar as well as an outdoor deck. Wireless internet is free but doesn't reach across the entire property; there's also a guest computer. $$$–$$$$

🏠 **Downtown Hotel** (59 rooms) Second Av & Queen St; ☎ 867 993 5346; e stay@downtownhotel.ca; www.downtownhotel.ca. The Downtown's rooms are rather ordinary, though there's nothing actually wrong with them. The hotel has a convenient, central location for those who don't like to walk – though, realistically, Dawson is small & no hotel is more than a 10min stroll from Front St. Wireless internet

---

THE 'SOILED DOVES' OF DAWSON

By 1899, Dawson's increasingly conventional society decided that it was not quite proper that it should share its streets with so-called scarlet women, and so the girls were driven from their rooms on Second Avenue and Paradise Alley to Fourth and Fifth Avenues. In 1901 they were banished from the main town altogether, and sent to the southern bank of the Klondike River at its confluence with the Yukon. This red-light district was known officially as Klondike City, but everyone called it Lousetown. Access was by a bridge over the Klondike – it was easy to see who came and went.

Laura Berton (see *The Berton family*, page 189) describes in her book *I Married the Klondike* how she and a colleague once climbed the hill above Lousetown. Pretending to pick berries, they pried on the forbidden world below where they saw the girls gossiping, washing their hair, and dressing for the evening. It seemed to them a scene so happy and colourful that it might have been lifted from a Brueghel canvas.

Prostitution was always carefully controlled in Dawson. From the beginning, girls were required to have twice-monthly medical inspections or face a fine. Business – and the girls that plied it – dwindled after the main stampede left town, but the single men employed on the dredges assured that trade was still viable for some. Dawson's last brothel didn't shut its doors till 1961.

9

costs $10 for 24hrs. This hotel's bar is the home to the famous sourtoe cocktail, see page 180. $$$

⌂ **Triple J Hotel** (20 cabins, 11 hotel rooms, 16 motel rooms) Fifth Av & Queen St; ☎ 867 993 5323, toll-free: ☎ 1 800 764 3555; e triplej@yknet.ca; www.triplejhotel.com. Cabins have kitchenettes. The rooms are all fine, but nothing to write home about. Free wireless internet. $$$

BED AND BREAKFASTS

⌂ **Dawson City B&B** (5 rooms) 451 Craig St; ☎ 867 993 5649, toll-free: ☎ 1 800 697 6539; e dawsonbb@dawsoncity.net; www.dawsonbb.com. This is the blue building bedecked with flowers & flags that you see overlooking the river as you drive into town from the Klondike Highway. It's a 5min walk from 'downtown'. The décor is fussier than that of the Fifth Avenue B&B, below, & the prices are steeper. But the flowers are pretty & it gets good reports. No children under 12. $$$$

⌂ **Midnight Sun Hotel** (44 rooms) Third Av & Queen St; ☎ summer: 867 993 5495, winter: 694 291 2652; e midnightsunhotel@hotmail.com; www.midnightsunhotel.com; ⏰ May–Sep. The rooms are rather dated & worn. The suites in Caley's Building, owned by the same operation & a national historic site, are better. Wireless internet in Caley's Building. $$–$$$$

⌂ **Fifth Avenue B&B** (11 rooms) Fifth Av & Church St; ☎ 867 993 5941, toll-free: ☎ 1 866 631 5237; e 5thave@5thavebandb.com; www.5thavebandb.com. Lovely rooms & outstanding b/fasts make this an excellent accommodation option. Steve & Tracy, the owners, live in a self-contained apartment on the 1st floor, so you're not always tripping over them & having to relate the events of your day. $$$

THE DEATH OF CIRCLE CITY

In early 1896, Circle City was a booming gold-mining town of more than a thousand inhabitants. Located on the Alaska side of William Ogilvie's border, 350km (220 miles) downstream from Dawson, it had an opera house, eight dance halls, 28 saloons, a library, a hospital, a school and a church. Carmack and his brothers-in-law struck gold in the Klondike in August that year but until the following January Circle's inhabitants knew little of the fortunes being made over the border. Vague rumours had reached the miners there, but they reckoned it was just Joe Ladue exaggerating in order to sell the lots in his crazy new town.

Then, in the very depths of that winter, musher and mailman Arthur Walden was employed to take a passenger from Circle to Fortymile. When he arrived, he was told of the wondrous riches being dug from the ground in the creeks of the Klondike River. His curiosity led him further upstream, where he saw the feverish activity for himself.

'As a large proportion of the men working at the diggings had partners in Circle City, they were very anxious to get letters down to them, and, as I happened to be the first man to go down after the new discoveries, I went back with quiet a large mail, each man howling to his partner to throw over everything and come up and be rich for life,' Walden wrote in his memoirs *A Dog Puncher on the Yukon*.

When he arrived back in Circle with the mail, Walden walked into Harry Ash's saloon, dumped the letters on the bar, and asked Ash for a cup of beef tea. Ash ignored him. Instead, he went for the mail pile: another musher had arrived from the Klondike just ahead of Walden, and had fuelled the earlier rumours. Ash riffled frantically through the pile looking for a letter addressed to him. On finding and reading it, he vaulted over the bar, and shouted to his customers, 'Boys! Hughie is right! Help yourselves to the whole shooting match! I'm off for the Klondike!'

Walden wrote, 'Then began the wildest excitement, as man after man got his letter and thought he was rich for life. Harry's invitation was promptly accepted and a wild orgy began. Corks weren't even pulled, and necks were knocked off bottles…The next morning Harry Ash pulled out, and the big stampede to the Klondike had started. My batch of mail had killed Circle City in less than an hour.'

Kate Rockwell arrived in Skagway in 1899, and took the brand-new White Pass and Yukon Route railway (see page 71) to Lake Bennett. From there she made her way to Whitehorse and Dawson, where she was employed as a dance-hall 'percentage girl', and became known as Klondike Kate.

The percentage girls earned commission on the drinks they sold. Kate, with her good looks and innocent expression, was a natural-born seller and soon she was said to be wearing a $1,500 Parisian gown and a belt made from gold pieces. She fell in love with a waiter, Alexander Pantages; legend has it that Pantages would fill empty champagne bottles with water, and Kate would sell these on to inebriated customers.

Together, the pair opened the Orpheum Theatre in Dawson with Kate performing the headline act. They left town in 1902 and Pantages went on to build a successful theatre chain – but, having spent much of her Klondike fortune, he then left Kate for another woman. She went to live in Oregon where she continued to enjoy publicity relating to her Klondike career until her death in 1957.

CABINS, HOSTELS, CAMPGROUNDS AND RV PARKS

Whitehouse Cabins (7 rooms/cabins, 1 wall tent) Front St between George & Judge Sts; ↘ 867 993 5576; e dcotter@yknet.ca; www.whitehousecabins.com; ⊕ May–Sep. The Gold Rush Cabin here is superb. It dates back to the very beginning – to 1897 – & the owners have lovingly restored it to modern standards with full kitchen with dining area, bathroom with antique clawfoot tub, cable TV, DVD & wireless internet. There are 6 other rooms of lower spec but all have kitchenettes with stoves & fridges, bathrooms, cable TV & interesting histories. 4 of the rooms are in Heritage House, which dates back to 1899, the other 2 are in the Riverside Cabin, which was reconstructed from gold-rush-era shipyard buildings in the 1940s. There's also a wall tent. The Whitehouse Cabins have an attractive, quiet riverside location (on the east bank, so the same side as the main town), & are a 5min walk from 'downtown'. $$$–$$$$

Klondike Kate's Cabins (15 cabins) Third Av & King St; ↘ 867 993 6527; e info@ klondikekates.ca; www.klondikekates.ca; ⊕ Apr–Sep. Cosy pine cabins each with their own small porch, bathroom stocked with locally made soaps & shampoos, & cable TV; some have fridge & microwave. They're rather closely spaced, & there's not much in the way of landscaping, but the location is good & the cabins themselves are lovely. Wireless internet. $$$–$$$$

Bonanza Gold Motel & Guggieville RV Park (150 RV sites, some full & some partial hook-up, 45 rooms) Located on the Klondike Highway, about 1.6km (1 mile) south of Dawson City, just before the Klondike River bridge; ↘ 867 993 6789, toll-free: ↘ 1 888 993 6789; e bonanzagold@ dawson.net; www.bonanzagold.ca. This place is a drive out of town but it's large & spacious & the people are friendly. There's wireless internet, hot showers & cable TV. Some of the motel rooms have kitchenettes. The Guggieville RV Park adjoins. Guggieville, incidentally, was the name given by Dawsonites to this patch of land in the years following the Klondike gold rush when it was mined by the dredges of the Yukon Gold Company, owned by the Guggenheims. Motel rooms $$–$$$$, RV sites $

Goldbottom (4 cabins) Km 14, mile 9 Hunker Creek Rd; ↘ 867 993 5023; e info@ goldbottom.com; www.goldbottom.com. Located a short drive out of Dawson City, the community of Goldbottom had a population of 5,000 during the heyday of 1898; now it's a working mining operation run by the wonderfully colourful Millar family. They rent out cabins that come complete with gold-panning equipment, & you can work the creek for all the gold you can find. There's also a week-long 'prospector' package, which gives you your own mini-sluice on one of the family's 69 claims. Goldbottom also runs fabulous mine tours; see pages 184–6. $$–$$$$

The Bunkhouse (8 economy rooms with shared bath & toilet, 5 en-suite rooms) Front St & Princess St; ↘ 867 993 6164; e info@ dawsoncitybunkhouse.com; www.dawsoncitybunkhouse.com; ⊕ Jun–Aug. The cheaper rooms are rather small & boxy, but they're

good value — in Dawson terms, at least. There's no internet. Economy rooms $$, en-suite rooms $$$
Å Gold Rush Campground (82 sites) Fourth Av & York St; ☏ summer: 867 993 5247, winter: 604 467 8858, toll-free in Canada: 1 866 330 5006; e goldrushcampground@shaw.ca; www.goldrushcampground.com; ☉ mid-May to mid-Sep. The only RV park in Dawson with a town-centre location. There are dry/tenting sites (though realistically it's better suited to RVs than tents — there are preferable tenting options across the river), & hook-ups with 15 amp & water, 15 amp water & sewerage, & 30 amp water & sewerage. There are also showers ($2) & a laundry ($5 wash & dry). Free wireless internet. $
🏠 Dawson City River Hostel & Tenting (40 beds in cabins inc 8 family & private rooms — bring your own sleeping bag or rent your sheets, plus tenting sites) Located on the west bank of the river — turn left as you come off the ferry & up the hill; ☏ summer only: 867 993 6823; e yukonhostels@yahoo.ca; www.yukonhostels.com; ☉ mid-May to Sep. This place has an outstanding location with good views over the river & of Dawson. It's eccentric, atmospheric & a little bit ramshackle; the tenting platforms are rather close together though this may be compensated for by the excellent 'sun deck' overlooking the water. There are good amenities: a large common cabin with wood stove, games & books; bicycle & canoe rentals; & van trips up the Dempster & along the Top of the World Highway. There's also a communal bathhouse with hot water, & a little shop, neither of which the government campground has. There's no electricity & they don't take credit cards. A member of Hostelling International. $

Å Yukon River (Top of the World Highway) Campground (98 sites) Km 0.3 Top of the World Highway — it's on the right as you come off the ferry & head up the hill. This is the government campground (see page 35) in Dawson, which has an excellent location on the west bank of the Yukon River overlooking the water & the dramatic cliffs beyond. The sites are well spaced & surrounded by trees. Both this & the Dawson City River Hostel above (they have very different vibes) are better for tenting than the Gold Rush Campground in town, which is a bit of a parking lot. The ferry service across the river is free & frequent. $

GEORGE DAWSON AND THE GEOLOGICAL SURVEY OF CANADA

Since Canada had become a Dominion of the British Commonwealth in 1867, the authorities had shown precious little interest in the far northwest of their new land. In 1883, however, the American Frederick Schwatka (see page 72) made his expedition from the Alaska coast to the Yukon interior and down the Yukon River. That an American should explore their territory before they had rankled the government bigwigs, and so they decided to send their own party of discovery.

The resulting expedition came under the auspices of the Geological Survey of Canada, a government body that had, for several decades, reported on the economic usefulness and mining potential of various parts of Canada. The Yukon-bound group was led by George Dawson, at the time an Assistant Director of the Geological Survey, and the man for whom Dawson City would later be named. William Ogilvie, the government surveyor who was in the Yukon at the time of the Klondike gold rush a decade later and subsequently became Commissioner of the Yukon, was also in the party.

Dawson, Ogilvie et al left for the Yukon in April 1887. Dawson and Ogilvie took separate paths, Dawson following Robert Campell's former route (see pages 142–3) up the Liard River, and Ogilvie taking the Chilkoot Pass over the Coast Mountains; one of Ogilvie's team was William Moore, who surveyed the White Pass as Ogilvie did the Chilkoot, and later staked the townsite of Skagway (see page 117).

Dawson recorded the geological features of this remote northwestern land while Ogilvie talked to the miners who were already prospecting in the Fortymile region. Returning to Ottawa, the two men concluded that so rich were the gold deposits in these parts that large quantities of the metal would soon be found. It was not so much a question of if, they concluded, but when the great gold rush would ensue.

✕ WHERE TO EAT

Dawson's most popular restaurants get very busy in the summer – it's a good idea to book.

✕ **The Table on 5th** Aurora Inn, Fifth Av & Harper St; ☏ 867 993 6860; e aurorainn@aurorainn.ca; www.aurorainn.ca; ⏲ mid-May to mid-Sep 5.30–9.30pm daily. Dawson's most high-class eatery, the Aurora Inn is worth the money if you're after a top-notch feed. The menu's global, with everything from pasta to wiener schnitzel to trout & lamb. **$$$**

✕ **The Drunken Goat Taverna** 950 Second Av; ☏ 867 993 5868; ⏲ summer: 5pm–11pm daily, winter: 5pm–10pm Mon–Sat. This is one of the most popular restaurants in town, & with good reason. It's a lively place & the food is yummy – moussaka, souvlaki, Greek salad & the like plus steaks & pizza. **$$$**

✕ **Klondike Kate's** Third Av & King St; ☏ 867 993 6527; e info@klondikekates.ca; www.klondikekates.ca; ⏲ Apr–Sep, 7am–10pm in peak season, shorter hrs in the shoulder season. This is probably Dawson's best option for a fabulously fattening b/fast, & it's good for lunch & dinner, too. Dishes include burgers, cowboy platters, salmon, steak, chicken & vegetarian options. **$$–$$$**

✕ **Jack London Grill** Downtown Hotel, Second Av & Queen St; ☏ 867 993 5346; e stay@ downtownhotel.ca; www.downtownhotel.ca; ⏲ 6am–10pm Sun–Thu, 6am–11pm Fri–Sat. A reliable year-round option, the Jack London Grill is a top spot if you're craving a tasty burger. **$$**

✕ **Back Alley Pizzeria** Located in the alley that runs between Second & Third Avs, attached to the back of the Drunken Goat; ☏ 867 993 5800; ⏲ summer: 4pm–10pm, winter: 4pm–9pm Mon–Sat. There are 2 small patio tables, but essentially this is a take-out joint. The pizzas are great. **$$**

✕ **Riverwest Bistro Restaurant and Coffee Bar** Front St & Queen St; ☏ 867 993 6339; ⏲ Apr–Sep, 7am–7pm daily in peak season, reduced hrs in the shoulder season. A really good option for a light lunch or a coffee break, the Riverwest serves delicious homemade soups, sandwiches & pastries alongside a variety of coffees & teas. **$**

ENTERTAINMENT AND NIGHTLIFE

♀ **Bombay Peggy's Victorian Inn & Pub** Second Av & Princess St; ☏ 867 993 6969; e info@ bombaypeggys.com; www.bombaypeggys.com. The bar is small but comfortable, & popular with locals & tourists alike.

♀ **The Pit** Westminster Hotel, 975 Third Av (it's the pink building); ☏ lounge/office: 867 993 5463, tavern: 867 993 5339; e info@thewestminsterhotel-1898.com; www.thewestminsterhotel-1898.com; ⏲ 9am daily, closes... I've never stayed up that late. The Westminster has been serving since 1898, & The Pit (short for The Snake Pit) is still where the local colour goes for refreshment. It's not a tourist joint, but it's friendly & full of atmosphere. It's a great place to drop by if you want to see a side of Dawson that's a far cry from the tour guides in their period garb.

♀ **Diamond Tooth Gertie's** Fourth Av & Queen St; ☏ 867 993 5575; e kva@dawson.net; www.dawsoncity.ca; $6 admission; ⏲ May–Sep 7pm–2am, extended hrs on summer w/ends, opens in winter for special events. This is about as far as you can get from the atmosphere of The Pit: it's a full-on squeaky-clean tourist experience complete with can-can shows & casino games. There's a minimum age limit of 19. Food is served here, too. The building was once the Arctic Brotherhood Hall, where Dawson City's high society held its major events. As for Diamond Tooth Gertie, she was a gold-rush era dancehall queen, nicknamed for the diamond she wore between her 2 front teeth. She went on to marry one of Dawson City's leading lawyers (always keeping the dental diamond); he, tragically, was later burned to death in one of Dawson's frequent fires.

♀ **Sourdough Saloon** Downtown Hotel, Second Av & Queen St; ☏ 867 993 5346; e stay@ downtownhotel.ca; www.downtownhotel.ca. You can have a perfectly ordinary beer here if you want to, but it's the sourtoe cocktail (see *The Sourtoe cocktail*, page 180) – a shot, usually of Yukon Jack whiskey liqueur, garnished with a genuine, severed human toe – that makes this bar stand out. The toe is revolting (it's brownish-yellow & shrivelled) but actually doing the sourtoe cocktail is marginally less repulsive than you might imagine. It's over quickly,

Back in the dark old days of 1973, a group of Dawsonites was debating how one could become an honorary sourdough (the name given by the early gold miners to those who had stayed in the Yukon from the freezing of the river in October to its break-up in May) without actually having to sit out the bitter months of winter. One of them, Dick Stevenson, had recently bought a cabin just outside Dawson from a couple of brothers who used to haul bootleg booze over the border into Alaska during the years of prohibition. They'd travelled by dogsled and, on one journey, one of them had put his foot through some overflow ice and his big toe had frozen. The toe had to be amputated to prevent gangrene but the brothers had no access to a doctor. So they just used those tools they had: they drank a fearsome quantity of the rum they were hauling, then one brother hacked off the other's frozen toe with their woodchopping axe. For reasons best known to themselves they preserved the toe in alcohol and stashed it in their cabin as a keepsake, and there it stayed until Dick inherited it. Maybe, Dick suggested, one could become a 'sourtoe' rather than a sourdough. Qualifiers must down a drink garnished with the preserved, frostbitten digit – and the toe must touch the drinker's lips.

Thanks to Dawson's summer tourist trade, today there are tens of thousands of members of the Sourtoe Cocktail Club (www.sourtoecocktailclub.com). The first toe met its end some years back: in July 1980, a placer miner named Garry Younger was trying for the sourtoe record. As he drank his 13th cocktail (in those days they were beer glasses full of champagne, though today you can order the tipple of your choice), he fell backwards off his bar stool, bumped his head and swallowed it.

'I've seen two people swallow the toes,' Matt Van Nostrand, co-owner of the Downtown, told me. 'And a few summers ago, I saw someone chew one up and spit it out. He was pretty intoxicated.' Fortunately for the Sourdough Saloon, generous amputees from far and wide have donated replacements. Van Nostrand currently has 12 in his collection – two big toes (one male, one female) and 10 little ones. The furthest-travelled toe came from Virginia. 'A woman emailed us and said that she had this toe she could send us,' Van Nostrand said. 'I think that one was a lawnmower accident.'

in any case, & you get a certificate for your scrapbook, so who can argue with that? The sourtoe cocktail is available 9pm–11pm daily in the summer; I dare say they'd bring out the box of toes in the winter, too, if you asked. The Sourdough Saloon also serves tasty food – it's a good place to stop by for a burger & a beer (**$$**).

SHOPPING

Dancing Moose Gifts Second Av between King St & Queen St; ☎ above freezing: 867 993 5549, below freezing: 867 993 6444; e dancingmoose@ dancingmoose.ca; www.dancingmoose.ca. Specializes in Yukon-made arts & crafts.
Dawson Hardware Store 1083 Second Av; ☎ 867 993 5433. A useful stop for practical stuff, & camping & fishing gear.
Dawson Trading Post 966 Front St; ☎ 867 993 5316. This place is quite interesting for its quirky array of goods, which ranges from mammoth ivory to fishing tackle.

Dog House Gifts & Supplies Front St & King St; ☎ 867 993 5405. Even if you don't need a new sled dog harness, this is a fun shop to poke your nose into. You'll find gifts here that make a change from T-shirts with pictures of moose on the front.
Maximilian's Gold Rush Emporium Front St & Queen St; ☎ 867 993 5486. Like most of the people in Dawson, Maximilian's has more than 1 job. It's a newsagent & bookstore (with an excellent stock of books on northern themes); it also sells jewellery & souvenirs.

Peabody's Photo Parlour Second Av & Princess St;
☎ 867 993 5209; e peabody@northwestel.net.
Sells photographic supplies as well as taking old-fashioned portraits for tourists.
Wild & Wooly Third Av between Princess St & Queen St; ☎ 867 993 5170; e romy@northwestel.net; ⏲ summer only, winter by appointment if Romy,

the owner, is in town. Probably the nicest gift shop in town, Wild & Wooly stocks clothing, jewellery, gift cards, & a good deal of other paraphernalia besides. A higher-than-usual proportion of it is stylish & tasteful; some of the jewellery & cards are made by Romy herself.

FOOD AND DRINK
Dawson City General Store Front St & Queen St; ☎ 867 993 5475. The larger of Dawson's 2 grocery stores stocks most things you'll want, including fresh bakery items.
Bonanza Market Second Av & Princess St; ☎ 867 993 6567. There's a good cheese counter at the back, as well as fresh meat & produce, & grocery staples.
Dawson City Liquor Store Third Av & Princess St (it's located in a replica of the Red Feather Saloon, an

old gold-rush bar); ☎ 867 993 5348; e ylcdc@gov.yk.ca; www.ylc.yk.ca; ⏲ mid-Sep to mid-May 10am–6pm Tue–Sat, mid-May to mid-Sep 9.30am–6pm Tue–Sat. If you want a drink on a Sun or Mon, you can buy offsales from the hotel bars. Grocery stores in the Yukon do not sell alcohol, & remember, all ye lax Europeans who aren't used to North America's alcohol laws: it's illegal to carry alcohol anywhere in your vehicle except in the trunk.

OTHER PRACTICALITIES

Dawson Health Centre 530 Church St; ☎ 867 993 4444, call the same number for out-of-hours emergencies; walk-in clinic ⏲ 10am–noon Mon, Wed, Fri, 8.30am–noon Tue, Thu.
A Ray of Sunshine Drug Store Second Av & Princess St; ☎ 867 993 5565. Non-prescription medicines are sold here.
RCMP Front St between Church & Turner; ☎ 867 993 5555
CIBC There's a branch at 978 Second Av (cnr of Queen St); ☎ 867 993 5447; ⏲ 9.30am–4pm Mon–Thu, 9.30am–5pm Fri, closed Sat–Sun; ATM available 24/7

Post office Third Av, between King St & Queen St
TastyByte Internet Café Front St, between King St & Queen St; ☎ 867 993 6100; e ron@tastybyte-internetcafe.com. Reliable internet connections & good coffee. Ron, who runs the place, also drives the school bus, so the café is closed at the beginning & end of the school day during term time. There are also internet computers in the **Downtown Hotel**, see pages 175–6, & most of the other hotels, B&Bs & so on have a wireless connection.
Shell station At the junction of Princess St & Fifth Av. For gas/petrol.

WHAT TO SEE AND DO: DOWNTOWN

For information on river trips, canoe and bike rental, see pages 173–5. For information on downtown walks, see pages 187–8.

DAWSON CITY MUSEUM (*Fifth Av & Turner St;* ☎ *867 993 5291;* e *info@dawsonmuseum.ca; www.dawsonmuseum.ca; adults $9, seniors/students under 18 $7, families $18;* ⏲ *mid-May to mid-Sep 10am–6pm daily*) This is a good museum (the Yukon's largest) with displays about First Nations history, the North West Mounted Police – oh yes, and the Klondike gold rush. There are also four restored narrow-gauge locomotives used by the Klondike Mines Railway from 1905 to 1913. Nerdy types (like me) will enjoy the archives upstairs, which houses huge numbers of photographs, newspaper cuttings, and intriguing documents such as the passenger lists from the steamers that came to the Klondike. In the winter, the museum screens classic movies: check its website for the latest program.

DÄNOJÀ ZHO CULTURAL CENTRE (*Front St, opposite visitor centre;* ☎ *867 993 6768;* e *cultural.centre@gov.trondek.com or freda.roberts@gov.trondek.com; www.trondek.com;*

ROBERT SERVICE

'I wanted the gold, and I sought it, I scrabbled and mucked like a slave,' wrote Robert Service in one of his best-loved poems, 'The Spell of the Yukon'. But, in actual fact, Service neither scrabbled nor mucked, nor so much as dirtied his fingernails with a sluicebox: he was not in the Yukon during the gold rush and he was not a prospector. Instead, he arrived in 1904 as a bank clerk and stayed in the north for just eight years. But while Service never sought nor made his fortune from mining, the gold-rush stories he heard during his years in the north inspired verses that saw him rich for life.

Service was born in Preston, England, in 1874; his family was Scottish and soon moved back across the border. He worked in a bank in Glasgow from the age of 15 until he was 21 when, lured by a sense of adventure, he travelled to Canada to become a cowboy (the story goes that his father bought him a Buffalo Bill cowboy outfit so he could be sure of looking the part). His dreams didn't quite work out: rather than a romantic cowboy, he became a farm labourer and his new life turned out to be tough. Dissatisfied, he drifted around North America until in 1902 he secured a job with the Canadian Bank of Commerce. He was transferred to Whitehorse two years later.

The gold rush had, by now, stampeded on by. But this vast land was still humbling and the old sourdoughs told stories of ripe characters and robust derring-do. Though he was a quiet man himself, and not at all given to roistering, Service managed to convey the spirit of the Klondike gold rush in his verse to such great effect that when he offered a publisher $100 to create a handful of books that he might give as gifts to family and friends, the publisher returned the cheque and offered him a contract. He'd shown the poems to a few people, he said, and had already taken 1,700 orders.

Service was transferred to the Dawson branch of the bank in 1908. A full ten years had passed since the rush, the dance halls were boarded up and the saloons were empty except for a few battered old-timers who sat nursing their memories.

Their reminiscences were Service's pay dirt. He soon became so wealthy from his royalties that he no longer needed his day job. He resigned, and took up residence in the little cabin on Eighth Avenue that still stands today. The doorway was – and continues to be – decorated with a pair of moose horns. In his autobiography, *Ploughman of the Moon*, Service wrote that they looked to him like the Winged Victory.

Service left Dawson in 1912, and worked as a correspondent for the Toronto Star covering the Balkan wars. He served in World War I as an ambulance driver. After the war he met and married a French woman, Germaine, and lived in France for most of the rest of his life. He never returned to the tiny northern town whose stories reaped such rich rewards: he had no wish, he said, to see it changed.

adults *$5, aged 12–18 $2.50, children under 12 free;* ⊕ *May–Sep 10am–6pm & by appointment at other times*) This is an excellent cultural centre dedicated to the Tr'ondëk Hwëch'in First Nation. Rotating exhibitions, videos and photographs tell of their history and contemporary experiences.

SS KENO (*Front St & Queen St; operated by Parks Canada* ☏ *867 993 7200;* e *dawson.info@pc.gc.ca; www.pc.gc.ca; $6.30;* ⊕ *tours at 2.30pm daily in summer*) This is a very similar attraction to the *SS Klondike* in Whitehorse – see page 69 – though, slightly bizarrely, the Dawson version is a few cents more expensive. Maybe it's the higher latitude.

DAWSON CITY FIREFIGHTERS MUSEUM (*Front St between Albert & Duke Sts;* ✆ 867 993 7407; *this is a volunteer-run museum & opening hrs vary – ask at the visitor centre for more information*) Back in the days of oil lamps and wood stoves, Dawson had an unfortunate tendency towards dramatic conflagrations. This museum displays the vintage fire engines that tried to damp the flames.

ROBERT SERVICE'S CABIN (*Eighth Av & Hanson St; operated by Parks Canada* ✆ 867 993 7200; e *dawson.info@pc.gc.ca; www.pc.gc.ca; $6.30;* ☉ *summer: 1.30pm daily*) The presentations at Service's cabin, like so much in Dawson, threaten to be hackneyed but turn out to be charming. A narrator wearing period dress reads a few of Service's poems and talks about his life. It's nicely done; after the presentation visitors can peer inside the cabin itself, which is furnished as it might have been when Service was resident. See *Robert Service*, page 182.

JACK LONDON CABIN AND INTERPRETIVE CENTRE (*Eighth Av & Firth St; operated by Klondike Visitors' Association* ✆ 867 993 5575; e *kva@dawson.net; www.dawsoncity.ca; $2;* ☉ *mid-May to mid-Sep daily*) The Jack London Centre sits just along the street from Robert Service's cabin. The story of the cabin's reconstruction at this site is a gripping one in itself. Author Dick North (see *Dick North*, below), who still lives in Dawson today, has long harboured a fascination with Jack London. Back in 1964, North followed the route of the gold rush travelling by railway over the White Pass and by canoe down the Yukon River. Part way through his paddling trip, he spent the night with a family called Burian, who lived in the remote wilderness. They told him that a couple of local trappers had once found a cabin on Henderson Creek that they thought Jack London must have lived in: London's name was inscribed on the wall. The trappers had cut out this autographed slab of wood and kept it. It was already known that London had spent the winter of 1897–98 in a cabin on Stewart Island. Poor nutrition had led to a severe bout of scurvy and, as soon the river had thawed in spring 1898, London and his companion had torn down their cabin and floated with the logs to Dawson. They'd sold the timber for $600 and London had taken himself and his money off to Father Judge's waterfront hospital (see *Father Judge*, page 188). But this story suggested the existence of a second cabin.

Over the following years, North travelled out into the wilds by dogsled and found the cabin; tracked down the slab of wood and had its autograph analyzed by handwriting experts; went back to the cabin and checked that the slab fitted in the slash on the back wall; and brought an expert to tree-ring date the cabin's logs. Finally, having concluded that this shack had indeed once been Jack London's home, in the spring of 1969 North and his team disassembled the entire cabin and carted the logs to Dawson. They then built two identical constructions from the old logs and new. One of those cabins was shipped to Oakland, California, London's hometown, while the other stayed in Dawson where visitors can see it

DICK NORTH

The most famous Dawson author still living is Dick North. His non-fiction books specialize in northern history, and especially the unsolved mysteries of the past. He spent many years trying to establish the identity of the Mad Trapper of Rat River, finally concluding it was a man named Albert Johnson (see *The Mad Trapper of Rat River*, pages 204–5). Dick North also wrote about the Lost Patrol (see *The Lost Patrol*, pages 200–1). His many books are for sale in Maximilian's on Front Street; they make great reading for anyone touring the north.

today. The interpretive centre, whose establishment was spearheaded by Dick North (he was curator here for many years), also has lots of photographs, letters and other documents relating to Jack London, and is an interesting place to spend half an hour or so.

The story of Dick North's journey to locate Jack London's cabin is told in his book *Sailor in Snowshoes: Tracking Jack London's Northern Trail*. For more on Jack London, see *Jack London*, opposite.

KLONDIKE INSTITUTE OF ART AND CULTURE (KIAC) (*Second Av & Princess St;* \ 867 993 5005; e kiac@kiac.ca; www.kiac.org; office ☺ 9am–5pm Mon–Fri) Dawson may be small but its community is creative, and the town enjoys a rich program of arts events throughout the year. Many of these take place at the KIAC building; KIAC hosts Dawson's annual short film festival each April and the Yukon Riverside Arts Festival in August. It has a small permanent art gallery, called the ODD Gallery (☺ *summer: 11am–5pm Tue–Fri, noon–5pm Sat, winter: 11am–5pm Mon–Fri, Sat as posted*), and an artist in residence program as well as a schedule of events including life drawing, and piano and guitar lessons. It also invites high-level musicians from far and wide to perform concerts. If you're going to be in Dawson for a few days, check out KIAC's website to see if any of these events will coincide with your visit.

INDOOR SWIMMING POOL (*Fifth Av & Turner St;* \ 867 993 7412; $4.50 adults, $2.50 children; ☺ mid-May to early Sep daily, limited hrs at w/ends) The pool's open for public swimming in the afternoons and evenings, and lessons in the mornings. Lane swimming and aquafit are also offered. Call or drop by the pool for the current schedule.

WHAT TO SEE AND DO: BEYOND DOWNTOWN

GOLDPANNING

Goldbottom Mine Tours (*Km 14, mile 9, Hunker Creek Rd;* \ 867 993 5023; e info@goldbottom.com; www.goldbottom.comtickets; $42 if you take their shuttle from town, $26.25 if you drive yourself, cash only, from the booth next to the Trading Post on Front St; 2 tours daily from beginning Jun to freeze-up (usually mid- to late Sep); shuttle leaves at 9.15am & 2.15pm, tours start at 10am & 3pm) When I did this tour a few summers ago, I wasn't entirely certain that I wanted to stand around in the rain watching huge quantities of mud being shovelled by hulking machinery. How wrong I was! The tour was truly fascinating despite the weather, due in large part to the

Jack London had been living in San Francisco, toiling ten hours a day in a steamy laundry, when Klondike fever struck. He convinced his sister and brother-in-law to stand him his grubstake; then he sailed to Skagway and climbed the Chilkoot Pass to the goldfields. London was in the Yukon for less than a year, and he never found his fortune in gold. Contrary to popular myth, he didn't make much from the most famous of his northern writings either: he sold *Call of the Wild* for a $2,000 flat fee, and so never received a cent in royalties. But it was the popularity of *Call of the Wild*, first published in 1903 just five years after London's return from the Yukon, that cemented his position as a great American writer.

Jack London had a tempestuous background. He left school aged 14 to work in a cannery. He subsequently made money as an oyster pirate, stealing from oyster beds and selling the booty at great profit, then turned gamekeeper by joining the Fish Patrol. At the age of 18 he spent 30 days in jail on a vagrancy conviction; the horrors of that experience marked him – and his writing – for life. Deciding he needed an education he returned to school, but dropped out just before he was expelled for his socialist activities. He then attended a crammer but was expelled. He subsequently studied alone and earned a place at the University of California, Berkeley – from which he dropped out. His trauma at discovering, aged 21, that his 'father' was no blood relation, and that his mother had attempted suicide when pregnant with him, did nothing to help his studies. He found work in a laundry; within months news of the Klondike strike reached San Francisco and London headed off in search of gold.

London had been writing before he went to the Klondike, but on his return he threw himself headlong into producing publishable work. His break came from *Overland Monthly* magazine, which bought his short story 'To the Man on the Trail'. By 1900, London was making good money from his writing. Then in early 1903 he penned *Call of the Wild*, which was published in July that year. While London would have made a great deal more money from *Call of the Wild* had he negotiated a royalty-based deal, $2,000 was nonetheless a good fee for the times. Furthermore, it came with the promise of substantial advertising backing and it's this that, arguably, made London's name.

Jack London married Bess Maddern in 1900. He openly admitted that he didn't love her, but thought they would breed well together. The result was two daughters – and a marriage that didn't last. Amid great public scandal, London divorced Bess and married Charmian Kittredge in 1905.

London remained restless for the remainder of his life. He drank heavily. Despite his ruthless productivity – he wrote a thousand words a day, wherever and however he was – he struggled financially due to his expensive tastes, and his obligation to support three households: his mother and adopted brother, his first wife and daughters, and his second wife all depended on him financially. Jack London died in 1916, at the age of 40. He was suffering from uremia and was taking morphine to combat the pain; there has been speculation that he committed suicide. Recent biographers, however, refute this and most now agree that London's death was caused by a fatal blend of uremia and accidental morphine overdose.

Dawson City   WHAT TO SEE AND DO: BEYOND DOWNTOWN

9

brilliantly colourful narration of members of the Millar family. This is a genuine, functioning placer mine (the only one that offers tours), whose operation is explained by tough-as-boots characters who have spent decades digging for Klondike gold. Afterwards you're invited to pan for your own gold in the creek; anything you find, you keep. In my opinion, this is the best of the gold-mining tourist attractions around Dawson; remember to wear stout shoes and pack mosquito repellent. The Millars rent out cabins, too; see page 177.

Claim Number 6 (*Km 16, mile 10, Bonanza Creek Rd;* ✆ *867 993 5575;* e *kva@ dawson.net; www.dawsoncity.ca*) You can pan for gold here for free, though you need to bring your own pan and shovel – and the pickings won't be rich.

Claim 33 (*Km 11, mile 7 Bonanza Creek Rd;* ✆ *867 993 6447;* ⊕ *summer: 9am–5.30pm*) At the time of writing, the future of Claim 33 is in some doubt following the sudden death of the operation's owner, Jerry Bryde, who drowned when Bonanza Creek flooded severely in May 2009. Ask at the visitor centre to find out if it's open, and if hours of operation have changed. Under Jerry, this gold-panning attraction guaranteed that you'd find gold, though many visitors also loved examining the mining paraphernalia that Jerry had collected over decades, and listening to the lively stories with which this popular character would regale his guests.

DREDGE NUMBER 4 (*Km 12.3, mile 7.8 Bonanza Creek Rd; operated by Parks Canada* ✆ *867 993 7200;* e *dawson.info@pc.gc.ca; www.pc.gc.ca; $6.30; tours summer only at 10am, 11am, 12pm, 1pm, 2pm, 3pm & 3.30pm Fri–Tue*) This is another genuinely interesting historical attraction. If I tell you it's the largest wooden-hull, bucket-line dredge in North America, your heartbeat may not quicken. But the sheer monstrosity of this vast edifice that for 47 years sucked in gravel from its gargantuan buckets, sluiced it for gold, and then spat out the debris to create the gigantic tailings that epitomize the Klondike landscape, is remarkable. The thing that really makes this tour, though, is that – at least on the day I went – the guide was no student on a summer job but a woman who had lived in area for decades and whose long personal history working the gold claims of the Klondike had bestowed on her knowledge, enthusiasm and storytelling powers that knew no

HOW DOES A SLUICE BOX WORK?

The theory is beautifully simple. Gold is heavy. It sinks. A sluice box, which along with the shovel and the gold pan was the principal tool of the Klondike gold-rush miners, works with gravity to extract the heavy gold dust and nuggets from the lighter sand and gravel in which they sit.

A sluice box is essentially a trough through which water flows. It's lined with a series of raised slats, called riffles. The sluice box is placed, angled downstream, in a creek, and gravel is shovelled into its upper entrance. As the water and gravel flow through, the riffles create eddies – that's to say backwards currents – that give the gold a chance to sink and stick behind the riffle while the lighter gravel is washed over the top. The trick is to get the water flowing through the sluice box at exactly the right speed. If it moves too slowly, the lighter material will settle in the riffles alongside the gold. If it moves too quickly, the gold too will be swept out. The bottom of the sluice box is lined with carpet or matting that collects the finest gold dust. From the dredges that replaced the individual stampeders, to the machinery of today's placer mines, the principal used is the same, though today's sluices tend to be made from aluminium or plastic.

Gold pans, too, rely on gravity. Scoop a mixture of gravel, sand and, hopefully, gold flakes into your pan, remove the larger rocks, and swirl, and the gold should sink to the bottom. As the rocks rise and the gold sinks, you sweep the debris from the top of the pan, until just the fine particles are left – and, if you've struck lucky, you should be able to pick out the glinting gold.

You don't need a licence to prospect – that's to say to locate and mine – for gold in the Yukon, as long as the land on which you're prospecting is available for mining purposes. However, if you want to assert rights over a piece of land, and stop anyone else mining there alongside you, you'll need to stake a claim.

Your first port of call should be the Mining Recorder's office – for Klondike claims you'll go to the Dawson Mining Recorder (*1242 Front St;* \ *867 993 5343;* e *dawsonmining@gov.yk.ca; www.yukonminingrecorder.ca*). Here you can look at maps to find out which areas are available for staking. A claim must usually be rectangular, and generally measures 500ft x 1,000ft (about 150m x 300m). Having found a patch that appeals to you, you'll need to obtain a couple of wooden posts, hike out to your desired plot, and hammer them into the ground. Then you need to go back to the Mining Recorder, record your claim and pay your first year's fee of $10. Then buy a sturdy shovel and a bumper supply of mosquito repellent, get out there and start digging.

There's one small hitch – you need to actually work the claim, and prove you are doing so by finding at least $200 of pay dirt each year. Otherwise you won't be allowed to renew. But it's perhaps academic: by the end of the first year, you may well have tired of being a gold miner anyway.

bounds. To go inside the dredge, you have to join a tour – you can't walk round on your own, though you can look at the dredge from the outside at any time. One last word to the wise: it can get very chilly inside the dredge. Bring warm clothing. See pages 168–70 for more on the history of the dredges.

TOP OF THE WORLD GOLF COURSE (*Off the Top of the World Highway, about 8km or 5 miles from downtown;* \ *867 993 5888; green fees $25, you can also rent a power cart or hand cart & clubs;* ⊕ *24hrs a day from end May to beginning Sep*) Not quite as on top of the world as its name implies, the golf course is actually on river level. It's a 5.3km (3.3-mile) drive down a gravel road from the Top of the World Highway. The greens aren't entirely top-notch (and there's no dress code in the club house – this is still Dawson) but you don't come here for perfect putting; you come for the experience of playing nine holes in a spectacular location, perhaps even under the midnight sun.

TOP OF THE WORLD HIGHWAY This is a really marvellous route that climbs quickly from the west bank of the Yukon River; even if you only go for a spin for an hour or two, you'll be gasping over the views. From 'downtown', you'll need to take the free car ferry over the river. The road is closed in winter.

TREK OVER THE TOP (e *eric@trekoverthetop.com; www.trekoverthetop.com*) Trek Over The Top comprises three separate snowmobile runs between Dawson and Tok, Alaska via the Taylor and Top of the World highways in February and March each year (when the highway is closed to normal road traffic). It's 320km or 200 miles each way; snowmobilers stay two days in Tok, then ride back to Dawson. There are also runs in the other direction, beginning and ending in Tok.

WALKS AND HIKES

PARKS CANADA GUIDED WALKING TOUR (*Tours at 9.30am & 3.30pm daily in summer, $6.30, tickets from Palace Grand Theatre on King St between Second Av & Third Av;* ⊕ *9.30am–5pm daily*) You may think that following a guide in period costume

Dawson City WALKS AND HIKES

9

around the dusty streets of Dawson sounds a little twee, but actually this is a fascinating way to spend 90 minutes as the guide takes you into refurbished, historic buildings that you wouldn't otherwise be able to see.

DAWSON CITY WALKING TOUR Yukon Tourism has produced walking tour leaflets for all the Yukon's towns. Dawson's is probably the best, given the large number of historic buildings with stories to tell. Pick up the *Dawson City Historic Buildings Walking Tour* brochure at the visitor centre – it has a map and blurb on 14 of the more interesting edifices.

CEMETERIES WALKING TOUR The leaflet *A Walking Tour of Dawson City Cemeteries* is available at the visitor centre, and leads you on a self-guided walk around the last resting places of great Dawson characters including Father Judge and Percy DeWolfe.

CROCUS BLUFF (*Distance: 500m, 0.3 miles; Difficulty rating: very easy; Trailhead: go up beyond the end of King St & follow the path – the trail goes off to the right just before you get to the cemetery*) This is a very short trail with interpretive panels on nature and history and a viewing deck over the river.

MIDNIGHT DOME (*Time: 3–4hrs round trip; Difficulty rating: moderate to strenuous; Trailhead: follow King St away from the waterfront – the road turns into Mary Macleod Rd, also known as Old Dome Rd, & from there the trail begins to climb steeply*) This is an energetic hike. After crossing the rockslide, you'll need to take the path to your right, then another trail to your right half a kilometre further on. There are fantastic views from the top, marred only slightly by the fact that there's a road up here, too, so you'll share the panorama with those who've driven up in their RVs.

MOOSEHIDE VILLAGE (*Time: about 6hrs round trip; Difficulty rating: moderate to strenuous – be aware that the trail is not maintained; Trailhead: the trail starts at the top of King St, at first following the same trail as the route to the Midnight Dome but, after the rockslide, you stay on the main trail to get to Moosehide*) Moosehide is a First Nations village just downstream of Dawson. There's a hiking trail that leads there via the hills behind town (you can see the trail traversing the large rockslide), but before going you must obtain permission from the Tr'ondëk Hwëch'in government (*Third Av & Queen St; ☎ 867 993 7100*). Also note that there are no services in Moosehide, so you'll need to pack food and water.

Every second year in July, the village celebrates northern heritage with the Moosehide Gathering. For three days, locals and visitors come together for traditional games, drumming, dancing, singing, storytelling and feasts. Visitors are welcome; ask at the Tr'ondëk Hwëch'in government office or at the visitor centre for information.

RIDGE ROAD HERITAGE TRAIL (*Distance: 32km, 20 miles; Trailhead: to get to the upper trailhead, drive south out of Dawson, then turn right into Bonanza Creek Rd. After 14km, 8.7 miles, you'll reach Upper Bonanza Rd, which you'll need to follow for about another 14km. The trail comes out the other end at Jackson Gulch on the Klondike Highway – the lower trailhead*) This trail runs along the ridge tops between Bonanza and Hunker Creeks. It's suitable for hiking or mountain biking (for information on bike rental see page 172).

The Ridge Road was built in 1899 to transport goods by wagon between Dawson City and the goldfields; it was abandoned in 1902 after better roads were built alongside Bonanza and Hunker creeks. Some gold-rush artefacts still lie along the way.

There are two basic but scenic campgrounds. The first, 15-mile Campground, was the site of Halfway House and Emile Mohr's Roadhouse; the stage coach between Dawson and Dominion Creek used to stop here. The second, 11-mile Campground, was once the site of two roadhouses. A brochure and trail map are available from the visitor centre.

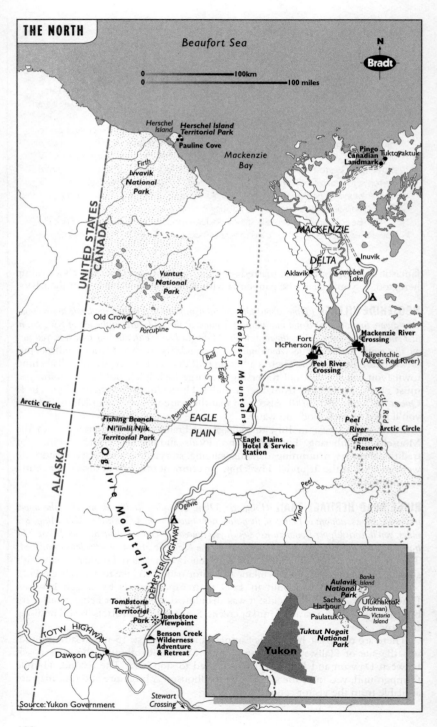

THE NORTH

Beaufort Sea

N

Bradt

0 ——————— 100km
0 ——————— 100 miles

Herschel
Island
Herschel Island
Territorial Park
Pauline Cove

Mackenzie
Bay

Pingo
Canadian
Landmark
Tuktoyaktuk

Firth
Ivvavik
National
Park

UNITED STATES
CANADA

MACKENZIE

DELTA

Inuvik

Vuntut
National
Park

Aklavik

Campbell
Lake

Old Crow

Porcupine

Bell

Eagle

Richardson Mountains

Fort
McPherson

Mackenzie River
Crossing

Tsiigehtchic
(Arctic Red River)

Peel River
Crossing

Arctic Circle

Porcupine

EAGLE

PLAIN

Fishing Branch
Ni'iinlii Njik
Territorial Park

Eagle Plains
Hotel & Service
Station

Peel
River
Game
Reserve

Arctic Red

Arctic Circle

Ogilvie Mountains

ALASKA

Peel

Ogilvie

DEMPSTER HIGHWAY

Wind

Tombstone
Territorial
Park

Tombstone
Viewpoint

Benson Creek
Wilderness
Adventure
& Retreat

KLONDIKE HIGHWAY

Dawson City

Stewart
Crossing

Source: Yukon Government

Aulavik
National
Park

Banks
Island

Sachs
Harbour

Ulukhaktok
(Holman)
Victoria
Island

Paulatuko

Tuktut Nogait
National Park

Yukon

10

The North

There's a romance to the Arctic. Even in the 21st century it maintains its mystique. It's still the great beyond, a place where nature rules – and a land of fantastical beauty. In winter, the temperatures are bitter and the sun doesn't rise from one month to the next – but spirits soar when the northern lights dance magically across the skies. In summer, the region basks beneath the buttery yellow light of the soft, midnight sun. This is a world of tremendous, spacious stillness where polar bears and musk oxen roam, where bowhead and beluga whales glide through the seas. It's a land of tundra that seems to stretch forever, that bursts with multi-coloured wildflowers in June and July and then, as August turns to September, transforms itself into hues of scarlet, yellow, orange and pink so vibrant that it's hard to believe they're natural. It's a terrain that climbs and falls through vastly differing mountain ranges, and whose constantly changing scenery keeps the senses delighted.

For hikers and paddlers with good outdoors survival skills, there are unparalleled adventure opportunities in the northern national parks. But you don't need rippling quadriceps to enjoy Canada's far northwest. Driving the Dempster Highway – the only road that crosses the Arctic Circle in Canada – is a truly marvellous adventure in itself. Many people rent a vehicle and go at their own pace, but there are van and bus tours for those who prefer somebody else to sit in the driving seat and, if you don't fancy a week-long yomp across the tundra, there are many scenic strolls of half an hour to half a day along the highway.

Just after you cross the Arctic Circle, you leave the Yukon and arrive in Canada's Northwest Territories (NWT) and this chapter follows the road over the border. In the Yukon, it covers the Tombstone Territorial Park just north of Dawson, as well as the Vuntut and Ivvavik national parks in the Yukon, plus the Yukon's most northerly community, the Vuntut Gwitchin village of Old Crow. Over the border in the NWT it includes the town of Inuvik at the end of the highway, the tiny communities of Fort McPherson, Tsiigehtchic (formerly Arctic Red River), Tuktoyaktuk, Aklavik, Paulatuk, Sachs Harbour and Ulukhaktok (formerly Holman), and Tuktut Nogait and Aulavik national parks. Remember to change your watch when you cross the territorial border: the Northwest Territories are one hour ahead of the Yukon.

If you're looking for more information on the Western Arctic than can be provided here, the Western Arctic Handbook Society has published the excellent *Canada's Western Arctic*, which offers a wealth of detail on the region's communities, culture, history, wildlife and wilderness trips.

THE DEMPSTER HIGHWAY

The Dempster Highway runs for 736km (457 miles) from the North Klondike Highway to Inuvik. This is one of the most spectacular road trips on earth – and yet few people have even heard of it. If you drive it in summer, yes, you'll meet others *en route*, but most of the time you'll share the road with just the occasional arctic ground squirrel and the tremendous expanses of surrounding wilderness where bears, wolves and caribou roam.

The highway traverses three mountain ranges – the Tombstones, the Ogilvies and the Richardsons. Geologists will have better language for them than I, but let me say that, even for the layman, it's the diversity of these ranges that is refreshing, surprising, and utterly spectacular. There's tremendous ecological range, too: of the 1,300 plant species found in the Yukon, 1,000 can be seen from the Dempster Highway. Wildlife spotters should look out for grizzly and black bears, Dall sheep, foxes, wolves, musk oxen, hoary marmots, collared pika and arctic ground squirrels (called sik-sik by the Inuit because of the sound they make). One of the major draws for wildlife enthusiasts is the 125,000-head Porcupine caribou herd, which winters near the more southerly reaches of the Dempster Highway from October to April, then migrates north to the coastal plain of Alaska's Arctic National Wildlife Refuge, often crossing the highway in large numbers as it moves.

This is also an incredible area for birding: 159 species have been recorded within 8km (5 miles) of the highway, including golden eagles, peregrine falcons, gyrfalcons, red-throated loons, long-tailed ducks, willow ptarmigan, golden plovers and long-tailed jaegers.

But it's the vastness of the land around the Dempster that blows the mind. Driving for hours across the Eagle Plains plateau when the autumn colours are in full riot, you have to wonder if there's any place on earth that's more mind-blowingly beautiful than this. You feel an immense and humbling sense of privilege in witnessing such a spectacle – and in knowing that the Dempster Highway is the only tiny, raggedy little road that cuts through it, opening up this incredible part of the planet for anyone with a vehicle and an adventurous spirit.

HISTORY 'I see a new Canada – a Canada of the North. This is the vision,' prime minister John Diefenbaker enthused to a Winnepeg hustings in February 1958. Diefenbaker was already in office – he'd formed a minority Conservative government eight months earlier, sweeping the Liberals from 22 years of power – but the forthcoming election would grant him a majority, and would see him lead the country for a further five years.

Diefenbaker's ambition was to open the Canadian north, and so reassert control over Canada's natural resources, which were being eyed up by foreign corporations. One of his most famous initiatives was his 'Roads to Resources' program, which built 2,270km (1,400 miles) of roads in the Canadian north; following his election victory, Diefenbaker allocated $100 million to the project. A highway running north from Dawson City to Eagle Plains – where oil had apparently been struck – was to be the program's first challenge.

And what a challenge it was. Surveying for the new all-weather road started in 1958. In the following three years, 116km (72 miles) of highway were built. But the project stalled when oil and gas explorations in Eagle Plains bore feeble results, and teetered to a standstill. It wasn't until 1968, when the Americans found oil at Prudhoe Bay, that the race for resources resumed. In 1970 oil was at last struck in the Canadian Beaufort Sea and the road project was resurrected. The Dempster Highway – named for Inspector Jack Dempster, the North West Mounted Police officer who led the expedition to recover the bodies of the Lost Patrol (see pages 100–1) – was finally opened on 18 August 1979, just two days after the death of John Diefenbaker, the man whose vision had started it all.

An insulating gravel pad – stretching in places to 2.4m (8ft) deep and creating sections of road that seem like raised bridges with no sides – sits beneath the road to protect the permafrost: if the permafrost melted, the road would sink. Bridges were built over the Ogilvie and Eagle rivers by the Canadian Armed Forces. It had originally been calculated that the highway would cost $5–8 million over a five-year construction period. In the end, the building of the road took almost 20 years, and the cost topped out at $103 million.

WHEN TO GO The road is open all year except during freeze-up and break-up when the ferries can't run on the two river crossings, and the ice isn't firm enough for an ice bridge. The very best time of year is the end of August and beginning of September, when the autumn colours are at their most sensational and the mosquitoes and blackflies have died off. You may even be lucky enough to see the northern lights as the days grow shorter. Many locals say the road is better in winter, as the snow and ice create a smoother surface; however, you should consider the implications of a cold-weather breakdown and travel prepared – the next vehicle may not come along for some time. If you want to drive the road in winter, March and April are the best months as temperatures are warmer and daylight is longer, yet the ice bridges across the rivers are still solid.

Parts of the highway close sporadically due to adverse weather. Check current road conditions at www.511yukon.ca or www.hwy.dot.gov.nt.ca/highways or call 511, 867 777 7344 or toll-free: 1 800 661 0750 before you travel.

HOW LONG DOES IT TAKE? You'll need between 12 and 16 hours in each direction, depending on road conditions and how often you stop to take photographs. Allow two days each way – and longer if you wish to do any decent hiking *en route* – plus, ideally, a couple of nights in Inuvik. If you're planning to stay at the Eagle Plains Hotel (see page 195) you should book your room in advance. Eagle Plains also has an RV park and campground.

LOGISTICS

Vehicles The Dempster Highway is unpaved except for the first 8km (5 miles) and the last 10km (6 miles). They call it a two-lane road, but it's narrow and most people drive straight down the middle, except when they need to pass. You should travel in a 4x4 and tell the car-hire company that you're planning to drive the Dempster. As there aren't any vehicle rental companies in Dawson, the only options – unless you're travelling as part of an organized tour (see page 194) are to hire one in Whitehorse and drive it from there, or to start and end your road trip in Inuvik.

Flat tyres Flat tyres are common; you should travel with two spares – vehicle rental companies will rent you a second. Flats can be repaired at Eagle Plains and Fort McPherson (and Inuvik and Dawson, of course).

Petrol/gas You shouldn't need to carry extra fuel on the Dempster – there are gas stations at the southern end of the highway at Klondike River Lodge, and at Eagle Plains, Fort McPherson and Inuvik. However, you'd be wise to take local advice before setting out just in case the situation changes – this is no place to run out of gas. Note that there's no propane at Fort McPherson.

River crossings The ferries over the Peel and Mackenzie/Arctic Red Rivers are free; they run 9am–12.30am (ie: half past midnight) daily from June to mid-October.

Speed The speed limit for the Dempster is 90km/h (55mph) but, if you're not experienced with gravel roads, you'd be well advised to take it slower – and in some sections you'll need to go very slowly indeed. When I drove the Dempster, I think we hit a bottom speed of about 25km/h (15mph) in the really rough sections – and though we were more cowardly than most, we were happy to complete the drive with no flat tyres or other headaches.

Food There's a restaurant at Eagle Plains and a grocery store at Fort McPherson. There's also a store at Tsiigehtchic, but you'll have to travel on an extra leg of the triangular ferry route to get there. Given that there are many hours driving between these stops, you'll want to stock up on food for lunches and snacks, and water, before you leave Dawson or Inuvik.

Further information The Northwest Territories Dempster Delta Western Arctic Visitor Reception Centre on Front Street in Dawson (see page 173) has up-to-date information on the Dempster Highway, as does the visitor centre in Inuvik (see page 207). They'll also give you a passport you can have stamped both ends of the highway to prove you made it.

THE DEMPSTER BY BIKE Plenty of people cycle the Dempster, though the going is rough in places. Talk to Tim in Dawson's **Circle Cycle** (*Seventh Av & King St;* ✎ *867 993 6270*). He's ridden the road, and will even rent you a bike or fix up yours.

TOUR OPERATORS Alternatively, you could let someone else do the driving while you sit back, gaze out of the window and ooh over the scenery. The following companies offer van tours up the Dempster (and you fly one way, so you don't have to drive it in both directions).

Arctic Chalet www.arcticchalet.com. Day trips & 2-day trips from Inuvik, see page 209.
Gray Line www.graylineyukon.com. Day trips out of Dawson, see page 25.

Nature Tours www.naturetoursyukon.com, see page 25.
Northern Tales www.northerntales.ca, see page 25.
Taiga Journeys www.taigajourneys.com, see page 26.
Up North Tours www.upnorthtours.ca, see page 208.

FISHING There are good fishing spots at the following. Note that you need a licence to fish in the Yukon (see page 44) and a separate licence to fish in the Northwest Territories (see *www.nwtwildlife.com/fishing/license.htm*).

Km 108, mile 67 Blackstone River (arctic grayling & arctic char)
Km 193, mile 119 Engineer Creek campground (arctic grayling)
Km 221, mile 138 Ogilvie River (arctic grayling, northern pike & arctic char)

Km 378, mile 235 Eagle River (arctic grayling)
Km 479, mile 298, NWT km 14 James Creek (arctic grayling)
Km 643, mile 400, NWT km 178 Rengling River (arctic grayling)

🏠 WHERE TO STAY

🏠 **Bensen Creek Wilderness Adventure & Retreat** (1 room in the lodge, plus 1 cabin) Km 29, mile 18; ✎ 867 993 5469; e g.cruchon@northwestel.net; www.bensencreek.com. This is the only lodge on the Dempster; the only other accommodation options (beyond camping) are the hotels at Eagle Plains & Fort McPherson. The main building is a pretty, cosy log cabin that can sleep between 2 & 5 (in 1 room); there's also a second cabin that sleeps 2. It's located a little less than an hour's drive from Dawson. Gerard Cruchon, the owner, can advise on self-guided hiking. Guided hiking & canoeing in summer & ice fishing, snowshoeing, dogsledding & skiing in winter can be arranged, & there's a wood-fired hot tub, perfect for northern lights viewing. $$$–$$$$
🏠 **Eagle Plains Hotel & Service Station** (32 rooms) Km 371, mile 229; ✎ 867 993 2453;

e info@eagleplainshotel.com; www.eagleplainshotel.com. At first, we laughed at the sign above the doorway proclaiming this to be 'an oasis in the wilderness' – this is a brown-tin motel & it's not exactly glamorous. There can be no question about the wilderness, however, & after a burger & a cold beer, we conceded to the oasis part of the slogan, too. In short, Eagle Plains Hotel isn't a lot to look at but, after many hrs on the road, it's a delightful place where truck drivers & tourists rub up together, & its display of historical photos on the walls is fascinating. Be warned – the restaurant

stops serving at 7pm in the winter & 8pm in the summer; these hrs could change so call ahead to check if you're thinking of cutting it fine (you'll need to phone from Dawson or Inuvik – there's no cell phone reception on the highway). There's bar food in the lounge after that, but it's somehow disappointing after a long day on the road not to have the full menu to choose from. Rooms are basic, but perfectly adequate. There's wireless internet access but it doesn't stretch to all rooms – you can always sit in the lobby, though. $$$

⌂ **Peel River Inn**, Fort McPherson. See page 201.

Campgrounds

⚑ **Tombstone Territorial Park Campground** (36 sites) Km 71, mile 44. This is a lovely government campground (see page 35), encircled by mountains. Come here in late Aug or early Sep & the hillsides are bright yellow & red as the trees & tundra plants change colour. The Tombstone Territorial Park Interpretive Centre is also here, see page 196. $

⚑ **Engineer Creek** (15 sites) Km 193, mile 119. Another government campsite (see page 35). This is a wooded site among poplar trees, but it feels rather bleak as it sits beneath the bare grey hills. The Tombstone campground scores more highly in prettiness points. The creek's water is coloured an unpleasant pale brown, apparently by iron hydroxide. It's supposed to be diluted enough to be safe to drink, but it looks utterly foul. If you're planning on stopping here, you may prefer to bring your own water. $

⚑ **Eagle Plains Hotel & Service Station** (12 sites) Km 371, mile 229; ☎ 867 993 2453; e info@eagleplainshotel.com; www.eagleplainshotel.com. Electrical hook-up for RVs, plus tenting, showers & laundry. There's also a restaurant, lounge, gas station & mechanical repairs – see above. $

⚑ **Rock River** (20 sites) Km 446, mile 275. Government campground, see page 35. Look out for northern wheatears, & for snowy owls in the winter & early spring. This is a good base for hiking in the Richardson Range. $

⚑ **Nitlainlaii Territorial Park** (23 sites) Km 541, mile 336, NWT km 76. There's an information centre here as well as firewood & a kitchen shelter. ⊕ 1 Jun–1 Sep. $

⚑ **Vadzaih Van Tshik/Caribou Creek Campground** (11 sites) Km 692, mile 430, NWT km 221. Has firewood, picnic tables, outhouses & BBQ pits. $

⚑ **Gwich'in Territorial Campground** (15 sites) Km 705, mile 438, NWT km 235. Just 30km (18.5 miles) short of Inuvik, this is a lovely site overlooking Campbell Lake. It has good facilities; this is a more pleasant site than the Vadzaih Van Tshik/Caribou Creek Campground a few kilometres earlier. $

⚑ **Juk Park** (32 sites without power, 6 sites with power) Km 731, mile 454, NWT km 266; ☎ 867 777 3613. Picnic tables, BBQ pits, firewood, water, kitchen shelter, toilets & showers, plus a 10m-high (33ft) lookout tower & walking trails. $

WHAT TO SEE AND DO There are many viewpoints and pull-outs along the Dempster Highway, all of which offer magnificent views. Those listed below are just a few of the highlights. For exhaustive information on the points of interest and wildlife along the way, download the free *Dempster Highway Travelogue* from www.environmentyukon.gov.yk.ca/pdf/DempsterFinalWeb.pdf or consult one of the books listed in *Further Information*, pages 255–7.

Tombstone Territorial Park Inhabited by the Tr'ondëk Hwëch'in First Nation for thousands of years (for more on the Tr'ondëk Hwëch'in people visit the Dänojà Zho Cultural Centre in Dawson, see pages 181–2), the spectacularly scenic Tombstone Territorial Park is now one of the Yukon's premier hiking areas and a major tourist draw. Access is easy – the park is intersected for 70km (43 miles) by the Dempster Highway – and there are hiking options from short strolls to multi-day backcountry thighbusters. The park is home to a rich diversity of wildlife –

grizzly and black bears, wolves, wolverine, caribou, moose and Dall sheep all inhabit the Tombstones, as do 137 species of bird, including arctic species such as the snow bunting, gyrfalcon, arctic tern and red-throated loon.

Those wishing to explore the park in a little more depth than a drive-through will allow can base themselves at the Tombstone Territorial Park Campground (*km 71, mile 44*) but, even if you're not planning to spend the night, you should nonetheless stop to visit the park's interpretive centre (*km 71.5, ⊕ late May to mid-Sep*). A new, $2 million facility opened in August 2009 providing displays, walks and trails, and general information. The interpretive centre's real asset, though, is its wardens, who are hugely knowledgeable about the area and current conditions. It's a good idea to enquire here about recent bear activity before you start hiking. The interpretive centre also rents bear-resistant containers ($40 deposit).

Note that the Tombstone Territorial Park has no established trails apart from Grizzly Creek: hikers will need good route-finding skills. Also, take heed of the fact that, while Dawson is only 1½ hours drive south, the weather in the Tombstones can be much cooler than in town. While snow is rare between June and mid-August, it's not unheard of. Take appropriate clothing.

Camping permits Between 1 June and 30 September, you need a permit if you're going to camp at Grizzly, Divide or Talus lakes. This is due to issues of overcrowding and the need to protect the fragile environment. Permits are free, but are limited to ten per lake per night (it's one permit per tent), and you can only camp at each lake for three consecutive nights. Permits can be obtained from the Tombstone Interpretive Centre. You don't need a permit to camp elsewhere in the backcountry of the Tombstone Territorial Park, and you don't need a permit for day hikes. For more information, e tombstone@gov.yk.ca or go to www.environmentyukon.gov.yk.ca/parksconservation/tombstonepark.php.

Five short hikes from the highway

From the campground (*Time: there are ½hr and 1hr trails; Difficulty rating: easy; Trailhead: campground*) These are self-guided nature walks with interpretive boards. There are also half-day and day routes leaving directly from the campground – ask at the interpretive centre for information.

Grizzly Creek (*Distance: 8km, 5 miles round trip; Time: 2–4hrs; Difficulty rating: moderate to strenuous; Trailhead: km 59, mile 36 Dempster Highway*) This is probably the most popular hike in the park and the only established trail – but the bears like it too; ask about recent bear activity at the interpretive centre before you set out. It's an easy-to-follow trail providing the quickest route into the heart of the Tombstone range. The trailhead is at the far end of a large gravel pit on the west side of the highway – it's easily identified by the other vehicles parked there, and there's an outhouse. If you're going to do the 8km round trip you'll have to turn round at the viewpoint over Mount Monolith; however, you can continue to Grizzly Lake and camp there. Energetic types can spend many days hiking in the Tombstones from this starting point. Ask at the interpretive centre for information, and see above for details on camping permits.

Goldensides (*Distance: 5km, 3 miles round trip; time: 2–3hrs; Difficulty rating: it's not far but is very steep with loose scree in places; Trailhead: km 75, mile 46 Dempster Highway – just 3km (1.8 miles) north of the interpretive centre & campground, & very shortly north of the viewpoint, there's an obvious road off to the right, as you head north, leading to a microwave tower. The start of the walk is clearly marked.*) This is a steep climb but the views from the top are extraordinary and well worth a bit of panting.

Angelcomb Peak (*Distance: 10km, 6 miles round trip; Time: 4–5hrs; Difficulty rating: moderate to strenuous; Trailhead: km 82, mile 51 Dempster Highway*) There's a gravel pit here in which you can park; the mountain to the east is Angelcomb Peak (also called Sheep Mountain). Follow any of the game trails along the creek and up the slope. This is an important Dall sheep lambing area in May and June. You should stay away from the mountain when the sheep are lambing. Look out also for the pair of golden eagles that nests on the cliffs here.

Hart Winter Road (*Distance: the road actually runs for about 70 miles, but there's a marshy section after 7km or 4.2 miles, which makes a good point for turning back if you're only after an amble; Time: about 4hrs round trip if you turn at the marshy bit; Difficulty rating: moderate; Trailhead: km 78, mile 49 Dempster Highway*) This is a fairly flat walk along a picturesque old mining road; you can either hike or mountain bike. Look out for caribou from the Hart River herd, and wolf, caribou, moose and bear tracks in the mud. Note that this route can be very wet in spring.

Further information For more information on hiking in the Tombstones, visit Environment Yukon's website at www.environmentyukon.gov.yk.ca/parksconservation/tombstonepark.php, or read the Canadian Parks and Wilderness Society's book *Yukon's Tombstone Range and Blackstone Uplands*.

Topo maps for the Tombstone Territorial Park
1:250,000 scale: Dawson (116 B and 116 C)
1:50,000 scale: Tombstone River (116 B/7), Upper Klondike River (116 B/8), North Fork Pass (116 B/9), and Seela Pass (116 B/10)

KM 74, MILE 46: TOMBSTONE VIEWPOINT You're unlikely to accidentally drive past this one. It gives onto the most iconic view of the whole highway – that of the jagged peak of the Tombstone Mountain (2,193m/7,193ft). The mountain's dramatic shape is due to its formation from a granitic rock called syenite, which pushed up in molten form into older sedimentary rock about 90 million years ago. This created pillars called plutons, which became exposed when glaciation and other forms of erosion removed the surrounding sedimentary rock.

KM 82, MILE 51: NORTH FORK PASS This is the highest point on the Dempster, at 1,300m (4,264ft). It's also a good spot for a short hike: look out for golden eagles.

KM 87–132, MILE 54–82: BLACKSTONE UPLANDS For birders, this is *the* area of the highway. Species include red-throated loons, long-tailed ducks, willow ptarmigan, American golden plovers, long-tailed jaegers, common and hoary redpolls, Lapland longspurs and snow buntings.

KM 104, MILE 64: TWO MOOSE LAKE There's another pull-out here with interpretive boards, and moose can sometimes be seen feeding, especially in the evening. Also look out for northern pintail, scaup, American wigeon, northern

WEEKEND ON THE WING

Tombstone Territorial Park hosts Weekend on the Wing, a birding festival, each June. It features walks and talks relating to the birds migrating overhead. Go to www.environmentyukon.gov.yk.ca/wildlifebiodiversity/birds.php or call ☎ 867 667 8299 for information.

shoveller and Harlequin duck. You can walk all the way around the lake if you choose. Three kilometres (1.8 miles) to the east, you'll see a gentle, northward-sloping hump. This terminal moraine was the northern limit of glaciation during the last ice age.

KM 115, MILE 72: PINGOS You've now left Tombstone Territorial Park – but don't worry, the scenery's still spectacular. After you've crossed the river and gained a bit of elevation, look upriver. About 8km (5 miles) away you'll see two conical mounds. These are pingos. See page 216.

KM 154, MILE 96: CARIBOU TRAILS On the grey mountain directly ahead you can see narrow trails that have been used by migrating caribou for centuries. These trails lie across hundreds of kilometres of tundra; the Porcupine caribou herd has wintered in this area for thousands of years.

KM 158, MILE 99: GYRFALCON NEST The location of the nest is revealed by the white smears of guano on the cliffs that flank the road.

KM 176–78, MILE 111–12: SHEEP LICK Look over to the hillside across the creek and you should see sheep tracks leading down to the water – it's rich in calcium and magnesium, and the sheep come here for their version of dietary supplements.

KM 193, MILE 119: ENGINEER CREEK CAMPGROUND See page 35.

KM 195, MILE 121: SAPPER HILL This hill provides a popular **short hike** off the highway (*Time: around 2hrs; Distance: 5km, 3 miles; Difficulty rating: moderate – there's a vigorous climb; Trailhead: park on the northeastern side of the Engineer Creek bridge – that's on the right-hand side, immediately across the first bridge after the Engineer Creek campground as you're driving north*). There's a trail – not brilliantly defined – climbing from the parking pull-out through the rubbly stuff, up the hill due east. After this it becomes fairly clear where you're heading, up and up to the rock formations, from which you'll enjoy mesmerizing views. You'll need to decide on a point to turn round and head back the way you came. Note that the cliffs here are nesting sites for peregrine falcons and gyrfalcons. You should avoid disturbing them: peregrine falcons have been known to throw their eggs out of their nests in times of stress. A 'sapper', by the way, is a nickname for an army engineer. The hill is named for the 3rd Royal Canadian Engineers, who built the Ogilvie River bridge.

KM 259, MILE 161: OGILVIE–PEEL VIEWPOINT This is one of the more dramatic viewpoints on the highway, looking over the northern Ogilvie Mountains. This is a point on the continental divide. West of the divide, the water flows into the Pacific Ocean; water to the east flows into the Arctic Ocean.

KM 371, MILE 229: EAGLE PLAINS HOTEL AND SERVICE STATION See page 195.

KM 406, MILE 252: ARCTIC CIRCLE You're now at 66°33' latitude, and crossing the point where the sun never sets on 21 June and never rises on 21 December – the further north you go, the longer the periods of continuous daylight and darkness. There's another viewpoint here (and what a view) as well as interpretive boards. In spring, you may see grizzly bears on the tundra; in autumn and winter you may see caribou from the Porcupine herd. Look out, in summer, for short-eared owls.

KM 465, MILE 289, NWT KM 0: YUKON–NORTHWEST TERRITORIES BORDER Just to confuse matters, the kilometre markers now start again from zero. The continental divide lies at the territories' border (it also crosses the Ogilvie–Peel viewpoint at km 259, see above). Also, you enter a different time zone here: the Northwest Territories are one hour ahead of the Yukon.

KM 509, MILE 316, NWT KM 44: MIDWAY LAKE The Midway Lake Music Festival is held here the first weekend of August. It's a Gwich'in jamboree with music, dancing (the Gwich'in 'traditional' dances incorporate jigs, waltzes and square dances learned from the 19th-century European fur traders), storytelling and canoe races on the lake. Note that the festival is dry: you'll be welcome, but your six-pack of beers will not. Go to www.tetlitgwichin.ca/MidwayLake for more information.

KM 530, MILE 329, NWT KM 71: TETLIT GWINJIK (PEEL RIVER) PARK AND PEEL RIVER PLATEAU VIEWPOINT What can I say? Yet more unbelievable views.

KM 539, MILE 335, NWT KM 74: PEEL RIVER CROSSING Ferry runs 9am–12.30am daily from June to mid-October. There's an ice bridge in the winter months. It is not possible to cross the river during freeze-up and break-up. The Peel River was named in 1826 by John Franklin (see *John Franklin*, page 210) after the British prime minister Sir Robert Peel.

CANOEING TO OLD CROW

Just after Eagle Plains, the road crosses the Eagle River. Canoeists can put in here to paddle the Eagle, Bell and Porcupine rivers to the community of Old Crow, which is accessed by scheduled air services. It's an easy run with no rapids. If you've time on your hands you can continue along the Porcupine into Alaska, past the Old Rampart village and through the southern part of the Arctic National Wildlife Refuge to Fort Yukon, from where you'll need to take a charter flight out. Or you can just keep going to the Yukon River and the Bering Sea beyond. The trip takes roughly two weeks to Old Crow or three weeks to Fort Yukon. To get to the Bering Sea, however, you'll need some serious time off work.

10

McDonald was an Anglican missionary, who arrived at Fort McPherson in the early 1870s. There he met and married a local Gwich'in girl, Julia Kutug, and with her he lived at Fort McPherson for more than 30 years.

McDonald is remembered principally as the first person to have created a written form of the Gwich'in language, and for his translations of the bible and other religious texts into Gwich'in. He also compiled a grammar book and a book designed to teach Gwich'in people to read. McDonald's books are still used by some of the older Gwich'in people who were taught to read by his system. (Younger generations can't make head or tail of it, since they've only learned a more contemporary form.)

It's also thought that McDonald was the first white man to discover gold in the Yukon. He found a quantity in 1863 and sent it for analysis to the British Museum, whose staff confirmed that he had, indeed, struck riches. McDonald, however, was more interested in his translations – or perhaps he foresaw the devastation a gold rush would wreak on his beloved Gwich'in people – and so he took the matter no further.

KM 541, MILE 336, NWT KM 76: NITAINLAII TERRITORIAL PARK There's an interpretive centre, with displays on the Gwich'in people and their traditions, and a campground (⊕ *1 Jun–1 Sep*).

KM 550, MILE 342, NWT KM 86: FORT MCPHERSON A side road leads off the highway to the Tetlit Gwich'in community of Fort McPherson. The settlement was first

THE LOST PATROL

Francis Fitzgerald was an outdoorsman of the highest order. He had excelled on a police expedition across arduous arctic terrain that lasted more than two years; he had shone as a sergeant during the Boer war; he was considered to be a man of integrity and intelligence. And so when, in 1903, it was decided that the Mounties needed to establish a presence at Fort McPherson in the Northwest Territories and on Herschel Island (see pages 217–19) – where the whalers were wreaking havoc plying the local islanders, the Qikiqtarukmiut, with alcohol and not paying duty on their lucrative trade to boot – Fitzgerald was chosen to command the new posts.

There was only one way that Fitzgerald could send his reports to his superiors, and check on the scattered prospectors and Indians that lived across the wilderness of the north, and that was via an annual dogsled patrol that was established between Dawson City, a well-developed town that had sprung up to house the miners of the Klondike gold rush just a few years before, and Fort McPherson. In 1904 the first patrol set out from Dawson: it was easier to supply an expedition from the more southerly town and from there Gwich'in guides, who knew the land and were expert huntsmen, were easy to hire.

But in the winter of 1910–11, Fitzgerald and his men travelled in the opposite direction. That year, Fitzgerald started at Herschel Island and made his way south towards Fort McPherson and Dawson, a journey of about 1,300km (800 miles). Breaking with tradition, he chose not to use an Indian guide but employed former constable Sam Carter instead. Constables George Francis Kinney and Richard O'Hara Taylor travelled with them.

The weather that winter was bitter. During the first week of January, temperatures averaged –46°C (–51°F); one day they fell –54°C (–65°F). And then the patrol missed the turn off the Little Wind River into Forrest Creek. The four men were lost. On 17 January Fitzgerald wrote in his journal, 'We have now only ten pounds of flour and eight established by John Bell of the Hudson's Bay Company. In 1849 he set up a trading post 6.5km (4 miles) four miles away; it was later moved to the present site due to flooding. The village is named for Murdoch McPherson of the Hudson's Bay Company (he whom Robert Campbell accused of tight-fistedness, see page 142); its Gwich'in name is Tetl'it Zheh, which means Town at the Head Waters.

A village of around 900 inhabitants, Fort McPherson doesn't offer a tremendous number of attractions for passing traffic. There's a visitor information centre in a restored log house (⊕ *May–Sep 9am–9pm daily*), a gas station with a food store, and a hotel, the **Peel River Inn** (*8 rooms, ⬎ 867 952 2373; www.peelriverinn; $$$$*) though most people prefer to stop at Eagle Plains, which is both better located at the highway's halfway point, and better value. I have found a few references to bed and breakfast accommodation in Fort McPherson though haven't actually seen any with my own eyes – call the Hamlet of Fort McPherson office on ⬎ 867 952 2428 or the Tetlit Gwich'in Tourism Society on ⬎ 867 952 2356 for current information.

Visitors can drop in to the **Fort McPherson Tent and Canvas Company** factory (⬎ *867 952 2179;* ⊕ *9am–5pm Mon–Fri*), which makes and sells tents and soft luggage. In case of emergencies, Fort McPherson has an **RCMP detachment** (⬎ *867 952 1111*) and a **health centre** (⬎ *867 952 2586*).

Of greater interest (hopefully!) is the cemetery, where you'll find the graves of the men of the Lost Patrol (see *The Lost Patrol*, below) – look for a large white-painted stone on which sits all four grave markers and a big white cross.

KM 608, MILE 378, NWT KM 142: MACKENZIE RIVER CROSSING This ferry operates at the confluence of the Mackenzie and Arctic Red rivers. It runs in a triangle shape

pounds of bacon and some dried fish. My last hope is gone, and the only thing I can do is return, and kill some of the dogs to feed the others and ourselves, unless we can meet some Indians. We have now been a week looking for a river to take us over the divide, but there are dozens of rivers and I am at a loss. I should not have taken Carter's word that he knew the way from the Little Wind River.'

The weather stayed against them as they attempted to find their way back to safety at Fort McPherson. They encountered neither game nor Indians. By the end of January, all four men were suffering from frostbite and scurvy. Their skin peeled to raw flesh, their feet swelled and their flesh grew discoloured. As starvation set in, their ribs protruded and their stomachs sank.

When by mid-February Fitzgerald and his men had not arrived in Dawson, concern deepened. Finally, on 20 February, Corporal Dempster – after whom the Dempster Highway was later named – was dispatched on a rescue mission with a team that included an Indian guide. Less than three weeks later, he found the bodies – first those of Kinney and Taylor and then, 16km (10 miles) downriver, those of Fitzgerald and Carter. Three had starved to death; Taylor had shot himself, whether to avoid the temptation of cannibalism or to eradicate a final couple of days of agony, nobody knows.

The trails of the north are rich with tales of triumph and tragedy, but there are few disasters that have cut to the heart of these tiny northern communities like that of the Lost Patrol. As the Qikiqtarukmiut said when they heard of Fitzgerald's demise, 'Too bad. Inspector good man.'

For more on the Lost Patrol, read Dick North's book, *The Lost Patrol*, available in Yukon bookshops, from www.yukonbooks.com, and from other online bookstores such as Amazon.

between the two points where the Dempster Highway meets the river, and the community of Tsiigehtchic (formerly Arctic Red river) which sits where the two waterways meet. The ferry runs 9am–12.30am daily from June to mid-October. There's an ice bridge in the winter months, and a separate spur road is created to lead to Tsiigehtchic. It is not possible to cross the river during freeze-up and break-up.

TSIIGEHTCHIC (FORMERLY ARCTIC RED RIVER) Originally a Gwich'in summer fishing camp, Tsiigehtchic is now home to the Gwichya Gwich'in people and has a permanent population of around 200, most of whom live from hunting, trapping and fishing. It officially changed its name in 1994 from Arctic Red River to Tsiigehtchic to reflect its residents' heritage. The community specializes in 'dryfish' made from Mackenzie River broad whitefish; it's often possible to buy some if you visit.

Tsiigehtchic benefits from being just off the highway – most drivers don't stop here – and so has a remoter feel than Fort McPherson despite its almost-on-the-road location. There are few services catering to tourists (that's to say, there's a shop and a fast-food joint) but visitors are welcome to pitch their tents on the flats or on the beach by the ferry stop. Note that Tsiigehtchic is a dry community: it's forbidden to bring alcohol here.

Timber Island Enterprises (↘ 867 678 2998; e timberisland@yahoo.ca) offers half-day boat and cultural camp tours out of Tsiigehtchic. Arctic Red River is navigable by canoe or kayak: you have to fly in to one of the lakes upstream and then paddle back towards the settlement and the Dempster. For charter flights, contact **Aklak Air** in Inuvik (↘ scheduled flights: 867 777 3777, charter flights: 867 777 3555, toll-free: ↘ 866 707 4977; e info@aklakair.ca; www.aklakair.ca), or one of the specialist canoeing operators listed on pages 207–9.

KM 701, MILE 436, NWT KM 232: CAMPBELL LAKE The highway follows the shore of this stunning lake for some time, but here there's a pull-out where you can park, and a short trail leads to the cliffs that give wonderful views over the water.

INUVIK

What the heck – let's start with the unpalatable. Inuvik's average annual temperature is –10°C (15°F). But this tiny town of 3,500 hardy souls, which sits 200km (124 miles) north of the Arctic Circle, is a place of contrasts. Summer temperatures can reach 30°C (86°F). Inuvik enjoys 54 days of continuous light each June, July and August – and in December and January it hunkers down for 30 days when the sun doesn't rise at all. (If you're wondering, there are more days of light than of darkness because of the hours of twilight, when the sun is below the horizon but the sky is light.)

I've been to Inuvik in both summer and winter and have found it to be a supremely warm place, whatever the temperature. It's hard to put my finger on why. It's a funny-looking town, though its brightly coloured 'Smartie-box' houses have their own charm, and the Igloo Church is pretty. I think, in the end, its attraction comes from the fact that the pace is slower here and, because it's out of the way, the people are friendly. They have time to stop and talk with visitors who've bothered to venture off the beaten track. If you're driving the Dempster Highway, it's definitely worth staying a couple of nights. There's plenty to do – if you make the onward journey to Tuk, you can even dip your toes in the Arctic Ocean – and the town provides perfect downtime between your days on the road.

HISTORY Following World War II, the Canadian government decided it need a permanent communications centre in the Western Arctic. Aklavik, the major existing community, was an obvious choice – but government planners decided it was too prone to flooding and erosion, and its delta location offered no room for growth.

In 1954, Ottawa's Department of Northern Affairs and National Resources sent a team to the Mackenzie Delta to locate a suitable site. They settled on a spot on the East Channel of the Mackenzie River, 100km (60 miles) south of the Beaufort Sea. There was no human settlement here; indeed, the land had changed little since 1789 when Alexander Mackenzie had sailed past on the river named for him (see *Alexander Mackenzie*, page 208). At first the new townsite was known simply as 'East Three'. The name Inuvik, meaning 'Place of Man' in the Inuit language, was adopted in July 1958.

Building a town from scratch this high in the Arctic invited immense complications. Construction, which was greatly hampered by permafrost (see *Why are the houses on stilts?* page 207), began in summer 1955 with crews working round the clock to make the most of the short arctic summer. But there were social problems, too. Many of the Gwich'in and Inuvialuit people found it difficult to abandon the village they had always known and their traditional lifestyle with its emphasis on the land, and to adapt to working fixed hours for the government or its contracted companies. There were also issues with schooling. Inuvik was created partly to fulfil a need for schools in the Mackenzie Delta: many of the region's children had no formal education until that time. Two hostels were built for those children whose parents had not chosen to move to Inuvik themselves: Stringer Hall was for the Protestant children and Grollier Hall for the Catholics. Grollier Hall, which didn't close its doors until 1997, later became notorious for the physical and sexual abuse that was meted out on the children in its care; six of its former supervisors subsequently served prison sentences.

Communications systems came to Inuvik, albeit slowly. The first long-distance telephone call was made from Inuvik in 1966; live television didn't arrive until 1973. The Dempster Highway (see pages 191–202) was completed in 1979, giving the town road access from the south, and increasing its tourist numbers.

By the late 1950s, oil and gas companies were exploring the Mackenzie Delta and Beaufort region. When in 1968 oil was discovered to the west, in Alaska's Prudhoe Bay, the corporate giants' quest for riches on the Canadian side of the border intensified; Imperial Oil struck oil at Atkinson Point, northeast of Inuvik on the Tuktoyaktuk Peninsula, in 1970. Oil and gas exploration rocketed and by the mid-1970s a Supreme Court Judge, Tom Berger, was dispatched to the Mackenzie Delta to investigate the potential effects of building a gas pipeline south through the northern Yukon. (An oil pipeline had recently been approved over the border in Alaska: construction on the Trans Alaska Pipeline, which to this day moves oil from Prudhoe Bay to Valdez, started in 1975 and was operational from 1977.) After two years of hearings, Berger suggested that the social impact of rapid development on the native people would be devastating. He further recommended that the Yukon route posed too great an environmental threat – he thought that any future energy corridor should follow the Mackenzie Valley instead – and proposed a ten-year moratorium on the pipeline to allow more research and the processing of native land claims. Berger's report shocked the government that appointed him, and caused oil and gas investment in the area to decline.

Another blow struck Inuvik in 1986, when the town's military base, which employed 267 personnel, closed. The military had played an important role in Inuvik's early years; the base's demise meant that 700 people left town.

Exploration in the Mackenzie Delta has sporadically peaked and troughed over the years, but has risen again since the turn of the millennium. As native land claims have been settled, the pipeline question has been broached once more. A conglomeration of oil and gas giants proposes to build a 1,220km (758-mile) pipeline from the Mackenzie Delta to Alberta, where it would connect with an existing gas pipeline system. The oil companies reached an understanding with the Aboriginal Pipeline Group in 2001; two years later it was agreed that aboriginal groups would own a third of the pipeline. However, regulatory hearings,

THE MAD TRAPPER OF RAT RIVER

On Christmas Day 1931, a local trapper went to the RCMP post at Arctic Red River. He complained that a man living in a cabin on Rat River was tampering with his traps. And so, on 26 December, two constables set off by dogsled to investigate.

It took the policemen two and a half days to reach the cabin. There was certainly somebody home – smoke was puffing from the stovepipe and the police saw a figure peer from a window – but nobody answered the Mounties' call. The police scented trouble, and so they returned to Aklavik – another night and two days' journey by dogsled – to ask for a warrant and reinforcements. Such was a northern policeman's beat.

It was New Year's Eve when the second contingent of Mounties arrived at the cabin on Rat River, and now they were four. One of them went to knock on the door – and the man within fired his rifle, wounding the policeman in the chest. His colleagues strapped him to a sled and mushed their already-tired dogs 130 miles back to Aklavik, stopping frequently to rub the unmoving man's flesh to stop it from freezing. Some 24 hours later they arrived. The wounded man was saved – and now the manhunt was on in earnest.

Nine Mounties, 42 dogs and a supply of dynamite returned to the cabin this time, but the man inside kept up a remarkable defence. From a foxhole he'd dug into the floor, he kept firing volleys of bullets at the police, even after they had blown the roof from his cabin with dynamite. The battle lasted 15 hours, by which time temperatures had plummeted into the minus 40s and the police were running short of supplies. Once more, they had to return to Aklavik. When they returned to the cabin for a fourth time its inhabitant, unsurprisingly, was gone.

The manhunt that followed was truly astonishing. It took the Mounties and the volunteers that helped them – all experienced arctic outdoorsmen – more than a month to track down the 'Mad Trapper'. They travelled with dogs; they had food and supplies; they could build fires to keep themselves warm. The Mad Trapper on the other hand could not build a fire unless he did so under a snow bank because the smoke would give away his location. He couldn't shoot game because the report, again, would tell police where he hid. He could only eat those small animals and birds he managed to snare yet, environmental concerns and bureaucratic meanderings have continued to stall the project, whose future remains uncertain.

GETTING THERE AND AROUND

By road The only road that connects Inuvik to the south is the Dempster Highway (see pages 191–202). There's an ice road to Tuktoyaktuk and Aklavik in the winter only (see pages 214–15).

For vehicle rentals, try **Norcan** (*you'll see it on the right as you're approaching town from the airport or Dempster Highway;* ✆ *867 777 2346, toll-free:* ✆ *1 877 881 5398 NWT, Yukon & Alberta only; www.norcan.yk.ca – note that it has moved from its old location on Franklin Rd, still shown on some town maps*) or Delta Auto Rentals at the **Arctic Chalet** (*25 Carn St;* ✆ *867 777 3535, toll-free:* ✆ *1 800 685 9417;* e *judi@ arcticchalet.com; www.arcticchalet.com*). For taxis, call **United Taxi** (*181 Mackenzie Rd;* ✆ *867 777 5050*).

By air The **Inuvik Mike Zubko Airport** (✆ *867 777 2467*) is 14km (8 miles) east of town; the entire runway rests on a thick gravel pad to protect it from corruption by the permafrost.

First Air (✆ *613 254 6200, toll-free:* ✆ *1 800 267 1247;* e *reservat@firstair.ca; www.firstair.ca*) operates across Canada's north; it connects to Yellowknife,

---

half-starved, he evaded capture by crossing the Richardson Mountains. Those that knew the terrain considered this feat to be all but impossible.

Finally, in mid-February, the Mad Trapper was killed in a police shoot-out and was buried in Aklavik. But although he was dead, the mystery of his identity remained. He carried no documents and, in his cabin, the police found no photographs, letters, or clues of any kind. Those who recognized his face from the death photographs claimed to have known him over the years by different names.

Decades later Dick North, the Dawson-based author (see page 183), took up the mystery with a near-obsessive interest. He spent 20 years, off and on, researching the story; his book *The Mad Trapper of Rat River* tells both the story of the manhunt and of North's own attempts to solve the mystery. North sought permission to have the Mad Trapper's body exhumed for identification, but his requests were turned down. Eventually, in the 1990s, he concluded that he must have been one Albert Johnson, an outlaw from the American West. But this wasn't the end of the story.

In March 2007, a TV production company, Myth Merchant, succeeded where North had failed (though they probably would not have done so had they not had local filmmaker Dennis Allen on board – see *My Father, My Teacher*, page 211). They persuaded the council and residents of Aklavik to vote in favour of the disinterment of the Mad Trapper's body. The producers proposed that they DNA test the remains, and make a documentary film about the mystery. The Mad Trapper's body was therefore exhumed in August that year. (After 75 years in the frozen ground, his hair, beard and fingernails were still intact.) The public was not allowed to be present at the disinterment and subsequent ceremony to rebury the remains; indeed the entire manoeuvre was controversial within Aklavik, where many claimed that it was disrespectful to disturb the dead. The film, titled *Hunt for the Mad Trapper*, was eventually aired in May 2009 on Discovery Channel Canada.

For more on the Mad Trapper, read Dick North's book *The Mad Trapper of Rat River*, available in Yukon bookshops, from www.yukonbooks.com, and from other online bookstores such as Amazon.

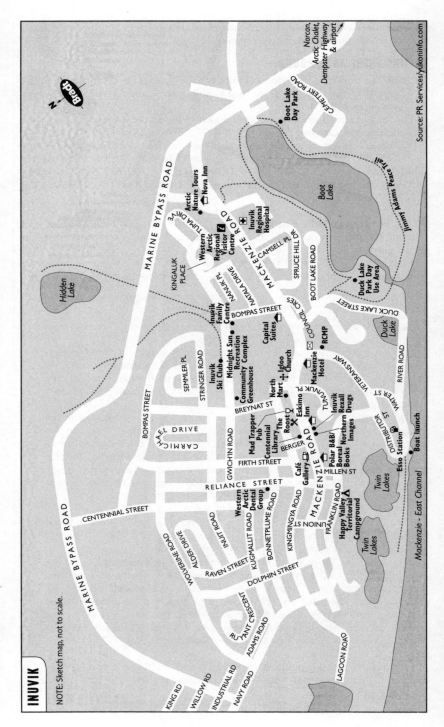

INUVIK

NOTE: Sketch map, not to scale.

Marine Bypass Road

King Rd
Willow Rd
Industrial Rd
Navy Road
Lagoon Road
Adams Crescent
Ant Crescent
Wolverine Road
Alder Drive
Raven Street
Dolphin Street
Inuit Road
Kugmallit Road
Bonnetplume Road
Kingmingya Road
Union St
Franklin Road
Millen St
Carmichael Drive
Bompas Street
Semmler Pl
Stringer Road
Gwich'in Road
Firth Street
Centennial Street
Reliance Street

Hidden Lake

Western Arctic Dental Group
Café Gallery
Centennial Library
Mad Trapper Pub
Happy Valley Territorial Campground
Mackenzie Road

Twin Lakes
Twin Lakes

Inuvik Ski Club
Midnight Sun Recreation Complex
Community Greenhouse
North Mart
Eskimo Inn
The Roost
Berger
Tununuk Pl
Polar B&B/ Boreal Books
Northern Images
Inuvik Rexall Drugs
Breynat St
Igloo Church
Mackenzie Hotel
RCMP
Capital Suites

Inuvik Family Centre
Bompas Street
Kingaluk Place
Naiyuk Pl
Natal'auq Drive
Tuma Drive
Western Arctic Regional Visitor Centre

Arctic Nature Tours
Nova Inn
Inuvik Regional Hospital
Council Cres
Spruce Hill Dr
Boot Lake Road
Mackenzie Road
Cemetery Road

Norcan, Arctic Chalet, Dempster Highway & airport

Boot Lake Day Park

Boot Lake

Jimmy Adams Peace Trail

Duck Lake Park Day Use Area
Duck Lake Street
Duck Lake

River Road
Veterans Way
Water St
Distributor St
Esso Station
Boat Launch

Mackenzie – East Channel

Source: PR Services/yukoninfo.com

206

Edmonton and other cities. **Air North** (❧ *867 668 2228, toll-free:* ❧ *1 800 661 0407; www.flyairnorth.com*) is the Yukon's airline; it connects to Yukon destinations including Dawson and Whitehorse, as well as Vancouver, Edmonton and Calgary. **Canadian North** (❧ *867 873 4484, toll-free:* ❧ *1 800 661 1505; www.canadiannorth.com*) is 100% aboriginal-owned; it has 30,000 Inuvialuit and Inuit of Nunavut shareholders. It connects to the major cities of Edmonton, Ottawa and Calgary, as well as to numerous destinations in the NWT, Nunavut and Quebec. **Aklak Air** (❧ *scheduled flights: 867 777 3777, charter flights: 867 777 3555, toll-free:* ❧ *1 866 707 4977;* e *info@aklakair.ca; www.aklakair.ca*) operates scheduled flights between Inuvik and Fort McPherson, Aklavik, Tuktoyaktuk, Paulatuk, Sachs Harbour and Ulukhaktok, and charter flights to pretty much everywhere else, including local navigable rivers and National Parks (see pages 221–4). They can transport canoes – and even have canoes for hire.

The following helicopter companies operate out of Inuvik: **Canadian Helicopters** (❧ *867 777 2424*); **Highland Helicopters** (❧ *867 777 5151*); **Gwich'in Helicopters** (❧ *867 678 2270, cell: 867 678 0270;* e *inuvik@ greatslaveheli.com; www.greatslaveheli.com*).

TOURIST INFORMATION AND TOUR OPERATORS The **Western Arctic Regional Visitor Centre** (*eastern end of Mackenzie Rd;* ❧ *867 777 4727;* e *travel_westernarctic@ gov.nt.ca;* ☉ *mid-May to mid-Sep 9am–8pm daily, in winter call Judith Venaas on* ❧ *867 777 7237 – she will open the visitor centre by appointment*) is an excellent facility with interpretive displays of local wildlife and history as well as a good selection of brochures and leaflets. It also has an interesting video and DVD collection. You can watch films on topics such as the Dempster Highway, Herschel Island and the caribou migration for free.

Arctic Nature Tours (*it's tucked away down the street behind the visitor centre & Nova Inn;* ❧ *867 777 3300, cell: 867 777 6360;* e *reservations@arcticnaturetours.com; www.arcticnaturetours.com;* ☉ *1 Jun to 1 Oct 8am–7pm Mon–Fri, 10am–5pm Sat–Sun*) has a portfolio of fascinating trips including cultural tours to Tuktoyaktuk, day and camping trips to Herschel Island, boat trips to see the pingos and through the Mackenzie Delta, a musk ox safari from Sachs Harbour, and an arctic char fishing trip beneath the midnight sun from Ulukhaktok. Advance booking is recommended.

Midnight Express Tours (❧ *867 777 4829*) operates boat trips on the Mackenzie Delta and cultural tours.

Siulig Tours (❧ *867 777 3833, cell: 867 678 5630;* e *siulig@northwestel.net*) Owner Gerry Kisoun offers eco-tourism trips in the Beaufort Delta by boat and snow machine. Gerry is Gwich'in–Inuvialuit and was raised in Inuvik. His dad was Victor Allen, see *My Father, My Teacher*, page 211.

Up North Tours (*69 Mackenzie Rd;* ☎ *867 678 0510;* e *info@upnorthtours.ca; www.upnorthtours.ca*) runs boating, fishing and national park tours in summer, snowmobiling and ice-road tours in winter, and trips down the Dempster Highway.

ALEXANDER MACKENZIE

Alexander Mackenzie was a fur trader with the North West Company – the Hudson's Bay Company's principal rival until the two companies merged in 1821. (Note that Alexander Mackenzie the explorer should not be confused with Alexander Mackenzie the second prime minister of Canada, who was 58 years the explorer's junior. The two share a name and a birthplace – Alexander Mackenzie the PM also started out in Scotland – but there's where the similarities end.)

Born on the Isle of Lewis in Scotland's Outer Hebrides in 1764, Mackenzie emigrated with his family to North America when he was 12 years old, and joined the North West Company four years later. When he was 22, the company offered him a partnership on the understanding that he would make explorations into 'Indian country'.

Mackenzie dreamed of finding a water route from the Atlantic to the Pacific Ocean. With this goal in mind, he and his entourage set off in canoes from Fort Chipewyan, Alberta, in 1789. Three months later they returned, sorry to have found a water route not to the Pacific but to the Arctic Ocean. Mackenzie named the great river that led them to the northern ocean Disappointment River; only later would it be named for his own accomplishment.

'Hardly a Shrub to be seen,' Mackenzie wrote in his journal on 11 July, from the stretch of river that now leads to Tuktoyaktuk from Inuvik. 'Close by the land is high and covered with short Grass and many Plants, which are in Blossom, and has a beautiful appearance, tho' an odd contrast, the Hills covered with Flowers and Verdure, and the Vallies full of Ice and Snow. The Earth is not thawed above 4 Inches from the Surface, below is a solid Body of Ice.'

Mackenzie and his men may not have found trees this far north, but they did come across local tribes.

'The Natives made a terrible uproar speaking quite loud & running up & down like perfect Madmen...I made them Presents of some small Articles but they were fonder of the Beads than anything else I gave particularly Blue Ones...There were 5 Families of them but I did not see them all as they kept in their hiding Places.'

In 1793 Mackenzie tried again to reach the Pacific. This time he headed upstream along the Peace River and over the Rocky Mountains, arriving at Bella Coona on the Pacific Coast on 22 July that year. He was the first European to cross North America by an overland route – and he achieved this a full 12 years before the USA's fabled Lewis and Clark made their acclaimed journey.

For an entertaining, contemporary travelogue on following Mackenzie's route to the Pacific, read *Voyageur: Across the Rocky Mountains in a Birchbark Canoe* by Robert Twigger. Over three summers, Twigger and his ragtag bunch of mates paddle, tow and portage their canoe upriver in the wake of Alexander Mackenzie. Twigger doesn't shy from relating the minutae – the arguments, the drugs, the arrests, the mosquitoes and bears, and the unfortunate but hilarious propensity that Dave has for mislaying his shoes (he ends up losing all three pairs and has to travel barefoot). It's a self-deprecating and very funny story about a group of men having a generally horrible time for no very good reason at all. And there's plenty on Mackenzie and his travails, as well.

- Inuvik has achieved world fame as a principal location of the blockbuster TV documentary *Ice Road Truckers*. The show's second season (aired worldwide from 2008–09) was filmed out of Inuvik.
- Inuvik's single traffic light, at the junction of Mackenzie Road and Distributor Street, is the northernmost traffic light in the world.
- The first child to squash a mosquito in Inuvik each summer wins a prize from the local newspaper, the *Inuvik Drum*.

White Husky Tours is run by **Arctic Chalet** (*25 Carn St;* ☎ *867 777 3535, toll-free:* ☎ *800 685 9417;* e *judi@arcticchalet.com; www.whitehuskies.com*). Judi and Olav's pure-white dogs are an unusual breed that originated from cross-breeding Alaskan Malamutes and Siberian huskies. In winter they offer half-day and day dogsledding trips during which guests drive their own team. They also host nine-day dogsledding trips to Tuktoyaktuk in March and April, and offer snowshoe trips to a secluded cabin near their lodge – you can either go and come back the same day, or spend the night there – plus winter van trips up the ice road to Tuktoyaktuk. In summer, White Husky Tours offers van tours down the Dempster, guided hikes with the dogs and flight tours to Tuk. Arctic Chalet has free canoes for its bed and breakfast guests (see *Where to stay*, below), rents canoes and kayaks, and offers transportation for longer river journeys as well as vehicle rental year round.

WHERE TO STAY

Mackenzie Hotel (97 rooms) 185 Mackenzie Rd; ☎ 867 777 2861; e mackenziehotel@ northwestel.net; www.inuvikhotels.com. One of the Inuvik hotel scene's more recent – & stylish – additions, the Mackenzie opened in summer 2006. 90% of its guests are business clients (predominantly in the oil & gas industries). It's kitted out to a high standard; all rooms have fridge, microwave & high-speed internet access via ethernet. There's also a business centre with guest computer & an exercise room. $$$$–$$$$$

Capital Suites (82 rooms) 198 Mackenzie Rd; ☎ 867 678 6300, toll-free reservations ☎ 1 877 669 9444; e inres@npreit.com; www.capitalsuites.ca. Very comfortable rooms all of which have fridge & microwave. The 1-bedroom suites are particularly attractive & have full kitchen facilities. There's DSL internet access in all rooms. Most of the guests here are on extended stays due to oil & gas company contracts. There's no bar or restaurant. $$$$–$$$$$

Nova Inn (41 rooms) 300 Mackenzie Rd; ☎ 867 777 6682; e novainninuvik@novahotels.ca; www.novahotels.ca. It's new & very clean-looking, but somewhat soulless. All rooms have fridges, fireplaces for the winter, & ethernet internet access. $$$–$$$$

Eskimo Inn (72 rooms) 133 Mackenzie Rd; ☎ 867 777 2801; e eskimoinn@northwestel.net; www.inuvikhotels.com/eskimo.htm. Owned by the same outfit as the Mackenzie, the Eskimo Inn is older & rather more tired, though some rooms have been renovated recently. There's high-speed internet, via ethernet, in all the rooms. $$$–$$$$

Arctic Chalet (10 rooms) 25 Carn St; ☎ 867 777 3535, toll-free: ☎ 800 685 9417; e judi@ arcticchalet.com; www.arcticchalet.com. This is my personal accommodation choice for Inuvik. Arctic Chalet is 2km (1.2 miles) out of the centre of Inuvik, has a delightfully relaxed atmosphere & its cabins are charming; all have electricity, hot running water & full kitchen facilities. Basic, unperishable food is supplied for b/fast but you'll probably want to supplement it. There's also a laundry & wireless internet, plus guest computer. Arctic Chalet has canoes, which are free for guests who want to paddle on Chuck Lake just behind the cabins. There are also nature trails & walks with Judi & Olav's white huskies (who are trained to be quiet at night!) Dogsledding is on offer in winter; see White Husky Tours, above. $$$

Polar Bed & Breakfast (4 rooms, 2 sgls & 2 dbls) 75 Mackenzie Rd; ☎ 867 777 2554; e kaufman@permafrost.com. Guests share a living

The British naval officer John Franklin led three Arctic expeditions; it was on the third that he and his men famously disappeared. The British were at the time intent on finding a route through the Northwest Passage, which connects the Atlantic and Pacific oceans above the Arctic Circle and was sought by mariners for hundreds of years as its discovery would dramatically shorten voyages between Europe and the west coast of America. Franklin's second Canadian journey brought him to the Mackenzie River area in June 1826. He and his men sailed up to the Delta and mapped a thousand kilometres of coastline before returning to spend the winter in the comforts of Fort Franklin on the shores of Great Bear Lake.

It was surprising, in many ways, that Franklin was chosen for this work, for although his second expedition was successful his first had been catastrophic – it had ended in the starvation to death of more than half of his party. In their desperation, Franklin and his men ate lichen from the rocks, which gave them dysentery. When there was no lichen, they ate their spare shoes. Remarkably, however, Franklin had returned home a hero. His triumph over adversity (even if that adversity had been partly his own fault) won the admiration of a public high on the romantic notion of the gentleman explorer. Franklin was the man who'd eaten his boots.

Franklin's third expedition, which left London in 1845, was supposed to map the last 500 miles (800km) of Canadian Arctic coastline, and to find the Northwest Passage. The ships *HMS Erebus* and *HMS Terror* and their crews were seen by two whalers off Lancaster Sound that July. And then they disappeared.

The search for the Franklin expedition lasted a full ten years, and cost in the region of £800,000, £35,000 of which was raised and spent by Sir John Franklin's loyal and energetic wife. A total of 39 expeditions set out to find the missing men. And at the end of it all, well, they found out that the men had died. They heard stories from local Inuit about men so sick they fell as they walked, and they found a few skeletons. They discovered, with some distaste, that the starving men appeared to have resorted to cannibalism. And that was the – exorbitantly expensive – end of that.

Anyone wanting to know more about the 19th-century quest for the Northwest Passage – and other British explorations of the period – should read Fergus Fleming's excellent book, *Barrow's Boys: A Stirring Story of Daring, Fortitude and Outright Lunacy*.

room with TV & a fully equipped kitchen with washer/dryer. Bathrooms are shared. $$$
⚠ Happy Valley Territorial Campground (28 sites, 20 with power) Franklin Rd; ☎ 867 777 3652; ⏰ late May/early Jun (they open when they ferry starts to operate) till first week Sep. It's a nice,

wooded site overlooking the Mackenzie River, yet centrally located. All sites have trees & a picnic table – it's better, therefore, than many gravel-yard RV park options. There's wireless internet, plus firewood ($5 a pile), laundry ($5) & showers (free). $

✕ WHERE TO EAT Inuvik's restaurant directory is slim, and note: the decent eateries close early. Also, given that you're practically in the Arctic Ocean and supplies have to be flown in, don't expect prices to be cheap.

✕ Mackenzie Hotel 185 Mackenzie Rd; ☎ 867 777 2861; e mackenziehotel@northwestel.net; www.inuvikhotels.com. The Mackenzie has a formal restaurant, Tonimoes (⏰ till 9pm), & when that's closed it serves up an extensive menu in its bar till

10pm. The food isn't amazing for the price, & the place has a big-hotel sterility about it, but it's not a bad option if you arrive in town late. $$$–$$$$
✕ The Roost 106 Mackenzie Rd; ☎ 867 777 2727; ⏰ 11am–midnight daily. Fast-food joint selling

burgers, pizzas, pasta, fish & chips, & Chinese. The surroundings aren't exactly luxurious but you nonetheless have the option of dining in the back room or taking out. The food is good enough & if you really come in late off the highway, this is the joint for you. **$$–$$$$**

✗ **Caribou Café** Eskimo Inn, 133 Mackenzie Rd; ☎ 867 777 3675; e eskimoinn@northwestel.net; www.inuvikhotels.com/eskimo.htm; ⏰ 7am–8pm daily. The Eskimo Inn is the drabber 'tourist' relation to sleeker sister the Mackenzie Hotel; however, its dining room is the one restaurant in Inuvik that, alongside the Café Gallery, is consistently recommended. The menu features burgers, fish & chips, chicken fingers & sandwiches at lunchtime; at dinner seafood pasta & steaks are thrown into the mix. It closes before its advertised time of 8pm if diners are thin on the ground, however, so either scoot along in good time or make a reservation. **$$–$$$**

⎁ **Café Gallery** 86 Mackenzie Rd; ☎ 867 777 2888; e robcafegallery@gmail.com; ⏰ 10am–8pm Mon–Fri, noon–8pm Sat, noon–5pm Sun. This is one of the best eating options in Inuvik. It's great for deli sandwiches, muffins, homemade soup & pizza. **$–$$$**

ENTERTAINMENT AND NIGHTLIFE For local colour go to the **Mad Trapper Pub**, opposite the Eskimo Inn (*124 Mackenzie Rd;* ☎ *867 777 2785;* ⏰ *11am–2am Mon–Sat*). There's live music at 10pm Monday–Saturday, and there's a jam session every Saturday afternoon from 4pm.

SHOPPING **Northern Images** (*115 Mackenzie Rd;* ☎ *867 777 4478;* e *ni.inuvik@ arctico-op.com; www.northernimages.ca*) is one of a chain of Inuit- and Dene-owned art galleries across the NWT and Nunavut; it has some genuinely lovely sculptures and paintings. For books, head to **Boreal Books** (*75 Mackenzie Rd;* ☎ *867 777 3748;* e *manager@borealbooks.com; www.borealbooks.com*), while bearing in mind that you may buy the same tome more cheaply in Whitehorse.

There's a good-sized **NorthMart** grocery store in Inuvik (*160 Mackenzie Rd;* ☎ *867 777 2582*). In addition to food, it sells myriad other goods from clothing to barbecues to fishing licences. **Inuvik Liquor Store** is at 64 Franklin Road; ☎ 867 777 4974.

MY FATHER, MY TEACHER

Flying back to Whitehorse after my first visit to Inuvik a few years ago, I found myself chatting to the man across the aisle. His name was Dennis Allen, and he was a filmmaker. His film, *My Father, My Teacher*, was being shown in Whitehorse that evening as part of the city's film festival. He suggested I go along, and so I did.

I found his film to be a touching and fascinating work. It depicts the upheaval experienced by Dennis's Inuvialuit–Gwich'in family when they moved to the new town of Inuvik in the 1960s, and were forced to abandon their traditional way of life. The central character is Victor, Dennis's father, and much of the movie was shot at Baby Island, where the family still goes each year to hunt whales for *muktuk* (whale blubber). Victor's wisdom shone through the movie. In his 70s when the film was shot, he seemed always to be smiling, even when he was talking about the most traumatic displacements of his community. Dennis also used the film to talk about his own struggle with addiction as he attempted to numb the pain of this displacement, his attempts as a young man to cut himself off from his culture, and his subsequent wish to reaffirm his links with his people's traditions. I later read that Victor has been Inuvik's first Santa Claus, and that with his trademark cheerfulness he came to the school on a dogsled – except that his dogs didn't want to run that day, and somebody had to jog the front of the gangline, pulling them along.

Very sadly Victor drowned, with three members of his family, in summer 2008 when the boat taking them to Baby Island capsized. The film, however, survives and can be bought as a DVD from the National Film Board of Canada (*www.nfb.ca*).

OTHER PRACTICALITIES

Inuvik Regional Hospital ✆ 867 777 8000; ambulance service ✆ 867 777 4444. The hospital is the big red-and-blue building on Mackenzie Road, opposite the visitor centre. It has an emergency department with doctors on call 24/7.
NorthMart 160 Mackenzie Rd; ✆ 867 777 2812. There is a pharmacy within the NorthMart supermarket.
Inuvik Rexall Drugs 125 Mackenzie Rd; ✆ 867 777 2266.
Western Arctic Dental Group 22 Reliance St – junction with Bonnetplume Rd; ✆ 867 777 3008

Police RCMP detachment, Veteran's Way; ✆ 867 777 1111
CIBC Bank 134 Mackenzie Rd; ✆ 867 777 4539. Has an ATM.
Canada Post 187 Mackenzie Rd; ✆ 867 777 2252
Gas Highway drivers will need to fill up at Inuvik's Esso station, which sits not on the main drag of Mackenzie Road but to the south of town at 17 Distributor Street (✆ 867 777 3974) – it's just before the Mackenzie River boat launch.

WHAT TO SEE AND DO The **Inuvik Centennial Library** (*100 Mackenzie Rd;* ✆ *867 777 8620;* e *IK_Library@gov.nt.ca; www.nwtpls.gov.nt.ca includes online catalogue;* ⊕ *10am–6pm & 7pm–9pm Mon–Thu, 10am–6pm Fri, 1pm–5pm Sat–Sun*) is a great stop for anyone interested in northern books due to its extensive Dick Hill Northern Collection. Dick Hill is a former mayor of Inuvik; when he moved house he didn't have space for his collection of 10,000 tomes on all things Arctic, so he donated it to the town. The library also has free internet access, and a collection of northern-themed videos that you can watch in its community room.

Visitors are welcome to tour the **Igloo Church** (*174 Mackenzie Rd;* ✆ *867 777 2236*), whose real name is Our Lady of Victory Church, by arrangement with the visitor centre (see page 212) in the summer months. The church was built by volunteers in the 1950s; it took two years to complete. Uniquely, the church does not sit on wooden pilings, but on a gravel pad.

DICK HILL AND THE ROYAL VISIT

The Queen, Prince Philip, Prince Charles and Princess Anne visited Inuvik in 1970, when Dick Hill was mayor of the town.

'One evening we had a reception and the Queen and Prince Philip were in separate rooms to give more people the opportunity to meet them,' Dick Hill is quoted as recalling in Jane Stoneman-McNichol's book *On Blue Ice: The Inuvik Adventure.* 'When Prince Philip entered the room where I thought the Queen was to be I blurted out that he was in the wrong room. He looked rather stunned. I didn't know the plans had been changed.

'The next morning we were walking together up the steps of the school to another reception. We arrived in front of all those doors and the Prince paused, looked at each door and turned to me: "Now, be very specific," he said. "Which door would you like me to go in?"'

For ten days in the middle of July each year, more than 100 visual and performing artists from communities across the Arctic put on exhibitions, demonstrations and workshops in skills from soapstone carving to moose hair tufting in Inuvik's Midnight Sun Recreation Complex. Groups including Inuit, Inuvialuit, Gwich'in, Dene and Métis are represented, as well as non-Aboriginal artists who have in previous years come from as far afield as Scotland's Orkney Islands. Artisans also sell their work, which includes paintings, carvings, jewellery and clothing. There are also live music and drumming performances, and northern games such as the blanket toss: a person on a blanket is tossed several metres into the air and is expected to land back on two feet. This activity originates from hunting – a person tossed high from an animal skin had a higher vantage point from which to spot whales and caribou. For more information, contact the **Great Northern Arts Festival** (\ *867 777 8638;* e *gnaf@town.inuvik.ca; www.gnaf.org*).

The **Inuvik Community Greenhouse** (*cnr of Gwich'in Rd & Breynat St, behind the Igloo Church;* \ *867 777 3267;* e *inuvikgreenhouse@yahoo.ca; www.inuvikgreenhouse.com;* ⊕ *May–Oct; call or ask at the visitor centre for tour times*) is a quirky attraction. The main floor is a giant allotment, arctic-style, where members of the community can grow their own fruit and veg – a cost-effective option in this town where air-freighted produce is expensive. The upper floor is a commercial growing area; money raised covers management costs. Every Saturday in July and August there are garden markets, where fresh produce, fudge and bakery items are sold.

The **Inuvik Family Centre** (*95 Gwich'in Rd;* \ *867 777 8640; opening hrs vary so call ahead or ask at the visitor centre*) is a fantastic resource for a town of this size. It's got a great indoor swimming pool with water slide, and a mini climbing wall and jungle gym for kids. There are also squash courts ($12 per hour, racquets available) plus a sauna and steam room. The adjoining **Midnight Sun Recreation Complex** (\ *867 777 8636; day membership $5;* ⊕ *24hrs daily but membership must be bought 8.30am–noon & 1pm–5pm Mon, 8.30am–10.30pm Tue–Fri, 2pm–7pm Sat, 1pm–9.30pm Sun*) has a gym. There are also public and family skating sessions most days on the ice rink. They're free of charge, and they'll lend you the boots for free, too. Call Kelly Noseworthy on \ 867 777 8609 or Josh McDonald on \ 867 777 8636 for the current schedule, or go to http://inuvik.ca/recreation/msrc.html.

The **Inuvik Ski Club** (*Gwich'in Rd;* \ *867 777 2303*) maintains four groomed trails in winter, of which one is lit.

Hiking trails For an easy stroll, try the **Jimmy Adams Peace Trail**, which runs round **Boot Lake** on the southern side of town. It's named for long-time Inuvik resident and trapper Jimmy Adams. You can access the trail either via Mackenzie Road and Duck Lake Street, or from the boat launch at Boot Lake Day Park.

Alternatively the ski trails that run from the ski club on Gwich'in Road make attractive summer hikes, or you can walk along the shore of the East Channel of the Mackenzie River – start (and park) at Inuvik Waterfront Park on Water Street, just past the Esso station.

Canoe rentals

Aklak Air \ 867 777 3777, toll-free: \ 1 866 707 4977; e info@aklakair.ca; www.aklakair.ca

Arctic Chalet 25 Carn St; \ 867 777 3535, toll-free: \ 1 800 685 9417; e judi@arcticchalet.com; www.arcticchalet.com

The Northern Games festival was launched in Inuvik in 1970 in response to fears that traditional arts were dying in the Western Arctic. Inuvik's Northern Games Society continues to hold annual Northern Games festivals each summer.

These traditional games were originally played both for fun and for survival, as they developed the strength that the Inuvialuit needed in order to live on their harsh, arctic land. Events include high-kick contests (competitors have to kick a roll of seal skin that's suspended at height with either one or two feet) knuckle hops and the blanket toss. They're remarkable to watch, requiring extraordinary agility – and, seemingly, a tremendous capacity for bearing pain.

For more information, contact the **Northern Games Society** (867 777 2737; e *northerngames@gmail.com; www.northerngames.org*).

You can canoe on Boot Lake, or in the East Channel of the Mackenzie River – you can paddle all the way to Tuktoyaktuk (see below) if you so wish, or to the community of Aklavik (see page 216) in the Mackenzie Delta. The Mackenzie River is generally broad and flat. Inuvik is also a good base for canoeing and kayaking remote northern rivers such as the Thomsen River in Aulavik National Park, Hornaday River in Tutktut Nogait National Park and Firth River in Ivvavik National Park. See *National Parks of the Western Arctic*, pages 221–4, for information.

TUKTOYAKTUK

Of all the smaller communities in the Western Arctic, Tuktoyaktuk (or Tuk to its friends) is the one best geared to tourism. In the summer, many visitors to Inuvik like to travel the final hundred-odd kilometres to Tuk where they can dip their toes in the Arctic Ocean while, in winter, driving the ice road is a truly beautiful experience (see *Getting there*, below). Tuk is also the closest settlement to the Pingo Canadian Landmark (see *Pingos*, page 216). But beyond that, it's a pleasant place – despite the first impressions that its beige, corrugated-metal houses may give – with a sensational location, and genuinely friendly people. If you have the time, spend a night here and give yourself a chance to chat with some of them.

HISTORY Inuvialuit people used to camp along the Beaufort Sea coast, where they hunted caribou and beluga whales. The largest gathering was at Kitigaaryuit, 28km (17 miles) southwest of Tuk. Following European contact, a transport camp was built at Tuk's present location in 1931, and the Hudson's Bay Company established a post in 1937. A DEW Line station was built here by the Americans in 1955; it became automated in 1994. Oil was struck at Atkinson Point, 90km (56 miles) to the south of Tuk, in 1970, which started a stampede of oil and gas exploration in the area; oil and gas companies are still a major employer, though many families in Tuk continue to live predominantly from hunting, fishing and trapping.

GETTING THERE In summer, Tuk is accessible only by air or boat. **Aklak Air** operates regular flights, see page 207. Alternatively, **Arctic Nature Tours** (see page 207) offers cultural and community tours of the hamlet, Tuk harbour tours and visits to traditional fishing camps, and boat trips up the Mackenzie River between Inuvik and Tuk. The energetic can paddle up the Mackenzie River from Inuvik.

In winter, an ice road is carved into the surface of the Mackenzie River and the Beaufort Sea, meaning that you can drive between Inuvik and Tuk (for information on vehicle rentals see *Getting there and around*, page 205). This road has featured in some episodes of the TV documentary *Ice Road Truckers*. It's 150km (93 miles) long, and usually takes around 2½ hours to drive. It's an incredible journey, and one I wholeheartedly recommend – though you should talk to locals in Inuvik about current conditions before you set out.

The road is wide and smooth, and makes for easy driving – as long as you take it slow. As you leave Inuvik, you pass ships frozen into the ice at the edge of the road. The spindly trees that grow on the banks now shrink, then disappear. You may pass another car every half hour or so, but other than that it's utterly silent. On a clear day, the low arctic sun reflects primrose yellow from the surface of the ice, while the snow banked on the side of the road casts shadows in deepest indigo. You spot snow-coated pingos (see *Pingos*, page 216). As you begin to cross the sea, you'll see that the snow, which now rises in peaks and troughs on the ocean's surface, is palest cornflower blue, while the sky turns from clear blue to dusky pink when it meets its faraway horizon. Finally you see specks on the horizon – the houses of Tuk – yet still you drive and you drive, and you don't reach them. It is a vast world out here, and your normal sense of perspective is entirely destroyed.

If you don't want to drive the ice road yourself, **Arctic Chalet/White Husky Tours** and **Up North Tours** (see pages 208–9) offer van tours.

TOURIST INFORMATION AND TOUR OPERATORS

Arctic Tour Company ✎ 867 977 2230;
e rtgruben@permafrost.com. Beluga whale watching, bird & wildlife viewing, as well as community tours of Tuk.
Beaufort Sea Adventures ✎ 867 977 2355;
e beaufortsea@hotmail.com. Guided tours to see the snow goose migration each year from mid-Aug to mid-Sep, as well as cultural tours.

Joanne's Taxi ✎ 867 977 2547. Takes visitors on community & cultural tours, & on boat tours to the pingos.
Ookpik Tours & Adventures ✎ 867 977 2170. Community tours of Tuk, boat tours, pingo tours, river rafting, canoeing & dogsledding.
Rendezvous Lake Outpost Camp ✎ 867 977 2406. Nature tours to Rendezvous Lake in the Anderson River area.

WHERE TO STAY For current information on accommodation in Tuk, call the **Hamlet Office** (✎ 867 977 2286) or ask at the visitor centre in Inuvik; see page 207.

ANDREW BEHR AND HIS GREAT REINDEER DRIVE

In 1929, a 70-year-old Lapp named Andrew Behr, with a group of fellow herders, started a journey with 3,000 domesticated reindeer from Alaska to the Mackenzie Delta. The idea was to establish a herd in the Canadian far north, and thus provide the Inuvialuit with a food source at a time when their traditional caribou herds were much depleted.

Behr's journey was an epic one. It took him more than five years to reach his destination; he arrived with a respectable 2,400 animals, yet terrible numbers had died – three quarters of those that arrived had been born *en route*. When the herders finally limped across the Mackenzie, having battled bogs, blizzards and everything in between, they settled at the new community of Reindeer Station, just south of Tuk on the East Channel of the Mackenzie River. The community is no longer, though those travelling by boat downriver from Inuvik will see its remains in the few buildings that still stand. The herd, however, lives on and grazes near Tuktoyaktuk.

The story of Andrew Behr and his reindeer drive has been told by Dick North in his book *Arctic Exodus: The Last Great Trail Drive*.

There are almost 1,500 pingos in the Western Arctic; they look like giant molehills bulging up across the land. They form when lakes drain, leaving a shallow, residual pond of water. When the lake was full, it was too deep to freeze to the bottom even in winter, and so the water kept the sandy lake bed from freezing. Once the lake has drained, however, the surrounding permafrost creeps in, freezes the residual pool, and covers it. The frozen water expands, and pushes upwards in a concave lens shape. The pingo continues to grow until the ground surrounding the ice core is entirely frozen.

The **Pingo Canadian Landmark**, managed by Parks Canada (*www.pc.gc.ca*), lies 5km (3 miles) west of Tuktoyaktuk. It contains eight of the 1,350 pingos found around the Beaufort Sea coast, including Canada's highest pingo (and the second-highest pingo in the world), Ibyuk Pingo, which soars to 49m (160ft) in height and stretches 300m (984ft) across its base.

There are no developed trails or facilities within the Pingo Canadian Landmark. In summer it is easily accessed from Tuk by motorboat or canoe. Access by foot can be complicated by tidal movement. Canoes are available for rent in Tuk, or you can hire the services of a guide. In winter, you can reach the pingos by snowmobile. Call the tour operators listed on pages 207–9 or the Hamlet Office (✆ 867 977 2286) for more information.

SHOPPING Tuktoyaktuk is known for its carvers, and you can often buy direct from the artists. Just ask around and the locals will direct you to the artists' homes, or call the Hamlet Office on ✆ 867 977 2286. Tuk has a small number of stores selling food and handicrafts.

OTHER PRACTICALITIES Tuk has an **RCMP detachment** (✆ 867 977 1111) and a **health centre** (✆ 867 977 2321). There's no bank, though there is an ATM in one of the stores.

AKLAVIK

A Gwich'in–Inuvialuit community of around 700 people, Aklavik has no summer road access; in winter vehicles have access via an ice road. It's not really geared towards tourists; many of the inhabitants live in traditional style, hunting, fishing and trapping.

Aklavik was the main community in this part of the Western Arctic until Inuvik was built in the 1950s. Gwich'in and Inuvialuit people traditionally gathered here to trade; the Hudson's Bay Company established a trading post at Aklavik in 1912. An Anglican mission followed in 1919, the RCMP set up a post in 1922, and the Roman Catholic mission came to town in 1926. The mission built hospitals, and residential schools were based here. By 1952, Aklavik had a population of 1,500. But the town was prone to flooding, so when the Canadian government decided to build a permanent administrative centre in the Mackenzie Delta, it was decided that Aklavik's location was too unstable. Moreover, Aklavik offered no room for growth: the hamlet is constrained on all sides by lakes and marshes. For this reason, the new town – Inuvik – was built 58km (36 miles) to the west.

Many relocated to the new town; children were required to go to school there, and parents didn't want their offspring to be subjected to the residential system. But others stayed, reluctant to give up their traditional ways of life.

The Mad Trapper of Rat River is buried in Aklavik – see *The Mad Trapper of Rat River*, pages 204–5. The festival named for him, the Mad Trapper Jamboree, takes place in Aklavik on Easter weekend each year, and features traditional contests – tea boiling and log-sawing competitions and the rest – as well as sled dog and snowshoe races and dancing. Visitors are welcome.

PRACTICALITIES For up-to-date information on accommodation call the **Hamlet Office** (✆ 867 978 2351) or ask at the visitor centre in Inuvik (see page 207). Aklavik has an **RCMP detachment** (✆ 867 978 1111) and **health centre** (✆ 867 978 2516) plus two grocery stores and two gas stations.

HERSCHEL ISLAND

This island, known by the Inuvialuit as Qikiqtaruk ('this is island'), lies 5km (3 miles) off the Yukon's Beaufort Sea coast. Designated a territorial park, it's now a protected area known for its early-summer wildflowers, and a haven of calm. It wasn't always that way.

It's thought that people have been coming to Herschel Island for around 9,000 years, and archaeologists have identified thousand-year-old Thule remains, some of which can still be seen. Descendants of the Thule were still living on the island when John Franklin, the first European to visit, arrived here in 1826 (see *John Franklin*, page 210). It was he who gave the island its English name, after his friend Sir John Herschel, a British astronomer, photographer and chemist.

In the late 19th century, European and American whalers caught on to the hunting possibilities in the Beaufort Sea. Bowhead whales were a valuable source of oil and of baleen – the flexible, cartilage-like 'whalebone' that acts like a sieve in the whale's mouth, and which was used to create the corsets and hooped skirts of fashionable 19th-century ladies. The baleen and oil of a single bowhead could sell for $15,000; in a 'good' season, a ship could reckon to slaughter $400,000 worth of whales. Herschel Island provided a sheltered spot for overwintering, which was necessary as it wasn't possible for the ships to make the journey north, hunt, and return south all in one summer season, and the freezing of the ocean made winter navigation impossible.

The first ships arrived at Herschel Island in 1889; it's reckoned that by the mid-1890s as many as 1,500 sailors were overwintering on the island. The hearty, sea-hardened men disrupted the islanders' traditional trading partnerships. They further damaged the islanders' wellbeing by exchanging alcohol for women, and by introducing disease: venereal diseases, measles and influenza decimated the island population.

The whaling crews attracted, in turn, traders, police and missionaries. Bishop Isaac Stringer (see *The bishop who ate his boots*, page 218) started visiting in 1893, then, with his wife, came to live at his newly established Anglican mission on the island in 1897. (This was not the mission house now inhabited by a colony of black guillemots – the building favoured by the birds was built later, in 1916, by one of Stringer's successors.) The Stringers were tolerant and well liked. They attempted to convert the Inuvialuit to Christianity; they also worked with the whaling captains to reduce the trade of alcohol with the islanders. The RCMP detachment, manned by Inspector Fitzgerald (who would later die as part of the Lost Patrol – see pages 200–1) was established in 1903.

Within a few years, however, the price of baleen plummeted – it sold for $6 a pound in 1890 but by 1907 the same weight was fetching just 50 cents – and the whalers went on their way. The Hudson's Bay Company established a fur-trading post on Herschel in 1915, which stayed until 1937.

The last permanent residents, the Mackenzie family, left Herschel Island in 1987. That same year, the Yukon government created Herschel Island Territorial Park in partnership with the Inuvialuit people, who share responsibility for its management and resources; Inuvialuit people still come to hunt and fish. Twelve historical buildings still stand at Pauline Cove; their vulnerability due to global

10

THE BISHOP WHO ATE HIS BOOTS

Bishop Isaac Stringer and his wife, Sadie, were stalwart characters. They were both from Ontario, but came north so that Stringer could answer his missionary calling. They lived for five years on Herschel Island, from 1896 to 1901; between them, they delivered two of their children in the Herschel Island mission house. In 1905 Stringer was consecrated Bishop of Selkirk and they moved to Dawson. But, since Stringer's diocese covered both the Yukon and the Mackenzie Delta, he needed to make long journeys across the vast, little-populated north in order to tend to his episcopal duties.

In the autumn of 1909, Stringer and another Church of England missionary, Charles Johnson, set out from Fort McPherson for Dawson. Their route took them by canoe down the Peel, Husky and Rat rivers; from there they'd trek over the Richardson Mountains and head south. They reckoned that the journey ought to take five days, and packed provisions for eight. Their departure had been delayed, however, due to illness, and the weather turned unseasonably cold. As they paddled south, the river started to freeze.

When the two men could travel by canoe no further, they left their boats and proceeded on foot. They hoped to walk to the missionary post at La Pierre's house, just on the other side of the mountain divide (and about 40km or 25 miles north of the point where the Dempster Highway now crosses the Richardson Mountains). But snow and fog obscured their way, and they became lost. For 51 days, they struggled above the treeline with little fuel and only the very few ptarmigan, sparrows and squirrels they could snare for food. As starvation threatened, the bishop hit on a plan. He'd heard that, in desperate times, the Indians used to boil beaver skins with the hair removed, and then drink the soup. He suggested that he and Johnson cook up their spare boots – which were made from seal skin and walrus skin – in a similar way. And so they cut their footwear into pieces and boiled it for hours, then baked the hide on hot stones.

'Travelled 15 miles, made supper of toasted rawhide sealskin boots. Palatable. Feel encouraged,' Stringer wrote in his journal on 17 October. His diary continued in the days that followed:

> October 18 – Travelled all day. Ate more pieces of my sealskin boots, boiled and toasted. Used sole first. Set rabbit snares.
>
> October 19 – No rabbit in snare. Breakfast and dinner of rawhide boots. Fine. But not enough.
>
> October 20 – Breakfast from top of boots. Not so good as sole.

After nearly two months in the wilderness, Stringer and Johnson finally stumbled into an Indian fishing camp. They were so emaciated that the Indians didn't recognize them. It was only on hearing Stringer's voice that one of them ventured, 'I think it must be the bishop.'

Sixteen years later, the Charlie Chaplin film *The Gold Rush* was released: it was Stringer's eating of his boots that inspired the famous boot-eating scene in the film.

warming, rising sea levels, an eroding coastline and melting permafrost led to Herschel Island's inclusion on the World Monuments Fund's Watch List of 100 Most Endangered Sites in 2008.

VISITING HERSCHEL ISLAND Today, visitors can hike and camp on the island ($12 per tent per night – permits available from park rangers at Pauline Cove; the historic Pacific Steam Whaling Company building is now used as a park office and visitor centre). Note that this is a wilderness environment: there are no shops or other facilities, so you must bring with you all food and camping supplies. For further information contact the Yukon Parks office at the Department of Environment in Whitehorse (✆ *867 667 5648, toll-free:* ✆ *1 800 661 0408;* e *environmentyukon@gov.yk.ca; http://environmentyukon.gov.yk.ca/parksconservation/ HerschelIslandQikiqtaruk.php*), in Dawson (✆ *867 993 6850*) or in Inuvik (✆ *867 777 4058*).

WILDLIFE Bowhead and beluga whales, and ringed seals can be spotted in the surrounding waters. Lemmings, tundra voles and arctic shrews are commonly seen on the island, and red and arctic foxes are sometimes sighted. Caribou, grizzly bears and musk oxen occasionally swim to the island, or walk over the ice in winter. In winter, a few female polar bears den on the island's northern slopes.

Herschel Island's birdlife includes more than 90 species, 40 of which nest on the island. The largest population of black guillemots in the Western Arctic nests in the old Anglican mission house. Arctic terns, American golden plovers, red-necked phalaropes, eiders, long-tailed jaegers, glaucous gulls, rough-legged hawks, snow buntings, Lapland longspurs and common redpolls can all be seen. The Yukon Bird Club has produced a checklist of the birds on Herschel Island. You can download it from http://www.environmentyukon.gov.yk.ca/pdf/herschelbirds.pdf.

FLORA Herschel Island is known for its abundant wildflowers including vetches, louseworts, arctic lupines, arnicas, and forget-me-nots. They bloom from late June to early August.

GETTING THERE Access to Herschel Island is generally by charter plane (see page 207). Arctic Nature Tours in Inuvik (see page 207) organizes trips to Herschel Island during the summer season.

OLD CROW

A Vuntut Gwitchin (note the different spelling to that of their Gwich'in breathren) community of just under 300 people, Old Crow has no road access, though Air North operates scheduled flights connecting to Dawson, Inuvik and Whitehorse. Named after a Vuntut Gwitchin chief, Walking Crow, who died in the 1870s, it's not a major tourist stopover, though canoeists from the Eagle and Porcupine rivers come through or take out here, and a few seasoned adventurers hike in the Vuntut National Park (see page 223).

Old Crow has two year-round accommodation options – **Ch'oodeenjik Accommodations** (*5 rooms;* ✆ *867 966 3008;* e *choodee@northwestel.net; http://choodee.oldcrow.ca; has wireless internet;* $$$) and **Porcupine Bed & Breakfast** (*3 rooms in self-contained building with shared bathroom, kitchen & laundry;* ✆ *867 966 3913;* e *bluefish_kennels@hotmail.com;* $$$) – and a few basic shops. There's an **RCMP detachment** (✆ *867 966 1111*) and a **nursing station** (✆ *867 966 4444*). Go to the extensive community website at www.oldcrow.ca for more information, or call the Vuntut Gwitchin First Nation office on ✆ 867 966 3622, or the Vuntut National Park office on ✆ 867 966 3622. Note that Old Crow is dry; no alcohol is allowed within 60km (37 miles) of the town.

PAULATUK

Paulatuk sits on Darnley Bay, near the mouth of the Hornaday River, 400km (248 miles) east of Inuvik. It's the base for trips into Tuktut Nogait National Park (see

The Vuntut Gwitchin are an isolated people, and because of this they have been able to maintain their language and traditions. Still today, they rely heavily on the Porcupine caribou herd for subsistence. They hunt the caribou as it migrates twice annually through their territory on its way to and from its calving grounds on the coastal plain of Alaska's Arctic National Wildlife Refuge (ANWR). They then use every part of the animal: they eat the meat and bone marrow, and use different parts of the animal to make moccasins, gloves, mittens, boots, baby slippers, tea pot and coaster sets, beaded baby belts, parkas, vests, purses, dresses and hair accessories.

The oil industry has, for decades, sought permission to drill on ANWR's coastal plain (the so-called 1002 lands, named for section 1002 of the 1980 Alaska National Interest Lands Conservation Act, which deferred a decision regarding future management of this part of the coastal plain). The oil lobby argues that ANWR is vast and they only want to drill on a tiny fraction of it; that the good health of the Central Arctic caribou herd across whose lands the Trans Alaska Pipeline runs proves that wildlife and oil drilling can co-exist; and that the quantities of oil extracted would be substantial.

Conservationists respond that, unlike the Central Arctic herd, the Porcupine caribou have no place to go if they are displaced; that drilling would be likely to disrupt the herd's migration and therefore its access to vital calving grounds; and that its numbers are in any case falling. The coastal plain is boggy terrain, difficult for wolves and unpopular with bears. If the caribou were forced to recreate their nursery in a spot more favourable to its predators, calf survival, which is already precarious, would very likely diminish.

Among the most vocal of the oil lobby's opponents have been the 19 Gwi'chin villages across Alaska, the Yukon and the NWT, including the Vuntut Gwitchin people of Old Crow. Arguing that oil drilling in the 1002 lands would irreparably damage their way of life, the Vuntut Gwitchin people have put up a robust defence of the caribou, travelling to Washington and lobbying vigorously for their cause, which has become a political issue of substantial controversy. During the Bush years the outcome seemed precarious; however, with the election of Barack Obama the caribou's nursery appears to be safe – for now. The President has spoken out against drilling in ANWR, and his Democrat majority supports him.

page 224). The village, whose population is less than 300, has a stunning location, and is surrounded by a wealth of wildlife: beluga and bowhead whales, polar and grizzly bears, barren-ground caribou, musk oxen and wolves. There is no road access, but there are scheduled flights from Inuvik with Aklak Air (see page 207).

Paulatuk has one hotel, the **Paulatuk Visitor Centre Hotel** (*10 rooms with en-suite shower,* ☎ *867 580 3051; kitchen facilities available – there's a grocery store attached to the hotel – or meals by prior arrangement;* $$$$$). There's also an **RCMP detachment** (☎ *867 580 1111*) and **health centre** (☎ *867 580 3231*). Local carvers sell their wares direct from their homes. Call the **Hamlet Office** (☎ *867 580 3531*) for more information.

For tours, try **Bekere Lake Outfitters** (☎ *867 580 3050*) and **Ruben's Outfitting & Guiding** (☎ *867 580 3890*) for fishing and wildlife, and **Saruq Guiding & Sports Hunting** (☎ *867 580 3002;* e *norarianne@hotmail.com*) for sport fishing and boat trips including to the Smoking Hills and Cape Parry Bird Sanctuary, which has the only nesting colony of thick-billed murres in the Western Arctic.

SACHS HARBOUR

This tiny hamlet on Banks Island has a population of around 100, but what it lacks in numbers it makes up for in history: archaeological remains found on Banks Island date back 3,500 years. In more recent times, the RCMP set up a post here in the 1950s, and the settlement – named for the ship Mary Sachs of the 1913 Canadian Arctic Expedition – gathered around it.

It's for the wildlife, particularly the high densities of musk oxen, and for Aulavik National Park (see page 223), that visitors come.

Access to Sachs Harbour is by plane from Inuvik, see page 207. Note that the National Park is 200km (124 miles) away from Sachs Harbour.

Overnight guests should head to **Kuptana's Guesthouse** (*5 rooms;* ✆ *867 690 4151; bathroom is shared;* $$$$$ *inc b/fast*). Sachs Harbour has a grocery store. The **police** can be contacted on ✆ 867 777 1111, the **health centre** on ✆ 867 690 4181, the **Hamlet Office** on ✆ 867 690 4351, and the **Aulavik National Park information office** on ✆ 867 690 3904.

John and Samantha Lucas run **Banks Island Tundra Tours** out of Sachs Harbour (✆ *867 690 4009*), with a focus on wilderness camping trips. **Kuptana's** (see above) also guides nature and wildlife tours.

ULUKHAKTOK

Formerly known as Holman, this village on Victoria Island has a population of around 450 people. The American and European whalers never came this far; it's thought that the explorer Vilhjalmur Stefansson was the first white man to visit the Copper Inuit people on the west side of Victoria Island in 1911. A trading post was established in 1940 to capitalize on the lucrative arctic fox fur trapping industry, and the permanent community of Holman grew from there.

Father Henri Tardi came to the settlement from France as an Oblate missionary in 1939. It was he who taught the local Inuit the skills of printmaking. Still, today, Ulukhaktok is known for its printmakers. Visitors can tour the **Ulukhaktok Eskimo Cooperative and Craft Shop** (✆ *867 396 3531*), where they can see the artists at work, and buy their wares. Strangely, Ulukhaktok is also known for its golf – the Billy Joss Open Golf Tournament takes place on the second weekend of July each year on the hamlet's nine-hole tundra course overlooking the Beaufort Sea.

Hiking, wildlife viewing and hunting trips are available from local outfitters. Try the **Arctic Hills Tour Company** (✆ *867 396 4455;* e *tours@arctichills.ca; www.arctichills.ca*) whose Inuvialuit owner and guide Louie Nigiyok offers dogsledding, snowmobiling and ice fishing in winter plus the chance to sleep in a traditional igloo, and wildlife tours in summer.

Access is by air from either Inuvik or Yellowknife. There's one hotel, the **Arctic Char Inn** (*8 rooms;* ✆ *867 396 3501; www.arcticcharinn.com;* $$$$$); it has a dining room. The **police** are on ✆ 867 396 1111, the **health centre**'s on ✆ 867 396 3111 and the **Hamlet Office** is on ✆ 867 396 8000.

NATIONAL PARKS OF THE WESTERN ARCTIC

The four national parks of the Western Arctic offer unparalleled wilderness hiking, paddling and backcountry skiing opportunities – but be warned, these parks are very remote. Access is usually by fly-in, and there are no facilities, developed trails or campgrounds. Unguided trips, therefore, are for those with good route-finding and wilderness survival skills only. A limited number of tour operators guide trips into these far-northern parks – see individual park entries for details.

Each year, Parks Canada gives six artists the opportunity to capture the spirit of Ivvavik National Park either as a painting, a photo, or as a short film. The artists, accompanied by Parks staff and a cook, spend seven to ten days in the park. The deadline for applications is usually in March. Email e inuvik.info@pc.gc.ca for more information.

The national parks listed below are all co-managed with aboriginal groups by Parks Canada. Aulavik, Ivvavik and Tuktut Nogait are all administered from the Parks Canada office in Inuvik (*the office is above the post office at 187 Mackenzie Rd;* ❧ *867 777 8800, 24hr emergency line in Jun, Jul & Aug: 867 777 4893;* e *inuvik.info@ pc.gc.ca; www.pc.gc.ca;* ☉ *summer: 8.30am–5pm*); Aulavik has a satellite office in Sachs Harbour (❧ *867 690 3904*) and Tutktut Nogait has an office in Paulatuk (❧ *867 580 3233*). The Vuntut National Park is administered from Old Crow (*contact Brenda Frost-Charlie* ❧ *867 667 3910;* e *brenda.frost-charlie@pc.gc.ca*) and Haines Junction (*contact Rhonda Markel* ❧ *867 634 2329, ext 291;* e *rhonda_markel@pc.gc.ca*).

Before leaving for any overnight trip, you must register with the relevant Parks office. When you've finished your trip, you must 'deregister', either in person or by telephone. You'll need a Northern Park Backcountry Excursion/Camping Permit, which costs $24.50 per day or you can buy an annual permit for $147.20 – it's valid in all Parks Canada parks in the Yukon, NWT and Nunavut, except for Kluane and Wood Buffalo, and can be bought from Parks Canada offices. If you're planning to fly in to one of the parks as a day visitor, you must apply for a free Parks Canada Aircraft Landing Permit – this is included with the overnight permit. It's worth asking the Parks staff in Inuvik if they know of other groups wishing to charter flights into these remote parts – you may be able to save money by sharing or dovetailing transport.

HUMAN HISTORY All the national parks listed below cover terrain on which humans have lived for thousands of years. The remains of Thule, Copper Inuit, Inuvialuit and Gwich'in peoples can be seen in tent rings, caches, rock alignments, meat drying areas, hunting blinds and the remains of driftwood homes. Those interested in the human history of the Arctic may like to read *The Last Imaginary Place: A Human History of the Arctic World* by Robert McGhee.

IVVAVIK NATIONAL PARK Ivvavik means 'a place for giving birth', in Inuvialuktun; it protects a portion of the calving grounds of the Porcupine caribou herd. The first national park in Canada to be created as a result of an aboriginal land claim agreement, it is dominated by the British Mountains, with a coastal plain to the north. The park is bordered by the Beaufort Sea to the north, and the international boundary and the Arctic National Wildlife Refuge to the west. Access is via charter flight from Inuvik, 200km (123 miles) away; see page 207 for information on charter flights. Air access points include Sheep Creek, Margaret Lake, Komakuk Beach and Stokes Point.

The big draw in Ivvavik is rafting or kayaking the Firth River. It's navigable for 130km (81 miles) from Margaret Lake, near the Alaska border, to the Beaufort Sea; rapids reach class IV+. The best time to do it is from the second week of June to the second week of August (the ice may not break on the river until the beginning of June, and note that even once the ice has thawed the water is *cold*, that's to say 4–7°C or 39–45°F). Parks Canada publishes the useful *Firth River Guide*, a copy of which can be obtained from the Parks Canada office in Inuvik.

The less experienced may want to raft the Firth River as part of a guided group. Trips last 12–13 days and are suitable for beginners. The following tour operators are licensed to lead rafting expeditions on the Firth River: **Nahanni River Adventures** (✆ *867 668 3180;* e *info@nahanni.com; www.nahanni.com*); **Rivers, Oceans and Mountains** (✆ *250 354 2056, toll-free:* ✆ *1 888 639 1114;* e *info@ iroamtheworld.com; www.iroamtheworld.com*); **Explorers' League World & Wilderness Rafting Expeditions** (✆ *778 686 3455;* e *info@explorersleague.ca; www.explorersleague.ca*).

Both paddlers and hikers stand a good chance of seeing the Porcupine caribou herd travelling from their calving grounds on the coastal plain between late June and early July; wildflowers are spectacularly abundant at this time, too. Hikers should note that there are no designated trails in the park. You should discuss your intended route with the Parks office in Inuvik, and supply them with a detailed route description on 1:50,000 scale before starting out. As with paddling, the best time for hiking is mid-June to mid-August.

VUNTUT NATIONAL PARK Vuntut encompasses 4,345km² (1,678 square miles) in the Yukon's northwestern corner. It's bordered by Ivvavik National Park to the north, the international boundary and the Arctic National Wildlife Refuge to the west, Black Fox Creek and the Old Crow River to the east and the Old Crow River to the south. Wilderness opportunities include canoeing on the Old Crow River, and backcountry hiking and skiing.

Parts of the Porcupine caribou herd are found in the park at various times of the year. The Old Crow Flats, sections of which fall within the park's boundaries, have been designated a wetland of international importance by the Ramsar Convention and are used as breeding, moulting and staging grounds by half a million birds each year. Muskrats are also plentiful in the flats.

The nearest community is Old Crow (see page 219), which lies about 50km (30 miles) south of the park by air, or 190km (117 miles) away by river. The Vuntut National Park is administered from Old Crow and Haines Junction; see page 222.

AULAVIK NATIONAL PARK The park comprises 12,000km² (4,633 square miles) of pristine arctic wilderness at the north end of Banks Island. It's home to the highest density of musk oxen in the world (there are 68,000 on the island, of which about 20% live in the park), as well as the endangered Peary caribou. Half a million lesser snow geese nest in Banks Island's two Migratory Bird Sanctuaries, one of which is in the northern part of Aulavik National Park. Flocks of snow geese are commonly seen during flights into the park. Polar bears, ringed seals, bearded seals, beluga whales and bowhead whales can be seen from the park's north coast.

Aulakvik lies 750km (463 miles) northeast of Inuvik and 250km (154 miles) northeast of the nearest community, Sachs Harbour (see page 221). The only practical way to access the park is by charter plane from Inuvik (see page 207). Note that once you've been dropped off, you're on your own till the plane comes back to collect you – and weather frequently delays flights. Pack plenty of extra supplies.

The highlight of Aulakvik for many is the Thomsen River, one of the most northerly navigable waterways in North America and a major wildlife corridor. Only one tour operator is licensed to guide on the Thomsen River and that's Canmore-based **Whitney & Smith Legendary Expeditions** (✆ *403 678 3052, toll-free:* ✆ *1 800 713 6660;* e *info@legendary.ca; www.legendaryex.com*). Their trip lasts 15 days out of either Inuvik or Edmonton. They use stable sea kayaks, and paddle for three to five hours daily, leaving time for hiking and relaxation.

TUKTUT NOGAIT NATIONAL PARK The Tuktut Nogait National Park is located 40km (25 miles) east of the community of Paulatuk, and 425km (262 miles) northeast of Inuvik. It's known for its spectacular hiking and paddling opportunities, as well as its wildlife: each June, 85,000 Bluenose West caribou travel to their calving grounds in Tuktut Nogait National Park. The park also has an impressive 360 archaeological sites.

Access is by charter flight from Inuvik, or by scheduled flight (Aklak Air, see page 207) from Inuvik followed by a chartered boat trip or a very long walk. For boat shuttles, contact **Paulatuk Community Corporation** (\ *867 580 3601*) or **Paulatuk Hunters and Trappers Committee** (\ *867 580 3004*).

The hiking season extends from mid-June to early August. The very best time to hike, however, is the end of June, when chances of seeing caribou are at their best and the wildflowers are in bloom. The best way to start planning a hiking trip into the park is to look at the four backpacking guides that the park has published: *Upper Hornaday River West, Hornaday River Canyon West, Hornaday River Canyon East* and *Roscoe River East*. They're available from the Parks Canada office in Inuvik (see page 222).

Paddlers come to Tutktut Nogait for the Hornaday River, which is known for its sensational canyons and waterfall. Trips take eight to 12 days and are best done in July. The two major routes are:

- Start at Hornaday Lake and access the Hornaday River via its main tributary, the Little Hornaday River (185km, 114-mile trip). This is for experienced paddlers only – the Little Hornaday River has class III rapids.
- Start directly on the main river (145km, 89-mile trip). This works for novice paddlers as the main river isn't technical. Obviously you'll need advanced wilderness camping skills, though.

Tuktut Nogait National Park has published a detailed river guide called, unsurprisingly, the *Hornaday River Guide*. Copies are available from the Parks Canada office in Inuvik (see page 222).

Sea to Sky Expeditions (\ *604 594 7701, toll-free:* \ *1 800 990 8735;* e *info@ seatoskyexpeditions.com; www.canadianexpeditions.com*) offers guided hiking in Tuktut Nogait. Trips last 14 days, are rated as 'strenuous', and depart from Whitehorse.

FISHING BRANCH NI'IINLII NJIK TERRITORIAL PARK In addition to the four national parks, the northern Yukon is also home to the ecological reserve of Fishing Branch Ni'iinlii Njik Territorial Park. Covering nearly 7,000km² (2,702 square miles), the park sits midway between Dawson and Old Crow and falls within the traditional lands of the Vuntut Gwitchin people. There's no road access – at its nearest point, the Dempster Highway is 100km (62 miles) away.

Fishing Branch Ni'iinlii'njik Park has a microclimate created by thermal energy stored in underground reservoirs and, despite extreme winter conditions, water flows year round. Each autumn, grizzly bears congregate near Bear Cave Mountain to feed on spawning salmon. From mid-September to the end of November, small groups of photographers, artists and naturalists can visit Bear Cave Mountain with Phil Timpany, a renowned bear specialist and wildlife photographer. His Whitehorse-based company, **Bear Cave Mountain Eco-Adventures** (\ *867 667 2283;* e *info@bearcavemountain.com; www.bearcavemountain.com*) has partnered with the Vuntut Development Corporation to create a unique cultural and wildlife experience. Four viewing areas are all close to comfortable but rustic cabins where guests spend the night; hiking and underwater photography are also possible. The helicopter taking you to Bear Cave Mountain leaves from Dawson.

Part Three

HIKING AND PADDLING

11

Wilderness Travel

The Yukon is one of the world's last great wildernesses. I have had few experiences that compare to the intense tranquillity and awe I've felt while paddling along a turquoise river as bald eagles soared overhead, or while hiking for days across tundra backed by mountains and glaciers without seeing another human soul. The tremendous peace, the spectacular landscapes and the occasional sightings of bears, moose or even porcupines raised my spirits and enlivened my senses.

The following pages focus on multi-day hiking and paddling adventures. You should have paddling and/or backcountry experience before setting out on these trips unguided. If you don't feel your own experience is sufficient, or you don't have time to make the necessary preparations for such a journey, all of these trips can be booked with an experienced guide. The detailed route information in this section has been provided by Stefan Wackerhagen, partner of **Northern Tales** (✆ 867 667 6054; e info@northerntales.ca; www.northerntales.ca), which specializes in custom-guided adventures in both summer and winter; see page 25. Otherwise, see pages 24–6 for a full list of Yukon tour operators, some of whom can organize both guided trips and transfers, and page 34 for details of float-plane companies.

The route descriptions in these pages incorporate GPS readings using the UTM coordinate system.

GENERAL INFORMATION

Much of the information below can be found in more detail in Environment Yukon's helpful booklet *Into the Yukon Wilderness*. It's available from any visitor information centre or Environment Yukon office, or you can download it in pdf form from www.environmentyukon.gov.yk.ca/pdf/ityw.pdf. It's definitely worth reading this before you head out into the wilds. There's also a useful bear safety video that you can watch at any of the Yukon's visitor centres.

CAMPING The campsites referred to in these pages are not, for the most part, developed campgrounds. They are simply flat, dry spots with a nearby water source. You shouldn't expect any kind of amenities.

Along the upper section of the Yukon River, and in Kluane National Park and Tombstone Territorial Park you'll find a few designated campsites with some amenities, such as outhouses and sometimes cooking shelters. The Chilkoot Trail's campsites have outhouses, shelters and tent platforms as well as bear-resistant containers on the Alaska side and at Happy Camp on the Canadian side. For hot showers, though, you'll have to wait till you're back in town.

LEAVE NO TRACE When you leave your camp, you should plan to leave no trace. Garbage, including toilet paper, should be packed out or burned thoroughly if you're out for too long to carry it all. Don't bury your rubbish: animals will dig it up. When you're hiking, keep to existing trails where possible, and try to walk in single file to avoid widening them.

There's detailed information on leaving no trace in Environment Yukon's *Into the Yukon Wilderness*, while Kathleen Meyer's book *How to Shit in the Woods: An Environmentally Sound Approach to a Lost Art* offers excellent and highly entertaining advice on how to relieve oneself with decorum – and without turning the backcountry into a big, festering, paper-festooned sewer.

BEARS Bear attacks are very rare and it's likely that, if you meet a bear, it will run away. However, you should take precautions. Bears are more likely to attack solitary hikers than those in pairs or groups. Carry bear spray (and know how to use it) when you're in wilderness areas. Bear spray can be bought from local outdoors shops; it can't be carried on commercial aircraft (it's pepper spray) either in your hand luggage or checked luggage so, if you're flying in, you'll have to buy it once you're in the Yukon. Alternatively, many tour operators will rent you a can of bear spray along with other outdoors equipment.

Never feed a bear, and make sure the 'kitchen' area of your camp is well away from the tents where you'll sleep. At night, make sure you have no food or cosmetics (including toothpaste) in your tent. All smelly items should be stashed either in sealed bins or hung from a tree, well away from your camp; in some parts of Kluane National Park and Reserve bear-resistant canisters, which you can borrow from the visitor centres, are mandatory. Burn rubbish thoroughly or pack it out. If you catch a fish, clean it well away from your camp, and throw the guts into deep and/or fast-flowing water downstream of your camp.

If you do meet a bear, don't attempt to get close to take photographs, and never stand between a sow and her cubs. If the bear doesn't run away, don't run yourself, and don't shout. Talk in a firm, calm voice while gently backing off in the direction from which you came. Give the bear the chance to get away. If you're carrying bear spray, hold it ready (you should always keep your bear spray in a holster on your waist or in another accessible place, never buried in your pack). You're supposed to try to stand in a position so that the wind is not blowing in your direction, though this can be difficult to arrange. But be aware if the spray blows back into your own face, you're the one that will be incapacitated. Make sure the nozzle is pointing at the bear and not at yourself. Remember that bear spray is ineffective until the bear is within a few metres, and that you must remove the brightly coloured safety clip before use.

If a bear does attack you must decide whether to play dead or fight back. (It's only considered an attack if it actually makes contact. Many bears will try to warn you off with a false charge. This doesn't count as an attack, but should succeed in scaring you sufficiently that you don't need to visit the outhouse for a while.) You should play dead if the bear is acting in self defence, for example if it's a grizzly with cubs, or a grizzly defending a carcass. You should fight back if you are attacked by any black bear, a grizzly not defending cubs or a carcass, or any bear that breaks into a tent or building.

How do I tell the difference between a grizzly and a black bear? You can't always rely on the colour. Look instead for the hump a grizzly has over its shoulders: this is the highest point on a grizzly, whereas a black bear's highest point is over its hind legs. A black bear has a long, straight muzzle, where a grizzly has a face that's more of a dish shape. And a black bear's front claws are dark, short and curved, where a grizzly's are light and long. But let's hope you don't get close enough to examine any bear's toenails.

Sounds complicated? Go to *Into the Yukon Wilderness*, download Environment Yukon's *How You Can Stay Safe in Bear Country* brochure (*www.environmentyukon.gov.yk.ca/*

pdf/howyoucanstaysafe.pdf) or watch the visitor centre's bear safety video to learn more. But above all, don't let a fear of bears put you off travelling into the backcountry. Aggressive encounters are very unusual.

CROSSING CREEKS You will have to cross creeks when hiking the Yukon's more challenging trails and routes. Sometimes you'll be able to hop easily from rock to rock. Other times, the creeks will be deep and fast. These can be dangerous. See *Crossing Creeks*, page 109, for information on the safe crossing of creeks, or ask Parks Canada wardens for advice.

FISHING If you're over the age of 16 and you wish to fish, you must have a fishing licence. If you're going to fish for salmon, you must also have a Salmon Conservation Catch Card. Licences are available at Environment Yukon's offices, most gas stations and sports and fishing stores. See page 44 for more information.

FIREARMS Most Yukoners and visitors do not carry firearms when on wilderness trips. Hunting is strictly regulated (see pages 44–5). Visitors who have permission from the Canadian Firearms Centre may carry a rifle or shotgun for protection against bears, except in national parks. Frankly, it's unlikely to be worth the trouble, but if you want to know more call the Canadian Firearms Centre toll-free on: ℡ 1 800 731 4000 (North America only) or go to www.cfc-cafc.gc.ca.

COMMUNICATIONS Cell phones don't work in the Yukon's wilderness areas. Some people like to carry a satellite phone in case of emergencies; many of the tour operators listed on pages 24–6 will be able to rent you a satellite phone along with other equipment. SPOT GPS Satellite Messengers and Personal Trackers are becoming increasingly popular, www.findmespot.com.

PICKING UP ANTLERS, ETC If you find cast-off antlers and so on when you're hiking in the backcountry, you can generally keep them. The rules say that you should go to an Environment Yukon office and ask for a permit; if everything is in order, this will usually be granted. If you wish to take antlers or other animal parts out of the Yukon, you'll need an export permit (again, from an Environment Yukon office). Some countries require import permits for parts of certain species.

FIREWOOD You're only permitted to cut timber in order to build a fire, and only dry or dead trees (standing or down) may be used. (In any case, green wood doesn't burn.)

CABINS Many of the cabins you'll find in the backcountry belong to trappers. They are private, and shouldn't be used except in an emergency. If you do have a genuine emergency and must use the cabin and the trapper's woodpile, you should replace the wood before you leave, and ensure that all tools are as you found them. The trapper's safety relies on his finding things as he left them.

Don't sleep in abandoned cabins you find along river banks or hiking trails. These cabins are popular with mice and bats and, quite apart from the fact that you may not wish to share your sleeping quarters with such critters, their faeces and urine can spread disease (including the rare but deadly hantavirus pulmonary syndrome). You should never use any timber from tumbledown cabins as firewood: these are historic artefacts.

MAPS AND BOOKS Mac's Fireweed Books (*203 Main St, Whitehorse;* ℡ *867 668 2434;* e *orders@macsbooks.ca; www.yukonbooks.com or www.macsbooks.ca;* ⊕ *summer: 8am–midnight daily, winter: 8am–9pm daily*) carries all the Yukon topographical maps

11

and wide selection of hiking and river guides. You can order both maps and books online if you want to buy them before you arrive in the Yukon.

SAMPLE PACKING CHECKLISTS

Obviously you'll need to tailor these lists to your own requirements; however, if you find you've packed dramatically more than they suggest, you're probably carrying too much.

CANOEING CHECKLIST

- Boats, paddles and lifejackets
- Sponge and scoop for each canoe
- Flotation throw bag for rescue
- Satellite phone or SPOT if desired
- Ropes of different lengths and strengths. You'll need it, for example, to secure load in the canoe (if the canoe tips and your gear is not securely stowed, you'll lose it); loose ropes should be attached to the front and back of the canoe and to secure the boats at night; rope is needed to suspend food etc from trees (away from bears); to secure a tarp in case of rain, and so on.
- Carabiners are useful for securing small items, e.g. cameras, that you want to access easily
- Dry bags and watertight barrels
- Tents and pegs
- Sleeping bags and mattresses
- Tarp and long pieces of rope for putting up tarp (makes a useful shelter in case of rain)
- Stove and fuel/gas
- Pots with handle, pan, grill, leather gloves
- Spatula, ladle, whisk
- Spare zip-lock bags, garbage bags
- Water bottles (at least one 1-litre bottle per person)
- Water treatment if you're not going to boil the water
- Biodegradable washing-up liquid and sponge
- Cups, bowls/plates and cutlery
- Thermos if desired
- Dish towel
- Paper towel
- Saw, axe
- Clothes
- Raingear (jacket and trousers)
- Matches/lighters
- Lanterns with candles for light in late August and early September
- Knife
- Sunglasses and sunscreen
- Headlight
- Camera/tripod and waterproof camera bag or box if desired
- GPS/map/compass
- Spare batteries for camera, GPS, headlight
- First aid kit
- Repair kit (for mattresses, tents and canoes)
- Orange garbage bag (if you need to be evacuated, you can use this to make yourself visible from the air – plus, it's useful and cheap)
- Fishing equipment if desired – remember you need a permit (see page 44)

- Bear spray
- Toilet paper
- Bug spray and bug shirt if desired
- Toothbrush/toothpaste and other personal items. Soap and shampoo should be biodegradable.
- Towel
- Nail clippers can be useful – it is hard to work with wood, ropes etc with overgrown nails
- Food

HIKING CHECKLIST This checklist is designed for a Chilkoot trip taking three or four days; however, you can tailor it for any hiking trip.

- Backpack
- Hiking boots and poles
- Running shoes/sandals for crossing creeks
- Gaiters
- Raingear (jacket and trousers)
- Backpack rain cover
- Tents and pegs
- Sleeping bags and mattresses
- Stove and fuel/gas
- Pots and handle
- Lighter
- Water bag and water treatment
- Water bottles (at least one 1-litre bottle per person)
- Biodegradable washing-up liquid and sponge
- Cups, bowls and cutlery
- Thermos
- Rope – for suspending food etc from trees where there are no bear-proof lockers.
- Bear-resistant canisters or bags if needed
- Dry bags
- 1 x trousers
- 1 x long johns
- 1 x shorts
- 1 x light windbreaker
- 1 x warm fleece
- 1 x medium fleece
- 3 x shirts
- 3 x underwear
- 3 x socks
- 1 x hat
- 1 x Buff
- 1 x gloves
- Matches/lighter
- Knife
- Sunglasses and sunscreen
- Headlight
- Camera
- Map
- Spare batteries
- First aid kit
- Repair kit for tents and mattresses

11

- Bear spray
- Satellite phone or SPOT if desired
- Toilet paper
- Bug spray
- Toothbrush/toothpaste
- Towel
- Nail clippers
- Food

12

Hiking

CHILKOOT TRAIL

Days	3–5
Distance	53km (33 miles)
Maximum elevation	1,074m (3,525ft)
Maps and books	You don't really need a map as the trail is well-trodden and well-marked (during the summer season). However, National Geographic's map number 254, *Chilkoot Trail/Klondike Gold Rush Trail*, is an interesting reference. It shows the route and also has detailed information on planning, equipment and logistics. Alternatively, try Alaska Geographic's *Hiker's Guide to the Chilkoot Trail*, which has similar information. Additionally, *Chilkoot Pass: A Hiker's Guide to the Klondike Gold Rush National Historical Park* by Archie Satterfield is a book rather than a map, but it's well worth reading for its fabulous gold-rush tales as well as information on hiking the trail today.

If you're looking for a vigorous three- to five-day hike, and don't mind meeting others *en route*, the Chilkoot is probably *the* trail to opt for. It has challenging sections – in particular the climb to the summit is steep. It's sensationally pretty, passing through coastal forest, alpine tundra, and boreal forest. But the Chilkoot has a further attraction, and that's its history.

Originally a Tlingit First Nations trading route – this is one of just three glacier-free corridors through Alaska's Coast Range – the Chilkoot Trail was one of the two major routes to the Klondike goldfields in the 1890s, and it's the ceaseless trail of stampeders struggling to the Chilkoot's snowy summit that provides the most abiding image of the gold rush. (The other popular trail was the White Pass, over which the White Pass and Yukon Route railway runs. If you're travelling to the trailhead from Whitehorse, it's fun to incorporate the railway journey from Carcross to Skagway into your trip, so that you travel both routes; see pages 70–1.) The trail is still littered with rusting gold-rush paraphernalia – picks, shovels and even collapsible boats – that the stampeders abandoned as they walked. The old telegraph line still hangs. So as well as being a truly fabulous, and fantastically scenic hike, the Chilkoot is also a journey through an incredible open-air museum. See pages 165–8 for more on the history of the Klondike gold rush.

A note on the trail's difficulty: I'd say its reputation is more fearsome than its reality. The stampeders may have called it 'the meanest 32 miles in history' but they had to ferry a ton of goods, comprising provisions to last them a year, before they were allowed into Canadian territory. Those who couldn't afford to hire packers needed three months or more to make as many as 40 ascents. And they were mostly city folk, unused to physical hardship. And it was winter. And they hadn't invented Goretex yet. If you're in good shape and you hike regularly, you should be able to complete – and enjoy – the trail. If you're in doubt, it may be worth using the services of a guide who knows the trail well and can deal with the logistics. Don't expect your guide to act as your porter, however. You'll still need to carry your share of the food and equipment: expect your backpack to weigh in at around 18kg (40lb).

LOGISTICS The Chilkoot Trail crosses the US/Canada international border; the boundary is at the summit of the pass. There's no passport control on the summit itself, but you do have to show your passport or other accepted ID at the **Skagway Trail Center** (*Broadway, between 1st & 2nd Avs;* \ *+1 907 983 9234;* ⊕ *8.30am–4.30pm daily*) when you pick up your permit. If you're hiking southbound, you need to show your documentation at the **Parks Canada office in Whitehorse** (*Suite 205–300 Main St;* \ *867 667 3910, toll-free:* \ *1 800 661 0486;* e *whitehorse.info@pc.gc.ca; www.pc.gc.ca*).

Due to the dual nationality of the trail, it's jointly managed by Parks Canada and the US National Parks Service. It's also worth noting that the Chilkoot Trail is not actually in the Yukon. It stretches from Alaska to the northwestern tip of BC; the Yukon Territory only begins a couple of kilometres after the trail ends. However, if you're basing yourself in Canada, it is from Whitehorse rather than BC that the connections are most easily made.

There's detailed information about the Chilkoot Trail at both the Parks Canada website (*www.pc.gc.ca/lhn-nhs/yt/chilkoot/index_e.asp*) and the National Parks Service website (*www.nps.gov/klgo/index.htm*).

Note that Alaska time is one hour behind Yukon time. Also worth observing is the fact that, if bears in the area approach humans, a bear warning is put in place and hikers may not be allowed to walk the trail in groups of less than four.

GETTING THERE AND AWAY The trailhead to the Chilkoot is not in Skagway itself but 16km (10 miles) away at Dyea (pronounced die-EE). The townsite was razed by the farmer who owned it after the gold rush and Dyea's buildings no longer stand. There is, however, a campsite (*US$6 per night*), which you may like to use the night before starting on the trail. Alternatively, there are many hotels in Skagway, see pages 123–4. Shuttle buses run from Skagway; companies vary from season to season so ask for information at the Skagway Trail Center. See pages 120–1 for information on how to get to Skagway.

Lake Bennett, at the end of the trail, is not accessible by road. There is no phone and there are no tourist services beyond a restaurant to feed the train passengers. You therefore need to organize your return transfer before you start hiking from Dyea. The options are:

- Take the White Pass and Yukon Route railway, which stops at Lake Bennett, back to either Carcross, Fraser or Skagway (see pages 70–1). The train leaves at 1pm on Monday, Tuesday, Thursday, Friday, Sunday. You can camp at Bennett if you're catching the train the day after you finish your hike.
- Hike out via the cut-off trail at km 47 (mile 26) of the trail just after Bare Loon Lake. The cut-off trail takes you to the railway, which you can follow to Log Cabin at km 44 (mile 27) of the South Klondike Highway from where you can get a bus or shuttle either to Skagway or Whitehorse. Try **Dyea Dave's Shuttle and Tours** (\ *+1 907 209 5031;* e *dyeadave@msn.com; www.dyeadavetours.com; Dyea Dave's real name is Dave McClelland if that helps at*

all); **Frontier Excursions** (☎ +1 907 983 2512, toll-free: ☎ 1 877 983 2512; e *info@frontierexcursions.com; www.frontierexcursions.com*); **Klondike Tours & Taxis** (☎ +1 907 983 2075, toll-free: ☎ 1 866 983 2075; e *klondiketours@ yahoo.com; www.klondiketours.com*); **Alaska Direct** (☎ 867 668 4833, toll-free: ☎ 1 800 770 6652; e *info@alaskadirectbusline.com; www.alaskadirectbusline.com*) or ask at the Skagway Trail Center or Parks Canada in Whitehorse.

- Fly from Lake Bennett to Whitehorse in style by getting **Alpine Aviation** (☎ 867 668 7725, cell: 867 393 1482; e *alpine@polarcom.com; www.alpineaviationyukon.com*) to pick you up in a float plane. It's a really pretty flight and makes a fantastic end to the journey.

WHEN TO GO Wardens (in Canada) and rangers (in the US) manage the trail from 1 June to Labour Day (the first Monday in September). Outside the summer season, you may hike the trail but do so at your own risk; you don't need a permit in winter, but you should tell someone where you're going and when you expect to return. You shouldn't embark on a winter trip unless you have excellent winter survival and avalanche hazard evaluation skills. You're advised to contact the US or Canadian park officials for information on trail conditions before embarking on a winter trip.

NORTH OR SOUTH? It's possible to hike the trail in either direction, but most people walk from south to north, starting at Dyea and ending at Lake Bennett. This is the direction the stampeders walked in, so it appeals on a historical note, but it's also the best direction from the point of view of the weather – most weather systems blow in from the coast. Moreover, it's easier to ascend the 'Golden Stairs' to the summit than to descend them. Walking from south to north, you'll pass very few people during the day, as you're all heading in the same direction, but will see the same faces in the camps each evening; most people enjoy catching up and comparing notes on the day's activity.

PERMITS If you're going to camp overnight on the trail, you must have a permit. At the time of writing this cost $53.50 (adult), $26.75 (youth) for the whole trail; reduced fees apply if you're going to hike on just the American or just the Canadian sides. There's an additional $11.70 reservation fee.

Parks Canada limits travel over the summit to 50 people per day; this translates to only 50 people being allowed to start on the trail each day. Of those, 42 permits are issued in advance, leaving eight tickets for walk-ins. Groups are limited to a maximum of 12 people, and only one large group (nine to 12 people) is allowed to start each day.

As the trail is very popular in high season, it's advisable to book well ahead of time – reservations can be made from early January each year (☎ 867 667 3910, toll-free: ☎ 1 800 661 0486). During the summer season reservations can also be made through the Skagway Trail Center.

Permits can be collected from the Skagway Trail Center the day before you start hiking, or on the morning you start. However, you must pick up your permit before noon or your reservations will automatically be cancelled. You're required to attach your permit to your backpack so that it's visible to wardens. Walk-in permits are issued from the Skagway Trail Center from 1pm on the day before the permit's start date. No-show permits are re-allocated at 1pm each day for same-day starts.

Day permits If you're going on a day walk on the Canadian side of the border, you must have a day permit ($9.80). Day walkers are permitted to use the trail without a permit on the American side. Day permits can be bought from Parks Canada in Whitehorse or from the Trail Center in Skagway.

CAMPING Overnighters must stick to designated campgrounds on the Chilkoot Trail. These are Finnegan's Point (km 7.7, mile 4.8), Canyon City (km 12, mile 7.5), Pleasant Camp (km 16.7, mile 10.4), Sheep Camp (km 18.9, mile 11.8), Happy Camp (km 33, mile 20.5), Deep Lake (km 37, mile 23), Lindeman City (km 41.8, mile 26) and Bare Loon Camp (km 46.7, mile 29). There are also campsites at both Dyea and Bennett.

You must specify which campsites you're planning to use, and on which dates, when you make your reservation. Open fires are not allowed at any of these campgrounds; you must carry a fuel (or gas) stove for cooking. You should use the outhouses provided (remember that the trail is walked by thousands each year) and pack out all rubbish and meal leftovers.

All the campsites on the Alaska side have bear bins for food and shelters with woodstoves, though you should only use the wood in the case of emergencies. On the Canadian side only Happy Camp and Lake Lindeman have bear-resistant storage facilities; at other sites you need to hoist your food etc onto bear poles. There's no enclosed shelter at Deep Lake or Bare Loon (though the latter has an open shelter).

RISKS Be aware that, while this is a popular and well-monitored trail, the weather can really stink (when I crossed the summit the temperature was 2°C and the rain hammered straight through our waterproofs). Carry appropriate clothing. For much of the season, the Golden Stairs are covered in snow. Watch for snow bridges (the snow melts from underneath as the rocks upon which it lies warm, and you can break through), and aim to cross the summit early in the day when the risk of avalanche is less. If you're not experienced in coping with adverse outdoor conditions, consider doing the hike guided.

Note that bears as well as humans use the Chilkoot Trail; when I hiked the trail, we shared our camp each evening with a man from Oregon and his son. They came face-to-face with a grizzly on the summit, and saw a black bear the following day. 'We've been real lucky,' the father beamed as he showed us his bear photos. 'Heck, if we get any luckier, you'll just see a big pool of blood out there on the trail.' Carry bear spray, and be 'bear aware' (see pages 228–9).

ARTEFACTS They may look like interesting bits of rusting old junk, but the objects left behind by the stampeders are historical artefacts, protected by law. You're not allowed to gather them up to adorn your mantelpiece back home; indeed, it is illegal to move or even touch them. If you burn wood from collapsed gold-rush buildings, you will go directly to hell.

HIKING THE TRAIL
Dyea to Sheep Camp (18.9km, 11.8 miles) If you're physically fit and start out early, it's easy to do this stretch in one day (it takes 7–10 hours depending on your level). An alternative, however – especially for those travelling down from Whitehorse – is to start hiking at around lunchtime or in the early afternoon and to stop for the first night at Finnegan's Point or Canyon City. This makes for a more relaxing first two days, and means that you're not exhausted when you come to the more difficult summit day.

The trail seems to tease hikers from the start: it begins with a very steep section. Don't panic. It only lasts half a kilometre (0.25 miles). The trail then levels out and soon (at km 2.5, mile 1.6) meets an old logging road that makes for easy walking. Now the trail starts to rise and dip, and after a while the terrain becomes flooded in places by clouded glacial streams. Boardwalks and bridges save hikers' feet from the worst of the wet, though, after bouts of rain, you may have to change your boots for sandals and wade a little.

There's a shelter with a wood stove at Finnegan's Point, which is named for a man who built a corduroy road over the marshy land and tried to charge stampeders $2 to use it – though many of them just ignored him. From here you can see the Irene Glacier to the left, across the Taiya River. In clear weather it spangles like a toothpaste commercial.

Canyon City Campground (km 12, mile 7.5) has a shelter and a wood stove. Just beyond the campground, the trail divides. Take the left fork if you want to visit the old townsite of Canyon City. There are a few tumbledown cabins and artefacts, plus a steam boiler that was used to generate electricity for Canyon City and to power a tramway.

Following the right fork, along the main trail, there's another steep ascent about a mile after Canyon City; many people find this challenging. Almost everyone is pleased to find, at the top, a pleasant spot for a break. Look out for the telegraph wire hanging in the stretch between Canyon City and Pleasant Camp. This section is not the original trail of '98; the river took over the historic trail, so the hikers' path was moved to the route along which the telegraph ran.

Sheep Camp to the summit (7.7km, 4.8 miles) Sheep Camp is well organized, with wooden platforms for tents. The platforms can create a bit of a problem for lines and pegs, which are difficult to anchor to the wooden slats. Experienced Chilkooters bring extra lengths of line so that they can peg their tents to the ground beneath the raised platform. There are also bear bins for stashing your food and other smelly items, and a shelter. Note that you're not allowed to sleep in the shelters along the trail. They are for cooking and eating only. Interpretive boards tell you that in 1898 Sheep Camp had a population of 8,000, and was a mile long and two streets deep. There were hotels, restaurants, saloons and a bathhouse.

There's a rangers' talk at Sheep Camp every evening at 7pm Alaska time during the summer season; it's well worth listening to. They offer advice on crossing the summit the next day, and provide information on trail conditions. The night I was in Sheep Camp, the ranger even took out his guitar and sang a little song!

The rangers advise you to make an early start on the morning of your summit, as there's a reduced risk of avalanche early in the day. Take the rangers' advice on the best time to set out – it differs according to the season and weather. If anything, try to leave slightly earlier than they say. This head start on your fellow hikers will allow you to pick the best camping spots in Happy Camp – this is especially desirable early in the season when many of the platforms are still covered in snow. But in any case, Happy Camp has a stunning location, and it's a delightful place to arrive early and to while away a leisurely afternoon.

The stretch between Sheep Camp and the summit is the most difficult stretch of the trail; it starts to climb almost immediately after you leave Sheep Camp and it's all uphill to the pass. You may have to cross the Taiya River (which is shallow and braided) several times.

'The Scales' are at km 25.7, mile 16; this is one tiny spot where the trail doesn't head upwards. The Scales are so-named because prospectors' gear was weighed here to ensure they were carrying their prescribed ton of goods. Those carrying too much dumped the surplus, or traded with others for missing items. Here you can also see the remains of the tramways that enterprising souls built to haul gear up to the summit – for a fee.

It's only 0.9km (0.5 miles) from The Scales to the summit, but it's a straight-up scramble – and the Golden Stairs are not stairs at all, but a vast, steep talus field. Early in the season, when the boulders are covered with snow, the rangers sometimes kick rough steps in, but in sunny weather these melt fast. It's good to be wearing heavy boots so that you can kick in steps for yourself. Later in the summer,

It was not all plain sailing. To reach Lake Bennett from Lake Lindeman, stampeders had to negotiate the one-mile rapids. Archie Satterfield, in his book *Chilkoot Pass*, tells the story of one young farmer from Idaho named John Matthews. Matthews hauled his ton of goods over the pass to the shores of Lake Lindeman, built himself a boat, set sail – and dashed his craft to smithereens in the rapids. He lost everything but saved himself, so he went back over the pass, returned to Dyea, bought another outfit, and ferried the lot over the trail once more. Arriving for a second time at the lake, he built himself another boat, but again smashed it to splinters in the rapids. For a second time, he lost his entire outfit but managed to swim to shore. 'My God, what will happen to Jane and the babies,' he is said to have cried. Then he held a gun to his head and shot himself.

when the snow has thawed, it's just a case of hauling yourself over the rocks: follow the orange beacons and rock cairns that mark the path the rangers consider to be best, and look out for loose rocks that may be dislodged by hikers above you.

There's a warden's post (which will be locked if the warden's not there) and an unlocked public shelter at the summit. If the weather's poor and you need somewhere to warm up and brew a hot drink, this is the spot for it. And if the weather's fine, well, you may feel like a cup of tea all the same. However, given the shelter's diminutive proportions, the wardens request that you don't dawdle there all afternoon. Take a break and then move on to make room for newly arriving hikers.

The summit to Happy Camp (6.4km, 4 miles) Many people choose to spend the night at Happy Camp and, assuming the weather is fine, this is a particularly beautiful section of the trail with its turquoise alpine lakes and wildflowers. Now you are in alpine tundra; the trail is good and wide and, after an initial downhill, more or less flat. Don't assume the work's all over, though. The snow lingers here till well into the summer. Watch out for the marked avalanche area just beyond the steep downhill section after the summit. You should walk straight through this part without stopping in the early season, though the avalanche threat should be over by mid-July. You may also have to cross creeks during this stretch.

Happy Camp to Bennett (20km, 12.4 miles) The last couple of days' hiking are comparatively easy, and the scenery is spectacular. There's a small but pretty campsite at Deep Lake. After the campsite, almost at the end of Deep Lake, look out for the skeleton of a collapsible boat. This is the rusting remains of a business enterprise of a company called Flowers & Smith, which had the idea of selling hundreds of such craft to the stampeders: unfortunately for them, they hadn't realized that they would need to cross into Canadian territory, and the Mounties sent them packing.

There are two campgrounds at Lindeman City as well as a wall tent with a photograph exhibition and a small library of northern books. There's not a great deal to choose between the two campgrounds. Both have cabins with wood stoves; the first has better tree cover, while the second is closer to the interpretive tent. Thousands of stampeders stopped to camp at Lindeman City in early 1898. While they waited for the ice to go out of the lakes, they sawed down trees to build boats that would take them across Lake Lindeman and Lake Bennett, to the mouth of the Yukon River, and to Dawson City beyond. Botanists reckon that it will take this fragile forest 300 years to recuperate. The ice broke on 29 May 1898. On that day around 30,000 people in 7,124 hand-hewn vessels set off across the water for the city of gold.

If you're not camping at Bare Loon Lake, it's an excellent spot for a long lunch, if the weather is fair. The lake is truly beautiful. In the last hour, the trail becomes sandy; some people find the going, so close to the end, a challenge.

DONJEK ROUTE

Days	8–15
Distance	100–120km (60–75 miles)
Maximum elevation	2,164m (7,100ft)
Maps and books	1:50,000 topo maps required: Bighorn Creek 115 G/3, Donjek Glacier 115 G/4, Steele Creek 115 G/5, Duke River 115 D/6, Burwash Landing 115 G/7 (NB The Donjek Glacier 115 G/4 map only covers a tiny section of the route, and this part of the hike is marked with a defined trail. You may be able to manage without carrying this map.)

This is a tremendously rewarding and scenic hike that takes in tundra, alpine panoramas and the Donjek glacier – but it is also very difficult. At times you will walk along eroded mining roads and old horse trails but essentially there is no trail: you must make your own way across the tundra and through the bush. There are many creek crossings; some of them dangerous.

You are unlikely to meet other hikers on this route. Given that there are no markings of any kind to indicate the way, you must be experienced with route finding and backcountry travel if you are to do it unguided.

There is no one set way of doing the Donjek Route. The notes below refer to the way we went in August 2008 – these were very long days and most hikers will prefer to divide the route into shorter sections than we did – but you may also like to look at the Parks Canada route description at www.pc.gc.ca/pn-np/yt/kluane/activ/activ1/activ1bxv_e.asp, which we followed for the most part, and Vivien Lougheed's description in her *Kluane National Park Hiking Guide*. Note that you may need to deviate from your intended route as weather, wildlife and other conditions dictate.

As a part (though not all) of this route falls within Kluane National Park, you'll need to register before you start either at the Haines Junction Visitor Centre (see page 103) or the Tachäl Dhäl (Sheep Mountain) Visitor Centre (see page 104). It's mandatory to register all overnight trips in the park, and there's a registration fee of $9.80 per person per night. You must also contact the visitor centre when you've finished to let them know of your safe return: you will be liable for the costs of any search parties sent out if you fail to do this.

The best time to do this route is probably late August or early September, when the fall colours are vibrant, and the mosquitoes fewer than in full summer. Be aware it may snow whichever month you hike.

HIKING THE TRAIL

Duke River 115 G/6 The route starts where the Duke River meets the Alaska Highway. Take the turn-off 9km (5.5 miles) past Burwash Landing (heading in the Beaver Creek direction), just after the Duke River bridge. The turn-off is on the left: you'll see two interpretive boards, one about the Donjek Route and the other about the Kluane First Nation, at the beginning of a gravel road, which you should be able to drive in a 4x4 unless the weather is dreadful. After 5km, you come to some cabins and a horse camp (7V 5979 68022). This is where the hike starts.

There's a clear trail – an old mining road – that leads past the cabins and off to the right. It heads steeply uphill for about one hour. When the trail forks (at 7V 5969 68029), keep left.

You'll soon have good views of the mountains and pass a lake as the trail becomes less steep and arrives in the subalpine. By now, the mining road is a grassy track, and it's eroding and sloughing off into small ponds on either side.

About 9km/5.5 miles (3 hours) from the start, you come to a creek. The flat land to the north of this creek is a reasonable spot for camping (7V 5913 68021). There's another good picnic/camping spot a further 3.5km/2.1 miles (approximately one hour) along the old mining road.

At this point there's a fork in the road to the left, heading towards Amphitheatre Mountain (which is clearly shaped like an amphitheatre). It's better not to follow this left fork, as the tundra makes for difficult going, but take the right of the two arms to continue for another 1.8km (1.1 miles) until the road disappears at 7V 5867 68033.

Now you need to strike out to the left (west) across the tundra, heading towards the saddle at the northwest end of Amphitheatre Mountain and to Burwash Creek. Going across the tundra is slow. It's soft, marshy and hummocky – every footstep sinks – and there are many mosquitoes. (To give you an idea, our speed over the tundra was about 2km/h or 1.2mph.) The landscape, though, makes up for the going: it is vast and impressive, with a huge plateau of tundra giving onto distant mountains. We met Burwash Creek at 7V 5823 68026. You can meet the creek further upstream: your total distance to the pass will be less this way, but you'll spend more time hiking across the difficult tundra, and less time walking along the relatively easier creek bed.

The walking becomes easier in the creek valley. It's firm, rocky terrain; sometimes you'll need to cross the water.

There are good, protected camp spots on the east (left) side of creek. We camped at 7V 5823 68012; it took us five hours (around 12km/7.5 miles) to get here from the camp spot at 7V 5913 68021. There are further possible campsites between here and the beginning of Hoge Pass.

From 7V 5823 68012, you continue to follow the creek upstream. After 4–5km (2.5–3 miles, about two hours) you come to a warden's cabin (7V 5824 67974). This is just inside the Kluane National Park boundary. The cabin is kept locked but its deck is a pleasant spot for a tea break.

After a further 1km (0.6 miles) a tributary comes into Burwash Creek from the west at 7V 5823 67968. It's possible to camp here. Now you have to climb up to an old mining road on the ridge to the south (left). It's a fair old scramble to get up there but once you're up the way is clear: a definite trail consisting of large broken-up rocks leads towards Hoge Pass, which lies about 2km (1.2 miles) to the west at 7V 5804 67966. It took us about 1½ hours to reach the pass from the warden's cabin.

Steele Creek 115 G/5 Don't follow the creek that leads directly down from Hoge Pass, even though this seems the obvious thing to do. Instead, you should climb the ridges to the south (from where there are outstanding views in clear weather, and we saw many Dall sheep; this is the point at which you'll first look down upon the Donjek River) then continue west along the ridge for as far you can (about an hour's walking). Then descend a scree slope on the left, which leads to a grass gully. Stay on the grass (on the left) until you can see the tributary to Hoge Creek. Now you'll see a steep scree slope that you need to hike down. From the correct descending point, you'll be able to see both a tributary that empties into Hoge Creek, and Hoge Creek itself. Beware of falling rocks from the hiker above, and slippery gravel on the bedrock. The descent of the scree slope ends at 7V 5787 67956, where the descent meets the tributary of Hoge Creek. Continue down

Hoge Creek canyon. It's full of large boulders that you'll need to climb and descend, and sometimes you'll need to cross the creek.

There's a good camp spot at 7V 5779 67957. This is about 1½ hours after you've arrived in the canyon, 10km (6 miles) or seven hours from Burwash Creek.

Follow Hoge Creek downstream for about another two hours; again, you'll sometimes need to cross. There's an old horse camp on the Donjek River at 7V 5751 67949. You need to climb up the bank on the left some 100m (110yds) after this horse camp. Follow the game trails in a southerly direction until you pick up a horse trail. (We picked up the horse trail at 7V 5756 67925.) The horse trail is well-defined; however, it is sometimes washed out by creeks and disappears. We lost it several times. After another 2.5km (1.5 miles), you'll cross a creek with pink-coloured rock at 7V 5768 67911.

Donjek Glacier II5 G/4 The trail enters a balsam poplar grove and crosses a clear creek at 7V 5780 67904. Then there's a section of dense, high shrubs for 2km (1.2 miles). After that you come to a large creek; it is always difficult with these large creek beds to find the horse trail again on the other side and you may want to drop your packs for a few minutes while you search for the trail. We found the trail at 7V 5803 67888.

Bighorn Creek II5/G3 Now you cross a series of meadows. After about 4km (2.5 miles), there's a good spot to camp on a hill overlooking the toe of the Donjek glacier (7V 5816 67863). This is about 15km (9 miles, seven hours) from Hoge creek; you leave the horse trail to climb the hill. The views are superb, as is the soundtrack – every now and then you'll hear a thunderous roar as the glacier calves – and there's a good supply of firewood. These benefits make up for the fact that the site is not perfectly flat (though there are enough flat patches), and you have to walk a few minutes down the hill to fetch water from a creek. We spent two nights in this camp, and went for a short half-day hike to the glacier on our much-needed 'day off'.

Continue along the horse trail; the terrain can be marshy here. After 30 minutes, there's a creek with steep banks. It's possible to camp here, close to the glacier.

After another hour or so, you'll come to a second, larger creek at 7V 5850 67824. Continue to follow the horse trail if you can, or, if you can't, just make for 7V 5867 67810. This is the head of a gully which you can fairly easily descend to Bighorn Creek.

From here there are three alternative routes. In low water, you can walk along the creek bed to the canyon (this took us 40 minutes), and then walk through the canyon for a further kilometre (0.6 miles). You will almost certainly have to cross wide sections of the creek several times and in places the water may be thigh deep. This can be highly dangerous and considerable caution is required. You'll come to the Chert Creek confluence just after the canyon at 7V 5898 67800.

If the water is too high to cross safely, you'll need to bypass the canyon by climbing a slope to the left (north) and contouring round to the east to a convenient slope that drops down to Chert Creek. This alternative route can take up to three hours.

The third alternative to this section is to hike to Atlas Pass via Expectation Pass. This route is described by Vivien Lougheed in her book *The Kluane National Park Hiking Guide*.

Assuming you took one of the first two routes through or round the canyon, you'll now follow Chert Creek upstream. The rocks here are bright orange. The creek branches 2km (1.2 miles) from the mouth of the creek: follow the right (east) fork. After another 600m (660yds) it branches again at 7V 5910 67821. Follow the left (west) arm and climb up the slopes to the right (east). There's a good camp at

7V 5917 67828, between the two arms of the creek (at this point, you'll be next to the right arm). This is around 16km (10 miles) from the glacier toe.

Now you'll follow the creek bed upstream. After about an hour, you'll arrive at a flat bowl, where camping is possible. To reach Atlas Pass, climb up the gentle slope to the right (east). The steeper slope straight ahead of the creek drainage is the wrong one (we speak from bitter experience). Atlas Pass is at 7V 5931 67853. In clear weather the view from the pass is meant to be stunning; when we did it, it was immersed in cloud.

From Atlas Pass, you'll see that the descent straight ahead looks treacherous. Don't go that way, but follow the clay and silt ridge to the left (north). There's a shallow climb to some dramatic rocky outcrops; go past the first, smaller outcrop and contour the second, larger one until you reach a broad, gently sloping, soft scree-and-silt ridge, which you can quite easily descend. Head towards a small saddle at 7V 5938 67853. From the saddle, you'll be able to see a distinct flat patch of green that looks somewhat like a putting green on a golf course. Descend the scree slope from the saddle to this green. From here, the easiest route down is to take the scree slope just to the right (east) of the green, down to Atlas Creek at 7V 5943 67853.

It's now about 6km (3.7 miles – 1½ hours or so) along the creek to Duke River. There are various places along the way that are suitable for camping. If you still have energy, however, it's worth continuing to the river as there's a lovely large campsite, with firewood, close to the river at 7V 5964 67895. To get there, follow the game trail that meets the creek just before the confluence. The camp spot is about 300m (330yds) along the game trail.

The Parks Canada directions now take you via Cache Lake and Copper Joe Creek. This route takes approximately two days. If you take this route, you'll need the topo map Burwash Landing 115 G/7. However, we deviated from the Parks route at this point due to the fact that it started to rain, and rain, and rain, and then it snowed. We walked out along the Duke River in one (long and tiring) day, as follows.

If you've camped at 7V 5964 67895, follow the trail back to the Duke River. If the water's low, you can hike downstream along the riverbed.

Duke River 115 G/6 There are two canyons between this point and the trail end. You'll have to climb up onto high ground to bypass these. Follow game trails upwards, and stay on the high meadows for as long as you can.

This section of the route is difficult and you shouldn't count on being able to do it in one day. You're bushwhacking a lot of the way, and must cross marshy areas, deep, soft moss, sections of uprooted timber, and other obstacles. There are many creek crossings; some of these creeks are full and fast. Granite Creek, particularly, can be difficult at high water.

For the last 5km (3 miles), you'll follow the old mining road beside the Duke River bed. The pick-up point (at the horse camp – the same as the drop-off point) is at 7V 5979 68022. It's around 22km (13.5 miles), or about nine hours' hiking, to here from the camp at 7V 5964 67895.

13

Paddling

Days	6–8
Distance	304km (189 miles)
Difficulty rating	Easy – wind and waves on Lake Laberge create the greatest danger. There are some bends and riffles on the Thirtymile section of the river. Between Carmacks and Dawson come the Five Finger Rapids and Rink Rapids, but you won't need to contend with these if you're only paddling as far as Carmacks.
Maps and books	Be sure to buy a copy of Mike Rourke's river guide *Yukon River: Marsh Lake to Dawson City*. It's excellent on historical detail as well as providing all the information necessary for canoeing the river today. You can buy it from Mac's Fireweed Books in Whitehorse, or from www.yukonbooks.com. You don't need topo maps as well as Rourke's river guide. However, we've used the topo guide numbers to subdivide this chapter and, if you want to look at them, they are: Whitehorse, map 105 D/11; Upper Laberge, map 105 D/14; Lake Laberge, map 105 E/03; Lower Laberge, map 105 E/06; Frank Creek, map 105 E/11; Hootalinqua, map 105 E/10; Big Salmon, map 105 E/15; Claire Lake, map 105 E/14; Frenchman Lake, map 105 L/04; Carmacks, map 115 I/01.

The Yukon River runs for 3,185 km (1,980 miles) from its headwaters in Marsh Lake, south of Whitehorse, to the Bering Sea. It's possible to paddle the entire course of the river; the journey usually takes around three months. Most people, however, paddle just a section of the river from Whitehorse to Carmacks, or to Dawson. This route description covers the Whitehorse–Carmacks stretch, which can be done at a very leisurely pace in around a week (the competitors of the Yukon River Quest race do it in a day or two, but those on vacation usually like to take things easier).

This portion of the river makes for easy paddling; it's suitable for novices. The river is wide and the current runs fast enough that you don't have to work too hard. Except for the Lake Laberge section, where the water's very slow movement means you'll have to use that paddle, you could realistically sit back with a cup of tea and float most of the way to Carmacks. There's no white water and little in the way of obstacles.

Paddling YUKON RIVER

13

One of the major draws of paddling the Yukon River is its history. This was the way the majority of the stampeders to the Klondike gold rush came, often in rudimentary, hand-hewn boats (see pages 165–8 for more on gold-rush history). After the gold rush, the river was the major transport route between Dawson and the Outside; sternwheeler traffic plied this waterway until the Whitehorse–Mayo road, and its Dawson spur, opened in the 1950s. And so, as you travel along the river, you continually pass points of historic interest – and old gold dredge sitting rusting in the shallows, a rotting sternwheeler hauled up on the shore and just left of there, the tumbledown remains of telegraph stations and wood camps. Anyone intending to paddle the Yukon out of Whitehorse should really make the effort to tour the SS Klondike, and watch the historic video that forms part of the tour (see page 69) – it brings the history of these ruins vibrantly to life.

Note that there are plenty of developed campsites along the Yukon River. While these are not managed, there is usually an outhouse and picnic tables. The local First Nation band sometimes supplies firewood at popular sites such as Hootalinqua, but don't count on it. Camping in these places is free of charge.

WHITEHORSE 105 D/11 The most popular put-in is the boat ramp downtown, behind Rotary Park. However, the Robert Service Campground (see page 62) is right on the river, so if you're staying there you could set out directly from the campground. Those wishing to canoe the river in its entirety will start south of Whitehorse, at the river's headwaters at Marsh Lake, and will need to portage around the hydroelectric dam at the end of Schwatka Lake; beginning from downtown Whitehorse avoids this.

As you pass all the big warehouses and buildings (the part of town were Walmart, etc is) at the northern end of town, keep to the river's right channel.

UPPER LABERGE 105 D/14 Just out of Whitehorse, you'll see high clay cliffs on the right side of the river. The trees on these cliffs are a favourite nesting spot for bald eagles so keep an eye out for them here.

At McIntyre Creek the water is wide, shallow and slow; keep right. Then, about 10km (6 miles) downstream of Whitehorse, the city's sewerage system drains into the river. The sewerage is treated by the time it reaches the river, and water quality has been greatly improved in recent years but, nonetheless, many people prefer not to drink the river water from here until about halfway across Lake Laberge. It's a good idea to fill up your water containers before you put in and, if you need to replenish them, to use creek water.

The river can sometimes become silty at the confluence with the Takhini River. There's a good camp on the front of Egg Island – this is the first island after the Takhini Confluence (and the Takhini is easily identified because a) there's a road bridge – the North Klondike Highway – across it near the confluence and b) it is the only river confluence near here). Walk around to the back of Egg Island and you'll find a beaver lodge.

Just before Policeman's Point, there's a sharp bend in the river, and a big island on the right-hand side. On the left side of this island, there's a good, open patch of land ideal for camping (it's marked on Rourke's map as 'good camp').

Policeman's Point is at Upper Laberge, just before the neck of the lake – there was once an RCMP post here, hence the name, though nothing much remains. In the river, just by Policeman's Point, you'll see a line of semi-submerged wooden posts poking out. This underwater fence was designed way back in 1899 to hold back the silty river bed – there used to be a sandbar here that almost entirely blocked the way. The pilings were meant to prevent the sandbar from forming, and force the water into the narrower, left-hand channel, so creating a good, navigable route through this shallow stretch of river. It didn't work as well as had been hoped, however, and within a few years it was severely damaged by ice. In the end, the White Pass and Yukon Route widened the channel to create a safer passage for their ships. When paddling past here, you should keep to the left – to the right of the posts the water is shallow.

Be wary of high waves on Lake Laberge. Sudden and severe storms can blow up without warning – and can drown careless paddlers. Always paddle close to the shore, and make for dry land at the first sign of high winds. The lake is about 50km (31 miles) long; reckon on taking ten to 12 hours to paddle its length. You may need to allow extra time to wait out strong winds. No recreational canoeist does it in a day; most people camp one or two nights on the lake's shore. This is usually the most arduous part of any Whitehorse–Carmacks paddling trip. This route description assumes you're going down the right (east) shore, which is the shorter way. The left side, however, has arguably better campsites.

There are remains of an abandoned First Nations village at 8V 4979 67612, as well as a brand-new lodge owned by Great River Journey (see page 25). Note that this is First Nations land, and you shouldn't camp here.

LAKE LABERGE 105 E/03 You'll see a cabin on the right (east) shore of the lake at 8V 4953 67753. This is owned by the Cathers family (they run Cathers Wilderness Adventures, see page 25); it's private property, and shouldn't be used except in an emergency.

There are good camping spots before and after the rocky point at approximately 8V 4916 67815.

LOWER LABERGE 105 E/06 There's an interesting historic site at at 8V 4879 68063 – this is the point where the lake empties into the Thirtymile River. There used to be a police station, post office, roadhouse and telegraph station here; the latter two still stand today. There's also a slowly oxidizing truck that sits amid fat blades of green grass – once used to haul timber for the steamers, it now just lies and rusts. There's also a developed campsite here.

The Thirtymile River (as the stretch of the Yukon between Lake Laberge and the confluence with the Teslin River is called) is fantastically pretty. Nominated a Canadian Heritage River, its water is clear and jade in colour, and is lined by sandy-coloured cliffs that are popular with bald eagles. Note that the water won't stay clear for long – it becomes silty after the confluence with the Teslin at Hootalinqua – so take your photos now. Many of the bends and creeks along the Thirtymile River are named for ships that found trouble there, for example Tanana Reef is named for the *Tanana*, which sank here in 1915, and La France Creek is for the steamer *La France* which chugged her last in 1911, when she became grounded on a nearby point. It's worth taking this part of the river slowly, as it's full of historical interest – stop every now and then to check out the derelict cabins that dot the shore.

There's another good camp (well used but officially undeveloped) behind the first cliff on the left after Lower Laberge, at roughly 8V 4881 68074. Mike Rourke marks this as a 'potential camp'; it has become popular since publication of his guide.

About 10km (6 miles) later you come to US Bend, which curves back tightly on itself: beware of riffles here.

FRANK CREEK 105 E/11 There's a good, developed camp on the right at approximately 8V 4942 68150, just beyond US Bend and before Johnston Island.

As is often the case with very well-used camps along the Yukon, suitable dead trees have been burned long ago and you may have to walk to find wood – or use a fuel stove instead.

HOOTALINQUA 105 E/10 There's a large developed camp on the left at 8V 5003 68265 between Cape Horn and Tyrell Bend with aspen trees and good grayling fishing as well as excellent hiking and photography opportunities.

Shortly after Tyrell Bend you come to Hootalinqua. Hootalinqua village once had a police station with two constables, a telegraph office, a store and a roadhouse. Now – on the opposite bank to the abandoned village – there's just a campsite (8V 5052 68278) with a covered area, outhouses, picnic tables and firepits. There's a fabulous short (but steep) hike from here up onto the hills overlooking the river and great expanses of wilderness beyond – the views are well worth a little shortness of breath. From the campsite walk along the shore downstream, and cross the creek. You'll pass a fallen-down cabin; then hike up a short, steep hill. The trail now splits. The right arm leads to some old Indian graves. Keep straight on to walk along the ridge, continuing until you come to a plateau with views. It takes around half an hour to walk to the top.

The Hootalinqua camp is well used; if you want to be alone, there's a good alternative spot on the opposite bank of the river just downstream of the old village. Wherever you sleep the night, though, be sure to stop in at Shipyard Island, just after Hootalinqua. Ships used to be pulled up here for repairs and winter storage (the ice on Lake Laberge thaws later each year than the ice of the river, and some ships were kept for the winter downstream of the lake so that they could begin operating early in the season) – and the sternwheeler *Evelyn* is still here. Though she's rather past her prime, she's pretty much intact, and an interpretive board explains her history. You can also camp on Shipyard Island.

At low tide, you can see the remains of the first *SS Klondike* at 8V 5067 68374. She sank on 12 June 1936. The captain had just gone below for breakfast, leaving the steering to his recently promoted second-in-command, who very quickly proved that he wasn't up to the job by crashing into a rocky bluff. One newly married couple on board lost all their possessions, including their furniture. The *SS Klondike* that you can tour today in Whitehorse was built to replace her sunken predecessor.

BIG SALMON 105 E/15 The Big Salmon River comes in from the right about 50km (around 30 miles) after Hootalinqua. Stop here to see the historic Indian village (8V 5042 68608) that sits at the confluence. Its cabins are now derelict but interesting to poke your head into. There are also picnic tables and so on – it's a pleasant spot for lunch or camping.

CLAIRE LAKE 105 E/14 Stay in the river's left arm around the island (it's the one at the very top of page 51 in Rourke's map, just beyond Fourth of July Bend). It's worth then paddling over to a point on the right (8V 4948 68656) where you'll find a gold dredge – it's the semi-submerged contraption with the 'Caterpillar' logo embossed into its rusting bodywork. It was built in 1940 by two men, Laurent Cyr and Boyd Gordon (part of their machine was made from the parts of an old Caterpillar, hence the logo). The dredge cost $10,000 to build, but Cyr and Gordon only operated it for three weeks that first summer, making around $2,300. They pulled it up onto the shore for winter – and there it still sits today, for they had a disagreement and never came back. There's a fair camp on the shore by the dredge.

Keep to the left again as you pass the first large island after the dredge – the left arm is narrower than the right, and quite a bit faster. The world won't come to an end if you miss it, but this is the easier passage.

FRENCHMAN LAKE 105 L/04 Just past the confluence with Little Salmon River you come to a First Nations seasonal fish camp, on the right-hand shore. During the salmon season (mid-July to August) you may see the First Nations people bringing in and smoking salmon here.

From Little Salmon village (8V 4645 68800) there's a trail that links to the Campbell Highway, which passes close by. This is the earliest opportunity for a highway take-out since leaving Whitehorse and, if you're short of time, you could cut your trip short by a day by finishing here.

A little more than 10km (6 miles) after Little Salmon you'll come to Eagle's Bluff, an obvious hump of a hill – it's about a 15-minute paddle from Mandanna Creek. Just after this, at approximately 8V 4522 68790, comes Columbia Slough on the right. It's named for the steamer *Columbia* who met her end here in September 1906 – she was carrying a supply of blasting powder and, when the ship's fireman tripped while carrying a rifle, he discharged a shot into the powder, which duly blasted. There were no passengers aboard (save a stowaway) but many of the crew died. This was the major tragedy of all the Yukon River's wreckages, with the greatest loss of life. There are more details in Mike Rourke's river guide.

Keep to the left as you go through Taylor's Cutoff, immediately after Columbia Slough (8V 4503 68811) – this narrow arm provides a helpful short cut, slicing off a wide bend in the main river. Don't take this route at very low water, however. There are many good places to camp in this area.

CARMACKS 115 I/01 The section between Taylor's Cutoff and Carmacks is characterized by long stretches with wide curves. The most popular take-out is at the Coal Mine Campground (see page 158) at 8V 4340 68869, which has power, water, and a restaurant; even if you're not stopping for the night, you can still take out and wolf down a burger before hitting the road for home.

BIG SALMON RIVER

Days	8–11
Distance	237km (147 miles)
Difficulty rating	Class I–II (novices should not attempt this river without a professional guide)
Maps and books	Mike Rourke's *Big Salmon River* is the river guide; it's available from Mac's Fireweed Books in Whitehorse, or www.yukonbooks.com. Paddlers will find this more useful than the corresponding 1:50,000 topo maps, of which there are seven: Crater Creek 105 F/03, Mount St Cyr 105 F/06, (no title) 105 F/05, Souch Creek 105 F/12, Teraktu Creek 105 E/09, Hootalinqua 105 E/10, and Big Salmon 105 E/15. Unless you're planning to combine your paddling trip with some day hikes (the hills in the Big Salmon range ascend into alpine landscape fairly quickly making for good outings on foot – but there are no trails so you need backcountry and route-finding experience) you don't need the topo maps in addition to Mike Rourke's river guide.

The Big Salmon is one of the Yukon's most popular paddling routes. It's easily accessible – both the put-in and take-out have road access, which keeps costs

13

down. Most people start at Quiet Lake, at km 99 (mile 61) of the South Canol Road, and finish at Carmacks on the North Klondike Highway, but it's possible to continue along the Yukon River to Dawson, or beyond.

The route starts with a succession of three lakes, which give onto wide panoramas. Then the river narrows into tightly winding valleys with glistening clear water. The river is known for its abundance of wildlife – moose, particularly, are frequently seen by paddlers, while wolves, lynx and bears may also be spotted.

There's no white water on the Big Salmon but it nonetheless has swift sections and takes tight turns. There are numerous sweepers and log jams; you'll need to portage in places. And while these hazards mean that the Big Salmon is no river for unguided novices, it's this very need for constant vigilance that makes it interesting for – and popular with – more experienced canoeists.

CRATER CREEK 105 F/03 The most popular put-in is at Quiet Lake Recreation Site, at km 99 (mile 61) of the South Canol Road (8V 6032 67809). This is a government campsite with 10 sites; see page 35.

It takes two to three hours to cross the lake, but be careful as you go: you should stay close to either the east or west shore, as high waves can blow up on the southerly winds. It's possible to camp on the east shore (right-hand side) at 8V 6011 67833. There's good fishing for lake trout around here.

There's a large space suitable for camping – it's free from bushes and shrubs but has tall tree cover – right at the end of the lake, just to the left of the river mouth. It's easily identified because it has a cabin, which is visible from the lake. Alternatively there's a smaller site (suitable for up to three tents) on the first river stretch at 8V 5967 67872. This spot is also good for grayling fishing.

After this point, the river narrows and becomes shallow. There's a fairly swift current: having just come out from Quiet Lake, you'll feel a substantial difference. Then the river leads into Sandy Lake; while this lake can have waves, it's smaller and safer than both Quiet Lake and Big Salmon Lake. You may find lake trout in the narrow section at the end of Sandy Lake.

MOUNT ST CYR 105 F/06 This section of river flows slowly and is easy to navigate. There's a possible camping spot on the left shore, before Big Salmon Lake (8V 5918 67920). This is a good place for grayling fishing. You may see moose drinking and grazing along the shore and in the shallows just before Big Salmon Lake.

Big Salmon Lake is a large body of water and, as with Quiet Lake, you should be wary of wind and waves, and stay close to the shore. There's an excellent, large camp on a point that juts out from the right-hand shore (8V 5928 67939): as you're coming into the lake, you'll see an island at two o'clock. Keep the island to your left and, just after you've passed it, you'll see the point on the right. There's a cabin at the end of the lake (8V 5893 67979). This is the property of the local First Nation and so should not be used except in emergencies, when it's a useful place to warm up. There is a stove; if you find and use chopped firewood, you must replace it before you leave. Again, you should be able to paddle the lake in two to three hours.

As you come out of Big Salmon Lake, you enter the most difficult section of the river: its course takes tight bends, the water runs fast, and there are frequent log jams. When the water's low, you'll see the splinters and shards of smashed-up canoes – take heed! For the whole of this section, you should keep alert, always looking out for log jams and sweepers, and trees and bushes in the water. A log jam totally blocks the river at 8V 5892 67994; you may sometimes be able to line the canoe through shallow water to the right, but more often you'll have to portage (again on the right), and the land you'll cross is muddy. Mike Rourke recommends a camp on the left at 8V 5875 68029; we haven't camped there ourselves.

There's a cut-through at 8V 5872 68028 – previously the river flowed in a tight loop, but eventually the water broke through the thin neck of land and the river now flows along this shorter route. Be particularly aware here of uprooted and fallen trees beneath the surface of the water – the river is flowing over what was recently forest floor, which harbours far greater obstacles than older riverbed. (Note also that, in the edition of the river guide we've been using, Mike Rourke says that the river has *almost* cut through at this point. The cut-through has become total since publication – though Rourke brings out new editions every now and then so your book may be different.)

There's a fair mid-water camp on a gravel bar to the left, in front of some willow trees, at 8V 5866 68030. Many people like to fish in the large eddy at the confluence with Sheep Creek; this is a popular spot for camping, too. Alternatively, there's a good camp on the left at 8V 5809 68104.

Watch out for fast riffles and a few rocks about 20 minutes after you pass Sheep Creek.

MAP 105 F/05 (NO TITLE) There's a good, large, well-used camp high on the left shore of the straight stretch of river between Sheep Creek and Moose Creek. The confluence of Moose Creek is good for fishing (8V 5790 68166). Moose Creek has two arms; the second is often dry. If this is the case, you can camp on the gravel of the dry arm. This is also a good spot for a lunch break, and you can walk easily from the camping/lunch site on the second arm to the confluence with its fishing.

After Moose Creek, the current of the river speeds up, and there's some danger from rocks for about 10km (6 miles).

SOUCH CREEK 105 F/12 Mike Rourke recommends a camping spot on the right-hand side of the river at 8V 5785 68208; there's also good grayling fishing here. There's a small lake close to the left shore, which is good for pike fishing. You can land your canoe at 8V 5774 52682 on the river bank and walk for a few metres over to the lake.

After this, the river straightens and the water runs faster again. Watch out for rocks, particularly in the section where the rock wall hugs the river to the left.

There are now many creeks coming in from the right offering good grayling fishing opportunities. You'll come to a total block from a log jam; a while back someone tried to cut through the blockage with a chain saw – last time we passed this 'gate' was no longer visible but, even if someone's come along and had another go, it's not recommended as the strength of the current makes it difficult to steer through accurately. It's better to stick to the tried-and-tested portage on the right end of the island: when you come to the log jam, paddle to the right, keeping the island to your left. You'll probably have to manoeuvre around some smaller log jams as you go. When this arm of the river, too, becomes totally blocked, you'll see a well-defined portage trail leading over the island, starting at 8V 5735 68259.

There's a good camp in the sharp right curve of the river, on the right, on the inside of the curve, at 8V 5720 68274, and another at the end of the gravel bar in the mouth of Souch Creek at 8V 5661 94683; this is fair spot for fishing.

There are several little lakes to the right of the river now, and there's a good short hiking trail along the shore of the first of them if you feel like stretching your legs. Pull over at 8V 5617 68235 and walk on a ridge beside the lake – there's a good view. This walk is also mentioned in Mike Rourke's book. It can take around an hour to walk there and back, though the exact length will depend on how high up on the ridge you venture.

There are three good camps to choose from along the following stretch of river. Mike Rourke recommends one on the right shore, near the second lake (8V 5605 68224), and another near the third lake, again on the right shore (8V 5588 68219). We prefer a spot on the left, however, just before the river curves to the right (8V 5573 68224) – it's a roomy campsite with a little creek; there's a large log in a sunny spot on the river bank which is great for drying out clothes...or just sitting and whiling away a beautiful afternoon.

TERAKTU CREEK 105 E/09 There's a possible high-water camp (ie: it's safe even in high water) behind the creek on the right, at 8V 5462 68239. The river now winds in U-turns until Headless Creek. There's a new cut-through at 8V 5366 68255, where the water has broken through a narrow neck of land; as explained on page 249, these cut-throughs create hazards due to the fact that the river is now flowing over the debris of recent forest floor.

There's a good high-water camp at 8V 5339 68288 – it's on the right, after the long, straight stretch of river – as well as a small camp at 8V 5300 68304, on the left side of the main river, directly behind the confluence with its southern arm (the South Big Salmon River). There's additionally a large camp on the opposite side of the river at 8V 5300 68306.

HOOTALINQUA 105 E/10 This section of the river winds at first, and then straightens out for long stretches making for a more relaxing paddle.

It's possible to camp on the right-hand shore, in the winding section of the river, at 8V 5259 68364. There's also a good high-water camp on the right at 8V 5259 68395.

BIG SALMON 105 E/15 There's a campsite suitable for three to four tents behind the confluence with the river's north arm (8V 5204 68476). It's a well-known spot, though, and if you arrive late in the day you may find other people have beaten you to it. If this is the case, you're probably going to have to press on for another 10–15km (6–9 miles); there are few suitable camping places along the stretch of river that follows. The solution is either to make sure you arrive early, or to look for camping opportunities in the section just before this recommended camping spot – there are some possibilities earlier on.

Once you've passed the confluence with the river's north arm, you come to another tricky section. For the next 2km (1.2 miles), the river runs fast, with large rocks and standing waves creating hazards for the unwary.

There are further hazards an hour or two downstream: after 8V 5140 68590, the river has many new channels, and is continually shifting, so it's impossible to give advice on which braid to follow.

There's an excellent camp on the left (opposite a high rock cliff on the right) at 8V 5108 68591. Shortly afterwards, you come to the confluence with the Yukon River. There's an abandoned Indian village here (8V 5042 68608) with picnic tables, an outhouse, and picturesque tumbledown cabins. It's a good spot for lunch, and you can camp here, too.

The route now continues down the Yukon River to the takeout at Carmacks; see pages 246–7. Note that Mike Rourke's *Big Salmon* guide includes this section of the Yukon River; you don't need to buy his *Yukon River* guide too.

LIARD RIVER

Days	8–12
Distance	209km (180 miles) or about 30–35hrs paddling time before breaks
Difficulty rating	Class I–II
Maps and books	1:50,000 top maps required: Caribou Lakes 105 B/13, Scurvy Lakes 105 B/14, Junkers Lake 105 G/3, Fire Lake 105 G/2, Scurvy Creek 105 B/15, Black River 105 B/16, Allan Creek 105 B/9, Sambo Creek 105 A/12, False Pass Creek 105 A/5, Watson Lake 105 A/2

The Upper Liard River in southeast Yukon is generally reckoned to be one of the territory's prettiest river trips. It's a remote wilderness waterway: people commonly paddle the whole route without meeting others. Most people start at Caribou Lakes, which is accessible only by float plane. The most common take-out is at Upper Liard village on the Alaska Highway, just west of Watson Lake.

There are plenty of gravel bars along the Liard River for camping and for lunch breaks. Some stretches of the Liard system are prone to log jams and sweepers. You may have to line or portage in sections: it's not a technical river but you'll need paddling experience if you're going to do it without a guide. You should be familiar with fast-moving water and the negotiation of obstacles.

Fishing is good throughout the Liard River: the Liard system is the only place in the Yukon that you'll catch bull trout and there are both bull trout and arctic grayling in most of the eddies and creek confluences. You'll occasionally find mountain white fish, too. Again, these are not common in the Yukon.

CARIBOU LAKES 105 B/13 Most people camp their first evening on the shores of Caribou Lakes. There's a good campsite at 9V 3591 67487.

Caribou Creek is shallow. You may need to line or portage. The waterway here is narrow with very tight bends, and the water, while not white, is fast.

There are pike where the lake meets the creek. The shores of Caribou Creek, which stretches from Caribou Lakes to the river, are marshy and wet – it's not advisable to camp here. It's therefore best to paddle the distance from Caribou Lakes to the river in one day. There's a good spot to break for lunch at 9V 3609 67553.

The last third of the creek stretch is the most difficult – it is narrow, winding and prone to log jams. Be sure to paddle in such a way that you can always reach the shore if you need walk to survey the river ahead. You may need to portage some sections. There's often a large log jam at 9V 3643 67578 just before the confluence with the Liard River. There's an eddy directly before the spot that jams. This is a good place to stop and observe the obstacle ahead. There's an arm leading off from the eddy – paddle down here and you'll be able to line your canoe around the log jam.

There's a good camp on the left, 1km (0.6 miles) past the Liard River confluence (9V 3652 67588). Most people take about 5 hours to get here from Caribou Lakes (3–3½ hours' actual paddling time).

SCURVY LAKES 105 B/14 The first stretch of the Liard River is narrow with sharp bends. Again, logs jam and pile up easily here, and you may have to line or portage. Look out particularly for a spot about 10 minutes after the camp (9V 3653 67595) where log jams are common – you may have to line or portage on the right. From 9V 3660 67642 there are plenty of gravel bars suitable for camping.

The river is full of boulders from 9V 3716 67626 to the mouth of Junkers Creek (9V 3748 67626). There are lots of possible campsites on the gravel bars in this area. Beware of the three tight bends around 9V 3787 67645; the most dangerous is the second one. Sweepers are common along this section. Tight corners and sweepers continue to keep paddlers alert until about one hour after Lonely Creek. There's a log jam completely blocking the river at 9V 3873 67706; you can portage on the left.

JUNKERS LAKE 105 G/3 This is probably the most scenic section in the Liard River trip, as you're surrounded by hills – the Pelly Mountains behind and the Cassiar Mountains in front. Make sure you remember to look behind you as well as to the front. It's a good spot for photos.

You then come to the Ings River confluence at 9V 3914 67718. The river braids, with log jams and sweepers, about half an hour after the confluence. The gravel bars here are constantly shifting, and it can be difficult to determine which is the main arm of the river.

FIRE LAKE 105 G/2 You'll only be using this map for a very short section. The primary point of interest is the adequate campsite at 9V 3927 67703. It's elevated, and therefore a useful spot to stop if the water is high.

SCURVY CREEK 105 B/15 Now the water slows down, and there are long, straight slow stretches from here to the end of your journey. Be ready, though, for fast water and turbulence at 9V 4085 67553 where Rainbow Creek and Dome Creek join simultaneously from either side.

There's an excellent campsite at 9V 4094 67531, which is three to four hours' paddling from the Ings River confluence. It can be difficult to reach, however, as the water immediately before it flows fast and the channels are constantly changing. Try to move towards the gravel bar on the right side as soon as you see the cut bank in front of you. The camp is on the sand bar to your right, after the sharp turn.

If you miss that camp, there are more cliffs with gravel bars suitable for camping just afterwards, and another good camp with plentiful fishing at the confluence with Quartz Creek (9V 4145 67472).

There's a trapping cabin but no fish where Scurvy Creek joins the river. Note that this, and the other cabins you pass, are private. They belong to trappers and should not be used except in emergencies. If you must use the cabin, and the trapper's woodpile and stove, you should replace the wood before you leave. Remember that tools and wood are here for a reason, and the trapper's comfort and safety will depend on these items being as he left them.

There's a possible hike 1km (0.6 miles) past Scurvy Creek, on the right (start at 9V 4164 67430). These hills are a burn area, so the terrain makes for easy progress and you can gain elevation quickly. It takes about an hour to climb the first hill and walk back; it's about a half-day round trip to hike to the higher hills behind. The hilltop at 9V 4160 67424 has an outstanding view to Pelly Mountains. Be aware that there are no trails here. You must make your own way through the bush, and it is steep in parts. Be sure to take bear spray and follow bear safety guidelines (see pages 228–9).

BLACK RIVER 105 B/16 This map only covers a short section of the route. The main point of interest is the wrecked boat at Sayyea Creek (9V 4263 67363). This was once used to support a mining camp on the creek. There's no good camping on this stretch.

ALLAN CREEK 105 B/9 Watch out for shallow gravel bars on this section of the river. There are two good spots for camping after Cabin Creek. The first is at the top of the second island (on the left) past Cabin Creek. The second is at the end of the island that lies about 20 minutes after Cabin Creek (9V 4345 67348). This is about 3–4 hours' paddling (usually about a 5-hour journey with breaks) from the recommended camp spot at 9V 4094 67531.

SAMBO CREEK 105 A/12 At the confluence with Hasselberg Creek (9V 4486 67219) the water is rapid with big waves. The shore is rocky and not attractive for camping. After this point, the river braids and even with a detailed topo map it can be difficult to know which arm you're in. Follow the arm that appears to have the most water – this may not be the widest. In places, where the braids narrow, the water flows faster and becomes choppy; there may well be sweepers.

There's a fair high-water camp on the right, 20 minutes past Hasselberg Creek (9V 4494 67187). The creek is named after Fred Hasselberg, who prospected in the area. You can still see the Hasselberg family's cabins on the left at 9V 4566 67150.

FALSE PASS CREEK 105 A/5 After this the river is long, straight and slow. There's a potentially difficult bend, which may be blocked by a log jam, just before the confluence with the Meister River (9V 4745 66880). Stay to the right side and be vigilant.

There's a possible camp spot on the sand bank on the left side just below the Meister River confluence at 9V 4744 66872.

After the Frances River joins the Liard, the river widens and slows considerably. There are lots of flat gravel bars good for camping from about one hour after the confluence. The river has carved a new channel at 9V 5005 66670; it's better to take the right arm, which has the most water, but stay on its inside as the outside is blocked with logs.

WATSON LAKE 105 A/2 The most common pick-up is about 4 hours from the Frances River confluence. The pick-up spot is at Upper Liard Village – there's a ramp on the right side of the river before the bridge (9V 5053 66569). Don't plan on arriving early in order to grab a nice meal in Upper Liard Village. The bar across the road doesn't open till 3pm, has a limited selection of food, and is in any case nothing to write home about. You'll do better to drive 12km (8 miles) to Nugget City (km 1003, mile 640 Alaska Highway) where Wolf It Down restaurant (see page 87) serves up outstanding homemade pie alongside fish and chips, steak, and the like.

Appendix

FURTHER INFORMATION

GENERAL GUIDES Yukon Tourism publishes a free vacation planner, which can be picked up from any government visitor centre or ordered online from http://travelyukon.com/planyourtrip/orderafreeyukonvacationplanner.

PR Services publish useful booklets on Whitehorse, Dawson City, Skagway, Watson Lake and Inuvik. These are free of charge and can be picked up from visitor centres and other distribution outlets across the Yukon (and Skagway and Inuvik, of course).

Canada's Western Arctic by the Western Arctic Handbook Society is an excellent guidebook to the very far north, with good accounts of the region's people and natural world.

Yukon: Travel Adventure Guide by Dieter Reinmuth is a detailed general guidebook to the Yukon self-published by a German who has lived for many years in Dawson.

Alaska: The Bradt Travel Guide by T T Terpening is Bradt's Alaska guide, written by a local, which provides good information on Skagway and Haines as well as the rest of that big frozen place to the west.

HIGHWAY GUIDES *The Milepost* gives a blow-by-blow account of pretty much every point of interest along the highways of the Yukon (and Alaska, BC, Alberta and NWT). It's detailed and accurate (it's updated every year), and a good highway companion, but note that its content is advertising-led – that's to say that those businesses that don't pay may not be included. It's also the size of a telephone directory. You can buy it in bookstores across the territories it covers.

HIKING AND OUTDOORS GUIDES The following – and many other local guides besides – should be available from Mac's Fireweed Books in Whitehorse; you can order them ahead of your trip from www.yukonbooks.com.

Hikes & Bikes by the Yukon Conservation Society covers the Whitehorse area.

The Kluane National Park Hiking Guide by Vivien Lougheed

Paddling the Yukon and its Tributaries by Don Maclean

Paddling in the Yukon: A Guide to Rivers, Lakes and the Arctic Ocean by Ken Madsen and Peter Mather

Yukon's Tombstone Range and Blackstone Uplands: A Traveller's Guide by the Canadian Parks and Wilderness Society

Along the Dempster: An Outdoor Guide to Canada's Northernmost Highway by Walter Lanz

Chilkoot Pass: A Hiker's Historical guide to the Klondike Gold Rush National Historical Pass by Archie Satterfield. This is fabulous for its historical stories of the Chilkoot and a must-read for anyone doing that hike.

How to Shit in the Woods: An Environmentally Sound Approach to a Lost Art by Kathleen Meyer does what it says on the tin – and includes a good dose of humour together with toe-curling anecdotes from those who've got it wrong. It wasn't available from Mac's when I checked, but you can get it from Amazon.

FLORA AND FAUNA

Flora of the Yukon Territory by William J Cody
Wildflowers Along the Alaska Highway by Verna E Pratt
Wildflowers of the Yukon, Alaska and Northwestern Canada by John Trelawny
Birds by the Dempster Highway by Bob Frisch
Birds of the Yukon Territory by Cameron D Eckert, Pamela H Sinclair, Wendy A Nixon and Nancy L Hughes is pretty but pricey at $150.
The Arctic: A Guide to Coastal Wildlife by Tony Soper. A beautifully illustrated guide for the layman naturalist; its other benefit is that it's small enough to carry with you when travelling.
A Naturalist's Guide to the Arctic by E C Pielou. This is a reasonably useful book but be warned: it ought to have been titled *A Naturalist's Guide to the North American Arctic*. Not a problem if you're in North America, though.
A Complete Guide to Arctic Wildlife by Richard Sale. This is an excellent, fully illustrated guide for Arctic enthusiasts. It's wonderful, but weighty.

KLONDIKE GOLD RUSH AND OTHER HISTORY

The Klondike Fever: The Life and Death of the Last Great Gold Rush by Pierre Berton. If you read just one book about the Klondike gold rush, I'd recommend you make it this.
I Married the Klondike by Laura Berton. Laura Berton was Pierre Berton's mother. She arrived in Dawson City just after the gold rush and stayed for 25 years. This is her delightful memoir.
Two Women in the Klondike by Mary E Hitchcock. Hitchcock and her friend Edith Van Buren were two society ladies who decided to 'do' the Klondike in style in 1898. The resulting book is eye-opening and hilarious.
A Dog Puncher on the Yukon by Arthur Walden. Walden ferried mail around the area from before gold-rush days. His memoir gives a great insight into the world of the pre-Klondike prospectors – and to the incredible excitement that engulfed them when the big strike was made.
Land of the Midnight Sun by Ken S Coates and William R Morrison. A good general history of the Yukon.
Prelude to Bonanza by Allan A Wright. An excellent history of European contact in the Yukon up to the gold-rush days, including Robert Campbell and the Hudson's Bay Company's explorations, the arrival of the missionaries, and the travails of the pre-Klondike miners.
The Lost Patrol by Dick North. A slim, easy-to-digest book about the Lost Patrol, a group of four Mounties who lost their way on a routine dogsled patrol in the winter of 1910–11. Temperatures dropped into the minus 50s Celsius. They ran out of food and ate their dogs one by one. Then the first three men starved to death. The fourth shot himself. Also try these – or any other of Dick North's far northern histories: *Sailor in Snowshoes: Tracking Jack London's Northern Trail*; *The Mad Trapper of Rat River*; and *Arctic Exodus: The Last Great Trail Drive*.
The Last Imaginary Place: A Human History of the Arctic World by Robert McGhee is good for anyone interested in the human history of the far north.
Barrow's Boys: A Stirring Story of Daring, Fortitude and Outright Lunacy by Fergus Fleming offers a gripping account of the quest to traverse the Northwest Passage, among other exploits.
The Cruellest Miles by Gay Salisbury and Laney Salisbury. This isn't actually about the Yukon but what the heck. It's about the serum run by dogsled to Nome, Alaska, in 1929, which saved the town from a diptheria epidemic. It's a cracking read.

ROBERT SERVICE
Robert Service's two volumes of autobiography make interesting reading; it's the first, *Ploughman of the Moon*, that covers his Yukon days, but it's out of print so may be hard to come by at a reasonable price. Always in print are volumes of Service's verse. The best-known of his Yukon verses are 'The Spell of the Yukon', 'The Shooting of Dan

McGrew' and 'The Cremation of Sam McGee' and these are generally included in any 'best of Robert Service' collection.

JACK LONDON From Jack London's pen *Call of the Wild* is the big one.

NARRATIVE TRAVEL BOOKS ON THE YUKON *Mad Dogs and an Englishwoman* by Polly Evans is my own book about learning to drive sled dogs in the Yukon.

Dorian Amos's two books *The Good Life* and *The Good Life Gets Better* tell the entertaining story of the author and his wife's move from Cornwall in the UK to Dawson City.

Voyageur: Across the Rocky Mountains in a Birchbark Canoe by Robert Twigger. is not about the Yukon (Twigger and his buddies follow Alexander Mackenzie's historic route to the Pacific) but it's a hilarious read; this is a good one for those going on paddling trips.

USEFUL DOWNLOADS Hard copies of most of these can be picked up from the government visitor centres.

Yukon's Wildlife Viewing Guide Along Major Highways (www.environmentyukon.gov.yk.ca/ mapspublications/documents/WVGuideEng2007.pdf)
Into the Yukon Wilderness (www.environmentyukon.gov.yk.ca/pdf/ityw.pdf)
How You Can Stay Safe in Bear Country (www.environmentyukon.gov.yk.ca/pdf/ howyoucanstaysafe.pdf)
Dempster Highway Travelogue (www.environmentyukon.gov.yk.ca/pdf/DempsterFinalWeb.pdf)
Yukon birds checklist (www.yukonweb.com/community/ybc)
Herschel Island birds checklist (www.yukonweb.com/community/ybc/herschelbirds.pdf)
Tombstone Territorial Park birds checklist (www.yukonweb.com/community/ybc/ tombstonebirds.pdf)
Birdwatchers' Guide to Whitehorse (www.yukonweb.com/community/ybc/birdingwhitehorse.pdf)
Yukon Butterflies (http://environmentyukon.gov.yk.ca/pdf/YukonButterflieswebfinal05.pdf)
Haines Wildlife Viewing Guide (www.haines.ak.us/hainesweb/tripplanning/viewingguide.pdf)
Birds of the Chilkat Valley: A Checklist (www.haines.ak.us/hainesweb/tripplanning/birds.pdf)

DVDS

Le Dernier Trappeur/The Last Trapper French film-maker Nicolas Vanier's work based on the life of Norman Winther, who traps and hunts in the Yukon.
Being Caribou Environmentalist Leanne Allison and wildlife biologist Karsten Heuer follow the migration of the Porcupine caribou herd from central Yukon to ANWR's coastal plain.
The Lone Trail Records the 20th-anniversary race of the Yukon Quest in 2004
Picturing a People: George Johnston, Tlingit Photographer see page 39
My Father, My Teacher see page 211

USEFUL WEBSITES

Yukon Tourism www.travelyukon.com
Parks Canada www.pc.gc.ca
Environment Yukon www.environmentyukon.com
Yukon Conservation Society www.yukonconservation.org
Arctic Borderlands Ecological Knowledge Society www.taiga.net
PR Services www.yukoninfo.com
The Bed & Breakfast Association of the Yukon www.yukonbandb.org
Northern lights forecast www.auroraforecast.com
Road reports www.yukon511.ca

WIN £100 CASH!

READER QUESTIONNAIRE

**Send in your completed questionnaire for the chance to win
£100 cash in our regular draw**

All respondents may order a Bradt guide at half the UK retail price – please
complete the order form overleaf.

(Entries may be posted or faxed to us, or scanned and emailed.)

We are interested in getting feedback from our readers to help us plan future Bradt
guides. Please answer ALL the questions below and return the form to us in order
to qualify for an entry in our regular draw.

Have you used any other Bradt guides? If so, which titles? . . . .
. . . .

What other publishers' travel guides do you use regularly? . . . .
. . . .

Where did you buy this guidebook? . . . .

What was the main purpose of your trip to the Yukon (or for what other reason did
you read our guide)? eg: holiday/business/charity etc.. . . . .
. . . .

What other destinations would you like to see covered by a Bradt guide?
. . . .

Would you like to receive our catalogue/newsletters?

YES / NO (If yes, please complete details on reverse)

If yes – by post or email? . . . .

Age (circle relevant category) 16–25   26–45   46–60   60+

Male/Female (delete as appropriate)

Home country . . . .

Please send us any comments about our guide to the Yukon or other Bradt Travel
Guides. . . . .
. . . .
. . . .
. . . .

Bradt Travel Guides

23 High Street, Chalfont St Peter, Bucks SL9 9QE, UK
☏ +44 (0)1753 893444 **f** +44 (0)1753 892333
e info@bradtguides.com
www.bradtguides.com

CLAIM YOUR HALF-PRICE BRADT GUIDE!

Order Form

To order your half-price copy of a Bradt guide, and to enter our prize draw to win £100 (see overleaf), please fill in the order form below, complete the questionnaire overleaf, and send it to Bradt Travel Guides by post, fax or email.

Please send me one copy of the following guide at half the UK retail price

Title	Retail price	Half price
....	....	....

Please send the following additional guides at full UK retail price

No	Title	Retail price	Total
...	....	....	....
...	....	....	....
...	....	....	....

Sub total ....

Post & packing ....

(£2 per book UK; £4 per book Europe; £6 per book rest of world)

Total ....

Name ....

Address ....

Tel .... Email ....

☐ I enclose a cheque for £........ made payable to Bradt Travel Guides Ltd

☐ I would like to pay by credit card. Number: ....

Expiry date: ... / ...   3-digit security code (on reverse of card) .....

Issue no (debit cards only) .....

☐ Please add my name to your catalogue mailing list.

☐ I would be happy for you to use my name and comments in Bradt marketing material.

Send your order on this form, with the completed questionnaire, to:

Bradt Travel Guides YUK1
23 High Street, Chalfont St Peter, Bucks SL9 9QE
✆ +44 (0)1753 893444   f +44 (0)1753 892333
e info@bradtguides.com   www.bradtguides.com

Index

Entries in **bold** indicate main entries; those in *italics* indicate maps